QATAR

FOREIGN POLICY & GOVERNMENT
GUIDE

International Business Publications, USA
Washington, DC, USA - Qatar

QATAR

FOREIGN POLICY & GOVERNMENT GUIDE

Editorial content: International Business Publications, USA
Editor-in-Chief: Dr. Igor S. Oleynik
Editor: Natasha Alexander
Managing Editor: Karl Cherepanya

Published by: International Business Publications, USA
P.O.Box 15343, Washington, DC 20003
Phone: (202) 546-2103, Fax: (202) 546-3275, E-mail: rusric@erols.com

UPDATED ANNUALLY

Databases & Information: Global Investment Center, USA
Cover Design: International Business Publications, USA

We express our sincere appreciation to all government agencies and international organizations which provided information and other materials for this guide

2004 International Business Publications, USA
ISBN 0-7397-5818-7

This guide provides basic information for starting or/and conducting business in the country. The extraordinary volume of materials covering the topic, prevents us from placing all these materials in this guide. For more detailed information on issues related to any specific investment and business activity in the country, please contact Global Investment Center, USA
Please acquire the list of our business intelligence and marketing reports and other business publications. We constantly update and expand our business intelligence and marketing materials. Please contact the center for the updated list of reports on over 250 countries.

in the USA: **Global Investment Center, USA.**
P.O.Box 15343, Washington, DC 20003
Phone: (202) 546-2103, Fax: (202) 546-3275, E-mail: rusric@erols.com

For additional analytical, marketing and other information please contact
Global Investment Center, USA

Printed in the USA

QATAR

FOREIGN POLICY & GOVERNMENT GUIDE

TABLE OF CONTENTS

**For additional analytical, business and investment opportunities information,
please contact Global Investment & Business Center, USA
at (202) 546-2103. Fax: (202) 546-3275. E-mail: rusric@erols.com
Global Business E-Books on Line: http://world.mirhouse.com**

For additional analytical, business and investment opportunities information,
please contact Global Investment & Business Center, USA
at (202) 546-2103. Fax: (202) 546-3275. E-mail: rusric@erols.com
Global Business E-Books on Line: http://world.mirhouse.com

For additional analytical, business and investment opportunities information,
please contact Global Investment & Business Center, USA
at (202) 546-2103. Fax: (202) 546-3275. E-mail: rusric@erols.com
Global Business E-Books on Line: http://world.mirhouse.com

**For additional analytical, business and investment opportunities information,
please contact Global Investment & Business Center, USA
at (202) 546-2103. Fax: (202) 546-3275. E-mail: rusric@erols.com
Global Business E-Books on Line: http://world.mirhouse.com**

For additional analytical, business and investment opportunities information,
please contact Global Investment & Business Center, USA
at (202) 546-2103. Fax: (202) 546-3275. E-mail: rusric@erols.com
Global Business E-Books on Line: http://world.mirhouse.com

For additional analytical, business and investment opportunities information, please contact Global Investment & Business Center, USA at (202) 546-2103. Fax: (202) 546-3275. E-mail: rusric@erols.com Global Business E-Books on Line: http://world.mirhouse.com

For additional analytical, business and investment opportunities information, please contact Global Investment & Business Center, USA at (202) 546-2103. Fax: (202) 546-3275. E-mail: rusric@erols.com Global Business E-Books on Line: http://world.mirhouse.com

STRATEGIC AND DEVELOPMENT PROFILES

STRATEGIC PROFILE

COUNTRY

Head of State: Sheikh Hamad bin Khalifa al-Thani
Independence: September 3, 1971 (from United Kingdom)
Population (1999E): 723,000
Location/Size: Persian Gulf/4,416 square miles, slightly smaller than Connecticut
Major Cities: Doha (capital), Umm Said, Dukhan, al-Khawr
Languages: Arabic (English widely spoken)
Ethnic Groups: Arab (40%), Pakistani (18%), Indian (18%), Iranian (10%), other (14%)
Religion: Muslim (95%)
Defense (8/98): Army (8,500), Navy (1,800), Air Force (1,500)

ECONOMY

Currency: Qatari Riyal
Market Exchange Rate (7/00): US$1 = 3.64 Qatari riyals
Nominal Gross Domestic Product (1999E): $9.6 billion **(2000E):** $10.0 billion
Real GDP Growth Rate (1999E): 3.3% **(2000E):** 4.6%
Inflation Rate (consumer prices) (1999E): 2.2% **(2000E):** 2.3%
Current Account Balance (1999E): -$1.3 billion **(2000E):** $1.5 billion
Major Trading Partners: Japan, United Kingdom, United States, Italy, Germany, France, South Korea
Merchandise Exports (1999E): $6.7 billion
Merchandise Imports (1999E): $5.5 billion
Major Export Products: Crude oil, LNG
Major Import Products: Machinery and transport equipment, manufactured goods, food and live animals
External Debt (1999E): $11.8 billion **(2000E):** $7.8 billion

ENERGY

Minister of Energy and Industry: Sheikh Abdullah bin Hamad al-Attiyeh
Proven Oil Reserves (1/1/00): 3.7 billion barrels
Oil Production (1999E): 806,000 barrels per day (bbl/d), of which 659,000 bbl/d was crude oil
OPEC Crude Oil Production Quota (effective 7/1/00): 658,000 bbl/d of crude oil (not including condensate)
Natural Gas Liquids Production (1999E): 111,000 bbl/d
Oil Consumption (1999E): 45,000 bbl/d
Net Oil Exports (1999E): 760,000 bbl/d
Crude Oil Refining Capacity (1/1/00): 57,500 bbl/d
Natural Gas Reserves (1/1/00): 300 trillion cubic feet (Tcf)
Natural Gas Production (1998E): 690 billion cubic feet (Bcf)

Natural Gas Consumption (1998E): 522 Bcf
Net Natural Gas Exports (1998E): 168 Bcf
Electric Generation Capacity (1/1/98): 1.4 gigawatts
Electricity Production (1998E): 6.7 billion kilowatthours

ENVIRONMENT

Total Energy Consumption (1998E): 0.6 quadrillion Btu* (0.2% of world total energy consumption)
Energy-Related Carbon Emissions (1998E): 9.1 million metric tons of carbon (0.1% of world carbon emissions)
Per Capita Energy Consumption (1998E): 898.3 million Btu (vs. U.S. value of 350.7 million Btu)
Per Capita Carbon Emissions (1998E): 13.1 metric tons of carbon (vs. U.S. value of 5.5 metric tons of carbon)
Energy Intensity (1998E): 64,900 Btu/ $1990 (vs U.S. value of 13,400 Btu/ $1990)**
Carbon Intensity (1998E): 0.9 metric tons of carbon/thousand $1990 (vs U.S. value of 0.21 metric tons/thousand $1990)**
Sectoral Share of Energy Consumption (1997E): Industrial (82.4%), Transportation (16.1%), Commercial (1.3%), Residential (0.2%)
Sectoral Share of Carbon Emissions (1997E): Industrial (80.3%), Transportation (18.2%), Commercial (1.3%), Residential (0.21%)
Fuel Share of Energy Consumption (1998E): Natural Gas (87.3%), Oil (12.7%)
Fuel Share of Carbon Emissions (1998E): Natural Gas (86.4%), Oil (13.6%)
Renewable Energy Consumption (1997E): 0.084 trillion Btu* (33% increase from 1996)
Status in Climate Change Negotiations: Non-Annex I country under the United Nations Framework Convention on Climate Change (ratified April 18th, 1996). Not a signatory to the Kyoto Protocol.
Major Environmental Issues: limited natural fresh water resources are increasing dependence on large-scale desalination facilities
Major International Environmental Agreements: A party to Conventions on Biodiversity, Climate Change, Hazardous Wastes and Ozone Layer Protection. Has signed, but not ratified, Law of the Sea

* The total energy consumption statistic includes petroleum, dry natural gas, coal, net hydro, nuclear, geothermal, solar and wind electric power. The renewable energy consumption statistic is based on International Energy Agency (IEA) data and includes hydropower, solar, wind, tide, geothermal, solid biomass and animal products, biomass gas and liquids, industrial and municipal wastes. Sectoral shares of energy consumption and carbon emissions are also based on IEA data.
**GDP based on EIA International Energy Annual 1998

OIL AND GAS INDUSTRIES

Organization: Qatar General Petroleum Corporation (QGPC) - exploration and production; National Oil Distribution Company (NODCO) - refining and distribution; Qatar

Petrochemical Company (QAPCO) - petrochemical production; Qatar Fertilizer Company (QAFCO) - fertilizer production; Qatar Liquefied Gas Company (Qatargas) and Ras Laffan LNG Company (Rasgas) - production and marketing of liquefied natural gas (LNG)

Major Foreign Oil Company Involvement: BP Amoco Arco, Chevron, Enron, Exxon, Gulfstream, Maersk, Marubeni, Mitsui, Mobil, MOL, Occidental, Phillips Petroleum, TotalFinaElf, Wintershall

Major Ports: Umm Said, Ras Laffan

Producing Oil Fields (production - bbl/d)(1998E): Dukhan (275,000), Id al-Shargi North Dome (120,000), Bul Hanine (80,000), Maydan Mahzam (50,000), al-Shaheen (100,000), al-Rayyan (32,000), and al-Khalij (30,000)

Major Pipelines: Dukhan-Umm Said, an offshore network connecting Halul Island to al-Khalij, Bul Hanine, and Maydan Mahzam, and Das Island (U.A.E.)-al-Bunduq

Major Refineries (capacity - bbl/d): Umm Said (57,500)

Background: During the late 1980s and early 1990s, the Qatari economy was crippled by a continuous siphoning off of petroleum revenues by the amir who had ruled the country since 1972. He was overthrown in a bloodless coup by his own son in 1995. Oil and natural gas revenues enable Qatar to have a per capita income not far below the leading industrial countries of Western Europe.

GEOGRAPHY

Location: Middle East, peninsula bordering the Persian Gulf and Saudi Arabia

Geographic coordinates: 25 30 N, 51 15 E

Map references: Middle East

Area:
total: 11,437 sq km
land: 11,437 sq km
water: 0 sq km

Area - comparative: slightly smaller than Connecticut

Land boundaries:
total: 60 km
border countries: Saudi Arabia 60 km

Coastline: 563 km

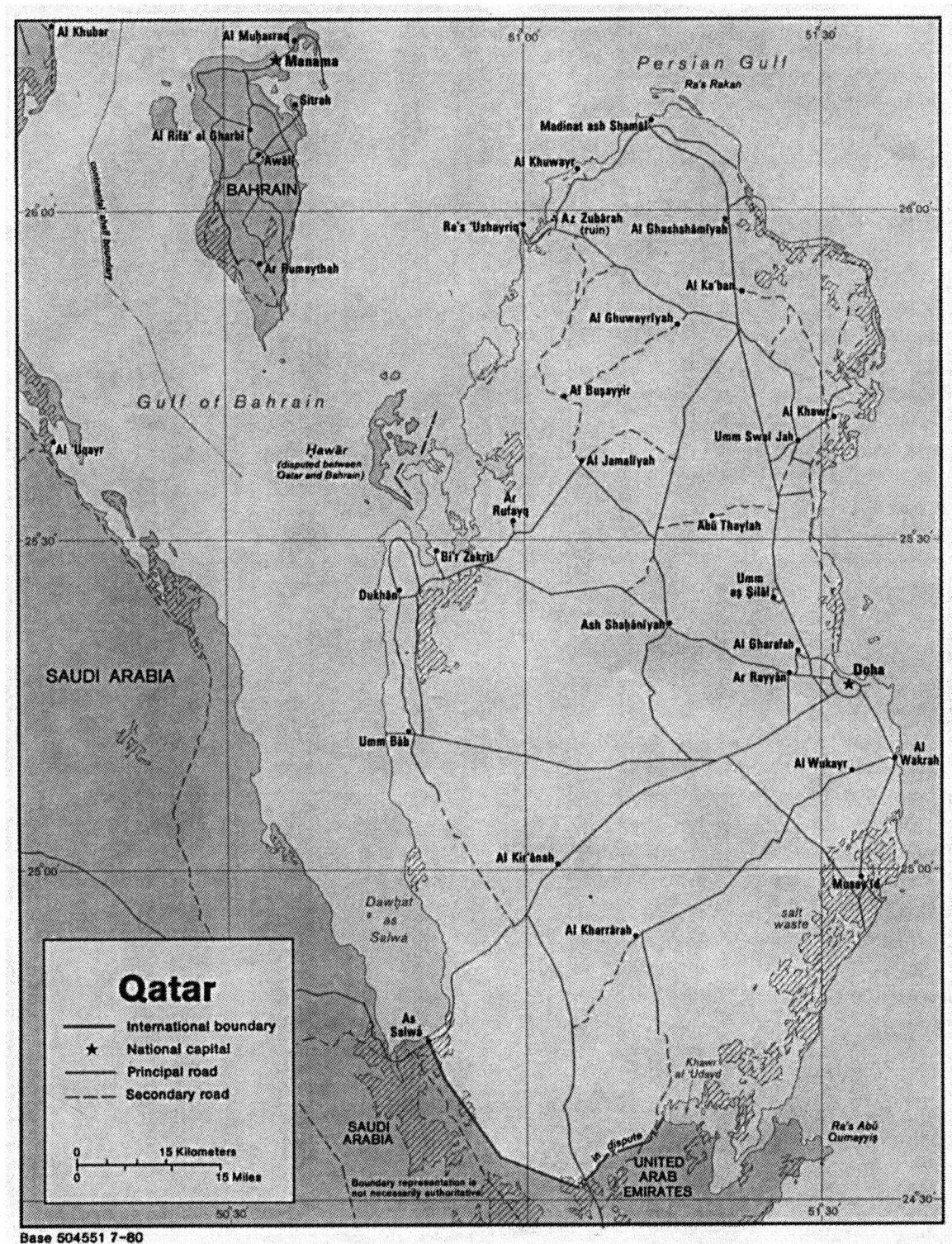

Maritime claims:
contiguous zone: 24 nm
exclusive economic zone: as determined by bilateral agreements, or the median line
territorial sea: 12 nm

Climate: desert; hot, dry; humid and sultry in summer

Terrain: mostly flat and barren desert covered with loose sand and gravel

Elevation extremes:
lowest point: Persian Gulf 0 m
highest point: Qurayn Abu al Bawl 103 m

Natural resources: petroleum, natural gas, fish

Land use:
arable land: 1%
permanent crops: 0%
permanent pastures: 5%
forests and woodland: 0%
other: 94% (1993 est.)

Irrigated land: 80 sq km (1993 est.)

Natural hazards: haze, dust storms, sandstorms common

Environment - current issues: limited natural fresh water resources are increasing dependence on large-scale desalination facilities

Environment - international agreements:
party to: Biodiversity, Climate Change, Desertification, Hazardous Wastes, Ozone Layer Protection
signed, but not ratified: Law of the Sea

Geography - note: strategic location in central Persian Gulf near major petroleum deposits

PEOPLE

Population: 744,483 (July 2000 est.)

Age structure:
0-14 years: 26% (male 99,702; female 95,960)
15-64 years: 71% (male 378,741; female 152,978)
65 years and over: 3% (male 12,120; female 4,982) (2000 est.)

Population growth rate: 3.35% (2000 est.)

Birth rate: 16.07 births/1,000 population (2000 est.)

Death rate: 4.19 deaths/1,000 population (2000 est.)

Net migration rate: 21.58 migrant(s)/1,000 population (2000 est.)

Sex ratio:
at birth: 1.05 male(s)/female
under 15 years: 1.04 male(s)/female
15-64 years: 2.48 male(s)/female
65 years and over: 2.43 male(s)/female
total population: 1.93 male(s)/female (2000 est.)

Infant mortality rate: 22.14 deaths/1,000 live births (2000 est.)

Life expectancy at birth:
total population: 72.37 years
male: 69.92 years
female: 74.94 years (2000 est.)

Total fertility rate: 3.25 children born/woman (2000 est.)

Nationality:
noun: Qatari(s)
adjective: Qatari

Ethnic groups: Arab 40%, Pakistani 18%, Indian 18%, Iranian 10%, other 14%

Religions: Muslim 95%

Languages: Arabic (official), English commonly used as a second language

Literacy:
definition: age 15 and over can read and write
total population: 79.4%
male: 79.2%
female: 79.9% (1995 est.)

GOVERNMENT

Country name:
conventional long form: State of Qatar
conventional short form: Qatar
local long form: Dawlat Qatar
local short form: Qatar
note: closest approximation of the native pronunciation falls between cutter and gutter, but not like guitar

Data code: QA

Government type: traditional monarchy

Capital: Doha

Administrative divisions: 9 municipalities (baladiyat, singular - baladiyah); Ad Dawhah, Al Ghuwayriyah, Al Jumayliyah, Al Khawr, Al Wakrah, Ar Rayyan, Jarayan al Batinah, Madinat ash Shamal, Umm Salal

Independence: 3 September 1971 (from UK)

National holiday: Independence Day, 3 September (1971)

Constitution: provisional constitution enacted 19 April 1972

Legal system: discretionary system of law controlled by the amir, although civil codes are being implemented; Islamic law is significant in personal matters

Suffrage: suffrage is limited to municipal elections

Executive branch:
chief of state: Amir HAMAD bin Khalifa Al Thani (since 27 June 1995 when, as crown prince, he ousted his father, Amir KHALIFA bin Hamad Al Thani, in a bloodless coup); Crown Prince JASSIM bin Hamad bin Khalifa Al Thani, third son of the monarch (selected crown prince by the monarch 22 October 1996); note - Amir HAMAD also holds the positions of minister of defense and commander-in-chief of the armed forces
head of government: Prime Minister ABDALLAH bin Khalifa Al Thani, brother of the monarch (since 30 October 1996); Deputy Prime Minister MUHAMMAD bin Khalifa Al Thani, brother of the monarch (since 20 January 1998)
cabinet: Council of Ministers appointed by the monarch
elections: none; the monarch is hereditary; note - in March 1999 Qatar held elections for representatives to its Central Municipal Council

Legislative branch: unicameral Advisory Council or Majlis al-Shura (35 seats; members appointed)
note: the constitution calls for elections for part of this consultative body, but no elections have been held since 1970, when there were partial elections to the body; Council members have their terms extended every four years since

Judicial branch: Court of Appeal

Political parties and leaders: none

International organization participation: ABEDA, AFESD, AL, AMF, CCC, ESCWA, FAO, G-77, GCC, IAEA, IBRD, ICAO, ICRM, IDB, IFAD, IFRCS, IHO (pending member), ILO, IMF, IMO, Inmarsat, Intelsat, Interpol, IOC, ISO (correspondent), ITU, NAM,

OAPEC, OIC, OPCW, OPEC, UN, UNCTAD, UNESCO, UNIDO, UPU, WHO, WIPO, WMO, WTrO

Diplomatic representation in the US:
chief of mission: Ambassador Saad Muhammad al-KUBAYSI
chancery: 4200 Wisconsin Avenue NW, Washington, DC 20016
telephone: [1] (202) 274-1600
consulate(s) general: Houston

Diplomatic representation from the US:
chief of mission: Ambassador Elizabeth MCKUNE
embassy: 22 February Road, Doha
mailing address: P. O. Box 2399, Doha
telephone: [974] 884 101
FAX: [974] 884 150
note: work week is Saturday-Wednesday

Flag description: maroon with a broad white serrated band (nine white points) on the hoist side

ECONOMY

Economy - overview: Oil accounts for more than 30% of GDP, roughly 80% of export earnings, and 66% of government revenues. Proved oil reserves of 3.7 billion barrels should ensure continued output at current levels for 23 years. Oil has given Qatar a per capita GDP three-fourths that of the leading West European industrial countries. Qatar's proved reserves of natural gas exceed 7 trillion cubic meters, more than 5% of the world total, third largest in the world. Production and export of natural gas are becoming increasingly important. Long-term goals feature the development of off-shore petroleum and the diversification of the economy. If high oil prices continue in 2000, Qatar will post its highest ever trade surplus - of more than $4 billion.

GDP: purchasing power parity - $12.3 billion (1999 est.)

GDP - real growth rate: 1.5% (1999 est.)

GDP - per capita: purchasing power parity - $17,000 (1999 est.)

GDP - composition by sector:
agriculture: 1%
industry: 49%
services: 50% (1996 est.)

Population below poverty line: NA%

Household income or consumption by percentage share:
lowest 10%: NA%
highest 10%: NA%

Inflation rate (consumer prices): 2% (1999)

Labor force: 233,000 (1993 est.)

Unemployment rate: NA%

Budget:
revenues: $5 billion
expenditures: $4 billion, including capital expenditures of $NA (FY99/00 est.)

Industries: crude oil production and refining, fertilizers, petrochemicals, steel reinforcing bars, cement

Industrial production growth rate: NA%

Electricity - production: 6.715 billion kWh (1998)

Electricity - production by source:
fossil fuel: 100%
hydro: 0%
nuclear: 0%
other: 0% (1998)

Electricity - consumption: 6.245 billion kWh (1998)

Electricity - exports: 0 kWh (1998)

Electricity - imports: 0 kWh (1998)

Agriculture - products: fruits, vegetables; poultry, dairy products, beef; fish

Exports: $6.7 billion (f.o.b., 1999 est.)

Exports - commodities: petroleum products 80%, fertilizers, steel

Exports - partners: Japan 50%, Singapore 12%, South Korea 9%, US, UAE (1997)

Imports: $4.2 billion (f.o.b., 1999 est.)

Imports - commodities: machinery and transport equipment, food, chemicals

Imports - partners: UK 25%, France 13%, Japan 10%, US 9%, Italy 6% (1997)

Debt - external: $10 billion (1998 est.)

Economic aid - recipient: $NA

Currency: 1 Qatari riyal (QR) = 100 dirhams

Exchange rates: Qatari riyals (QR) per US$1 - 3.6400 riyals (fixed rate)

Fiscal year: 1 April - 31 March

COMMUNICATIONS

Telephones - main lines in use: 146,980 (1995)

Telephones - mobile cellular: 18,469 (1995)

Telephone system: modern system centered in Doha
domestic: NA
international: tropospheric scatter to Bahrain; microwave radio relay to Saudi Arabia and UAE; submarine cable to Bahrain and UAE; satellite earth stations - 2 Intelsat (1 Atlantic Ocean and 1 Indian Ocean) and 1 Arabsat

Radio broadcast stations: AM 6, FM 5, shortwave 1 (1998)

Radios: 256,000 (1997)

Television broadcast stations: 2 (plus three repeaters) (1997)

Televisions: 230,000 (1997)

Internet Service Providers (ISPs): NA

TRANSPORTATION

Railways: 0 km

Highways:
total: 1,230 km
paved: 1,107 km
unpaved: 123 km (1996 est.)

Pipelines: crude oil 235 km; natural gas 400 km

Ports and harbors: Doha, Halul Island, Umm Sa'id

For additional analytical, business and investment opportunities information,
please contact Global Investment & Business Center, USA
at (202) 546-2103. Fax: (202) 546-3275. E-mail: rusric@erols.com
Global Business E-Books on Line: http://world.mirhouse.com

Merchant marine:
total: 24 ships (1,000 GRT or over) totaling 721,756 GRT/1,132,510 DWT
ships by type: cargo 10, combination ore/oil 2, container 7, petroleum tanker 5 (1999 est.)

Airports: 4 (1999 est.)

Airports - with paved runways:
total: 2
over 3,047 m: 2 (1999 est.)

Airports - with unpaved runways:
total: 2
914 to 1,523 m: 1
under 914 m: 1 (1999 est.)

Heliports: 1 (1999 est.)

MILITARY

Military branches: Army, Navy, Air Force, Public Security

Military manpower - military age: 18 years of age

Military manpower - availability:
males age 15-49: 306,850
note: includes non-nationals (2000 est.)

Military manpower - fit for military service:
males age 15-49: 160,899 (2000 est.)

Military manpower - reaching military age annually:
males: 6,471 (2000 est.)

Military expenditures - dollar figure: $816 million (FY99/00)

Military expenditures - percent of GDP: 8.1% (FY99/00)

TRANSNATIONAL ISSUES

Disputes - international: the territorial dispute with Bahrain over the Hawar Islands and the maritime boundary dispute with Bahrain are currently before the International Court of Justice (ICJ); June 1999 agreement has furthered the goal of definitively establishing the border with Saudi Arabia

For additional analytical, business and investment opportunities information,
please contact Global Investment & Business Center, USA
at (202) 546-2103. Fax: (202) 546-3275. E-mail: rusric@erols.com
Global Business E-Books on Line: http://world.mirhouse.com

IMPORTANT INFORMATION FOR UNDERSTANDING QATAR

Official Name: State of Qatar

PROFILE

GEOGRAPHY

Area: 11,437 sq. km. (4,427 sq. mi.); about the size of Connecticut and Rhode Island combined.
Cities: *Capital*--Doha 313,600 (1992). *Other Cities*--Umm Said, Al-Khor, Dukhan, Ruwais.
Terrain: Mostly desert, flat, barren.
Climate: Hot and dry, sultry in summer.

CLIMATE

Qatar is characterized by a hot summer starting from June till August (or the middle of September). Winter is warm, with little rainfall. It starts from December till the end of February. The weather is generally pleasent during March, April, May, October and November.

PEOPLE

Nationality: *Noun and adjective*--Qatari(s).
Population: 550,000 (est.) 80% foreign workers.
Population Growth Rate (1996 est): 2.39%.
Ethnic Groups: Arab 40%, Pakistani 18%, Indian 18%, Iranian 10%, other 14%.
Religion: Islam (state religion, claimed by virtually all of the indigenous population).
Languages: Arabic (official); English (widely spoken).
Literacy: 79.4%--total population, 79.2%--male, 79.9%--female.
Education: *Compulsory*--ages 6-16. *Attendance*--98%.
Health: *Infant Mortality Rate*--20.4 deaths/1,000 live births. *Life Expectancy At Birth*--73.03 years.
Work Force (primarily foreign): 290,000. *Industry, services and commerce*--70%, *Government*--20%, *Agriculture*--10%.

The people of Qatar are the descendants of ancient Arabian lines of kinship. The Arab tribes who immigrated from the neighboring areas, mainly *Najd*, *Al-Ihsa* and *Oman* in various periods during the 17th and 18th centuries, form the basis for the composition of the present population which is estimated at approximately 550,000 inhabitants

PEOPLE

The total population of Qatar is presently somewhere over 600,000 and has been increasing at a rate of about 9% annually in recent years.

However, prior to the discovery and exploitation of oil in the 1950's the population of Qatar in the early part of this century, which can only be guessed at due to lack of accurate records, varied between 16,000 and 30,000, according to times of relative prosperity or slump.

Of these numbers, a substantial proportion were foreign workers from Africa, and a smaller proportion were Iranians, usually occupied in trading or boat building.

The real boom in foreign workers began in the 1970's. Between the first census, carried out in 1970, which revealed a total population of roughly 111,000 and 1977, the population doubled.

By 1986 the figure had reached 370,000 and by 1992, nearly 500,000. The present number is made up of about 25% of Qatari nationals, with the rest being expatriates.

Of the latter, by far the largest groups come from the Indian subcontinent (dominated by Pakistanis and Indian Keralites), other Arab countries (notably Egypt, Jordan, Palestine and Syria) and the Philippines.

For additional analytical, business and investment opportunities information, please contact Global Investment & Business Center, USA at (202) 546-2103. Fax: (202) 546-3275. E-mail: rusric@erols.com Global Business E-Books on Line: http://world.mirhouse.com

The European / North American / Australasian population still numbers less than ten thousand (although it has virtually doubled over the last two or three years, due to increased recruitment for the oil and gas industries).

Overall there are representatives of a huge number of different nationalities resident in Qatar. These range from people from various African countries, to East Europeans, to South Americans, to Far Eastern nations.

Exact statistics on the population of Qatar are obtainable through the government Central Statistical Office, which conducts census surveys about every five years. The last one was carried out in 1997. Should you wish to find out the fact and figures in great detail, contact the CSO on 497497.

Qataris tend to have large families, many with over five children. The improvement in health care, and resultant dramatic drop in infant mortality rates has meant that the national population is growing at a considerable and healthy rate.

Qatari nationals are often of somewhat mixed race themselves, coming both from a variety of tribes that have inhabited the region for centuries (including what are now Bahraini and Saudi Arabian families) and from overseas countries, such as Iran and East Africa.

This accounts for the variety of physical characteristics observable among the Qatari people. Most of the population (over 60%) lives in Doha, with the rest distributed in the smaller towns, such as Wakrah, Al Khor, Dukhan and Messaieed. A negligible number live in rural areas.

Overall, the population mix in the State of Qatar constitutes one of the most fascinating aspects of life in the country. The new resident will find it possible to meet and get to know people from all over the world, and to absorb many aspects of the varied and interesting cultures that prevail.

For additional analytical, business and investment opportunities information, please contact Global Investment & Business Center, USA at (202) 546-2103. Fax: (202) 546-3275. E-mail: rusric@erols.com Global Business E-Books on Line: http://world.mirhouse.com

It is especially noticeable and commendable for children, who mix with a great variety of nationals in their schools, and grow up with none of the prejudice or racism that so often affects Western nations.

GOVERNMENT

Type: Traditional emirate.
Independence: September 3, 1971.
Constitution: 1970 Basic Law, revised 1972.
Branches: *Executive*--Council of Ministers. *Legislative*--Advisory Council (appointed; has assumed only limited responsibility to date). *Judicial*--independent.
Subdivisions: Fully centralized government; nine municipalities.
Political Parties: None.
Suffrage: None.
Flag: Maroon with white serrated band (nine white points) on the hoist side.

ECONOMY

GDP: $10.7 billion
Real Growth Rate: -1%
Per Capita Income: $20,820
Natural Resources: Petroleum, natural gas, fish.
Agriculture: Accounts for less than 2% of GDP. *Products*--fruits and vegetables (most food is imported).
Industry: Oil production and refining (31% of GDP), natural gas development, mining, manufacturing, construction, and power. Trade: *Exports*--$3.26 billion (1996 est.), principally oil (75-80%). *Partners*--Japan 61%, Australia 5%, UAE 4%, Singapore 4% (1994). *Imports*--$4.9 billion (1996 est.), principally consumer goods, machinery, food. *Partners*--Germany 14%, Japan 12%, UK 11%, U.S. 9%, Italy 5% (1994).

People

Natives of the Arabian Peninsula, most Qataris are descended from a number of migratory tribes that came to Qatar in the 18th century to escape the harsh conditions of the neighboring areas of Nejd and Al-Hasa. Some are descended from Omani tribes. Qatar has over 0.5 million people, the majority of whom live in Doha, the capital. Foreign workers with temporary residence status make up about four-fifths of the population. Most of them are South Asians, Egyptians, Palestinians, Jordanians, and Iranians. About 3,000 U.S. citizens resided there as of 1996.

For centuries, the main sources of wealth were pearling, fishing, and trade. At one time, Qataris owned nearly one-third of the Persian Gulf fishing fleet. With the Great Depression and the introduction of Japan,s cultured-pearl industry, pearling in Qatar declined drastically.

The Qataris are mainly Sunni "Wahhabi" Muslims. Islam is the official religion, and Islamic jurisprudence is the basis of Qatar,s legal system. Arabic is the official language

For additional analytical, business and investment opportunities information, please contact Global Investment & Business Center, USA at (202) 546-2103. Fax: (202) 546-3275. E-mail: rusric@erols.com Global Business E-Books on Line: http://world.mirhouse.com

and English is the lingua franca. Education is compulsory and free for all Arab residents 6-16 years old. Qatar has an increasingly high literacy rate.

GEOGRAPHY

Qatar is a peninsula, 11,437 sq. kms in area, that projects from the Arabian mainland. It is approximately 160 kms in length and 80 kms in width at its widest point. Overall, the country is very flat, rising to only 110 m at its highest point , and the land mass largely consists of scrubby desert terrain, covered in sand and loose gravel. The country is largely formed of limestone deposits and clays, laid down in various geologically defined eras. A broad North-South arch dominates the structure of the land, with the Dukhan anticline to the west, while the coastal areas are mostly characterised by salt flats, with an area of high sand dunes in the south-east. Lying in the path of strong prevailing south-easterly winds, the peninsula owes many of its features to wind erosion, in addition to significant fluctuations in the level of the sea-bed. The latter is responsible for the fact that Qatar is now separated from Bahrain and from the small islands that surround the peninsula, all of which, at one time, formed a complete land mass.

There are several small islands dotted around the coastline of Qatar. The most significant of these are Halul, located 90 kms off the east coast and used as an oil processing, storage and export terminal, and the Hawar Islands to the west, which are currently the subject of an ownership dispute between Qatar and Bahrain. The resolution of this conflict is in the hands of the International Court of Justice.

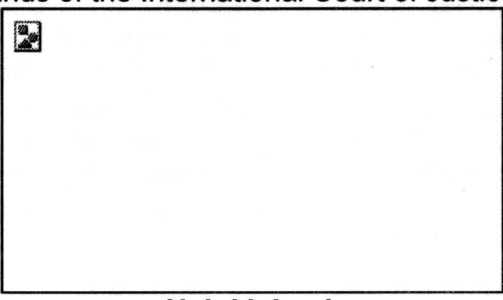

Halul Island

By far the majority of the country is surrounded by the waters of the Arabian Gulf - the coastline of Qatar extends for some 560 kms, while the only land border of 60 kms separates the country from Saudi Arabia. There are several shallow natural harbours, Doha, Wakrah and Messaieed being the most notable of these.

For additional analytical, business and investment opportunities information, please contact Global Investment & Business Center, USA at (202) 546-2103. Fax: (202) 546-3275. E-mail: rusric@erols.com Global Business E-Books on Line: http://world.mirhouse.com

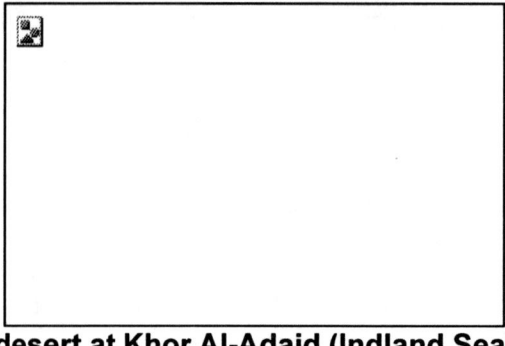

desert at Khor Al-Adaid (Indland Sea)

Qatar enjoys (although that is hardly the appropriate word) a typical desert climate, with mild winters subject to very limited, though erratic, rainfall, often in the form of violent storms. The average winter temperatures are from 20 - 30 C, while during the hot, humid summers the thermometer frequently registers over 40C.

The winter months are generally October through April, with the remaining period suffering from blistering heat and high humidity.

These climactic conditions give rise to sparse vegetation throughout the country and poor soil conditions, capable of sustaining a bare minimum of plant life. Those with a serious interest in desert flora will be pleasantly surprised by the variety to be found in Qatar. To the layman, however, the place looks dry and brown most of the time, while the infrequent rain showers cause the almost instantaneous growth of greenery - the desert literally seems to bloom for a few days. The little agriculture that is practiced in the country survives only through irrigation, and even the date palms that are liberally scattered throughout the towns and in "farming" areas owe their existence to frequent watering. There are a few underground wells providing limited water for irrigation in the central part of the peninsula, but most of the water comes from desalination plants.

DOHA

By far the majority of the population of Qatar is concentrated in Doha, the capital. Originally a scantily inhabited fishing village (the capital of the area being Zubara, in the north-west until the eighteenth century), Doha rose to relative eminence in the nineteenth century and became the chief town and residence of the Al-Thani family, later to become the rulers of Qatar. The population explosion that has taken place in Doha, however, is entirely a late twentieth-century phenomenon, due to Qatar's oil wealth. It is estimated that 80% of the population of Qatar (in excess of 670,000) live in Doha. The town is constantly expanding in all directions (except eastward, of course) and is characterised by what seems to be a never ending process of construction.

The focus of the semi-circular shaped city, hugging the contours of the broad, artificially extended bay is undoubtedly the Corniche, a 7 km coastal path, along which many of the key buildings are located, including the Emiri Diwan (royal palace), several ministries and three of the main hotels.

As the capital city, Doha is, as one would expect, the location of the country's government, airport, seaport, main communications centres, hotels and recreational facilities, sports facilities and just about everything else except the oil and gas and related industries.

There are many impressive new buildings in Doha, and occasional examples of interesting architecture are to be found. Sadly, few old buildings remain, but careful searching of the down town souk area will reveal some examples of pre-oil indigenous architecture, particularly featuring wind-towers, which were used as a way of exploiting breezes to keep structures cool. The National Museum houses a couple of fine old dwellings, used by previous rulers as residences, which are particularly noteworthy for their surprising economy of scale. There are many impressive new buildings in Doha, and occasional examples of interesting architecture are to be found.

Sadly, few old buildings remain, but careful searching of the down town souk area will reveal some examples of pre-oil indigenous architecture, particularly featuring wind-towers, which were used as a way of exploiting breezes to keep structures cool. The National Museum houses a couple of fine old dwellings, used by previous rulers as residences, which are particularly noteworthy for their surprising economy of scale.

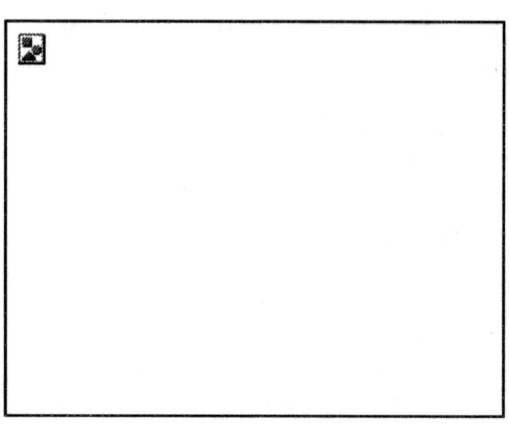

Although the first time visitor may find Doha a confusing place to get around in, it is actually quite well planned, with arterial roads forming concentric arcs parallel to the bay. There is no designated town centre as such, and key locations are to be found scattered all over. Considerable effort has been made in planting trees and shrubs along the roadsides and on central reservations, and this, coupled with the parks dotted around the town give a pleasantly green effect.

Although hardly a booming metropolis in the Western sense of the word, Doha has a definite city feel about it, with its ever increasing traffic, population and amenities.

DUKHAN

Dukhan, located on the central west coast of Qatar, is the heart of the onshore oil and gas industry. Its landscape, characterised by limestone rock formations and hillocks, makes it a little more interesting than most of the rest of the country, and the area boasts some excellent beaches. The town is almost entirely populated by oil and gas personnel and their families and has developed into a small but significant community in its own right. By far the majority of Dukhan's population work for QGPC, the national oil and gas company. Boasting a small school (with more planned for the near future), several restaurants and shops and a social club for residents, it appeals to those who prefer small town life.

As driving to Doha from Dukhan takes about an hour on a reasonably good road, most residents travel frequently to the capital, both to shop and for leisure activities.

AL-KHOR

Al Khor, until very recently a small, picturesque fishing village on the north-east coast, is poised to become Qatar's second largest urban centre. The focus of the North Field Gas industry, Al Khor is not only being developed as an industrial complex but will also become a major residential area. A beautification programme is currently being implemented in the Corniche area, which, it is hoped, will encourage leisure and tourism

For additional analytical, business and investment opportunities information, please contact Global Investment & Business Center, USA at (202) 546-2103. Fax: (202) 546-3275. E-mail: rusric@erols.com Global Business E-Books on Line: http://world.mirhouse.com

activities, while the vital infrastructure required for any urban development is now being developed in the form of schools, a hospital, sports clubs, restaurants etc. Large housing complexes, both villas and apartment blocks, are under construction.

Al-Khor Corniche

Living in Al-Khor, in its present underdeveloped state, is not necessarily appealing to expatriates, but it is hoped that this will change in the near future, as the town grows. Close to Al-Khor lies the port of Ras Laffan, the terminal for processing and export of LNG from Qatar's North Field. The development of the vast facilities required for LNG compression, storage and shipping has occurred with amazing speed, and a full port has been constructed within the last five years, capable of handling several gas tankers.

MESSAIED

Messaieed, located some 45 kms south of Doha on the south east coast of Qatar, is the centre of the oil processing and export industry. The town boasts a commercial port and several refineries and industrial plants. A significant percentage of Messaieed's workers live in the town, which has a pleasant Corniche area, a few useful shops and cafes, in addition to a clinic and a couple of schools. However, it is a very small place, and many families choose to live in Doha, commuting being relatively easy.

NATURE

Most of the wildlife indigenous to Qatar is typical of a desert environment, and consists of insects such as grasshoppers, crickets, scorpions and praying mantis. Lizards, geckos and skinks are common features of the country, as are small nocturnal mammals, such as desert hares, sand rats and jerboas.

In earlier times, herds of Arabian Oryx roamed the countryside, using the natural wells and oases as breeding and settling points.

For additional analytical, business and investment opportunities information, please contact Global Investment & Business Center, USA at (202) 546-2103. Fax: (202) 546-3275. E-mail: rusric@erols.com Global Business E-Books on Line: http://world.mirhouse.com

Sadly, this magnificent creature is now only to be found in captivity. The government has embarked upon a stringent oryx breeding and conservation programme, with notable results.

Qatar is an excellent place for observing bird life, especially during the migratory months in Spring and Autumn. Throughout the year, sparrows, parakeets, gulls, cormorants and other sea birds can be found, but the population is significantly augmented by visiting species, taking advantage of the many fine trees and gardens that are cultivated in the towns to rest for a few days during their long journeys.

The best places for observing bird life are to be found just south of Doha, an area of effluent natural ponds, and around the Messaieed Sewage Works.

There is a certain amount of marine life in Qatar's coastal waters, although this is more limited than one might expect, due to the shallowness of the waters and the high degree of salinity. Crabs, lobsters and the famous Gulf Shrimp are common features of the coasts, as, less attractively, are jellyfish. In the deeper waters further offshore are to be found hammour (grouper) - the most popular edible fish in the region -, channad, snapper, tuna and certain varieties of shark

Those wishing to know more about the flora and fauna of Qatar are encouraged to contact the Natural History Society. Contact **Clare Gillespie** on **684731.**
The Qatar National Museum also has a good natural history section, including an aquarium. Many of the flora and fauna mentioned above are on display, (all stuffed of course, except the fish) and the descriptions are comprehensive and reasonably well done.
Open daily 8am - 12pm and 4pm - 7pm. Telephone 442191

HISTORY

Qatar has been inhabited for millennia. In the 19th century, the Bahraini Al Khalifa family dominated until 1868 when, at the request of Qatari nobles, the British negotiated the termination of the Bahraini claim, except for the payment of tribute. The tribute ended with the occupation of Qatar by the Ottoman Turks in 1872.

When the Turks left, at the beginning of World War I, the British recognized Sheikh Abdullah bin Jassim Al Thani as Ruler. The Al Thani family had lived in Qatar for 200 years. The 1916 treaty between the United Kingdom and Sheikh Abdullah was similar to those entered into by the British with other Gulf principalities. Under it, the Ruler agreed not to dispose of any of his territory except to the U.K. and not to enter into relationships with any other foreign government without British consent. In return, the British promised to protect Qatar from all aggression by sea and to lend their good offices in case of a land attack. A 1934 treaty granted more extensive British protection.

In 1935, a 75-year oil concession was granted to Qatar Petroleum Company, a subsidiary of the Iraq Petroleum Company, which was owned by Anglo-Dutch, French, and U.S. interests. High-quality oil was discovered in 1940 at Dukhan, on the western side of the Qatari peninsula. Exploitation was delayed by World War II, and oil exports did not begin until 1949.

During the 1950s and 1960s gradually increasing oil reserves brought prosperity, rapid immigration, substantial social progress, and the beginnings of Qatar,s modern history.

When the U.K. announced a policy in 1968 (reaffirmed in March 1971) of ending the treaty relationships with the Gulf sheikdoms, Qatar joined the other eight states then under British protection (the seven trucial sheikdoms--the present United Arab Emirates--and Bahrain) in a plan to form a union of Arab emirates. By mid-1971, however, the nine still had not agreed on terms of union, and the termination date (end of 1971) of the British treaty relationship was approaching. Accordingly, Qatar sought independence as a separate entity and became the fully independent State of Qatar on September 3, 1971.

RELIGION

The official religion of Qatar is Islam, and the vast majority of Qataris are Sunni Moslems. The country adopted Islam without any controversy in the 7th century and has remained devout to the faith ever since.

There are five main pillars or tenets of the Islamic faith, namely :

- The Islamic profession of faith (shahhada)
- Prayer (salah) - to be performed five times daily
- Zakat (alms for the poor, levied in the form of a religious tax)
- Fasting, which takes place annually during the Holy Month of Ramadhan between dawn and dusk

- The pilgrimage to Mecca or Hajj, which must be performed at least once in a lifetime, if possible

Unlike other cultures and religions, Moslems follow a lunar calendar, which means that no prayer time or religious festival is fixed. Generally, key events, such as Ramadhan and the Eid Al Fitr festival which immediately follows, shift backwards by 10 days per year, while prayer times are determined by the hours of dawn and dusk.

Moslems are free to pray where they wish, should they be unable to reach a mosque, and it is a common phenomenon for workers to take time during the day to perform prayers.

Prayers must be preceded by ablutions, and prayer and washing facilities are provided in most buildings and public places to accommodate this.

Friday prayers are of especial significance and take place in the many mosques located throughout Qatar. The Calls to Prayer, which issue from the minarets of the mosques five times a day, are a noted feature of life in Qatar.

During the Holy Month of Ramadhan, as noted above, Moslems are required to fast between dawn and dusk.

Non-Muslims are expected to conform to this in public, and respect the prevailing conditions. Many shops do not therefore open in Qatar during Ramadhan until after sunset. Night time during Ramadhan tends to be busy, as Moslems gather with family and friends to break their fast, and subsequently go about their business and leisure activities during the rest of the night.

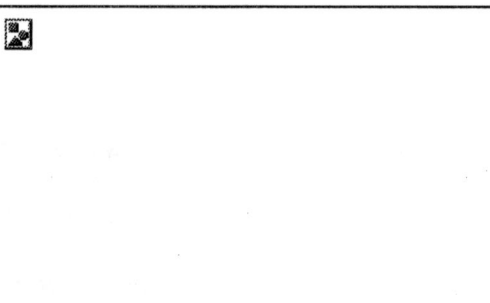

Public holidays in Qatar, apart from National Day, are also religious holidays. The main ones are Eid Al Fitr (which follows Ramadhan) and Eid Al Adha, which follows 40 days after Eid Al Fitr.

It is expected that non-Muslims resident in Qatar should respect the laws and customs of the religion. This means adhering to modest standards of dress and behaviour in public, in addition to not mocking or denigrating Islam in any way.

EDUCATION

Qatar's education policy constantly reaffirms its firm principles of commitment towards quality education for all, equal opportunities and adherence to its islamic heritage and personality. This goes side by side with the constant development of school curricula and educational systems whilst benefiting from modern achievements and new technologies.

The State's comprehensive educational system provides Arabic speaking expatriates with the full range of schooling requirements starting from primary school education through to University studies. There are also a number of Community schools in Doha which cater for expatriate non-Arabic speaking children. These include American, English, French and Indian schools to name just a few

GOVERNMENT AND POLITICAL CONDITIONS

GOVERNMENT

His Highness Sheikh Abdulla Bin Khalifa Al-Thani **The Prime Minister**	**His Highness Sheikh Hamad Bin Khalifa Al-Thani** **The Emir**	**His Highness Sheikh Jassim Bin Hamad Al-Thani** **The Heir Apparaent**

The arrival in Qatar of the Al-Thani family goes back to the eighteenth century. The Name of Al-Thani is derived from that of the family's ancestor Thani Bin Mohamed, father of Mohamed Bin Thani who was the first Sheikh to rule over the Qatari peninsula during the mid 19th Century. The family is a branch of the ancient Arab tribe, the Bani Tameem. The Present Emir is HH Sheikh Hamad Bin Khalifa Al-Thani, who took over the reigns of power on 27th of June 1995.

The Advisory Council, comprising of notable senior members of Qatari society, was convened for the first time on 15th May 1972. The Council advises on and reviews proposals related to State affairs and legislation.

The arrival in Qatar of the Al-Thani family goes back to the eighteenth century. The Name of Al-Thani is derived from that of the family's ancestor Thani Bin Mohamed, father of Mohamed Bin Thani who was the first Sheikh to rule over the Qatari peninsula during the mid 19th Century. The family is a branch of the ancient Arab tribe, the Bani Tameem. The Present Emir is HH Sheikh Hamad Bin Khalifa Al-Thani, who took over the reigns of power on 27th of June 1995.

The Advisory Council, comprising of notable senior members of Qatari society, was convened for the first time on 15th May 1972. The Council advises on and reviews proposals related to State affairs and legislation.

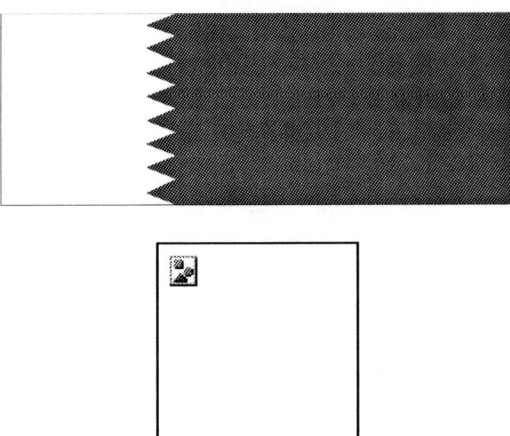

Flag and State Offical Logo

The ruling Al Thani family continued to hold power following the declaration of independence in 1971. The head of state is the Emir, and the right to rule Qatar is passed on within the Al Thani family. Politically, Qatar is evolving from a traditional society into a modern welfare state. Government departments have been established to meet the requirements of social and economic progress. The Basic Law of 1970 institutionalized local customs rooted in Qatar,s conservative Wahhabi heritage, granting the Emir preeminent power. The Emir,s role is influenced by continuing traditions of consultation, rule by consensus, and the citizen,s right to appeal personally to the Emir. The Emir, while directly accountable to no one, cannot violate the *Shari,a* (Islamic law) and, in practice, must consider the opinions of leading notables and the religious establishment. Their position was institutionalized in the Advisory Council, an appointed body that assists the Emir in formulating policy. There is no electoral system. Political parties are banned.

The influx of expatriate Arabs has introduced ideas that call into question the tenets of Qatar,s traditional society, but there has been no serious challenge to Al Thani rule.

In February 1972, the Deputy Ruler and Prime Minister, Sheikh Khalifa bin Hamad, deposed his cousin, Emir Ahmad, and assumed power. This move was supported by the key members of Al Thani and took place without violence or signs of political unrest.

On June 27, 1995, the Deputy Ruler, Sheikh Hamad bin Khalifa, deposed his father Emir Khalifa in a bloodless coup. Emir Hamad and his father reconciled in 1996.

PRINCIPAL GOVERNMENT OFFICIALS

Emir, Commander in Chief of the Armed Forces, and Minister of Defense--HH Sheikh Hamad bin Khalifa Al Thani.
Deputy Ruler and Crown Prince--HH Sheikh Jassim bin Hamad bin Khalifa Al Thani.
Prime Minister and Interior Minister--HH Sheikh Abdullah bin Khalifa Al Thani.
Minister of Foreign Affairs--HE Sheikh Hamad bin Jassim bin Jabir Al Thani.
Ambassador to the U.S.--HE Saad Mohamed al-Kobaisi.

Qatar maintains an embassy in the United States at 4200 Wisconsin Ave. NW, Suite 200, Washington, DC 20016 (tel. 202-274-1600) and expects to open a consulate in Houston in November 1997. Qatar,s Permanent Mission to the United Nations is at 747 Third Ave., 22nd floor, New York, NY 10017 (tel. 212-486-9335).

DEFENSE

Qatar,s defense expenditures accounted for approximately 4.2% of GNP in 1993. Qatar maintains a modest military force of approximately 11,800 men, including an army (8,500), navy (1,800) and air force (1,500). In August 1994, Qatar signed a defense agreement with France in which it agreed to purchase several Mirage 2000-5 aircraft. Qatar has also recently signed defense pacts with the U.S. and U.K. Qatar plays an active role in the collective defense efforts of the Gulf Cooperation Council (the regional organization of the Arab states in the Gulf; the other five members are Saudi Arabia, Kuwait, Bahrain, the UAE, and Oman). Qatari forces played a disproportionately important role in the Gulf War.

ECONOMY

CURRENCY

Currency in Qatar is the *Qatari Riyal*, which has full IMF backing. At present there are no restrictions on money transfer into or out of Qatar, and it is possible to effect remittences in any currency. Bank notes are in denominations of 1, 5, 10, 50, 100 & 500 QR. in paper, and 50 & 25 *Dirhams* in coins (1 QR. = 100 DHs). 1 US$ = 3.65 QRs approximately.

Oil is the cornerstone of Qatar,s economy and accounts for more than 70% of total government revenue. In 1973, oil production and revenues increased sizeably, moving Qatar out of the ranks of the world,s poorest countries and providing it with one of the highest per capita incomes. Despite a marked decline in levels of oil production and prices since 1982, Qatar remains a wealthy country.

Qatar,s economy was in a downturn from 1982 to 1989. OPEC (Organization of Petroleum Exporting Countries) quotas on crude oil production, the lower price for oil, and the generally unpromising outlook on international markets reduced oil earnings. In turn, the Qatari Government,s spending plans had to be cut to match lower income. The resulting recessionary local business climate caused many firms to lay off expatriate staff. With the economy recovering in the 1990s, expatriate populations, particularly from Egypt and South Asia, have grown again.

Oil production will not long return to peak levels of 500,000 barrels per day (b/d), as oil fields are projected to be mostly depleted by 2023. Fortunately, large natural gas reserves have been located off Qatar,s northeast coast. Qatar,s proved reserves of gas are the third-largest in the world, exceeding 7 trillion cubic meters. The economy was boosted in 1991 by completion of the $1.5-billion Phase I of North Field gas development. In 1996, the Qatargas project began exporting liquefied natural gas (LNG) to Japan. Further phases of North Field gas development costing billions of dollars are in various stages of planning and development.

Qatar,s heavy industrial projects, all based in Umm Said, include a refinery with a 50,000 b/d capacity, a fertilizer plant for urea and ammonia, a steel plant, and a petrochemical plant. All these industries use gas for fuel. Most are joint ventures between European and Japanese firms and the state-owned Qatar General Petroleum Corporation (QGPC). The U.S. is the major equipment supplier for Qatar,s oil and gas industry, and U.S. companies are playing a major role in North Field gas development.

Qatar pursues a vigorous program of "Qatarization," under which all joint venture industries and government departments strive to move Qatari nationals into positions of greater authority. Growing numbers of foreign-educated Qataris, including many educated in the U.S., are returning home to assume key positions formerly occupied by expatriates. In order to control the influx of expatriate workers, Qatar has tightened the administration of its foreign manpower programs over the past several years. Security is the principal basis for Qatar,s strict entry and immigration rules and regulations.

INDUSTRY

Under the wise and able rule of His Highness Sheikh Hamad Bin Khalif Al-Thani, the State of Qatar emerged as a modern industrial nation within a short period of 20 years.

For additional analytical, business and investment opportunities information, please contact Global Investment & Business Center, USA at (202) 546-2103. Fax: (202) 546-3275. E-mail: rusric@erols.com Global Business E-Books on Line: http://world.mirhouse.com

OIL AND GAS

Before the discovery of oil, the pearling and fishing represented Qatar's only source of wealth. There was a time when Qatari Pearling Dhows made up to a third of the entire Gulf fleet. But the development of cultured pearls by Japan, in the 1930's sharply depressed the Gulf's pearling trade. As a result, the Qatari economy experienced difficulties, but fortunately hard days did not last for long, as oil was discovered a little after the decline of the pearl market.

The Ras Laffan LNG project is being developed as a market-driven multi-train LNG plant, aimed at supplying world market with at least the next MMTA of Qatari LNG.

Production capacity will initially be 5 MMTA from two 2.5 MMTA trains with the option of future expansion to accommodate more than six further trains as markets develop and demand increases.

FOREIGN RELATIONS

Qatar achieved full independence in an atmosphere of cooperation with the U.K. and friendship with neighboring states. Most Arab states, the U.K., and the U.S. were among the first countries to recognize Qatar, and the state promptly gained admittance to the United Nations and the Arab League. Qatar established diplomatic relations with the U.S.S.R. and China in 1988. It was an early member of OPEC and a founding member of the GCC, whose rotating presidency it holds until December 1997.

In September 1992 tensions arose with Saudi Arabia when a Qatari border post was allegedly attacked by Saudi forces resulting in two deaths. Relations have since improved and a joint commission has been set up to demarcate the border as agreed between the two governments.

Qatar and Bahrain dispute ownership of the Hawar islands. The case is before the International Court of Justice in The Hague, while Saudi-led mediation efforts continue.

PRINCIPAL U.S. OFFICIALS

Ambassador--Patrick N. Theros
Deputy Chief of Mission--Todd P. Schwartz
Political Military Officer--Shaun Murphy
Economic/Commercial Officer--Benjamin Watson
Consular Officer--Clarence A. Hudson, Jr.
Administrative Officer--Raphael Semmes III
Public Affairs Officer--Jeffrey Hill

The U.S. Embassy in Qatar is located in Doha at 149 Ahmed bin Ali Street, Fariq bin Omran. Mailing address: P.O. Box 2399, Doha. Telephone: 974-864701/2/3; fax 861669. The embassy is open Saturday through Wednesday (Qatar,s workweek), closed for U.S. and Qatari holidays.

U.S.-QATARI RELATIONS

Bilateral relations are cordial. The U.S. Embassy was opened in March 1973. The first resident U.S. ambassador arrived in July 1974. In the summer of 1986, the then-Minister of Education, Sheikh Mohammed bin Hamad Al Thani, third-ranking official in the government, visited the U.S. as a guest of U.S. Secretary of Education William J. Bennett. In October 1987, Energy Secretary John S. Herrington led a delegation on a visit to Qatar that included calls on the Emir and the Heir Apparent and meetings at the Ministry of Finance and Petroleum. Secretary of Energy Henson Moore led a delegation to Doha in October 1991. The late Secretary of Commerce Ron Brown visited Doha in February 1995, and Secretary of Defense Perry visited in November 1996. More than 400 Qataris study at U.S. universities.

US AMBASSADOR

MAUREEN E. QUINN

Maureen E. Quinn, a career member of the Senior Foreign Service, was confirmed by the United States Senate as Ambassador to the State of Qatar in August 2001. She assumed her duties in Doha in September , 2001.

From July 1998 to March 2001, Ambassador Quinn served as Deputy Chief of Mission to the Embassy in Rabat, Morocco. Before serving in Morocco, she was Deputy Executive Secretary in the Department of State from 1997 to 1998, Executive Assistant and Special Assistant to the Undersecretary for Economic, Business and Agricultural Affairs from 1994 to 1997, and Economic Counselor at the U.S. Embassy in Panama from 1991 to 1994.

From 1990 to 1991, Ambassador Quinn was a Pearson Fellow at the U.S. House of Representatives. She served in the Economic Bureau's Office of International Development Finance from 1988 to 1990 and the Western Hemisphere's Bureau of Regional Economic Affairs from 1986 to 1988.

From 1984 to 1986, Ambassador Quinn was Economic Officer and Commercial Attaché at the U.S. Embassy in Conakry, Guinea. She served as Vice Consul and General Services Officer at the U.S. Consulate General in Karachi, Pakistan from 1982 to 1984.

Ambassador Quinn speaks French, Spanish and some Urdu. She earned a Bachelor's Degree at Newcomb College of Tulane University and a Master's Degree at Georgetown University. Ambassador Quinn is a native of Spring Lake, New Jersey.
U.S. Embassy
P.O. Box 2399, Doha, Qatar
Email: usisdoha@qatar.net.qa
OFFICE AND HOURS OF OPERATION

OFFICE

Position	Phone	Fax

For additional analytical, business and investment opportunities information, please contact Global Investment & Business Center, USA at (202) 546-2103. Fax: (202) 546-3275. E-mail: rusric@erols.com Global Business E-Books on Line: http://world.mirhouse.com

Public Affairs Officer	488-4101 ext.6065	488-4173
Public Affairs Specialist	488-4101 ext.6068	488-4173
Information Asst.	488-4101 ext.6247	488-4173
Information Resource Center	488-4101 ext.6009	488-4173

HOURS OF OPERATION

Office	Days	Hours
Public Affairs Section	Sunday through Thursday	8:00 AM - 4:30 PM
Information Resource Center	Sunday through Thursday	10:00 AM - 2:00 PM
U.S. Embassy	Sunday through Thursday	8:00 AM - 4:30 PM

IMPORTANT OFFICIAL MATERIALS ON FOREIGN POLICY ISSUES

QATAR'S FOREIGN POLICY[1]

Sheikh Hamad Bin Jassem Bin Jabr Al-Thani has been Qatar's minister of foreign affairs since 1992. This exclusive interview was conducted for Middle East Insight by Gulf specialist Louay Bahry, adjunct professor of political science at the University of Tennessee, who visited Qatar this year.

MEI: What is the role of Qatar in the Gulf Cooperation Council (GCC) and what is the future of the council as a unifying mechanism among Gulf countries?

Hamad Bin Jassem Al-Thani: Qatar is deeply committed to the strengthening of relations between Gulf countries. We therefore accord absolute priority to the solidarity of the members of the GCC, and the promotion of its ability to realize the goals assigned to it in the political, economic, military, and security domains. We know that we owe it to our people to offer them tangible results that they can

---

[1] Interview with Foreign Minister of Qatar, His Excellency Sheikh Hamad Bin Jassem Bin Jabr Al-Thani

---

For additional analytical, business and investment opportunities information, please contact Global Investment & Business Center, USA at (202) 546-2103. Fax: (202) 546-3275. E-mail: rusric@erols.com Global Business E-Books on Line: http://world.mirhouse.com

"In a world where democracy is increasingly being chosen as a system of governance, the steps taken by Qatar should not antagonize any state in the region."
feel in daily life, rather than the mere spectacle of meetings and conferences. We also consider differences of opinion a healthy sign that furthers joint efforts.

In a world of massive groupings, we consider it our duty to achieve peace and stability for our region through cooperation. This should occur through the implementation of agreed projects and the formulation of new ones, in such a way as to shape a new map for our region that is characterized by security and prosperity for our Arab and Muslim brothers.

MEI: Following his visit to Saudi Arabia, Iranian President Muhammad Khatami visited Qatar in 1999. How do you see relations between Qatar and Iran? How do GCC countries regard Iran today as compared to a decade ago?

Hamad Bin Jassem Al-Thani: I can confidently state that Qatari and GCC relations with Iran are better now than 10 years ago. Evidently the political changes witnessed by that country improved Iran's external relations, particularly its relations with its neighbors. This has promoted the adoption of policies based on mutual interest. Gulf participation in the Islamic summit held in Tehran in 1998, is perhaps best proof of our desire to improve relations with Iran. Regional proximity, religion, and reciprocal interests influence those relations. Besides, Iran is a regional economic and military power that cannot be ignored, and is capable of contributing to the security of the region.

Another facet of improving relations is the exchange of visits among GCC and Iranian officials, and the invitations extended by the Iranian leadership to Gulf leaders to visit Tehran. One such invitation was extended to H.H. Sheikh Hamad Bin Khalifa Al-Thani, the emir of Qatar. The date for that visit will soon be set.

However, the biggest hindrance to the development of that relationship is the Iranian occupation of the U.A.E. islands. If wisdom prevails, a negotiated settlement could be reached to safeguard the interests of both Iran and the U.A.E. We hope that the tripartite commission-Qatar, Saudi Arabia, and Oman-working on that problem will be successful in finding an acceptable solution.

For additional analytical, business and investment opportunities information, please contact Global Investment & Business Center, USA at (202) 546-2103. Fax: (202) 546-3275. E-mail: rusric@erols.com Global Business E-Books on Line: http://world.mirhouse.com

MEI: This year Libya withdrew its ambassador from Doha in protest against a program broadcast by Al-Jazeera that it considered negative. Do Al-Jazeera programs influence Qatari relations with other Arab countries? What is the official stand on the role of Al-Jazeera in Arab information?

Hamad Bin Jassem Al-Thani: We regret that action and hope that Libya will rethink its position. Let me reiterate that the foreign policy of Qatar is based on mutual respect and noninterference in internal affairs. We intend no mischief for any country.

Concerning Al-Jazeera, I'd like to affirm that it does not reflect official policy in Qatar, rather it is a consequence of freedom of information, an option that the emir has chosen. I'd like to add that the Ministry of Foreign Affairs is also not happy with the climate created from time to time by Al-Jazeera. Nonetheless, freedom of information remains a basic choice. We hope to see similar freedom in the rest of the Arab world to enable its citizens to know the truth and to participate in shaping policies and freely expressing their views.

ADDRESS BY HIS HIGHNESS SHEIKH HAMAD BIN KHALIFA AL THANI EMIR OF THE STATE OF QATAR AT THE MILLENIUM SUMMIT IN THE UNITED NATIONS

7 September 2000

In the Name of God the Merciful and Compassionate

Your Majesties, Highnesses and Excellencies,

Your Excellency Mr. President of the United Nations General Assembly

Your Excellency Mr. Secretary-General of the United Nations,

Ladies and Gentlemen:

It is a source of pleasure and pride for us to talk, on behalf of the State of Qatar and its people, in the Millennium Session held by the General Assembly at the United Nations Headquarters, address this honorable gathering and salute His Excellency Secretary General Kofi Annan and his staff for the fruitful efforts they exerted in organizing this session.

Ladies and Gentlemen,

It is no coincidence that most speeches delivered in this podium have, since the beginning of our meeting, concentrated on the subject of Globalization.

This phenomenon, which is the product of economic, social, cultural and technological developments and breakthroughs in the field of information, has not become only a major factor in the process of political decision, making, but the essential source for defining the components of international relations.

We find ourselves talking about a world with diminished distances and dimensions, easy means of communications and linkage among nations, by virtue of the emerging means that the informatics revolution has provided; a world in which we witness with great admiration the giant strides taken and the impressive results achieved through scientific research, particularly during the last decade of the century that is coming to an end.

But it is regrettably in this selfsame wonderful world that technological illiteracy, even alphabetical illiteracy, is spread among the majority of its peoples, and about a billion of its inhabitants suffer from abject poverty that is disgraceful to human dignity and, as a result of economic invasion, the economies of its countries are threatened with permanent crises and suffocating indebtedness. Moreover, its natural environment is deteriorating due to abusive exploitation, although this runs counter to the recommendations of numerous international forums, particularly the conference held at Rio de Janeiro. Is this not the reality? Is this state of affairs not too far form the ideal of building on earth and honoring human beings, which is advocated by the heavenly religions and cherished by international norms and covenants? Are we not, as we take part in this international forum which embodies the universality of man, supposed to stand together, think and ask ourselves about the ideal formula to bring things back to normal and make up for what is lost, before it is too late. We, both individuals and groups, have a great responsibility that we have to bear with integrity in the service of the present and future generations.

Dear Colleagues,

To achieve a better future for humanity and realize the principles of the United Nations is impossible without collective political will, wherein all parties in the international community help each other in one concerted effort with the aim of adopting a strategy geared basically towards narrowing the economic and cultural gap among states, and getting to the optimum and fair utilization of the fruits of technological progress. We believe that the United Nations organization is qualified to formulate an international system that comprehends globalization and spreads its blessings on all humanity, while putting checks on its negative effects.

Here, we should like to introduce our viewpoint concerning the procedural steps that may ensure the success of such a strategy:

First, we firmly believe that the objective condition for bringing nations closer together lies in establishing a comprehensive educational plan based on eliminating alphabetical illiteracy, promulgating compulsory education, and providing opportunities for harnessing information technology in the service of the goals of development.

The Third Millennium man is not satisfied only to know how to write, but is supposed to master the use of the modem means of communication, and qualify to freely express his ideas and discuss the ideas of other people.

Second, to improve the economic situation of developing countries, and the poor ones among them in particular, efforts to write off the debts of poor states should, in our view, be taken seriously, and we believe that it is useful to have these debts transformed into capitals invested in development projects that revive the production process and generate employment opportunities which will, in turn, reduce, if not eliminate, the flux of emigration to developed countries. It would be appropriate, in this respect, to gear special support to those states that take fundamental steps towards democracy.

Third, it is fairly regrettable that donor countries' development assistance is not proportionate with their gross domestic product (GDP). This runs counter to good judgment.

Fourth and last, we believe that it is in the interest of developed countries to be mindful of the great damage that will, by reason of their economic policies, befall the developing countries. We shall briefly refer, in this respect, to three indicators.

The first indicator relates to the developing countries that produce and export raw materials. Industrial developed countries lend a deaf ear to the high prices of their own products, while they raise objecting voices when the prices of raw materials, such as petroleum, rise in international markets, although this price-rise is the result of high taxes imposed by those developed countries.

The second indicator relates to industrial countries' resort to various excuses with the aim of weakening the competitive power of some developing countries.

The third indicator relates to the increasing restrictions those developed countries and their giant corporations impose on utilizing the vast progress in the different spheres of human knowledge and technology development, under the pretext of protecting intellectual prosperity.

Ladies and Gentlemen,

We endorse the constructive proposals submitted by His Excellency the Secretary-General in his report concerning the elimination of armed conflicts in the world" and the role of the U.N. in this respect, and emphasize the particular importance of three issues:

First, the United Nations should be urged to activate its role in bringing the Arab-Israeli conflict to an end. At the same time, we welcome any other efforts that could be made outside the United Nations in this regard, provided they pay due respect to the rights of the Palestinian and Syrian peoples established by international resolutions.

In the same context, we consider that the issue of Holy Jerusalem should be granted the extreme importance that it deserves, by reason of its distinct place in the hearts and minds of Arabs and Muslims, and since it is the cornerstone of any prospective peace in the Middle East.

The second issue is the necessity of moving fast towards making the Middle East a nuclear-weapon-free zone. From this forum, we call on Israel to accede to the Treaty on the Nonproliferation of Nuclear weapons.

The third issue relates to the necessity of putting checks on the way international sanctions are imposed. These checks should establish a time frame to stop the continuation of sanctions forever.

Ladies and Gentlemen,

As we look forward to contributing to the improvement of the performance of the United Nations Organization, we feel that the only way to realize this goal is to extend democratic practice and equal opportunities within the various international organizations. It is also high time for expanding representation in the Security Council to include, fairly and equitably, all regions of the world. By reason of its importance, the Arab World should have a permanent seat in the Council.

Ladies and Gentlemen,

While we are on the threshold of the Third Millennium, we look forward to a peaceful and safe world, pervaded by justice, security and prosperity, free of division, harm or wars, moving smoothly towards change, development and betterment, and contributing to the progress of all humanity.

Peace be upon you all and may the mercy of God and His blessings be with you.

2002 DOHA CONFERENCE ON U.S. RELATIONS WITH THE ISLAMIC WORLD

EMIR OF QATAR'S OPENING REMARKS

Sheik Hamad bin Khalifa Al Thani:

In the Name of God, the most compassionate, the most merciful,

Mr. Chairman, Your Excellencies, Honorable Guests, Esteemed Audience,

First, I would like to welcome you in Doha, wishing you pleasant stay and success for you conference on U.S. relations with the Islamic world.

For additional analytical, business and investment opportunities information, please contact Global Investment & Business Center, USA at (202) 546-2103. Fax: (202) 546-3275. E-mail: rusric@erols.com Global Business E-Books on Line: http://world.mirhouse.com

The relations between the United States and the Arab and Islamic worlds are of paramount importance. We consider them as a vital foundation, which we seek to reinforce in order to realize our common interests and ambitions. We advocate the principle of dialogue aimed at deepening the scope of understanding and establishing the bases of mutual respect, friendship and cooperation between our countries and societies.

The significance of relations between our Arab and Muslim countries and the West in general, and the United States in particular, is neither new nor accidental to our strategic and political concepts. It represents a real expression of historical facts which nobody can ignore or overlook the realities they involve. Our relations with the Untied States are not dictated upon us by common interests only, but we are also in agreement wit it on many basic matters inherent in our beliefs and ambitions. A good deal of the founding principals of the American society, which are in fact pillars of contemporary Western civilization, are not isolated from the sublime values and tenets which we cherish in our Arab and Islamic civilization.

We believe in justice, liberty, equality, respect for human rights, equal opportunities, encourage the spirit of initiative, and seek hard to establish popular participation as a basis for the decision making process and conducting government and administration affairs in our country. Moreover, we are keen on laying the basis of our foreign policy on the principles of international legality, coexistence and mutual respect. If these principles are sometimes not properly applied in some of our societies, this is not due to a deficiency in these principles and beliefs, but rather due to the way they are applied.

These principles are derived from the teachings of our true Islamic religion, which instructs us to respect other heavenly religions and open up to their followers. We also derive from them our contemporary view of the West, its civilization and communities as a major partner in our endeavor to realize the objectives of development and progress in our country.

However, this partnership and friendship does not mean detailed conformity in viewpoints, or the loss of identity. Allies and friends could never agree on every thing; what is important is that they need to be candid and deal with each other on the basis of friendship, equality, and mutual confidence. We agree with the United States on many issues and bearings and consider the close relations that bind us a strategic priority in our foreign policy.

From this standpoint, we did not hesitate to condemn the September 11 terrorist attacks against the U. S. A., and expressed our deep sympathy with the victims of those attacks and the resulting losses and suffering of the innocent civilians. In view of the dimensions of this event, its style, immensity, and the gravity of its consequences we called for the necessity of a deep search for its real causes and motives of its perpetrators. However, at the same time we stressed, and still do stress, the importance of differentiating between terrorism in all its forms and guises and the legitimate right of peoples to defend themselves, liberating their lands as well as their struggle to regain their rights.

We equally emphasized the importance of not making the mistake of attaching terrorism to a particular religion or a specific culture or civilization or one nationality of people. I am referring here to the misleading attempts that had, unfortunately, spread in some western political, informational and social circles, especially the American, in the wake of last year?s events, which sought to brand Islam with terrorism.

Islam as a religion and culture and civilization is clear of terrorists and terrorism. As for those who try to practice terrorism under the slogans of Islam, there are not different than the rest of extremists who engage in preaching the calls to fanaticism and isolation in all religions, societies and countries, whether they are oriental or occidental, Muslim or Christian or Jewish or otherwise. Fanaticism is fanaticism and terrorism is terrorism whatever slogans, calls, methods, or the affiliations of its perpetrators might be.

Ladies and gentlemen, we call upon the United States to deal with Arab and Muslim issues with a greater measure of evenhandedness, fairness and equality.

Let me be explicit on this point. We are not asking the United States to give up its special relationship with Israel. We call upon it as a superpower to perform its international, political and moral responsibilities and obligations towards the Palestinian question and the Arab-Israeli conflict in accordance with the resolutions of international legality, and exert the necessary efforts and pressures on Israel to end its occupation of the Arab territories. In this respect, we appreciate the conception announced by President George W. Bush as a basis of settlement; yet we are still hoping to see the practical mechanism and timetables by which this conception can be put to application.

Honorable audience, you undoubtedly agree with me as to the difficult and critical circumstances prevalent in the Gulf region and the Middle East. Our world is at a crucial crossroad. Perhaps the questions of relations between the U.S. and the Arab and Islamic worlds, which is the axis of your deliberations at this conference, represents the best evidence for the importance of the issues we are facing and the urgent need for finding the adequate solutions for them. We hope to start here to make the first basic steps required in this respect, which is the first basic step required in this respect, which is the indispensable and unavoidable dialogue.

I would like to take this opportunity to propose to you establishing a permanent forum for an Islamic-American dialogue, for the purpose of discussing the vital issues of interest to our countries and peoples. There is no alternative but to sit together and jointly arrive at solutions for our problems. Through such solutions, we can start planning for a joint future where we cooperate for the benefit of our peoples and societies to realize a better world for the present and future generations; a world based on a common belief in the principles of justice, human rights, and mutual openness among all peoples, nations, and cultures.

Thank you for your attendance and attention. I wish you all success in your mission. May the peace and blessings of God be upon you.

POST-SADDAM IRAQ: LINCHPIN OF A NEW OIL ORDER[2]

Only in the most direct sense is the Bush administration's Iraq policy directed against Saddam Hussein. In contrast to all the loud talk about terrorism, weapons of mass destruction, and human rights violations, very little is being said about oil. The administration has been tight-lipped about its plans for a post-Saddam Iraq and has repeatedly disavowed any interest in the country's oil resources. But press reports indicate that U.S. officials are considering a prolonged occupation of Iraq after their war to topple Saddam Hussein. It is likely that a U.S.-controlled Iraq will be the linchpin of a new order in the world oil industry. Indeed, a war against Iraq may well herald a major realignment of the Middle East power balance.

OIL FOREVER

The Bush administration's ties to the oil and gas industry are beyond extensive; they are pervasive. They flow, so to speak, from the top, with a chief executive who grew up steeped in the culture of Texas oil exploration and tried his hand at it himself; and a second-in-command who came to office with a multi-million dollar retirement package in hand from his post of CEO of Halliburton Oil. Once in office, the vice president developed an energy policy under the primary guidance of a cast of oil company executives whose identities he has gone to great lengths to withhold from public view. Since taking office, the president and vice president have assembled a government peopled heavily with representatives from the oil culture they came from. These include Secretary of the Army Thomas White, a former vice president of Enron, and Secretary of Commerce Don Evans, former president of the oil exploration company Tom Brown, Inc., whose major stake in the company was worth $13 million by the time he took office.

The Bush administration's energy policy is predicated on ever-growing consumption of oil, preferably cheap oil. U.S. oil consumption is projected to increase by one-third over the next two decades. The White House is pushing hard for greater domestic drilling and

---

[2] By Michael Renner, Worldwatch Institute

For additional analytical, business and investment opportunities information, please contact Global Investment & Business Center, USA at (202) 546-2103. Fax: (202) 546-3275. E-mail: rusric@erols.com Global Business E-Books on Line: http://world.mirhouse.com

wants to open the Arctic National Wildlife Refuge to the oil industry. Even so, the administration's National Energy Policy Development Group, led by Vice President Cheney, acknowledged in a May 2001 report that U.S. oil production will fall 12% over the next 20 years. As a result, U.S. dependence on imported oil—which has risen from one-third in 1985 to more than half today—is set to climb to two-thirds by 2020.1

Since the 1970s, the U.S. has put considerable effort into diversifying its sources of supply, going largely outside of OPEC and outside the Middle East. The current administration is advocating greater efforts to expand production in such far-flung places as the Caspian area, Nigeria, Chad, Angola, and deep offshore areas in the Atlantic basin and is looking to leading Western Hemispheric suppliers like Canada, Mexico, and Venezuela.2 West Africa is expected to account for as much as a quarter of U.S. oil imports a decade from now.3

But there is no escaping the fact that the Middle East—and specifically the Persian Gulf region—remains the world's prime oil province, for the U.S. and for other importers. Indeed, the Cheney report confirms that "by any estimation, Middle East oil producers will remain central to world oil security." The Middle East currently accounts for about 30% of global oil production and more than 40% of oil exports. With about 65% of the planet's known reserves, it is the only region able to satisfy the substantial rise in world oil demand predicted by the Bush administration.4 The Cheney report projects that Persian Gulf producers alone will supply 54-67% of world oil exports in 2020.5

Saudi Arabia is a pivotal player. With 262 billion barrels, it has a quarter of the world's total proven reserves and is the single largest producer.6 More importantly, the Saudis have demonstrated repeatedly—after the Iranian revolution, and following Iraq's invasion of Kuwait—that they are prepared to compensate for losses from other suppliers, calming markets in times of turmoil. Today, Riyadh could raise its production of 8 million barrels per day (b/d) to 10.5 million b/d within three months, making up for any loss of Iraqi oil during a U.S. military assault.7

IRAQ: FROM PARIAH TO FABULOUS PRIZE

The pariah state of Iraq, however, is a key prize, with abundant, high-quality oil that can be produced at very low cost (and thus at great profit). At 112 billion barrels, its proven reserves are currently second only to Saudi Arabia's. The Energy Information Administration (EIA) of the U.S. Department of Energy estimates that additional "probable and possible" resources could amount to 220 billion barrels. And because political instability, war, and sanctions have prevented thorough exploration of substantial portions of Iraqi territory, there is a chance that another 100 billion barrels lie undiscovered in Iraq's western desert. All in all, Iraq's oil wealth may well rival that of Saudi Arabia.8

At present, of course, this is mere potential—the Iraqi oil industry has seriously deteriorated as a result of the 1980-88 Iran-Iraq War, the 1991 Gulf War, and inadequate postwar investment and maintenance. Since 1990, the sanctions regime has effectively frozen plans for putting additional fields into production. It has also caused a severe shortage of oil field equipment and spare parts (under the sanctions regime, the U.S. has prevented equipment imports worth some $4 billion). Meanwhile, questionable methods used to raise output from existing fields may have damaged some of the reservoirs and could actually trigger a decline in output in the short run.9

But once the facilities are rehabilitated (a lucrative job for the oil service industry, including Vice President Cheney's former employer, Halliburton) and new fields are brought into operation, the spigots could be opened wide. To pay for the massive task of rebuilding, a post-sanctions Iraq would naturally seek to maximize its oil production. Some analysts, such as Fadhil Chalabi, a former Iraqi oil official, assert that Iraq could produce 8-10 million b/d within a decade and eventually perhaps as much as 12 million.10

The impact on world markets is hard to overstate. Saudi Arabia would no longer be the sole dominant producer, able to influence oil markets single-handedly. Given that U.S.-Saudi relations cooled substantially in the wake of the September 11, 2001, terrorist attacks—rifts that may widen further—a Saudi competitor would not be unwelcome in Washington. An unnamed U.S. diplomat confided to Scotland's *Sunday Herald* that "a rehabilitated Iraq is the only sound long-term strategic alternative to Saudi Arabia. It's not just a case of swapping horses in mid-stream, the impending U.S. regime change in Baghdad is a strategic necessity."11

Washington would gain enormous leverage over the world oil market. Opening the Iraqi spigot would flood world markets and drive prices down substantially. OPEC, already struggling with overcapacity and a tendency among its members to produce above allotted quotas (an estimated 3 million barrels per day above the agreed total of 24.7 million b/d), might unravel as individual exporters engage in destructive price wars against each other.12

A massive flow of Iraqi oil would also limit any influence that other suppliers, such as Russia, Mexico, and Venezuela, have over the oil market. Lower prices could render Russian oil—more expensive to produce—uncompetitive, which would cloud the prospects for attracting foreign investment to tap Siberian oil deposits.13 Russia's weak economy is highly dependent on oil export revenues. Its federal budget is predicated on prices of $24-25 per barrel.14 Aleksei Arbatov, deputy chairman of the Russian parliament's defense committee, predicts that if a new Iraqi regime sells oil without limits, "our budget will collapse."15

OIL COMPANY INTERESTS

To repair and expand its oil industry, Iraq will need substantial foreign investment. Thus, for eager oil companies, Iraq represents a huge bonanza—a "boom waiting to happen," according to an unnamed industry source.16

LEADING OIL COMPANIES, 2000

The 10 leading companies in each category are highlighted in the respective columns.

For additional analytical, business and investment opportunities information,
please contact Global Investment & Business Center, USA
at (202) 546-2103. Fax: (202) 546-3275. E-mail: rusric@erols.com
Global Business E-Books on Line: http://world.mirhouse.com

	Oil Reserves (billion barrels)	Oil Production (million b/d)	Refining Capacity (million b/d)	Product Sales (million b/d)
Saudi Aramco	261.8	8.6	2.1	3.0
INOC (Iraq)	112.5	2.6	0.4	0.4
KPC (Kuwait)	96.5	1.7	1.0	0.9
NIOC (Iran)	89.7	3.8	1.5	1.3
PDV (Venezuela)	77.7	3.3	3.1	3.2
ADNOC (United Arab Emirates)	53.8	1.4	0.2	0.2
Pemex (Mexico)	28.3	3.5	1.5	2.1
NOC (Libya)	23.6	1.3	0.3	0.3
Lukoil (Russia)	14.3	1.6	0.5	0.9
NNPC (Nigeria)	13.5	1.3	0.4	0.3
ExxonMobil (U.S.)	12.2	2.6	6.2	8.0
PetroChina	11.0	2.1	1.9	1.1
Royal Dutch/Shell (UK/Netherlands)	9.8	2.3	3.2	5.6
British Petroleum	7.6	1.9	3.2	5.5
TotalFinaElf (France)	7.0	1.4	2.6	3.1
ChevronTexaco (U.S.)	8.5	2.0	2.1	4.0
Petrobras (Brazil)	8.4	1.3	1.9	2.2
Sinopec (China)	3.0	0.7	2.6	1.3
Nippon Mitsubishi (Japan)	0.05	0.05	1.3	1.4
WORLD	1,046.2	74.5	81.6	

Source: Adapted from Energy Intelligence Group.
State-owned companies are in italics (state ownership is 100 percent, except for the following: PetroChina (90 percent), Sinopec (57 percent), and the majority privately owned Petrobras (32.5 percent) and Lukoil (14.1 percent)).

Prior to the OPEC revolution in the early 1970s, a small number of companies (referred to as the "majors" or "Seven Sisters") called the shots in the industry, controlling activities from exploration and production to refining and product sales. But they lost much of their reserve base, as nationalization spread through the Middle East and OPEC nations. Today, state oil companies own the vast majority of the world's oil

For additional analytical, business and investment opportunities information, please contact Global Investment & Business Center, USA at (202) 546-2103. Fax: (202) 546-3275. E-mail: rusric@erols.com Global Business E-Books on Line: http://world.mirhouse.com

resources. Even though private companies still do much of the exploring, drilling, and pumping, in many countries they have access to the oil only under prices and conditions set by the host government. Although oil companies have managed to adjust to this situation, a directly owned concession would offer them far greater flexibility and profitability.

The dominant private companies (ExxonMobil and Chevron-Texaco of the U.S., Royal Dutch-Shell and BP of Britain and the Netherlands, TotalFinaElf of France), which are largely the result of recent megamergers, sell close to 29 million barrels per day in gasoline and other oil products. But production from fields owned by these "super-majors" came to 10.1 million barrels per day in 2001, or just 35% of their sales volume.17 Although these corporations have poured many billions of dollars into discovering new fields outside the Middle East, their proven reserves stood at just 44 billion barrels in 2001, 4% of the world's total and sufficient to keep producing oil for only another 12 years at current rates.18 The situation is similar for other oil companies. Thus, the oil-rich Middle East, and particularly Iraq, remains key to the future of the oil industry.

If a new regime in Baghdad rolls out the red carpet for the oil multinationals to return, it is possible that a broader wave of denationalization could sweep through the oil industry, reversing the historic changes of the early 1970s. Squeezed by a decade of sanctions, the current regime has already signaled that it is prepared to provide more favorable terms to foreign companies.19 Such an invitation by Baghdad would be in tune with larger changes that are afoot, as a growing number of oil producing countries are opening their industries to foreign direct investment.20

RIVALRIES & QUID PRO QUOS

Several European and Asian oil companies have in recent years signed deals with Iraq that, if consummated, would give them access to reserves of at least 50 billion barrels and a potential output of 4-5 million barrels per day (another estimate says that Russian companies alone have signed deals involving about 70 billion barrels). In addition, a number of contracts have been signed for exploration in the western desert.21

Russian, Chinese, and French companies in particular have tried to position themselves to develop new oil fields and to rehabilitate existing ones, once UN sanctions are lifted. Russia's Lukoil, for instance, signed an agreement in 1997 to refurbish and develop the West Qurna field (with 15 billion barrels of oil reserves). China's National Petroleum Corporation signed a deal for the North Rumailah reservoir. And France's TotalFinaElf has set its eyes on the giant Majnoon deposits (holding 20-30 billion barrels).22

Iraq has sought to use the lure of oil concessions to build political support among three permanent Security Council nations—France, Russia, and China—for a lifting of sanctions. Although the international consensus in favor of sanctions has badly eroded, this gamble has failed to pay off in the face of determined U.S. and British opposition. (In December 2002, Iraq cancelled a contract with three Russian companies, out of frustration that the firms—in deference to sanctions—had not commenced oil exploration

For additional analytical, business and investment opportunities information,
please contact Global Investment & Business Center, USA
at (202) 546-2103. Fax: (202) 546-3275. E-mail: rusric@erols.com
Global Business E-Books on Line: http://world.mirhouse.com

work.) As long as Saddam Hussein stays in power, U.S. and British companies will be kept out of Iraq, but ongoing sanctions will also thwart existing oil development plans.

"Regime change" in Baghdad would reshuffle the cards and give U.S. (and British) companies a good shot at direct access to Iraqi oil for the first time in 30 years—a windfall worth hundreds of billions of dollars. U.S. companies relish the prospect: Chevron's chief executive, for example, said in 1998 that he'd "love Chevron to have access to" Iraq's oil reserves.23

In preface to the passage of Security Council Resolution 1441 on November 8, there were thinly veiled threats that French, Russian, and Chinese firms would be excluded from any future oil concessions in Iraq unless Paris, Moscow, and Beijing supported the Bush policy of regime change. Ahmed Chalabi, leader of the Iraqi National Congress (INC), an exile opposition group favored by the Bush administration, said that the INC would not feel bound by any contracts signed by Saddam Hussein's government and that "American companies will have a big shot at Iraqi oil" under a new regime. U.S. and British oil company executives have been meeting with INC officials, maneuvering to secure a future stake in Iraq's oil.24 Meanwhile, the State Department has been coaxing Iraqi opposition members to create an oil and gas working group involving Iraqis and Americans.25

Nikolai Tokarev, general director of Russia's Zarubezhneft, a state-owned oil company, reflected in late 2002: "Do Americans need us in Iraq? Of course not. Russian companies will lose the oil forever if the Americans come."26 Fears of being excluded from Iraq's oil riches and losing influence in the region have fed Russian, French, and Chinese interest in constraining U.S. belligerence. These countries nonetheless are eager to keep their options open in the event that a pro-U.S. regime is installed in Baghdad, avoiding the "risk of ending up on the wrong side of Washington," as the *New York Times* put it.27

Rival oil interests were a crucial behind-the-scenes factor as the permanent members of the UN Security Council jockeyed over the wording of Resolution 1441, intended to set the conditions for any action against Iraq. It is likely that backroom understandings regarding the future of Iraqi oil were part of the political minuet that finally led to the resolution's unanimous adoption. U.S. promises that the other powers would get a slice of the pie, hinted at in broad terms, were apparently inducement enough to win their nod. It is thus unlikely that French, Russian, and Chinese companies will be completely locked out of a post-Saddam Iraq, though they could find themselves in a junior position.

FROM SURROGATES TO DIRECT CONTROL

Throughout the history of oil, sorting out who gets access to this highly prized resource and on what terms has often gone hand in hand with violence. At first it was Britain, the imperial power in much of the Middle East, that called the shots. But for half a century, the U.S.—seeking a preponderant share of the earth's resources—has made steady progress in bringing the Persian Gulf region into its geopolitical orbit. In Washington's calculus, securing oil supplies has consistently trumped the pursuit of human rights and democracy.

U.S. policy toward the Middle East has long relied on building up proxy forces in the region and generously supplying them with arms. After the Shah of Iran, the West's regional policeman, was toppled in 1979, Iraq became a surrogate of sorts when it invaded Iran. Washington aided Iraq in a variety of ways, including commodity credits and loan guarantees, indirect arms supplies, critical military intelligence in Baghdad's long battle against Iran, a pro-Iraqi tilt in the "tanker war," and attacks on Iran's navy.

Beginning in the 1970s, but particularly in the wake of the 1991 Gulf War, the U.S. supplied Saudi Arabia and allied Persian Gulf states with massive amounts of highly sophisticated armaments. After the Gulf War, U.S. forces never left the region completely. By prepositioning military equipment and acquiring access to military bases in Saudi Arabia, Kuwait, Bahrain, and Qatar, Washington prepared the ground for future direct intervention as needed.

In the Persian Gulf and adjacent regions, access to oil is usually secured by a pervasive U.S. military presence. From Pakistan to Central Asia to the Caucasus and from the eastern Mediterranean to the Horn of Africa, a dense network of U.S. military facilities has emerged—with many bases established in the name of the "war on terror."

Although the U.S. military presence is not solely about oil, oil is a key reason. In 1999, General Anthony C. Zinni, then the head of the U.S. Central Command, testified to the Senate Armed Services Committee that the Persian Gulf region is of "vital interest" to the U.S. and that the country "must have free access to the region's resources."28

Bush administration officials have, however, categorically denied oil is one of the reasons why they are pushing for regime change in Iraq. "Nonsense," Defense Secretary Donald Rumsfeld told *60 Minutes'* Steve Kroft in mid-December 2002. "It has nothing to do with oil, literally nothing to do with oil."

But oil industry officials interviewed by *60 Minutes* on December 15 painted a different picture. Asked if oil is part of the equation, Phillip Ellis, head of global oil and gas operations for Boston Consulting replied, "Of course it is. No doubt."

In fact, oil company executives have been quietly meeting with U.S.-backed Iraqi opposition leaders. According to Ahmed Chalabi, head of the Iraqi National Congress, "The future democratic government in Iraq will be grateful to the United States for helping the Iraqi people liberate themselves and getting rid of Saddam." And he added that "American companies, we expect, will play an important and leading role in the future oil situation in Iraq."

ENDNOTES

For additional analytical, business and investment opportunities information,
please contact Global Investment & Business Center, USA
at (202) 546-2103. Fax: (202) 546-3275. E-mail: rusric@erols.com
Global Business E-Books on Line: http://world.mirhouse.com

1. National Energy Policy Development Group, *Reliable, Affordable, and Environmentally Sound Energy for America's Future* (Washington: U.S. Government Printing Office, May 2001), pp. x and 1-13.
2. Ibid., pp. 8-3 and 8-7.
3. James Dao, "In Quietly Courting Africa, White House Likes Dowry," *New York Times*, September 19, 2002.
4. Production and reserves are from *BP Statistical Review of World Energy 2002*; exports are from *OPEC Annual Statistical Bulletin 2001* (Vienna: 2002), Table 26.
5. National Energy Policy Development Group, *Reliable, Affordable, and Environmentally Sound Energy for America's Future* (Washington: U.S. Government Printing Office, May 2001), p. 8-4.
6. *BP Statistical Review of World Energy 2002*. Ultimately recoverable estimate is from U.S. Department of Energy, Energy Information Administration (EIA), *Saudi Arabia Country Analysis Brief*, October 2002, <http://www.eia.doe.gov/cabs/saudi.html>.
7. Past Saudi production increases are from *BP Statistical Review of World Energy 2002*; potential for current increase is from Jeff Gerth, "U.S. Fails to Curb Its Saudi Oil Habit, Experts Say," *New York Times*, November 26, 2002.
8. U.S. Department of Energy, Energy Information Administration (EIA), *Iraq Country Analysis Brief*, October 2002, <http://www.eia.doe.gov/cabs/iraq.html>. Iraqi oil officials agree, estimating reserves at 270-300 billion barrels in "Iraq's Oil Industry: An Overview," Platts, <http://www.platts.com/features/Iraq/oiloverview.shtml>.
9. U.S. Department of Energy, Energy Information Administration (EIA), *Iraq Country Analysis Brief*, October 2002, <http://www.eia.doe.gov/cabs/iraq.html>.
10. Fadhil J. Chalabi, "Iraq and the Future of World Oil," *Middle East Policy*, vol. vii, no. 4, October 2000, <http://www.mepc.org/public_asp/journal_vol7/0010_chalabi.asp>.
11. Trevor Royle, "The World's Petrol Station: Iraq's Past Is Steeped in Oil ... and Blood," *Sunday Herald*, October 6, 2002, <http://www.sundayherald.com/print28226>.
12. OPEC overproduction data is from Neela Banerjee, "As Its Members Flout Oil Quotas, OPEC Considers New Approach," *New York Times*, December 12, 2002.
13. Dan Morgan and David B. Ottoway, "In Iraqi War Scenario, Oil Is Key Issue," *Washington Post*, September 15, 2002.
14. Stratfor, "War in Iraq: What's at Stake for Russia?" November 22, 2002 (distributed electronically).
15. Arbatov quoted in Sabrina Tavernise, "Oil Prize, Past and Present, Ties Russia to Iraq," *New York Times*, October 17, 2002.
16. Quote from James A. Paul, "Iraq: The Struggle for Oil," August 2002, Global Policy Forum website, <http://www.globalpolicy.org/security/oil/2002/08jim.htm>.
17. Calculated from *OPEC Annual Statistical Bulletin 2001* (Vienna: 2002), Table 77.
18. Ibid.
19. U.S. Department of Energy, Energy Information Administration (EIA), *Iraq Country Analysis Brief*, October 2002, <http://www.eia.doe.gov/cabs/iraq.html>.
20. "The Iraq Oil Industry After Sanctions," Middle East Institute conference proceedings summary, February 29, 2000, as reposted on the Global Policy Forum website, <http://www.globalpolicy.org/security/oil/2000/0229mei.htm>.
21. Deutsche Bank estimates, reported in U.S. Department of Energy, Energy Information Administration (EIA), *Iraq Country Analysis Brief*, October 2002, <http://www.eia.doe.gov/cabs/iraq.html>. The higher estimate is from Zarubezhneft, a Russian state-owned company. See Sabrina Tavernise, "Oil Prize, Past and Present, Ties Russia to Iraq," *New York Times*, October 17, 2002.
22. U.S. Department of Energy, Energy Information Administration (EIA), *Iraq Country Analysis Brief*, October 2002, <http://www.eia.doe.gov/cabs/iraq.html>.

23. Speech by Kenneth T. Derr, <http://www.chevrontexaco.com/news/archive/chevron_speech/1998/98-11-05.asp>.
24. Chalabi quote is from Dan Morgan and David B. Ottoway, "In Iraqi War Scenario, Oil Is Key Issue," *Washington Post*, September 15, 2002. Peter Beaumont and Faisal Islam, "Carve-Up of Oil Riches Begins," *The Observer* (United Kingdom), November 3, 2002.
25. Stratfor, "War in Iraq: What's at Stake for Russia?" November 22, 2002 (distributed electronically).
26. Sabrina Tavernise, "Oil Prize, Past and Present, Ties Russia to Iraq," *New York Times*, October 17, 2002.
27. Serge Schmemann, "Controlling Iraq's Oil Wouldn't Be Simple," *New York Times*, November 3, 2002.
28. Zinni quote is from James A. Paul, "Iraq: The Struggle for Oil," August 2002, Global Policy Forum website, <http://www.globalpolicy.org/security/oil/2002/08jim.htm>. Testimony of April 13, 1999.

For additional analytical, business and investment opportunities information, please contact Global Investment & Business Center, USA at (202) 546-2103. Fax: (202) 546-3275. E-mail: rusric@erols.com Global Business E-Books on Line: http://world.mirhouse.com

PERCIAN GULF HISTORY & QATAR

THE FIVE COUNTRIES covered in this volume--Kuwait, Bahrain, Qatar, the United Arab Emirates, and Oman--are all Arab states on the Persian Gulf that share certain characteristics. But they are not the only countries that border the gulf. Iran, Iraq, and Saudi Arabia share the coastline as well, and they too shared in the historical development of the area. Of the five states covered in this volume, Oman has a particular culture and history that distinguish it from its neighbors. It also is the state with the shortest coastline along the Persian Gulf. Most of Oman lies along the Gulf of Oman and the Arabian Sea (see fig. 1).

The main element that unites these countries is the nature of their involvement with people and nations beyond the region. The gulf has been an important waterway since ancient times, bringing the people who live on its shores into early contact with other civilizations. In the ancient world, the gulf peoples established trade connections with India; in the Middle Ages, they went as far as China; and in the modern era, they became involved with the European powers that sailed into the Indian Ocean and around Southeast Asia. In the twentieth century, the discovery of massive oil deposits in the gulf made the area once again a crossroads for the modern world.

Other factors also bring these countries together. The people are mostly Arabs and, with the exception of Oman and Bahrain, are mostly Sunni (see Glossary) Muslims. Because they live in basically tribal societies, family and clan connections underlie most political and economic activity. The discovery of oil and the increasing contact with the West has led to tremendous material and social changes.

Important distinctions exist, however, among the five countries. Bahrain is an island with historical connections to the Persian Empire. Kuwait is separated from the others by Saudi Arabia. In Oman high mountain ranges effectively cut off the country's hinterland from the rest of the region. Moreover, various tribal loyalties throughout the region are frequently divisive and are exacerbated by religious differences that involve the major sects of Islam-- Sunni and Shia (see Glossary)--and the smaller Kharijite sect as well as Muslim legal procedures.

TRADE IN THE GULF

The Persian Gulf lies between two of the major breadbaskets of the ancient world, the Tigris-Euphrates area (Mesopotamia, meaning "between the rivers") in present-day Iraq and the Nile Valley in Egypt. Mesopotamia, a part of the area known as the Fertile Crescent, was important not only for food production but also for connecting East to West.

Rivers provided the water that made agriculture possible. Agriculture, in turn, enabled people to settle in one area and to accumulate a food surplus that allowed them to pursue tasks besides growing food, namely, to create a civilization. They chose leaders, such as kings and priests; they built monuments; they devised systems of morality and religion; and they started to trade.

Mesopotamia became the linchpin of ancient international trade. The fertile soil between the Tigris and the Euphrates produced a arge surplus of food; however, it did not support forests to produce the timber necessary to build permanent structures. The region also lacked the mineral resources to make metals. Accordingly, the early inhabitants of Mesopotamia were forced to go abroad and trade their food for other raw materials. They found copper at Magan, an ancient city that lay somewhere in the contemporary state of Oman and, via Magan, traded with people in the Indus Valley for lumber and other finished goods.

Trade between Mesopotamia and India was facilitated by the small size of the Persian Gulf. Water provided the easiest way to transport goods, and sailors crossed the gulf fairly early, moving out along the coasts of Persia and India until they reached the mouth of the Indus. Merchants and sailors became middlemen who used their position to profit from the movement of goods through the gulf. The people of Magan were both middlemen and suppliers because the city was a source of copper as well as a transit point for Indian trade. Over time, other cities developed that were exclusively entrepôts, or commercial way stations. One of the best known of these cities was Dilmun.

Dilmun probably lay on what is now the island state of Bahrain. Excavations on the island reveal rich burial mounds from the Dilmun period (ca. 4000 to 2000 B.C.). Scholars believe the monuments on the island indicate that residents, in addition to farming, earned money from the East-West trade and that other cities on the gulf coast survived similarly.

The trading cities on the gulf were closely linked to Mesopotamia, reflected in the similarities between the archaeological finds in the two areas. The similar finds suggest that the people of the gulf coast and the people of the Tigris and Euphrates valley developed increasingly complex societies and beliefs.

The people of the gulf coast differed from those of the interior of the Arabian Peninsula. The people in the interior were nomads who had no time to build cities or monuments and no need to develop elaborate social structures. When the desert provided insufficient food for their flocks, the tribes pushed into the date groves or farmlands of the settled towns. Centers on the gulf coast were subject to such nomadic incursions, as were the people of Mesopotamia. As a result, after the second millennium B.C. the gulf began to take on an increasingly Arab character. Some Arab tribes from the interior left their flocks and took over the date groves that ringed the region's oases, while others took up sailing and began to take part in the trade and piracy that were the region's economic mainstays. These nomadic incursions periodically changed the ethnic balance and leadership of the gulf coast.

Meanwhile, trade flourished in the second millennium B.C., as reflected in the wealth of Dilmun. In about 1800 B.C., however, both the quality and the amount of goods that passed through Dilmun declined, and many scholars attribute this to a corresponding decline in the Mesopotamian markets. Concurrently, an alternate trade route arose that linked India to the Mediterranean Sea via the Arabian Sea, then through the Gulf of Aden, thence into the Red Sea where the pharaohs had built a shallow canal that linked

For additional analytical, business and investment opportunities information, please contact Global Investment & Business Center, USA at (202) 546-2103. Fax: (202) 546-3275. E-mail: rusric@erols.com Global Business E-Books on Line: http://world.mirhouse.com

the Red Sea to the Nile. This new route gave access not only to Mediterranean ports but also, through the Mediterranean ports, to the West as well.

One of the ways that rulers directed goods toward their own country was to control transit points on the trade routes. Oman was significant to rulers in Mesopotamia because it provided a source of raw materials as well as a transshipment point for goods from the East. Although a valuable prize, Oman's large navy gave it influence over other cities in the gulf. When Mesopotamia was strong, its rulers sought to take over Oman. When Oman was strong, its rulers pushed up through the gulf and into Mesopotamia. One of the basic conflicts in gulf history has been the struggle of indigenous peoples against outside powers who sought to control the gulf because of its strategic importance.

Competition between Red Sea and Persian Gulf trade routes was complicated by the rise of new land routes around 1000 B.C. Technological advances in the second and first millennia B.C. made land routes increasingly viable for moving goods. The domestication of the camel and the development of a saddle enabling the animal to carry large loads allowed merchants to send goods across Arabia as well. As a result, inland centers developed at the end of the first millennium B.C. to service the increasing caravan traffic. These overland trade routes helped to Arabize the gulf by bringing the nomads of the interior into closer contact with their relatives on the coast.

THE GULF IN THE ANCIENT WORLD

Archaeological evidence suggests that Dilmun returned to prosperity after the Assyrian Empire stabilized the TigrisEuphrates area at the end of the second millennium B.C. A powerful ruler in Mesopotamia meant a prosperous gulf, and Ashurbanipal, the Assyrian king who ruled in the seventh century B.C., was particularly strong. He extended Assyrian influence as far as Egypt and controlled an empire that stretched from North Africa to the Persian Gulf. The Egyptians, however, regained control of their country about a half-century after they lost it.

A series of other conquests of varying lengths followed. In 325 B.C., Alexander the Great sent a fleet from India to follow the eastern, or Persian, coast of the gulf up to the mouth of the Tigris and Euphrates rivers and sent other ships to explore the Arab side of the waterway. The temporary Greek presence in the area increased Western interest in the gulf during the next two centuries. Alexander's successors, however, did not control the area long enough to make the gulf a part of the Greek world. By about 250 B.C., the Greeks lost all territory east of Syria to the Parthians, a Persian dynasty in the East. The Parthians brought the gulf under Persian control and extended their influence as far as Oman.

The Parthian conquests demarcated the distinction between the Greek world of the Mediterranean Sea and the Persian Empire in the East. The Greeks, and the Romans after them, depended on the Red Sea route, whereas the Parthians depended on the Persian Gulf route. Because they needed to keep the merchants who plied those routes under their control, the Parthians established garrisons as far south as Oman.

For additional analytical, business and investment opportunities information, please contact Global Investment & Business Center, USA at (202) 546-2103. Fax: (202) 546-3275. E-mail: rusric@erols.com Global Business E-Books on Line: http://world.mirhouse.com

In the third century A.D., the Sassanians, another Persian dynasty, succeeded the Parthians and held the area until the rise of Islam four centuries later. Under Sassanian rule, Persian control over the gulf reached its height. Oman was no longer a threat, and the Sassanians were strong enough to establish agricultural colonies and to engage some of the nomadic tribes in the interior as a border guard to protect their western flank from the Romans.

This agricultural and military contact gave people in the gulf greater exposure to Persian culture, as reflected in certain irrigation techniques still used in Oman. The gulf continued to be a crossroads, however, and its people learned about Persian beliefs, such as Zoroastrianism, as well as about Semitic and Mediterranean ideas.

Judaism and Christianity arrived in the gulf from a number of directions: from Jewish and Christian tribes in the Arabian desert; from Ethiopian Christians to the south; and from Mesopotamia, where Jewish and Christian communities flourished under Sassanian rule. Whereas Zoroastrianism seems to have been confined to Persian colonists, Christianity and Judaism were adopted by some Arabs. The popularity of these religions paled, however, when compared with the enthusiasm with which the Arabs greeted Islam.

EARLY DEVELOPMENT OF ISLAM

Islam is a system of religious beliefs and an allencompassing way of life. Muslims believe that God (Allah) revealed to the Prophet Muhammad the rules governing society and the proper conduct of society's members. It is incumbent on the individual, therefore, to live in a manner prescribed by the revealed law and incumbent on the community to build the perfect human society on earth according to holy injunctions. Islam recognizes no distinctions between the religious institution and the state. The distinction between religious and secular law is a recent development that in part reflects the more pronounced role of the state in society and Western economic and cultural penetration. The impact of religion on daily life in Muslim countries is extensive, usually greater than that found in the West.

The area that constitutes the present-day Persian Gulf states was on the immediate periphery of the rise of Islam. In A.D. 610, Muhammad--a merchant of the Hashimite branch of the ruling Quraysh tribe in the Arabian town of Mecca--began to preach the first of a series of revelations that Muslims believe was granted him by God, some directly and some through the angel Gabriel. A fervent monotheist, Muhammad denounced the polytheism of his fellow Meccans. Because the town's economy was based in part on a thriving pilgrimage business to the shrine called the Kaaba and to numerous other pagan religious sites in the area, his censure earned him the enmity of the town's leaders. In 622 he and a group of followers accepted an invitation to settle in the town of Yathrib, later known as Medina (the city), because it was the center of Muhammad's activities. The move, or hijra (see Glossary), known in the West as the hegira, marks the beginning of the Islamic era and of Islam as a force in history; the Muslim calendar begins in 622. In Medina, Muhammad continued to preach, and he eventually defeated his detractors in battle. He consolidated the temporal and the spiritual leadership in his person before his death in 632. After Muhammad's death, his

For additional analytical, business and investment opportunities information,
please contact Global Investment & Business Center, USA
at (202) 546-2103. Fax: (202) 546-3275. E-mail: rusric@erols.com
Global Business E-Books on Line: http://world.mirhouse.com

followers compiled those of his words regarded as coming directly from God into the Quran, the holy scripture of Islam. Others of his sayings, recalled by those who had known him, became the hadith (see Glossary). The precedent of Muhammad's deeds is called the sunna. Together they form a comprehensive guide to the spiritual, ethical, and social life of an orthodox Sunni Muslim.

The major duties of Muslims are found in the five pillars of Islam, which set forth the acts necessary to demonstrate and reinforce the faith. These are the recitation of the *shahada* ("There is no god but God [Allah], and Muhammad is his prophet"), daily prayer (*salat*), almsgiving (*zakat*), fasting (*sawm*), and pilgrimage (hajj). The believer is to pray in a prescribed manner after purification through ritual ablutions each day at dawn, midday, midafternoon, sunset, and nightfall. Prescribed genuflections and prostrations accompany the prayers, which the worshiper recites while facing toward Mecca. Whenever possible, men pray in congregation at the mosque with an imam (see Glossary), and on Fridays they are required to do so. The Friday noon prayers provide the occasion for weekly sermons by religious leaders. Women may also attend public worship at the mosque, where they are segregated from the men, although most frequently women pray at home. A special functionary, the muezzin, intones a call to prayer to the entire community at the appropriate hour.

The ninth month of the Muslim calendar is Ramadan, a period of obligatory fasting in commemoration of Muhammad's receipt of God's revelation. Throughout the month, all but the sick and the weak, pregnant or lactating women, soldiers on duty, travelers on necessary journeys, and young children are enjoined from eating, drinking, smoking, or sexual intercourse during the daylight hours. Those adults excused are obliged to endure an equivalent fast at their earliest opportunity. A festive meal breaks the daily fast and inaugurates a night of feasting and celebration. The pious well-to-do usually do little or no work during this period, and some businesses close for all or part of the day. Because the months of the lunar year revolve through the solar year, Ramadan falls earlier in the solar year each successive year. A considerable test of discipline at any time of the year, a fast that falls in summer imposes severe hardship on those who must do physical work.

All Muslims, at least once in their lifetimes and if circumstances permit, should make the hajj to Mecca to participate in special rites held there during the twelfth month of the lunar calendar. Muhammad instituted this requirement, modifying pre-Islamic custom, to emphasize sites associated with God and Abraham (Ibrahim), founder of monotheism and father of the Arabs through his son, Ismail.

The lesser pillars of the faith, which all Muslims share, are jihad, or the permanent struggle for the triumph of the word of God on earth, and the requirement to do good works and to avoid all evil thoughts, words, and deeds. In addition, Muslims agree on certain basic principles of faith based on the teachings of the Prophet Muhammad: there is one God, who is a unitary divine being in contrast to the trinitarian belief of Christians; Muhammad, the last of a line of prophets beginning with Abraham and including Moses and Jesus, was chosen by God to present God's message to humanity; and there is a general resurrection on the last, or judgment, day.

For additional analytical, business and investment opportunities information, please contact Global Investment & Business Center, USA at (202) 546-2103. Fax: (202) 546-3275. E-mail: rusric@erols.com Global Business E-Books on Line: http://world.mirhouse.com

During his lifetime, Muhammad held both spiritual and temporal leadership of the Muslim community. Religious and secular law merged, and all Muslims have traditionally been subject to the sharia, or religious law. A comprehensive legal system, the sharia developed gradually through the early centuries of Islam, primarily through the accretion of interpretations and precedents set by various judges and scholars. During the tenth century, legal opinion began to harden into authoritative rulings, and the figurative *bab al ijtihad* (gate of interpretation) closed. Thereafter, rather than encouraging flexibility, Islamic law emphasized maintenance of the status quo.

After Muhammad's death, the leaders of the Muslim community consensually chose Abu Bakr, the Prophet's father-in-law and one of his earliest followers, to succeed him. At that time, some persons favored Ali ibn Abu Talib, Muhammad's cousin and the husband of his daughter, Fatima, but Ali and his supporters (the Shiat Ali, or Party of Ali) eventually recognized the community's choice. The next two caliphs (successors)--Umar, who succeeded in 634, and Uthman, who took power in 644--enjoyed the recognition of the entire community. When Ali finally succeeded to the caliphate in 656, Muawiyah, governor of Syria, rebelled in the name of his murdered kinsman, Uthman. After the ensuing civil war, Ali moved his capital to Iraq, where he was murdered shortly thereafter.

Ali's death ended the last of the so-called four orthodox caliphates and the period in which the entire community of Islam recognized a single caliph. Muawiyah proclaimed himself caliph from Damascus. The Shiat Ali refused to recognize him or his line, the Umayyad caliphs, and withdrew in the great schism of Islam to establish the dissident sect, known as the Shia, who supported the claims of Ali's line to the caliphate based on descent from the Prophet. The larger faction, the Sunnis, adhered to the position that the caliph must be elected, and over the centuries they have represented themselves as the orthodox branch.

SUNNI ISLAM

Although originally political in nature, the differences between Sunni and Shia interpretations rapidly took on theological overtones. In principle, a Sunni approaches God directly: there is no clerical hierarchy. Some duly appointed religious figures, such as imams, however, exert considerable social and political power. Imams usually are men of importance in their communities, but they need not have any formal training. Committees of socially prominent worshipers usually are responsible for managing major mosque-owned lands. In most Arab countries, the administration of waqfs (religious endowments) has come under the influence of the state. Qadis (judges) and imams are appointed by the government.

The Muslim year has two religious festivals: Id al Adha, a sacrificial festival held on the tenth day of Dhu al Hijjah, the twelfth, or pilgrimage, month; and Id al Fitr, the festival of breaking the fast, which celebrates the end of Ramadan on the first day of Shawwal, the tenth month. To Sunnis these are the most important festivals of the year. Each lasts three or four days, during which time people put on their best clothes and visit, congratulate, and bestow gifts on each other. In addition, cemeteries are visited. Id al

For additional analytical, business and investment opportunities information,
please contact Global Investment & Business Center, USA
at (202) 546-2103. Fax: (202) 546-3275. E-mail: rusric@erols.com
Global Business E-Books on Line: http://world.mirhouse.com

Fitr is celebrated more festively because it marks the end of Ramadan. Celebrations also take place, although less extensively, on the Prophet's birthday, which falls on the twelfth day of Rabi al Awwal, the third month.

With regard to legal matters, Sunni Islam has four orthodox schools that give different weight in legal opinions to prescriptions in the Quran, to the hadith, to the consensus of legal scholars, to analogy (to similar situations at the time of the Prophet), and to reason or opinion. Named for their founders, the earliest Muslim legal schools were those of Abd Allah Malik ibn Anas (ca. 715-95) and An Numan ibn Thabit Abu Hanifa (ca. 700-67). The Maliki school was centered in Medina, and the lawbook of Malik ibn Anas is the earliest surviving Muslim legal text, containing a systematic consensus of Medina legal opinions. The Hanafi school in Iraq stressed individual opinion in making legal decisions. Muhammad ibn Idris ash Shafii (767-820), a member of the tribe of Quraysh and a distant relative of the Prophet, studied under Malik ibn Anas in Medina. He followed a somewhat eclectic legal path, laying down the rules for analogy that were later adopted by other legal schools. The last of the four major Sunni legal schools, that of Ahmad ibn Muhammad ibn Hanbal (780-855), was centered in Baghdad. The Hanbali school, which became prominent in Arabia as a result of Wahhabi (see Glossary) influence, gave great emphasis to the hadith as a source of Muslim law but rejected innovations and rationalistic explanations of the Quran and the traditions

SHIA ISLAM

Shia Muslims hold the fundamental beliefs of other Muslims (see Sunni Islam , this ch.). In addition to these tenets, however, Shia believe in the imamate, which is the distinctive institution of Shia Islam. Whereas Sunni Muslims view the caliph as a temporal leader only and consider an imam to be a prayer leader, Shia Muslims hold a hereditary view of Muslim leadership. They believe the Prophet Muhammad designated Ali to be his successor as Imam (when uppercase, Imam refers to the Shia descendant of the House of Ali), exercising both spiritual and temporal leadership. Only those who have *walayat* (spiritual guidance) are free from error and sin and have been chosen by God through the Prophet. Each Imam in turn designated his successor--through twelve Imams--each holding the same powers.

The imamate began with Ali, who is also accepted by Sunni Muslims as the fourth of the "rightly guided caliphs" to succeed the Prophet. Shia revere Ali as the First Imam, and his descendants, beginning with his sons Hasan and Husayn, continue the line of the Imams until the twelfth. Shia point to the close lifetime association of the Prophet with Ali. When Ali was six years old, he was invited by the Prophet to live with him, and Shia believe Ali was the first person to make the declaration of faith in Islam. Ali also slept in the Prophet's bed on the night of the hijra, when it was feared that the house would be attacked by unbelievers and the Prophet stabbed to death. He fought in all the battles the Prophet did, except one, and the Prophet chose him to be the husband of one of his favorite daughters, Fatima.

Among Shia, the term *imam* traditionally has been used only for Ali and his eleven descendants. None of the twelve Imams, with the exception of Ali, ever ruled an Islamic

For additional analytical, business and investment opportunities information, please contact Global Investment & Business Center, USA at (202) 546-2103. Fax: (202) 546-3275. E-mail: rusric@erols.com
Global Business E-Books on Line: http://world.mirhouse.com

government. During their lifetimes, their followers hoped that they would assume the rulership of the Islamic community, a rule that was believed to have been wrongfully usurped. Because Sunni caliphs were cognizant of this hope, Imams generally were persecuted under the Umayyad and Abbasid dynasties. Therefore, the Imams tried to be as unobtrusive as possible and to live as far as was reasonable from the successive capitals of the Islamic empire.

During the eighth century, Caliph Al Mamun, son and successor to Harun ar Rashid, was favorably disposed toward the descendants of Ali and their followers. He invited Imam Reza, the Eighth Imam (765-816), to come from Medina to his court at Marv (Mary in present-day Turkmenistan). While Reza was residing at Marv, Al Mamun designated him as his successor in an apparent effort to avoid conflict among Muslims. Reza's sister, Fatima, journeyed from Medina to be with her brother but took ill and died at Qom, in present-day Iran. A major shrine developed around her tomb, and over the centuries Qom has become a major Shia pilgrimage site and theological center.

Al Mamun took Reza on his military campaign to retake Baghdad from political rivals. On this trip, Reza died unexpectedly in Khorasan. Reza was the only Imam to reside in, or die in, what is now Iran. A major shrine, and eventually the city of Mashhad, grew up around his tomb, which is the major pilgrimage center in Iran. Several theological schools are located in Mashhad, associated with the shrine of the Eighth Imam.

Reza's sudden death was a shock to his followers, many of whom believed that Al Mamun, out of jealousy for Reza's increasing popularity, had the Imam poisoned. Al Mamun's suspected treachery against Imam Reza and his family tended to reinforce a feeling already prevalent among his followers that Sunni rulers were untrustworthy.

The Twelfth Imam is believed to have been only five years old when he became Imam in 874 on the death of his father. Because his followers feared he might be assassinated, the Twelfth Imam was hidden from public view and was seen only by a few of his closest deputies. Sunnis claim that he never existed, or that he died while still a child. Shia believe that the Twelfth Imam never died, but disappeared in about 939. Since then, the greater occultation of the Twelfth Imam has been in force, which will last until God commands the Twelfth Imam to manifest himself on earth again as the mahdi or messiah. Shia believe that during the occultation of the Twelfth Imam, he is spiritually present--some believe that he is materially present as well--and he is besought to reappear in various invocations and prayers. His name is mentioned in wedding invitations, and his birthday is one of the most jubilant of all Shia religious observances.

The Shia doctrine of the imamate was not fully elaborated until the tenth century. Other dogmas developed still later. A characteristic of Shia Islam is the continual exposition and reinterpretation of doctrine.

A significant practice of Shia Islam is that of visiting the shrines of Imams in Iraq and in Iran. In Iraq, these include the tomb of Imam Ali in An Najaf and that of his son, Imam Husayn, in Karbala, because both are considered major Shia martyrs. Before the Iran-Iraq War (1980-88), tens of thousands made the visits each year. Other principal pilgrimage sites in Iraq are the tombs of the Seventh Imam and the Ninth Imam at Kazimayn near Baghdad. In Iran, pilgrimage sites include the tomb of the Eighth Imam in Mashhad and that of his sister in Qom. Such pilgrimages originated in part from the difficulty and the expense of making the hajj to Mecca in the early days.

In commemoration of the martyrdom of Husayn, killed near Karbala in 680 during a battle with troops supporting the Umayyad caliph, processions are held in the Shia towns and villages of southern Iraq on the tenth day of Muharram (Ashura), the anniversary of his death. Ritual mourning (*taaziya*) is performed by groups of five to twenty men each. Contributions are solicited in the community to pay transportation for a local group to go to Karbala for *taaziya* celebrations forty days after Ashura. There is great rivalry among groups for the best performance of the *taaziya* passion plays.

Shia practice differs from Sunni practice concerning divorce and inheritance in that it is more favorable to women. The reason for this reputedly is the high esteem in which Fatima, the wife of Ali and the daughter of the Prophet, was held.

Like Sunni Islam, Shia Islam has developed several sects. The most important of these is the Twelver, or Ithna-Ashari, sect, which predominates in the Shia world generally. Not all Shia became Twelvers, however. In the eighth century, a dispute arose over who should lead the Shia community after the death of the Sixth Imam, Jaafar ibn Muhammad (also known as Jaafar as Sadiq). The group that eventually became the Twelvers followed the teaching of Musa al Kazim; another group followed the teachings of Musa's brother, Ismail, and were called Ismailis. Ismailis are also referred to as Seveners because they broke off from the Shia community over a disagreement concerning the Seventh Imam. Ismailis do not believe that any of their Imams have disappeared from the world in order to return later. Rather, they have followed a continuous line of leaders represented in early 1993 by Karim al Husayni Agha Khan IV, an active figure in international humanitarian efforts. The Twelver Shia and the Ismailis also have their own legal schools.

Another group, the Kharijites, arose from events surrounding the assassination of Uthman, the third caliph, and the transfer of authority to the fourth caliph, Ali. In the war between Ali and Muawiyah, part of Ali's army objected to arbitration of the dispute. They left Ali's camp, causing other Muslims to refer to them as "kharijites" (the ones who leave). The term *Kharijites* also became a designation for Muslims who refused to compromise with those who differed from them. Their actions caused the Sunni community to consider them assassins.

In the eighth century, some Kharijites began to moderate their position. Leaders arose who suppressed the fanatical political element in Kharijite belief and discouraged their followers from taking up arms against Islam's official leader. Kharijite leaders emphasized instead the special benefits that Kharijites might receive from living in a small community that held high standards for personal conduct and spiritual values. One of these religious leaders, or imams, was Abd Allah ibn Ibad, whose followers founded communities in parts of Africa and southern Arabia. Some of Abd Allah's followers, known as Ibadis, became the leaders of Oman.

THE SPREAD OF ISLAM

Early Islamic polity was intensely expansionist, fueled both by fervor for the faith and by economic and social factors. After gaining control of Arabia and the Persian Gulf region, conquering armies swept out of the peninsula, spreading Islam. By the end of the eighth century, Islamic armies had reached far into North Africa and eastward and northward into Asia.

Traditional accounts of the conversion of tribes in the gulf are probably more legend than history. Stories about the Bani Abd al Qais tribe that controlled the eastern coast of Arabia as well as Bahrain when the tribe converted to Islam indicate that its members were traders having close contacts with Christian communities in Mesopotamia. Such contacts may have introduced the tribe to the ideal of one God and so prepared it to accept the Prophet's message.

The Arabs of Oman also figure prominently among the early converts to Islam. According to tradition, the Prophet sent one of his military leaders to Oman to convert not only the Arab inhabitants, some of whom were Christian, but also the Persian garrison, which was Zoroastrian. The Arabs accepted Islam, but the Persians did not. It was partly the zeal of the newly converted Arabs that inspired them to expel the Persians from Oman.

Although Muhammad had enjoined the Muslim community to convert the infidel, he had also recognized the special status of the "people of the book," Jews and Christians, whose scriptures he considered revelations of God's word and which contributed in some measure to Islam. By accepting the status of *dhimmis* (tolerated subject people), Jews and Christians could live in their own communities, practice their own religious laws, and be exempt from military service. However, they were obliged to refrain from proselytizing among Muslims, to recognize Muslim authority, and to pay additional taxes. In addition, they were denied certain political rights.

THE GULF IN THE MIDDLE AGES

In the Islamic period, the prosperity of the gulf continued to be linked to markets in Mesopotamia. Accordingly, after 750 the gulf prospered because Baghdad became the seat of the caliph and the main center of Islamic civilization. Islam brought great prosperity to Iraq during this period, thus increasing the demand for foreign goods. As a result, gulf merchants roamed farther and farther afield. By the year 1000, they were traveling regularly to China and beyond, and their trading efforts were instrumental in spreading Islam, first to India and then to Indonesia and Malaysia.

The Islam they spread, however, was often sectarian. Eastern Arabia was a center for both Kharijites and Shia; in the Middle Ages, the Ismaili Shia faith constituted a particularly powerful force in the gulf. Ismailis originated in Iraq, but many moved to the gulf in the ninth century to escape the Sunni authorities. Whereas the imam was central to the Ismaili tradition, the group also recognized what they referred to as "missionaries" (*dua*; sing., *dai*), figures who spoke for the imam and played major political roles. One of these missionaries was Hamdan Qarmat, who sent a group from Iraq to Bahrain in the ninth century to establish an Ismaili community. From their base in Bahrain, Qarmat's followers, who became known as Qarmatians, sent emissaries throughout the Muslim world.

The Qarmatians are known for their attacks on their opponents, including raids on Baghdad and the sack of Mecca and Medina in 930. For much of the tenth century, the Ismailis of Bahrain were the most powerful force in the Persian Gulf and the Middle East. They controlled the coast of Oman and collected tribute from the caliph in Baghdad as well as from a rival Ismaili imam in Cairo, whom they did not recognize.

By the eleventh century, Ismaili power had waned. The Qarmatians succumbed to the same forces that had earlier threatened centers on the gulf coast--the ambitions of strong leaders in Mesopotamia or Persia and the incursion of tribes from the interior. In 985 armies of the Buyids, a Persian dynasty, drove the Ismailis out of Iraq, and in 988 Arab tribes drove the Ismailis out of Al Ahsa, an oasis they controlled in eastern Arabia. Thereafter, Ismaili presence in the gulf faded, and in the twentieth century the sect virtually disappeared.

Ibadis figured less prominently than the Shia in the spread of Islam. A stable community, the Ibadi sect's large following in Oman has helped to distinguish Oman from its gulf neighbors. Ibadis originated in Iraq, but in the early eighth century, when the caliph's representative began to suppress the Ibadis, many left the area. Their leader at the time, Jabir ibn Zayd, had come to Iraq from Oman, so he returned there. Jabir ibn Zayd's presence in Oman strengthened the existing Ibadi communities; in less than a century, the sect took over the country from the Sunni garrison that ruled it in the caliph's name. Their leader, Al Julanda ibn Masud, became the Ibadi imam of Oman.

In the Ibadi tradition, imams are elected by a council of religious scholars, who select the leader that can best defend the community militarily and rule it according to religious principles. Whereas Sunnis and Shia traditionally have focused on a single leader, referred to as caliph or imam, Ibadis permit regions to have their own imams. For instance, there have been concurrent Ibadi imams in Iraq, Oman, and North Africa.

Because of the strong sense of community among Ibadis, which resembles tribal feelings of community, they have predominated in the interior of Oman and to a lesser degree along the coast. In 752, for example, a new line of Sunni caliphs in Baghdad conquered Oman and killed the Ibadi imam, Al Julanda. Other Ibadi imams arose and reestablished the tradition in the interior, but extending their rule to the coastal trading cities met opposition. The inland empires of Persia and Iraq depended on customs duties from East-West trade, much of which passed by Oman. Accordingly, the caliph and his successors could not allow the regional coastal cities out of their control.

As a result, Oman acquired a dual nature. Ibadi leaders usually controlled the mountainous interior while, for the most part, foreign powers controlled the coast. People in the coastal cities have often been foreigners or have had considerable contact with foreigners because of trade. Coastal Omanis have profited from their involvement with outsiders, whereas Omanis in the interior have tended to reject the foreign presence as

For additional analytical, business and investment opportunities information, please contact Global Investment & Business Center, USA at (202) 546-2103. Fax: (202) 546-3275. E-mail: rusric@erols.com Global Business E-Books on Line: http://world.mirhouse.com

an intrusion into the small, tightly knit Ibadi community. Ibadi Islam has thus preserved some of the hostility toward outsiders that was a hallmark of the early Kharijites.

While the imam concerned himself with the interior, the Omani coast remained under the control of Persian rulers. The Buyids in the late tenth century eventually extended their influence down the gulf as far as Oman. In the 1220s and 1230s, another group, the Zangids--based in Mosul, Iraq--sent troops to the Omani coast; around 1500 the Safavids, an Iranian dynasty, pushed into the gulf as well. The Safavids followed the Twelver Shia tradition and imposed Shia beliefs on those under their rule. Thus, Twelver communities were established in Bahrain and to a lesser extent in Kuwait.

Oman's geographic location gave it access not only to the Red Sea trade but also to ships skirting the coast of Africa. By the end of the fifteenth century, however, a Persian ruler, the shaykh of Hormuz, profited most from this trade. The shaykh controlled the Persian port that lay directly across the gulf from Oman, and he collected customs duties in the busy Omani ports of Qalhat and Muscat. Ibadi imams continued to rule in the interior, but until Europeans entered the region in the sixteenth century, Ibadi rulers were unable to reclaim the coastal cities from the Iranians.

COLONIAL PERIOD

During the Middle Ages, Muslim countries of the Middle East controlled East-West trade. However, control changed in the fifteenth century. The Portuguese, who were building ships with deep hulls that remained stable in high seas, were thus able to make longer voyages. They pushed farther and farther down the west coast of Africa until they found their way around the southern tip of the continent and made contact with Muslim cities on the other side. In East Africa, the Portuguese enlisted Arab navigators there to take them across to India, where they eventually set themselves up in Calicut on the Malabar Coast in the southwestern part of the country.

Once in India, the Portuguese used their superior ships to transport goods around Africa instead of using the Red Sea route, thus eliminating the middlemen in Egypt. The Portuguese then extended their control to the local trade that crossed the Arabian Sea, capturing coastal cities in Oman and Iran and setting up forts and customs houses on both coasts to collect duty. The Portuguese allowed local rulers to remain in control but collected tribute from them in exchange for that privilege, thus increasing Portuguese revenues.

The ruler most affected by the rise of Portuguese power was the Safavid shah of Iran, Abbas I (1587-1629). During the time the shaykh of Hormuz possessed effective control over gulf ports, he continued to pay lip service and tribute to the Safavid shah. When the Portuguese arrived, they forced the shaykh to pay tribute to them. The shah could do little because Iran was too weak to challenge the Portuguese. For that the shah required another European power; he therefore invited the British and the Dutch to drive the Portuguese out of the gulf, in return for half the revenues from Iranian ports.

Both countries responded to the shah's offer, but it was the British who proved the most helpful. In 1622 the British, along with some of the shah's forces, attacked Hormuz and drove the Portuguese out of their trading center there. Initially, the Dutch cooperated with the British, but the two European powers eventually became rivals for access to the Iranian market. The British won, and by the beginning of the nineteenth century Britain had become the major power in the gulf.

Struggles between Iranians and Europeans contributed to a power vacuum along the coast of Oman. The British attacks on the Portuguese coincided with the rise of the Yarubid line of Ibadi imams in the interior of Oman. The Yarubid took advantage of Portuguese preoccupation with naval battles on the Iranian side of the gulf and conquered the coastal cities of Oman around 1650. The imams moved into the old Portuguese stronghold of Muscat and so brought the Omani coast and interior under unified Ibadi control for the first time in almost 1,000 years.

A battle over imamate succession in the early eighteenth century, however, weakened Yarubid rule. Between the 1730s and the 1750s, the various parties began to solicit support from outside powers. The Yarubid family eventually called in an Iranian army, which reestablished Iranian influence on the Omani coast. But this time the Iranian hold on Oman was short-lived. In 1742 the Al Said, an Ibadi family from one of the coastal cities, convinced the local population to help it expel the Iranians; this put the leader, Ahmad ibn Said Al Said, in control of the Omani coast. His success sufficiently impressed the Ibadi leaders so that they made him imam several years later.

The title of imam gave Ahmad ibn Said control over all of Oman, and under him and his successors the country prospered for more than a century. The Omanis extended their influence into the interior and into part of the present-day United Arab Emirates (UAE), consisting of the states of Abu Dhabi, Ajman, Al Fujayrah, Dubayy, Ras al Khaymah, Sharjah, and Umm al Qaywayn. They also collected tribute from as far away as present-day Bahrain and Iraq. The Omanis conquered the Dhofar region, which is part of present-day Oman but was not historically part of the region of Oman.

Oman also strengthened its hold on the Muslim cities of East Africa. These cities had been established by Omani traders in the tenth and eleventh centuries, but their connection to Oman had grown somewhat tenuous. At the beginning of the nineteenth century, however, the Al Said reasserted Omani authority in the area. Said ibn Sultan (1806-65) encouraged Omanis to settle in Zanzibar, an island off the African coast that had retained strong connections with Oman and, from Zanzibar, sent expeditions to take over several cities on the mainland

Although Ahmad ibn Said had succeeded in uniting Oman under an Ibadi imamate, the religious nature of his family's authority did not last long. His son, Said ibn Ahmad Al Said, was elected to the imamate after him, but no other family member won the official approval of the religious establishment. As a result, the Al Said called themselves *sultans*, a secular title having none of the religious associations of imam. They further distanced themselves from Ibadi traditions by moving their capital from Ar Rustaq, a traditional Ibadi center in the interior, to the trading center of Muscat. As a result of the move, the dichotomy between coast and interior that had traditionally split Oman was reinstituted.

For additional analytical, business and investment opportunities information, please contact Global Investment & Business Center, USA at (202) 546-2103. Fax: (202) 546-3275. E-mail: rusric@erols.com Global Business E-Books on Line: http://world.mirhouse.com

The relationship between coast and interior was becoming a major feature within the gulf. In the eighteenth century, tribes from the interior increasingly began to move and settle into the coastal centers. Although the economy on the Arab side of the gulf did not match past prosperity, coastal conditions remained better than those in central Arabia. Limited agriculture existed, and the gulf waters were the site of rich oyster beds for harvesting pearls. The area's easy access to India, a major market for pearls, made the pearling industry particularly lucrative, and this drew the attention of tribes in the interior. The tribal migrations that occurred around 1800 put in place the tribes and clans that in 1993 controlled Kuwait, Bahrain, Qatar, and the UAE.

The Bani Utub moved from central Arabia into the northern gulf in the early 1800s, and one of its families, the Al Sabah, established itself as leaders of present-day Kuwait; another family, the Al Khalifa, established itself in present-day Bahrain. In the early 1800s, a number of other tribes were living along the gulf. Thus, Al Sabah and Al Khalifa control meant that these families ruled loosely over other tribes. Before taking Bahrain, the Al Khalifa had first established a settlement across the water on the peninsula that is present-day Qatar. Although the Al Khalifa were successful in taking Bahrain, they were unable to hold Qatar. They lost the peninsula to the Al Thani, the leading family from another tribe that, like the Bani Utub, had recently moved into the area.

The exact origins of the Al Thani are unknown, but they were already in Qatar when the Al Khalifa came. The origins of the Bani Yas and the Qawasim tribes that rule in the present-day UAE are somewhat clearer. The Bani Yas originated in central Arabia and probably established themselves on the coast at Abu Dhabi around 1700; they later extended their influence to Dubayy. Historical evidence indicates that the Qawasim lived along the gulf during the pre-Islamic period and engaged in trade, pearling, and piracy.

WAHHABI ISLAM AND THE GULF

The eighteenth and nineteenth centuries were a turbulent time for Arabia in general and for the gulf in particular. To the southeast, the Al Said of Oman were extending their influence northward, and from Iraq the Ottoman Turks were extending their influence southward. From the east, both the Iranians and the British were becoming increasingly involved in Arab affairs.

The most significant development in the region, however, was the Wahhabi movement. The name *Wahhabi* derived from Muhammad ibn Abd al Wahhab, who died in 1792. He grew up in an oasis town in central Arabia where he studied Hanbali law, usually considered the strictest of Islamic legal schools, with his grandfather. While still a young man, he left home and continued his studies in Medina and then in Iraq and Iran.

When he returned from Iran to Arabia in the late 1730s, he attacked as idolatry many of the customs followed by tribes in the area who venerated rocks and trees. He extended his criticism to practices of the Twelver Shia, such as veneration of the tombs of holy men. He focused on the central Muslim principle that there is only one God and that this God does not share his divinity with anyone. From this principle, his students began to

For additional analytical, business and investment opportunities information,
please contact Global Investment & Business Center, USA
at (202) 546-2103. Fax: (202) 546-3275. E-mail: rusric@erols.com
Global Business E-Books on Line: http://world.mirhouse.com

refer to themselves as *muwahhidun* (sing., *muwahhid*), or "unitarians." Their detractors referred to them as "Wahhabis."

Muhammad ibn Abd al Wahhab considered himself a reformer and looked for a political figure to give his ideas a wider audience. He found this person in Muhammad ibn Saud, the amir (see Glossary) of Ad Diriyah, a small town near Riyadh. In 1744 the two swore a traditional Muslim pledge in which they promised to work together to establish a new state (which later became present-day Saudi Arabia) based on Islamic principles. The limited but successful military campaigns of Muhammad ibn Saud caused Arabs from all over the peninsula to feel the impact of Wahhabi ideas.

The Wahhabis became known for a fanaticism similar to that of the early Kharijites. This fanaticism helped to intensify conflicts in the gulf. Whereas tribes from the interior had always raided settled communities along the coast, the Wahhabi faith provided them with a justification for continuing these incursions to spread true Islam. Accordingly, in the nineteenth century Wahhabi tribes, under the leadership of the Al Saud, moved at various times against Kuwait, Bahrain, and Oman. In Oman, the Wahhabi faith created internal dissension as well as an external menace because it proved popular with some of the Ibadi tribes in the Omani interior.

Wahhabi thought has had a special impact on the history of Qatar. Muhammad ibn Abd al Wahhab's ideas proved popular among many of the peninsula tribes, including the Al Thani clan, before the Al Khalifa attempted to take over the area from Bahrain at the beginning of the nineteenth century. As a result, Wahhabi beliefs motivated Al Thani efforts to resist the attempt of the Al Khalifa, who rejected Wahhabism, to gain control of the peninsula. In the early 1990s, Wahhabism distinguished Qatar religiously from its neighbors.

Wahhabi fervor was also significant in the history of the present-day UAE. The Qawasim tribes that had controlled the area since the eighteenth century adapted Wahhabi ideas and transferred the movement's religious enthusiasm to the piracy in which they had traditionally engaged. Whereas Wahhabi thought opposed all that was not orthodox in Islam, it particularly opposed non-Muslim elements such as the increasing European presence in the Persian Gulf.

TREATIES WITH THE BRITISH

The increased European presence resulted in large part from widespread Qawasim piracy in the early nineteenth century. The British asked the sultan in Oman, to whom the pirates owed nominal allegiance, to end it. When the sultan proved unable, British ships launched attacks on Qawasim strongholds in the present-day UAE as early as 1809; the navy did not succeed in controlling the situation until 1819. In that year, the British sent a fleet from India that destroyed the pirates' main base at Ras al Khaymah, a Qawasim port at the southern end of the gulf. From Ras al Khaymah, the British fleet destroyed Qawasim ships along both sides of the gulf.

The British had no desire to take over the desolate areas along the gulf; they only wished to secure the area so that it would not pose a threat to shipping to and from their possessions in India. Knowing that the sultan in Oman could not be relied upon to control the pirates, the British decided to leave in power those tribal leaders who had not been conspicuously involved with piracy; they concluded a series of treaties in which those leaders promised to suppress all piracy.

As a result of these truces, the Arab side of the gulf came to be known as the "trucial coast." This area had previously been under the nominal control of the sultan in Oman, although the trucial coast tribes were not part of the Ibadi imamate. The area has also been referred to as "trucial Oman" to distinguish it from the part of Oman under the sultan that was not bound by treaty obligation.

In 1820 the British seemed primarily interested in controlling the Qawasim, whose main centers were Ras al Khaymah, Ajman, and Sharjah, which were all small ports along the southeastern gulf coast. The original treaties, however, also involved Dubayy and Bahrain. Although Dubayy and Bahrain were not pirate centers, they represented entrepôts where pirates could sell captured goods and buy supplies. The inclusion of these ports brought two other extended families, the Bani Yas and the Al Khalifa, into the trucial system.

During the next 100 years, the British signed a series of treaties having wide-ranging provisions with other tribes in the gulf. As a result, by the end of World War I, leaders from Oman to Iraq had essentially yielded control of their foreign relations to Britain. Abu Dhabi entered into arrangements similar to those of Dubayy and Bahrain in 1835, Kuwait in 1899, and Qatar in 1916. The treaty whose terms convey the most representative sense of the relationship between Britain and the gulf states was the Exclusive Agreement of 1882. This text specified that the signatory gulf states (members of the present-day UAE) could not make any international agreements or host any foreign agent without British consent.

Because of these concessions, gulf leaders recognized the need for Britain to protect them from their more powerful neighbors. The main threat came from the Al Saud in central Arabia. Although the Turks had defeated the first Wahhabi empire of the Al Saud around 1820, the family rose again about thirty years later; it threatened not only the Qawasim, who by this time had largely abandoned Wahhabi Islam, but also the Al Khalifa in Bahrain and the Ibadi sultan in Oman. In the early 1900s, the Al Saud also threatened Qatar despite its Wahhabi rulers. Only with British assistance could the Al Thani and other area rulers retain their authority.

The Al Saud were not the only threat. Despite its treaty agreement with Britain, Bahrain on several occasions has claimed Qatar because of the Al Khalifa involvement on the peninsula. The Omanis and Iranians have also claimed Bahrain because both have held the island at various times. Furthermore, the Ottomans claimed Bahrain occasionally and tried throughout the latter part of the nineteenth century to establish their authority in Kuwait and Qatar.

The British wished to maintain security on the route from Europe to India so that merchants could safely send goods between India and the gulf. Britain also sought to exclude the influence in the area of other powers, such as Turkey and France.

East-West trade through the Persian Gulf dried up in the nineteenth century after the opening of the Suez Canal, which provided a direct route to the Mediterranean Sea. Gulf merchants continued to earn substantial income from the slave trade, but international pressure, mostly from Britain, forced them to abandon this by 1900. Thereafter, the region continued to profit from the gulf pearl beds, but this industry declined in the 1930s as a result of the world depression, which reduced demand, and as a result of the Japanese development of a cheaper way to "breed" pearls, or make cultured pearls.

Oman, which was technically cut off from the gulf after 1820 when it lost the southern portion of the present-day UAE, fared little better during the late nineteenth century. The fifth sultan in the Al Said line, Said ibn Sultan, ruled for almost the entire first half of the nineteenth century, increasing Omani influence and revenue tremendously. The resulting prosperity, however, was short-lived. The Omani fleet could not compete with the more technologically advanced European ships; thus the sultan gradually lost much of the income he had earned from customs duties on the Indian trade. At the same time, the increasing pressure to restrict the slave trade eliminated much of the revenue the Omanis had earned from East Africa.

The final blow to Oman's economic and political viability came after the death of Said ibn Sultan. When the Al Said could not agree on a successor, the British acted. They divided the Al Said holdings and gave Oman proper to one of the claimants to the throne and awarded Omani possessions in East Africa to another. Thus, after 1856, there were two Al Said rulers. The one in Muscat, with a weakened merchant fleet and no East African revenues, was left with little support. Because of the different centers of power, the country became popularly known as Muscat and Oman.

The sultan's financial weakness contributed to his difficulty in maintaining his hold on the interior. The devout Ibadi population of the interior had long resented the more secular orientation of the coastal centers. As the sultan grew weaker, groups in the interior raised revolts against him on several occasions. Only with British help could the sultan remain in control, and his growing dependence on outsiders caused his relations with the Ibadi population to deteriorate. Whereas other gulf rulers used the British to protect them from their more powerful neighbors, the sultan needed the British to protect him from his subjects.

DISCOVERY OF OIL

At the end of World War I, the Arab states of the gulf were weak, with faltering economies and with local rulers who maintained their autonomy only with British assistance. The rulers controlled mainly the small port cities and some of the hinterland. The sultan in Oman claimed a somewhat larger area, but resistance to his rule made it difficult for him to exert his authority much beyond Muscat.

For additional analytical, business and investment opportunities information, please contact Global Investment & Business Center, USA at (202) 546-2103. Fax: (202) 546-3275. E-mail: rusric@erols.com Global Business E-Books on Line: http://world.mirhouse.com

The discovery of oil in the region changed all this. Oil was first discovered in Iran, and by 1911 a British concern, the Anglo-Persian Oil Company (APOC), was producing oil in Iran. The British found oil in Iraq after World War I. In 1932 Standard Oil Company of California (Socal) discovered oil in commercial quantities in Bahrain. Socal then obtained a concession in Saudi Arabia in 1933 and discovered oil in commercial quantities in 1938.

A flurry of oil exploration activity occurred in the gulf in the 1930s with the United States and Britain competing with one another for oil concessions. One reason for the increased activity was that in 1932 the new Iranian government of Reza Shah Pahlavi revoked APOC's concession. Although the shah and the British later agreed on new terms, the threat of losing Iranian oil convinced the British in particular that they must find other sources. The small states of the Persian Gulf were a natural place to look. Geological conditions were similar to those in Iran, and, because of treaties signed between 1820 and 1920, the British had substantial influence and could restrict foreign access.

Oil exploration did not mean immediate wealth for Arab rulers of the area. Although the oil companies struck large deposits of oil in Bahrain almost immediately, it took longer in other countries to locate finds of commercial size. Oman, for instance, was unable to export oil until 1967. World War II delayed development of whatever fields had been discovered in the 1930s; so it was not until the 1950s that countries still technically dependent on Britain for their security began to earn large incomes. The oil fields in Kuwait were developed the fastest, and by 1953 that nation had become the largest oil producer in the gulf. Considerably smaller fields in Qatar came onstream in commercial quantities in the 1950s, and Abu Dhabi began to export offshore oil in 1962. Dubayy began to profit from offshore oil deposits in the late 1960s.

Until the 1970s, foreign companies owned and managed the gulf oil industry. In most cases, European- and United States-based concerns formed subsidiaries to work in specific countries, and these subsidiaries paid fees to the local rulers, first for the right to explore for oil and later for the right to export the oil. When the first arrangements were made, local rulers had a weak bargaining position because they had few other sources of income and were eager to get revenues from the oil companies as fast as possible. Moreover, in 1930 no one knew the size of gulf oil reserves.

As production increased and the extent of oil deposits became known, indigenous rulers improved their terms. In the 1950s, rulers routinely demanded an equal share of oil company profits in addition to a royalty fee. By the 1970s, most of the gulf countries, which by then were independent of British control, bought major shares in the subsidiary companies that worked within their borders. By the early 1990s, many of these subsidiaries had become completely state-owned concerns. They continued to employ Western experts at the highest decisionmaking levels, but the local government had ultimate responsibility and profits.

For additional analytical, business and investment opportunities information, please contact Global Investment & Business Center, USA at (202) 546-2103. Fax: (202) 546-3275. E-mail: rusric@erols.com Global Business E-Books on Line: http://world.mirhouse.com

INDEPENDENCE

With the exception of Saudi Arabia and Iraq, the Arab coast of the gulf was ruled by ten families: in Kuwait the Al Sabah; in Bahrain the Al Khalifa; in Qatar the Al Thani; in the present-day UAE the Al Nuhayyan in Abu Dhabi, the Al Nuaimi in Ajman, the Al Sharqi in Al Fujayrah, the Al Maktum in Dubayy, the Al Qasimi in Ras al Khaymah and Sharjah, and the Al Mualla in Umm al Qaywayn; and the Al Said in present-day Oman. These families owed their positions to tribal leadership; it was on this traditional basis that the British had negotiated treaties with their leaders in the nineteenth century and the early twentieth century.

A major provision of these treaties was the recognition of sovereignty. The British were concerned that rulers of the weaker gulf families would yield some of their territory under pressure from more powerful groups, such as the Al Saud or the Ottomans. Accordingly, the treaties signed between 1820 and 1916 recognized the sovereignty of these rulers within certain borders and specified that these borders could not be changed without British consent. Such arrangements helped to put tribal alliances into more concrete terms of landownership. This meant that the Al Nuhayyan of Abu Dhabi, for example, not only commanded the respect of tribes in the hinterland but also owned, as it were, the land that those tribes used--in this case, about 72,000 square kilometers of Arabia.

Controlling, or owning, land became more important with the discovery of oil. When oil companies came to explore for oil, they looked for the "owner" of the land; in accordance with British treaties, they went to the area's leading families and agreed to pay fees to the heads of these families. As oil revenues increased, the leaders became rich. Although the leaders spent much of their new wealth on themselves, they also distributed it in the area they controlled according to traditional methods, which initially consisted mostly of largesse: gifts for friends and food for whomever needed it. As time passed, the form of largesse became more sophisticated and included, for example, the construction of schools, hospitals, and roads to connect principal cities to towns in the interior.

Oil revenues did not change traditional tribal ideas about leadership. New money, however, increased the influence of area leaders by giving them more resources to distribute. Because of oil exploration, tribal boundaries became clearer, and areas were defined more precisely. Distinctions among tribes also became more evident. A new sense of identity appeared in gulf shaykhdoms and aroused a growing expectation that they should rule themselves. To do this, shaykhs had to cut themselves off from British control and protection.

By the early 1960s, this was something to which the British had little objection. India and Pakistan won their independence in 1947; this meant that Britain no longer had to worry about protecting the western flank of the subcontinent. Britain was also burdened by the tremendous sacrifices it made during World War II and could not be as globally involved as it had been before the war. Therefore, Britain yielded many of its strategic responsibilities to the United States in the postwar period or gave them up entirely. However, the British were bound to the gulf by treaties and so remained in the region, but it was clear by the 1960s that they sought to leave the gulf.

For additional analytical, business and investment opportunities information, please contact Global Investment & Business Center, USA at (202) 546-2103. Fax: (202) 546-3275. E-mail: rusric@erols.com Global Business E-Books on Line: http://world.mirhouse.com

Kuwait was the first state to terminate the agreement connecting it with Britain. Oil production in Kuwait had developed more quickly than in neighboring states; as a result, Kuwaitis were better prepared for independence. They declared independence in 1961 but ran into immediate trouble when Iraq claimed the territory. The Iraqis argued that the British had recognized Ottoman sovereignty over Kuwait before World War I and, because the Ottomans had claimed to rule Kuwait from what was then the province of Iraq, the territory should belong to Iraq.

The British immediately sent troops to Kuwait to deter any Iraqi invasion. British and Kuwaiti positions were supported by the newly formed League of Arab States (Arab League), which recognized the new state and sent troops to Kuwait. The Arab League move left the Iraqis isolated and somewhat intimidated. Accordingly, when a new Iraqi government came to power in 1963, one of its first steps was to give up its claim and recognize the independence of Kuwait.

The experience of Kuwait may have increased the anxiety of other gulf leaders about declaring their independence. Even into the 1970s, Iran and Saudi Arabia continued to make claims on territory in Bahrain and the UAE, although by the end of 1971 those states were independent, and nothing came of those claims. Gulf leaders also faced uncertainty about the form their state should take. Should they all, with the exception of Oman whose situation was different in that its treaty relationship with Britain did not guarantee its borders as did treaties of the other gulf states, band together in the largest entity possible? Or should they break up into nine separate states, the smallest of which had little territory, few people, and no oil?

British action forced gulf leaders to decide. Because of domestic financial concerns, Britain decided in the late 1960s to eliminate its military commitments east of Suez. As a result, the gulf shaykhs held a number of meetings to discuss independence. Initially, leaders considered a state that would include all nine shaykhdoms; Qatar had even drawn up a constitution to this effect. In the end, however, so large a federation proved unworkable.

An obstacle to creating a "superstate" was the status of Bahrain, which had been occupied by Iran at various times. The shah of Iran argued that he had a stronger claim to the island than the Al Khalifa, who had only come to Bahrain in the eighteenth century. Furthermore, the shah indicated that Iran would not accept a federation of Arab states that included Bahrain.

In the end, the United Nations (UN) considered the issue of Bahrain; it decided to deny the Iranian claim to the island and to allow the Bahrainis to form an independent state. Bahrain was better suited to independence than some of the other shaykhdoms because the island had been a center of British administration and had a more developed infrastructure and education system than its neighbors. Ironically, the greater British presence on Bahrain made residents more resentful of treaty ties to Britain. Bahrain was the only place in the gulf where demonstrations against Britain occurred.

Backed by the UN decision, Bahrain declared its independence on August 15, 1971. On September 3, 1971, Qatar followed, removing another state from any potential federation. Although Qatar had minimal contact with Britain, it was well suited to independence because it had a history of support from the Al Saud that went back to the beginnings of the Wahhabi state. Accordingly, at independence, Qatar could expect continued support from Saudi Arabia. It could also anticipate substantial oil revenues that had been increasing since the 1950s.

The same was not true for the other gulf states. The five southern shaykhdoms--Ajman, Al Fujayrah, Ras al Khaymah, Sharjah, and Umm al Qaywayn--had little oil in their territory and so could not afford self-sufficiency as countries. Although substantial deposits had been discovered in Abu Dhabi and Dubayy, these two states preferred the security of a confederation rather than independence. Abu Dhabi, for example, had an outstanding border dispute with Saudi Arabia and a history of poor relations with that country because of Abu Dhabi's opposition to Wahhabi Islam. Abu Dhabi might have protected itself by forming a federation with the five southern shaykhdoms, but this would not have suited Dubayy. Although Dubayy had oil of its own, its rulers, the Al Maktum, had a history of hostility toward their relatives in Abu Dhabi, the Al Nuhayyan, from whom they split in the early nineteenth century. The Al Maktum would not have liked the Al Nuhayyan to dominate a confederation of gulf leaders while they were isolated in Dubayy.

Powers beyond the gulf coast also had an interest in the state to be formed. The Saudis no longer sought to control the gulf coast, but they remained concerned about stability on the eastern border. The British and other oil-consuming countries in the West were similarly concerned, and all parties believed that the largest state would also be the most stable. Accordingly, many forces were applying pressure in 1970 to convince the seven shaykhs to stay together.

Thus, in 1971 soon after Qatar became independent, the remaining shaykhs, with the exception of the Al Qasimi in Ras al Khaymah, took the preliminary constitution that Qatar had originally drawn up for a nine-member confederation and adapted it to a six-member body. On December 2, 1971, one day after the British officially withdrew, these six shaykhdoms declared themselves a sovereign state.

Ras al Khaymah originally refused to join the confederation. The Al Qasimi, who ruled the area, claimed a number of islands and oil fields within the gulf to which Iran laid claim as well. In the negotiations to form the UAE, the Al Qasimi sought support for their claims from Arab states on the peninsula as well as from some Western powers. When their efforts proved unsuccessful, the Al Qasimi pulled out of the negotiations. They quickly realized, however, that they could not exist on their own and joined the union in February 1972.

Oman was never considered a possible confederation member. Always geographically separate from its neighbors to the north, Oman had never entered into the agreements with Britain that governed other gulf rulers. The British had been closely involved in

Oman since the middle of the nineteenth century, but they were under no official obligation to defend it.

The issue in Oman was one of internal unity rather than of sovereignty over foreign affairs. The historical split between coast and interior had continued through the second half of the nineteenth century and the first part of the twentieth. In 1920 the Al Said sultan, Taimur ibn Faisal, came to terms with this split by granting limited sovereignty to the tribes of the interior. Because of ambiguous language, the peoples of the interior believed that the treaty cut them off from the Al Said; the Al Said, however, never gave up their claim to all of Oman.

The dispute between the two groups was exacerbated by the exploration for oil, which began in Oman in 1924. The oil fields lay in the interior, and the oil companies negotiated for access to them with the Al Said in Muscat. This Al Said sultan gladly sold them rights to the Omani oil fields, although the tribes of the interior claimed sovereignty over the area. When the oil men went inland to explore, they were attacked by the tribes, whom the sultan considered to be rebels, leading the oil companies to complain to the British government. Their complaints encouraged the British to continue their aid to the sultan, hoping that he would pacify the area and ensure Western access to Omani oil.

The sultan was eventually successful. In 1957 forces loyal to Said ibn Taimur captured the town of Nazwah, which the Al Said had not controlled since the nineteenth century. In 1958 the sultan withdrew to his palace in the coastal city of Salalah in Dhofar, a southern province that the Al Said had annexed in the nineteenth century, and took little interest in maintaining stability in the country. While keeping his military relationship with the British, he restricted Oman's contact with the rest of the world, discouraged development, and prohibited political reform.

In the end, the Al Said control over a united Oman survived, but Said ibn Taimur did not. Although the sultan had partially reestablished his authority in the Omani interior, he was unable to handle the increasing complexity of domestic politics. By the 1960s, Omani affairs had become international issues. Western oil companies sought to work in the interior of the country, and foreign governments, such as the Marxist state of the People's Democratic Republic of Yemen, were sending arms to the rebels in Dhofar.

The Al Said hold over the region remained problematic, however, and in 1964 another rebellion arose, this time in Dhofar. The Dhofar rebellion, which was not brought under control until 1976, obliged the sultan to seek foreign military assistance; therefore, British forces, particularly the air force, resumed action in the country. The rebels pointed to British involvement as an indication of the sultan's illegitimacy and brought their case to the UN, which eventually censured Britain for its continuing involvement in Oman.

Said ibn Taimur's policies frustrated many, not only in Oman but also in Britain, whose citizens were heavily involved in the sultan's military and intelligence apparatus. By 1970 these elements decided they could bear with the situation no longer; a coalition of Omani military and civilian forces, as well as British forces, attacked the palace and forced Said ibn Taimur to abdicate. They replaced him with his son, Qabus ibn Said Al Said, who

For additional analytical, business and investment opportunities information, please contact Global Investment & Business Center, USA at (202) 546-2103. Fax: (202) 546-3275. E-mail: rusric@erols.com Global Business E-Books on Line: http://world.mirhouse.com

had played no role in Said ibn Taimur's government. The sultan had actually locked his son in the palace for fear that Qabus ibn Said, who had been educated in Britain, would challenge his archconservative policies.

On his release, Qabus ibn Said consolidated the sultanate's hold over the interior and then solicited regional rather than British help to put down the rebellion in Dhofar. Other Arab leaders, as well as the shah of Iran, sent troops to Oman in response to Qabus ibn Said's requests; with the help of this coalition, by 1976 the sultan ended the Dhofar rebellion.

Qabus ibn Said was not an Ibadi imam as the first rulers in his line had been, but in 1970 this was less important than it had been in earlier times. Only about 60 percent of Oman's population was Ibadi, concentrated in the northern mountains. Furthermore, the province of Dhofar had a relatively short history of association with the rest of Oman.

DEVELOPMENTS SINCE INDEPENDENCE

Since the early 1970s, increased oil production and regional instability have dominated events in the Persian Gulf. Revenues from the oil industry grew dramatically after oil producers raised their prices unilaterally in 1973; as a result, funds available to gulf rulers increased. Governments began massive development projects that brought rapid material and social change. As of 1993, the turmoil that these changes caused had not yet stabilized. Those states that had benefited longest from oil money, such as Kuwait and Bahrain, made the greatest progress in adjusting to the new oil wealth. Oman-- which has used its oil reserves only since the early 1970s and which had suffered under the repressive policies of Said ibn Taimur--saw substantially less progress.

The Iranian Revolution of 1979 challenged gulf stability. Many gulf leaders agreed with some of the social goals of the revolution and its efforts to tie Iran more firmly to its Islamic roots. But Iran's desire to spread the movement beyond its borders clearly threatened gulf leaders. Furthermore, several gulf states have significant Shia or Iranian minorities (Bahrain has a Shia majority although the ruling family is Sunni), and gulf rulers feared that Iran would use ethnic or sectarian loyalties to stir up such minorities.

As of 1993, however, Shia of the western gulf had not responded enthusiastically to the Iranian call. Kuwait and Bahrain, which have the largest Shia populations, experienced some limited pro-Iranian demonstrations in 1979. In general, however, Shia in both these states feel that they have more to gain by supporting the existing regimes than by supporting the convulsive changes that have taken place in Iran.

Iran was perhaps more threatening to gulf stability because of its strong anti-Western stance in world and in regional politics. The new Iranian position stood in stark contrast to the gulf amirs' long history of involvement with the British and the close ties to the West that the oil industry entailed. Thus, the Iranian political worldview was one to which rulers in the gulf states could not subscribe.

For additional analytical, business and investment opportunities information, please contact Global Investment & Business Center, USA at (202) 546-2103. Fax: (202) 546-3275. E-mail: rusric@erols.com Global Business E-Books on Line: http://world.mirhouse.com

In 1980 the outbreak of the Iran-Iraq War made the Iranian threat more concrete. For the first six years of the conflict, the gulf states sought to mediate between the two countries and to remain neutral. Their position changed, however, in 1986, when fighter aircraft attacked tankers belonging to Saudi Arabia and Kuwait. Whether Iran or Iraq was responsible for the first attacks remains uncertain, but the gulf states decided to blame the Iranians and began to take Iraq's side in the war. Iran responded by opening up a limited secret campaign against the gulf states. A number of explosions occurred in Kuwait and Bahrain for which many believed Iran was responsible. Such attacks made all the states in the region more concerned about external threats.

In 1981, partly in response to these concerns, Kuwait, Bahrain, Saudi Arabia, Qatar, Oman, and the UAE formed the Gulf Cooperation Council (GCC) . The goal of the GCC has been to provide for regional defense and to coordinate policy on trade and economic issues. Although the GCC has taken steps to increase the military capabilities of various members, the region has remained dependent to a great extent on the protection of the Western powers. For instance, when the Iran-Iraq War made the gulf unsafe for oil tankers in the late 1980s, it was ships from Europe and the United States that protected shipping and cleared the area of mines.

Whereas broader, regional alliances in the gulf have changed dramatically since the 1970s, individual political systems have remained relatively unchanged. All the gulf countries grant ultimate power to a single family, whose leading member rules as amir, but they also provide for an advisory body whose members are drawn from outside the royal family. Kuwait and Bahrain have gone beyond this and have set up separate parliaments with limited power to draft legislation. However, the Al Sabah and the Al Khalifa have sometimes dissolved these bodies; thus, it remains uncertain whether parliaments will become a permanent feature of gulf politics.

The ruling families' hold on power has been challenged at various times. More problematic is the manner in which the gulf states have distributed individual citizenship. Since the 1930s, the population has increased dramatically because of the oil boom, but the number of citizens has not increased correspondingly. Most of the gulf states place restrictions on citizenship, requiring that an individual trace his or her roots in the country to before 1930. Accordingly, the millions of people that have poured into the region since the 1940s have only partial legal status and lack political rights in the countries in which they reside. Although they may have lived there for two generations, they can be asked to leave at any time.

TRIBAL NATURE OF GULF SOCIETY

Gulf states have not granted citizenship freely for two reasons. First, they are reluctant to share wealth with recent arrivals; second, the tribal nature of gulf society does not admit new members easily. A tribe usually traces its lineage to a particular eponymous ancestor. The standard Arabic reference to tribe is *bani fulan*, or "the sons [*bani*] of so-and- so." The Bani al Murrah in Saudi Arabia, for example, trace their line back to a figure named Murrah, who lived some time before the Prophet.

Over a period of 1,500 years, the sons of Murrah, or any other ancient figure, have tended to become numerous, making further distinctions necessary. Accordingly, tribes are divided into clans and then into households (*fukhud*; sing., *fakhd*). Households include groups of single families. Together this extended group of families calls itself a tribe. Each tribe has certain characteristics, such as different speech, dress, and customs. But since the 1950s, speech has become less of a distinguishing factor because of the fluidity of gulf society.

The name of a tribe may also reflect some past event. For example, the name *Utub*--the tribe to which the Al Sabah of Kuwait and the Al Khalifa of Bahrain belong--comes from the Arabic word for wander (*atab*). In 1744 the tribe "wandered" out of the desert and into the gulf area and became the Utub.

Two of the most important tribal groups in Arabia are the Qahtan and the Adnan, whose roots stem from the belief that tribes in the north of the peninsula were descended from Adnan, one of Ismail's sons, and that tribes in the south were descended from Qahtan, one of Noah's sons. People in the gulf often attribute the structure of tribal alliances to this north-south distinction, and many still classify their tribes as Adnani or Qahtani.

Historically, the tribal nature of society has occasioned petty warfare in the gulf. Arab tribes have attacked each other since before Islam, but tribal customs have prevented these attacks from turning into random violence. Clans, however, have defected from their tribe and made alliances with other tribes, and tribes have sometimes banded together to form a more powerful group.

Moreover, although some tribes may trace their lineage to some heroic figure, the real identity of the tribe lies in the people that currently compose it. In the tribe, an individual bases his or her sense of self-esteem on the honor of the tribe as a whole.

In Arabia it was impossible to survive in the desert alone, and so families banded together to find water and move their flocks to new grazing lands. Once they established the necessary resources through collective effort, they guarded them jealously and refused to share them with outsiders. It therefore became necessary to set up boundaries between members of the group or between the tribe and outsiders. The tribe worked to restrict membership in order to preserve its sense of solidarity. As a result, birth into the right family tended to be the only way to become a member of a tribe. Marriage sometimes extended the tribal line beyond blood lines, but, in general, people tended to marry within the tribe and only went outside to establish alliances with other tribes.

The emphasis on the group precluded the rise of a strong leader. Accordingly, tribal leadership is often described as "the first among equals," suggesting a collective leadership in which one among a number of leaders is recognized as the most authoritative. This principal leader must continue to consult with his lesser colleagues and so rules by consensus.

For additional analytical, business and investment opportunities information, please contact Global Investment & Business Center, USA at (202) 546-2103. Fax: (202) 546-3275. E-mail: rusric@erols.com Global Business E-Books on Line: http://world.mirhouse.com

An extension of this pattern of leadership is the concept of leading families within the tribe. Although tribalism tends to discourage inherited authority, traditions of leadership are nevertheless passed down, and tribes expect that certain families will furnish them with leaders generation after generation. This pattern occurred when tribes that were previously nomadic settled down in oases or coastal areas. It then became more likely that certain families would accumulate wealth, whether in food or in goods, and with this wealth would increase their authority. In this way, the individual families that in the 1990s controlled the gulf states established themselves around 1800. Relations with the British and the discovery of oil continued that process.

The existence of these ruling families is perhaps the most obvious manifestation of Arab tribalism in gulf society in 1993. Another manifestation is the collective manner in which these families rule. In most of these states, the position of amir is not passed from father to son but alternates among different parallel patrilineal lines. This makes the appointment of the next amir an open issue and something on which the entire family must agree. The family also participates in the various consultative bodies that exist to advise the leader. Such bodies, which include figures outside the ruling family, help to institutionalize the first among equals system in these states.

The way that government officials are appointed reflects the importance of tribal connections. Members of the ruling family are accommodated first, followed by families and tribes with whom the rulers have been traditionally allied. In Bahrain, for example, the ruling Al Khalifa have given the major positions in the bureaucracy to Sunni Arabs from tribes that helped them rule the island in the nineteenth century. The Al Khalifa have given lesser positions to Shia Arabs from merchant families with whom they engaged in the pearl industry but with whom they had no tribal alliances. But the Al Khalifa have been reluctant to give positions of authority to Shia farmers of Iranian descent to whom they had neither tribal nor economic ties.

Tribal cohesiveness is also reflected in the efforts of the gulf states to restrict citizenship. The gulf has always been relatively cosmopolitan, and its port cities have included Arab Shia from Iraq, freed slaves from Africa, Indian pearl traders, and Iranian farmers and merchants, in addition to tribal Sunni Arabs. (In 1939, for example, before the oil boom started, 39 percent of Qatar's population was non-Arab.) The dominant Arab tribes have accommodated many of these groups, and those who arrived in the region before 1930 became full citizens of the gulf states, albeit without the connections of tribal Arabs. The tremendous influx since 1940, however, has caused the naturally restrictive nature of tribal society to reassert itself to prevent a further dilution of tribal identities.

Ironically, those foreigners closest to the tribal Arabs, the nontribal Arabs, represent the greatest threat. Only Arabs from other Arab states might conceivably stay in the gulf and expect to be citizens. Others, even Muslims from the coasts of Pakistan and India, whose history is intertwined with that of the gulf, would have a difficult time arguing in the twentieth century that they should be citizens of an Arab state.

Modern Arab politics, however, often speaks of a single Arab nation in which all Arabs might be citizens. This has led to the notion that Arabs should have rights in the gulf states simply because of their ethnicity. The continuing exodus of millions of Palestinian Arabs since 1948, and their subsequent residence throughout the Arab world, has added urgency to the demand that individual Arab states define their qualifications for citizenship. Many Arabs argue that Palestinians in particular, but other Arabs as well, should be accepted as citizens in the gulf. Gulf leaders have understandably opposed this for fear that nontribal Arabs would challenge traditional ways of rule. Although people from all over the world may come to the gulf to work, sovereignty and citizenship are closely guarded by the predominantly tribal population that has its roots in the Arabian Peninsula. In this way, the Persian Gulf coast has preserved its ties with the Arab interior that form the essence of its identity.

HISTORY OF QATAR

The early history of the Gulf region was dominated by that of its powerful neighbours - The Assyrian Empire in Mesopotamia (modern day Iraq) and the various dynasties that ruled the Persian Empire.

Rock inscription found at Al-Kharrara, central Qatar

Their interests lay in keeping the waters of the Gulf open and accessible for trade and military purposes, ensuring free passage for their armies and supplies. The varying prosperity of these empires ensured that the small communities that flourished along the Western Gulf coast survived and benefitted from their influence.

There is evidence that Alexander the Great sent an expeditionary force along the Gulf waters in 325BC, although the resultant Greek influence soon gave way to domination by the Persian Parthians. This strong trading nation fortified the Gulf coast to protect their interests and held sway until the third centry AD, when the Sassanians, another Persian dynasty, rose to ascendancy and ruled the area until the advent of Islam in the seventh century. The people of the pre-Islamic Gulf region were therefore exposed to a variety of cultures and religions, and evidence exists of early Christian and Jewish settlements in the area, along with Zoroastrians. These all disappeared rapidly with the conversion of the Arabs to Islam. However, the traditional mingling of peoples of Arab and Persian origin in the Gulf region continues to be a feature of the modern Gulf States.

The livelihood of the early inhabitants of Qatar would have been almost totally dependent on seafaring activities, such as pearling, fishing and trading. They would have had to import many of their foodstuffs and raw materials, while agriculture was limited to bedouin animal husbandry and the cultivation of date palms.

Pearl diver

In this respect, things did not change significantly until after the discovery of oil.

THE DEVELOPMENT OF ISLAM

The Prophet Mohammed (P.B.U.H.) first came to prominence as a preacher in AD 610, in Mecca, on the western side of the Arabian Peninsula. His fervour and conviction soon earned him both a loyal band of followers, and the emnity of the polytheistic rulers of Mecca. As a result, he and his devotees moved to what is now Medina, and the date of this move (622 AD) became the first year of the new Muslim calendar. After the death of Mohammed in 632, his followers gathered together all his teachings, and created the Quran, or holy book of Islam, containing all the words of Mohammed, regarded as having come directly from God.

The faith of Islam spread rapidly after the death of Mohammed and the area which included Qatar converted peacefully in the late seventh century. From this time, until the arrival of the Portuguese in the fifteenth century, the region prospered, benefitting from the control both Persia and Mesopotamia exercised over East-West trade routes. Various tribes in the Qatar area rose to ascendancy and the territory was strongly linked to Bahrain, often falling under its rule. The main town in Qatar during this period was Zubara, on the North-West coast.

THE COLONIAL ERA

For additional analytical, business and investment opportunities information, please contact Global Investment & Business Center, USA at (202) 546-2103. Fax: (202) 546-3275. E-mail: rusric@erols.com Global Business E-Books on Line: http://world.mirhouse.com

With the arrival of the Portuguese in East Africa and India in the fifteenth century, the pattern of dominance in the Gulf region changed dramatically. These conquerers established forts in the Gulf, thereby enabling them to control trade and levy duties on all ships using the sea route.

Traditional sailing Dhow

This situation continued until the early seventeenth century, when the British arrived on the scene, invited by a disgruntled Persian Shah, who no longer wished to pay revenues to the Portuguese. A period of on-off warfare ensued for a couple of centuries, until the British established their dominance in the nineteenth century, motivated by the desire to protect and enhance their trade routes to India.

Ruins near the town of Zubarah

During this period of shifting colonial influences, various tribes held sway in the Qatar / Bahrain area and Zubara became a town of considerable influence. These tribes included the Al-Musallam, the Maahid, the Bani Ali and the Al Bu Kawara, in addition to various nomadic bedouin tribes.

Tribal society was ruled by the leader of each group, who held responsiblity and judicial authority over his people. Alliances ensured support for neighbours based on political expediency, but on the whole these tribes co-existed peacefully, each holding sway over its territory and peoples.

The settled tribes of the Qatar area were based around the coast, and largely engaged in fishing, pearling and trade, while the nomads of the interior wandered around on a seasonal basis, and were generally left undisturbed. It was during the latter part of this era that Doha came to prominence as an urban settlement.

In the late eighteenth century a new force within Islam rose to prominence in the Arabian peninsula. This was known as Wahhabism, after its founder Mohammed Ibn Abd Al Wahhab, and it sought to return Islam to its purest and strictest form, from which it was deemed to have strayed. The leader of the Ibn Saud tribes from the Riyadh area joined forces with Al-Wahhab and these tribes embarked upon an aggressive mission of conquest on the eastern side of the Arabian Peninsula, inspired by their desire to spread the true word of Islam. The tenets of Wahhabism proved appealing to various local tribes in the Qatar region, notably the Al-Thani. However, the Al-Khalifas of Bahrain, who currently ruled in the region, did not embrace the new religious principles, and moved to invade the peninsula of Qatar as a result. This was fiercely resisted by the Al-Thani and their followers, and by the early 1890's Qatar was established as an isolated Wahhabi community on the east coast. This proved highly significant for the subsequent history of the country, and established the Al-Thani for the first time as a dominant ruling entity in the region.

Around the same time, the British Political Resident for the Gulf (appointed by the East India Company) came to Qatar for the first time, extending his support for the Al-Thani against the Al-Khalifa. In 1868 an agreement was signed between the Resident and Mohammed Al-Thani, whereby the British offered protection in return for a guarantee of peace by the local residents. This treaty gave stature and prominence to Mohammed Al-Thani and contributed to the rise of influence of his family in the area.

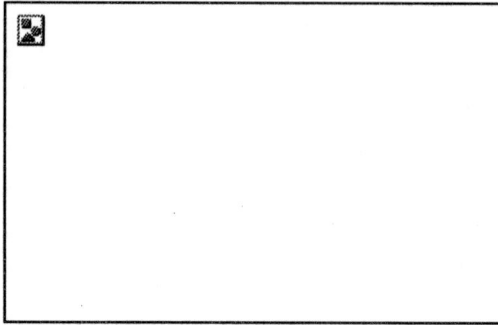

Shortly thereafter, the Ottoman Turks invaded the Arabian peninsula, and Qatar came under their rule. The head of the Al-Thani by this time was Mohammed's son Qasim, who accepted Ottoman rule, counterbalancing this against maintaining links with the British.

Matters continued peacefully until 1893, when the Turks moved against Doha and a battle ensued, which, against the odds, the Al-Thani tribes won. This victory established yet more firmly the hegemony of the Al-Thani and gave the newly emerging country a sense of independence and political cohesion. For the first time, roads were built and a few religious schools were established. Although the Ottomans continued to dominate the region, their direct inflluence was scarcely felt in Qatar itself.

In 1913 the Wahhabis, under the leadership of Ibn Saud, underwent a resurgence and reasserted their influence in the eastern part of Arabia, driving the Ottoman Turks from the area. Shortly afterwards, Abdulla, the son of Qasim Al-Thani, succeeded his father and decided to cast his lot in with the British. An exclusive treaty was signed in 1916 whereby Qatar agreed not to enter into political relations with any other power without the permission of the British, and agreed not to engage in piracy or slave trading, while the British guaranteed the safety of Qatar by land and sea. Under the terms of this treaty, Abdulla was recognised as the independent ruler of Qatar, and the hegemony of the Al-Thani was formally established.

THE EARLY TWENTIETH CENTURY - THE DISCOVERY OF OIL

The early part of the twentieth century saw the rapid rise to power of the Wahhabi movement in the Arabian Peninsula. Ibn Saud, leader of this movement came to conquer most of the Arabian peninsula and by 1932 he was proclaimed King of Saudi Arabia. Although the Gulf States were never directly invaded by his forces, the influence of the Wahhabis remained strong, and Abdulla Al-Thani was constantly aware of the potential threat to his security from the new Kingdom of Saudi Arabia.

For additional analytical, business and investment opportunities information, please contact Global Investment & Business Center, USA at (202) 546-2103. Fax: (202) 546-3275. E-mail: rusric@erols.com Global Business E-Books on Line: http://world.mirhouse.com

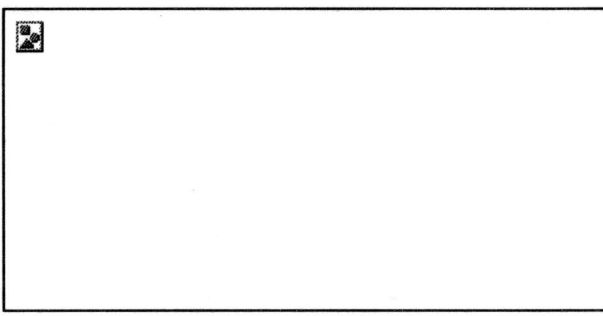

Al-Zubarah Forth

British promises of protection never materialised, and the Qataris eventually paid a tribute to the Al Sauds to preserve their sovereignty and ward against invasion.

In the 1930's, however, the picture changed dramatically and irrevocably with the discovery of oil The first strike in Bahrain in 1932 by Socal (an American consortium) led to a rush of interest by the British, alarmed that the Americans might come to dominate this new found source of wealth in the Gulf. An option had already been granted to the British by Qatar as early as 1926, athough the company (the Anglo Persian Oil Company - APOC), had chosen not to exploit it further. The ruler, Abdulla, used this new-found enthusiasm of the British in the 1930's to gain increased commitment from them with regard to the safety of Qatar, and the guarantee of succession for his son and heir, Hamad. In 1935 the first oil concession was granted to Petroleum Development Qatar Limited (PDL) - a newly created subsidiary of APOC, for a period of 35 years. In 1939, oil first flowed from a well near Zakrit on the west coast of the country. Exploitation was delayed due to the Second World War, and it was not until 1949 that production was undertaken in a major way. In 1963 the Qatar Petroleum Company was founded. Concessions were eventually granted to a number of other companies, notably Shell.

Offshore production began in 1964 and by 1976 the newly formed State of Qatar had gained control of all oil production within the country and offshore.

MODERN TIMES - THE STATE OF QATAR

In the 1950's the main developments for the foundation of a modern state were begun. Schools began to be built, along with roads, power stations and a hospital.

right to left : Sh. Abdullah Bin Qassim Al Thani, Sheikh Ali, and Sheikh Hamad, grandfather of present Emir

After the abdication of Sheikh Abdullah in 1949, Qatar was ruled first by Sheikh Ali Al-Thani, then by his son Ahmad until 1972, although Khalifa, the son of Hamad, Sheikh Abdulla's oldest son, was de facto ruler for much of this latter period. During this time the British announced their intention of withdrawing from of all their treaties of protection and defence commitments in the Middle East by 1971. The Gulf States, which had all effectively been guaranteed by these treaties, decided to unite and form a federation of Arab Emirates. This was due to consist of Bahrain, Qatar, Abu Dhabi, Dubai, Sharjah, Ras Al Khaimah, Ajman, Umm Al Qawain and Fujairah. Lengthly negotiations ensued and ultimately Qatar and Bahrain opted for independence from the other states, which subsequently formed the United Arab Emirates in December 1971.

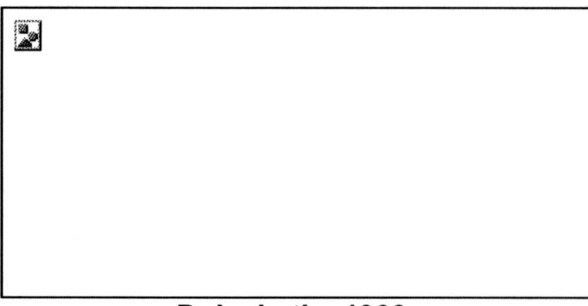

Doha in the 1960s

Qatar formulated a constitution in 1970 and formally declared independence on September 3rd, 1971. This date has remained as the country's National Day since then.

In February 1972 it was decided by the Al-Thani family that Khalifa should formally take over as ruler from Ahmad.
He reigned from 1972 to mid-1995, when his eldest son and Heir Apparent, Sheikh Hamad, assumed power. During Khalifa's reign, oil revenues increased significantly, due both to increased production and to the dramatic rise in the price of oil. Qatar entered a new phase of substantial prosperity and the population benefitted from this wealth by government establishment of free housing, education and health care for all

citizens. Doha grew from a small settlement to a large city within the space of a few years, and the trappings of modern life began to appear throughout the country. It was during this period also that large numbers of expatriate workers were hired to assist in the rapid and dramatic growth and modernisation of the State.

Since 1995, and the assumption of power by Sheikh Hamad, Qatar has opened its doors wider to international investment, and has increased its potential for growth even further.

The Emir of Qatar, Shaikh Hamad Bin Khalifa Al Thani at the opening of Ras Laffan Port.

Various production sharing agreements have brought overseas oil companies back into the country to maximise the potential of reserves, while the discovery and development of the huge gas field to the North East of the country promise to augment the State's national wealth even further. This is particularly crucial at the present time, as falling oil prices threaten to have an adverse impact on the economy. Qatar has always striven to make itself known for sound foreign policy and international diplomacy. Shortly after the foundation of the State, Qatar joined the United Nations and the Arab League. Shortly afterwards, it became a member of the International Monetary Fund and the World Bank. These overseas links have been maintained and strengthened during recent years, while internal changes are constantly taking place to modernise the State. The council of Ministers was rationalised shortly after Sheikh Hamad's accession and 1999 will see the first ever municipal council elections. On a local level Qatar, is an active member of the Gulf Cooperation Council and often hosts summits in Doha. The most recent of these was in 1996. Equally prestigious was the hosting of the 1997 Middle East and North Africa summit, which was attended by many dignitaries, including the American Secretary of State Madeleine Albright.

Qatar, in conclusion, has had a long and distinguished history within the context of its strategic position on the Gulf coast. It heads toward the new milennium confident in its prosperity, stable in its political and economic outlook and ready and eager to face the challenges of the next century.

QATAR IS A SMALL COUNTRY dominated by the Persian Gulf's largest ruling family, the Al Thani. The amir, Shaykh Khalifa ibn Hamad Al Thani, is the country's ruler, but his son, Shaykh Hamad ibn Khalifa Al Thani, in addition to being the heir apparent and minister of defense, wields considerable power in the day-to-day running of the country. The Al Thani regime tolerates no political opposition. The social mores of the country are

For additional analytical, business and investment opportunities information, please contact Global Investment & Business Center, USA at (202) 546-2103. Fax: (202) 546-3275. E-mail: rusric@erols.com Global Business E-Books on Line: http://world.mirhouse.com

shaped by a somewhat milder version of Wahhabi (see Glossary) Islam than is found in neighboring Saudi Arabia. Women are permitted to drive if they obtain permits, for example, and non-Qatari women need not veil in public.

Occupying a barren peninsula scorched by extreme summer heat, Qatar was transformed between the mid-1960s and the mid-1980s from a poor British protectorate noted mainly for pearling into an independent state with modern infrastructure, services, and industries. The state was built using mostly foreign labor and expertise, with funding from oil revenues. And as in other states where oil dominates the economy, Qatar's fortunes have followed those of the world oil market. The late 1980s and early 1990s were times of relative austerity, with development projects canceled or delayed. But those years were also a period of significant transition when Qatar began its shift from an economy reliant almost entirely on oil to one that would be supported by the exploitation of natural gas from the North Field, the world's largest natural gas field.

The early 1990s also constituted a watershed period in foreign relations because the invasion of Kuwait by Iraq on August 2, 1990, changed regional and world alignments. Qatar sent troops to fight for Kuwait's liberation and, reversing its previous opposition to the presence of foreign forces in the region, permitted United States, Canadian, and French air force fighter aircraft to operate from Doha (also seen as Ad Dawhah). This placed Qatar firmly on the anti-Iraq side of the great rift that split the Arab world after the invasion and weakened the full support for the Palestine Liberation Organization that the country had previously shown.

Human habitation of the Qatar Peninsula dates as far back as 50,000 years, when small groups of Stone Age inhabitants built coastal encampments, settlements, and sites for working flint, according to recent archaeological evidence. Other finds have included pottery from the Al Ubaid culture of Mesopotamia and northern Arabia (ca. 5000 B.C.), rock carvings, burial mounds, and a large town that dates from about 500 B.C. at Wusail, some twenty kilometers north of Doha. The Qatar Peninsula was close enough to the Dilmun civilization (ca. 4000 to 2000 B.C.) in Bahrain to have felt its influence. A harsh climate, lack of resources, and frequent periods of conflict, however, seem to have made it inevitable that no settlement would develop and prosper for any significant length of time before the discovery of oil.

The peninsula was used almost continuously as rangeland for nomadic tribes from Najd and Al Hasa regions in Saudi Arabia, with seasonal encampments around sources of water. In addition, fishing and pearling settlements were established on those parts of the coast near a major well. Until the late eighteenth century, the principal towns were on the east coast--Al Huwayla, Al Fuwayrit, and Al Bida--and the modern city of Doha developed around the largest of these, Al Bida. The population consisted of nomadic and settled Arabs and a significant proportion of slaves brought originally from East Africa.

The Qatar Peninsula came under the sway of several great powers over the centuries. The Abbasid era (750-1258) saw the rise of several settlements, including Murwab. The Portuguese ruled from 1517 to 1538, when they lost to the Ottomans. In the 1760s, the

For additional analytical, business and investment opportunities information, please contact Global Investment & Business Center, USA at (202) 546-2103. Fax: (202) 546-3275. E-mail: rusric@erols.com Global Business E-Books on Line: http://world.mirhouse.com

Al Khalifa and the Al Jalahima sections of the Bani Utub tribe migrated from Kuwait to Qatar's northwest coast and founded Az Zubarah (see fig. 9). Because the Bani Utub had important trading connections with Kuwait and were close to the rich oyster banks, Az Zubarah became a thriving center of trade and pearling, despite hostilities between the Al Khalifa and the Al Jalahima.

In response to attacks on Az Zubarah by an Omani shaykh who ruled Bahrain from Bushehr in Iran, the Bani Utub of Kuwait and Qatar, as well as some local Qatari tribes, captured Bahrain in 1783. The Al Khalifa claimed sovereignty over Bahrain and ruled it for several years from Az Zubarah. This angered the Al Jalahima, who felt they were deprived of their share of the spoils, and so they moved a few kilometers up the Qatari coast to establish Al Khuwayr, which they used as a staging point for maritime raids against the shipping of the Al Khalifa and the Iranians.

Most of the Al Khalifa migrated to the more desirable location of Bahrain and established a shaykhdom that endures to this day. That they left only a token presence in Az Zubarah meant initially that the Al Jalahima branch of the Bani Utub could achieve ascendancy in Qatar, with their leader, Rahman ibn Jabir Al Jalahima, earning a reputation as one of the most feared raiders on the surrounding waters. It also meant that with the economic decline of Az Zubarah (because the Al Khalifa shifted their trade connections to Bahrain), the peninsula would once more become a relative backwater. With no dominant local ruler, insecurity and rivalry characterized tribal relations. Settled tribes built walled towns, towers, and small forts to keep raiding beduin at bay.

In the late eighteenth and early nineteenth centuries, continuing bloody conflict involved not only the Al Khalifa, the Al Jalahima, and the Iranians but also the Omanis under Sayyid Said ibn Sultan Al Said, the nascent Wahhabis of Arabia, and the Ottomans. The period also saw the rise of British power in the Persian Gulf as a result of their growing interests in India. Britain's desire for secure passage for East India Company ships led it to impose its own order in the gulf. The General Treaty of Peace of 1820 between the East India Company and the shaykhs of the coastal area--which became known as the Trucial Coast because of the series of treaties between the shaykhs and the British-- was a way of ensuring safe passage. The agreement acknowledged British authority in the gulf and sought to end piracy and the kidnapping of slaves. Bahrain also became a party to the treaty, and it was assumed by the British and the Bahrainis that Qatar, as a dependency, was also a party to it.

But when, as punishment for piracy, an East India Company vessel bombarded Doha in 1821, destroying the town and forcing hundreds to flee, the residents had no idea why they were being attacked. The situation remained unsettled in 1867, when a large Bahraini force sacked and looted Doha and Al Wakrah. This attack, and the Qatari counterattack, prompted the British political agent, Colonel Lewis Pelly, to impose a settlement in 1868. His mission to Bahrain and Qatar and the peace treaty that resulted were milestones in Qatar's history because they implicitly recognized the distinctness of Qatar from Bahrain and explicitly acknowledged the position of Muhammad ibn Thani ibn Muhammad, an important representative of the peninsula's tribes. The Al Thani were originally beduin from Najd, but after settling in Qatar, they engaged in fishing, pearling, date palm cultivation, and trade.

For additional analytical, business and investment opportunities information, please contact Global Investment & Business Center, USA at (202) 546-2103. Fax: (202) 546-3275. E-mail: rusric@erols.com Global Business E-Books on Line: http://world.mirhouse.com

With the expansion of the Ottoman Empire into eastern Arabia in 1871, Qatar became vulnerable to occupation. Muhammad ibn Thani opposed Ottoman designs on Qatar, but his son, Qasim ibn Muhammad Al Thani, accepted Ottoman sovereignty in 1872. Although Qasim ibn Muhammad privately complained of the Ottoman presence, he hoped that with Ottoman support he could dominate those shaykhs in other towns who opposed him and rebuff Bahrain's claims on Az Zubarah. The question of Az Zubarah became moot in 1878, however, when Qasim ibn Muhammad destroyed the town as punishment for the piracy of the Naim, a tribe that resided in the north of Qatar but was loyal to the shaykh of Bahrain. Moreover, Qasim ibn Muhammad's ambivalent relations with the Ottomans deteriorated to the point that in 1893 they sent a military force to Doha to arrest him, ostensibly over his refusal to permit an Ottoman customhouse in Doha. Fighting broke out, and Qasim ibn Muhammad's supporters drove out the Ottoman force. This defeat, and Qasim ibn Muhammad's embrace after the turn of the century of the resurgent Wahhabis under Abd al Aziz ibn Saud, marked the de facto end of Ottoman rule in Qatar.

The Ottomans officially renounced sovereignty over Qatar in 1913, and in 1916 the new ruler, Qasim ibn Muhammad's son, Abd Allah ibn Qasim Al Thani, signed a treaty with Britain bringing the peninsula into the trucial system. This meant that in exchange for Britain's military protection, Qatar relinquished its autonomy in foreign affairs and other areas, such as the power to cede territory. The treaty also had provisions suppressing slavery, piracy, and gunrunning, but the British were not strict about enforcing those provisions.

Despite Qatar's coming under British "protection," Abd Allah ibn Qasim was far from secure: recalcitrant tribes refused to pay tribute; disgruntled family members intrigued against him; and he felt vulnerable to the designs of Bahrain, not to mention the Wahhabis. Despite numerous requests by Abd Allah ibn Qasim--for strong military support, for weapons, and even for a loan--the British kept him at arm's length. This changed in the 1930s, when competition (mainly between Britain and the United States) for oil concessions in the region intensified. In a 1935 treaty, Britain made more specific promises of assistance than in earlier treaties in return for the granting of a concession to the Anglo- Persian Oil Company.

The scramble for oil, in turn, raised the stakes in regional territorial disputes and put a dollar value on the question of national borders. In 1936, for example, Bahrain claimed rule over a group of islands, the largest of which is Hawar, on the west coast of Qatar because it had established a small military garrison there. Britain accepted the Bahraini claim over Abd Allah ibn Qasim's objections, in large part because the Bahraini shaykh's personal British adviser was able to frame Bahrain's case in a legal manner familiar to British officials. The question of domain continued in the early 1990s. Triggered by a dispute involving the Naim, the Bahrainis once again laid claim to the deserted town of Az Zubarah in 1937. Abd Allah ibn Qasim sent a large, heavily armed force and succeeded in defeating the Naim. The British political resident in Bahrain supported Qatar's claim and warned Hamad ibn Isa Al Khalifa, the ruler of Bahrain, not to intervene militarily. Bitter and angry over the loss of Az Zubarah, Hamad ibn Isa imposed a crushing embargo on trade and travel to Qatar.

Oil was discovered in Qatar in 1939, but its exploitation was halted between 1942 and 1947 because of World War II and its aftermath. The disruption of food supplies caused by the war prolonged a period of economic hardship in Qatar that had begun in the 1920s with the collapse of the pearl trade and had increased with the global depression of the early 1930s and the Bahraini embargo. As they had in previous times of privation, whole families and tribes moved to other parts of the gulf, leaving many Qatari villages deserted. Even Shaykh Abd Allah ibn Qasim went into debt and, in preparation for his retirement, groomed his favored second son, Hamad ibn Abd Allah Al Thani, to be his successor. Hamad ibn Abd Allah's death in 1948, however, led to a succession crisis in which the main candidates were Abd Allah ibn Qasim's eldest son, Ali ibn Abd Allah Al Thani, and Hamad ibn Abd Allah's teenage son, Khalifa ibn Hamad Al Thani.

Oil exports and payments for offshore rights began in 1949 and marked a turning point in Qatar. Not only would oil revenues dramatically transform the economy and society, but they would also provide the focus for domestic disputes and foreign relations. This became frighteningly clear to Abd Allah ibn Qasim when several of his relatives threatened armed opposition if they did not receive increases in their allowances. Aged and anxious, Abd Allah ibn Qasim turned to the British, promised to abdicate, and agreed, among other things, to an official British presence in Qatar in exchange for recognition and support for Ali ibn Abd Allah as ruler in 1949.

The 1950s saw the cautious development of government structures and public services under British tutelage. Ali ibn Abd Allah was at first reluctant to share power, which had centered in his household, with an infant bureaucracy run and staffed mainly by outsiders. Ali ibn Abd Allah's increasing financial difficulties and inability to control striking oil workers and obstreperous shaykhs, however, led him to succumb to British pressure. The first real budget was drawn up by a British adviser in 1953. By 1954 there were forty-two Qatari government employees.

A major impetus to the development of the British-run police force came in 1956 when about 2,000 demonstrators, who coalesced over issues such as Gamal Abdul Nasser's pan-Arabism and opposition to Britain and to Shaykh Ali ibn Abd Allah's retinue, marched through Doha. This and other demonstrations led Ali ibn Abd Allah to invest the police with his personal authority and support, a significant reversal of his previous reliance on his retainers and beduin fighters.

Public services developed haltingly during the 1950s. The first telephone exchange opened in 1953, the first desalination plant in 1954, and the first power plant in 1957. Also built in this period were a jetty, a customs warehouse, an airstrip, and a police headquarters. In the 1950s, 150 adult males of the Al Thani received outright grants from the government. Shaykhs also received land and government positions. This mollified them as long as oil revenues increased. When revenues declined in the late 1950s, however, Ali ibn Abd Allah could not handle the family pressures this engendered. That Shaykh Ali ibn Abd Allah spent extravagantly, owned a villa in Switzerland, and hunted in Pakistan fueled discontent, especially among those who were excluded from the regime's largesse (non-Al Thani Qataris) and those who were not excluded but thought they deserved more (other branches of the Al Thani). Seniority and proximity to the shaykh determined the size of allowances.

For additional analytical, business and investment opportunities information,
please contact Global Investment & Business Center, USA
at (202) 546-2103. Fax: (202) 546-3275. E-mail: rusric@erols.com
Global Business E-Books on Line: http://world.mirhouse.com

Succumbing to family pressures and poor health, Ali ibn Abd Allah abdicated in 1960. But instead of handing power over to Khalifa ibn Hamad, who had been named heir apparent in 1948, he made his son, Ahmad ibn Ali, ruler. Nonetheless, Khalifa ibn Hamad, as heir apparent and deputy ruler, gained considerable power, in large part because Ahmad ibn Ali, as had his father, spent much time outside the country.

Although he did not care much for governing, Ahmad ibn Ali could not avoid dealing with family business. One of his first acts was to increase funding for the shaykhs at the expense of development projects and social services. In addition to allowances, adult male Al Thani were also given government positions. This added to the antiregime resentment already felt by, among others, oil workers, low-ranking Al Thani, dissident shaykhs, and some leading individuals. These groups formed the National Unity Front in response to a fatal shooting on April 19, 1963, by one of Shaykh Ahmad ibn Ali's nephews. The front called a general strike, and its demands included a reduction of the ruler's privileges, recognition of trade unions, and increased social services. Ahmad ibn Ali cracked down by jailing fifty leading individuals and exiling the front's leaders. He also instituted some reforms, eventually including the provision of land and loans to poor Qataris.

Largely under Khalifa ibn Hamad's guiding hand, the infrastructure, foreign labor force, and bureaucracy continued to grow in the 1960s. There were even some early attempts at diversifying Qatar's economic base, most notably with the establishment of a cement factory, a national fishing company, and small-scale agriculture.

In 1968 Britain announced its intention of withdrawing from military commitments east of Suez, including those in force with Qatar, by 1971. For a while, the rulers of Bahrain, Qatar, and the Trucial Coast contemplated forming a federation after the British withdrawal. A dispute arose between Ahmad ibn Ali and Khalifa ibn Hamad, however, because Khalifa ibn Hamad opposed Bahrain's attempts to become the senior partner in the federation. Still giving public support to the federation, Ahmad ibn Ali nonetheless promulgated a provisional constitution in April 1970, which declared Qatar an independent, Arab, Islamic state with the sharia (Islamic law) as its basic law. Khalifa ibn Hamad was appointed prime minister in May. The first Council of Ministers was sworn in on January 1, 1970, and seven of its ten members were Al Thani. Khalifa ibn Hamad's argument prevailed with regard to the federation proposal. Qatar became an independent state on September 3, 1971. That Ahmad ibn Ali issued the formal announcement from his Swiss villa instead of from his Doha palace indicated to many Qataris that it was time for a change. On February 22, 1972, Khalifa ibn Hamad deposed Ahmad ibn Ali, who was hunting with his falcons in Iran. Khalifa ibn Hamad had the tacit support of the Al Thani and of Britain, and he had the political, financial, and military support of Saudi Arabia.

In contrast to his predecessor's policies, Khalifa ibn Hamad cut family allowances and increased spending on social programs, including housing, health, education, and pensions. In addition, he filled many top government posts with close relatives.

For additional analytical, business and investment opportunities information, please contact Global Investment & Business Center, USA at (202) 546-2103. Fax: (202) 546-3275. E-mail: rusric@erols.com Global Business E-Books on Line: http://world.mirhouse.com

In 1993 Khalifa ibn Hamad remained the amir, but his son, Hamad ibn Khalifa, the heir apparent and minister of defense, had taken over much of the day-to-day running of the country. The two consulted with each other on all matters of importance.

GEOGRAPHY

Qatar occupies 11,437 square kilometers on a peninsula that extends approximately 160 kilometers north into the Persian Gulf from the Arabian Peninsula. Varying in width between fifty-five and ninety kilometers, the land is mainly flat (the highest point is 103 meters) and rocky. Notable features include coastal salt pans, elevated limestone formations (the Dukhan anticline) along the west coast under which lies the Dukhan oil field, and massive sand dunes surrounding Khawr al Udayd, an inlet of the gulf in the southeast known to local English speakers as the Inland Sea. Of the islands belonging to Qatar, Halul is the most important. Lying about ninety kilometers east of Doha, it serves as a storage area and loading terminal for oil from the surrounding offshore fields. Hawar and the adjacent islands immediately off the west coast are the subject of a territorial dispute between Qatar and Bahrain (see Foreign Relations , this ch.).

The capital, Doha, is located on the central east coast on a sweeping (if shallow) harbor. Other ports include Umm Said, Al Khawr, and Al Wakrah. Only Doha and Umm Said are capable of handling commercial shipping, although a large port and a terminal for loading natural gas are planned at Ras Laffan, north of Al Khawr. Coral reefs and shallow coastal waters make navigation difficult in areas where channels have not been dredged.

Qatar shares its land border with the United Arab Emirates (UAE), with which in 1993 it continued to have a dispute in the Khawr al Udayd area. The boundary with Saudi Arabia was settled in 1965 but never demarcated. Qatar's northwest coast is fewer than thirty kilometers from Bahrain.

Doha is the capital of the country and the major administrative, commercial, and population center. In 1993 it was linked to other towns and development sites by a system of about 1,000 kilometers of paved roads. Doha's international airport has an approximately 4,500-meter main runway, capable of receiving all kinds of aircraft.

The long summer (June through September) is characterized by intense heat and alternating dryness and humidity, with temperatures exceeding 55° C. Temperatures are moderate from November through May, although winter temperatures may fall to 17° C, which is relatively cool for the latitude. Rainfall is negligible, averaging 100 millimeters per year, confined to the winter months, and falling in brief, sometimes heavy storms that often flood the small ravines and the usually dry wadis. Sudden, violent dust storms occasionally descend on the peninsula, blotting out the sun, causing wind damage, and momentarily disrupting transport and other services.

The scarcity of rainfall and the limited underground water, most of which has such a high mineral content that it is unsuitable for drinking or irrigation, restricted the population and the extent of agricultural and industrial development the country could support until desalination projects began. Although water continues to be provided from underground sources, most is obtained by desalination of seawater.

POPULATION

The population of Qatar before independence must be estimated because, until oil revenues created a reason to stay on the peninsula, individuals and whole tribes migrated when the economic or security situation became intolerable. Some sought work elsewhere; others joined neighboring branches of their tribe. In 1908 a British observer estimated there were 27,000 inhabitants; 6,000 were described as foreign slaves and 425 as Iranian boatbuilders. (By 1930 the number of Iranians had increased to 5,000, or almost 20 percent of the population.) The population probably remained fairly stable until the 1930s and 1940s, when economic hardship and regional insecurity caused people to migrate to other areas, leaving Qatar with a population of only 16,000 in 1949, according to one estimate.

After oil exports increased in the 1950s, employment opportunities attracted Arabs from other Persian Gulf countries and foreign workers (mostly Indians, at first) to Qatar. In 1970 the Qatari government, assisted by British experts, carried out a census that reported a population of 111,113, of whom 45,039, or more than 40 percent, were identified as Qataris. With the oil boom of the 1970s and the resultant influx of foreign workers came the largest population growth, so that by 1977 it was estimated that 200,000 people lived in the country, about 65 percent of whom were non-Qataris. During the 1960-75 period, the population grew at an average annual rate of 8.9 percent; in the 1970-75 period it grew at 12.7 percent.

The census of March 16, 1986, counted a population of 369,079, and an estimate for 1990 brought the total to 371,863, including up to 70,000 Qataris. The July 1992 estimate was 484,387, with a 1992 growth rate of 3.2 percent. The 1989 birth rate was 31.8 per 1,000 population and the death rate 2.5 per 1,000, for a natural increase per 1,000 of 29.3, a high rate for a developing country. The 1986 census showed that 84 percent of the population was concentrated in Doha and in the neighboring town of Ar Rayyan. Other towns included Al Wakrah (population 13,259) and Umm Said (population 6,094). In total, 88 percent of the population was urban. Reflecting the high number of migrant workers, about 67 percent of the population was male. The age breakdown was as follows: under fifteen, 27.8 percent; fifteen to twenty-nine, 29.3 percent; thirty to forty-four, 32.3 percent; forty-five to fifty-nine, 8.6 percent; and sixty and over, 2.0 percent.

South Asians (mainly Indians, Pakistanis, Bangladeshis, and Filipinos) made up about 35 percent of the population; Qataris, 20 percent; Arabs, 25 percent; Iranians, 16 percent; and others, 4 percent. Roughly 90 percent of the population was Muslim (mostly Sunni--see Glossary), and the remainder were Christian, Hindu, Bahai, and other.

EDUCATION AND WELFARE

For additional analytical, business and investment opportunities information, please contact Global Investment & Business Center, USA at (202) 546-2103. Fax: (202) 546-3275. E-mail: rusric@erols.com Global Business E-Books on Line: http://world.mirhouse.com

EDUCATION

The tentative beginnings of education in Qatar were in the first half of the twentieth century when boys and girls were taught in the traditional 'katateeb' schools. They were taught many subjects but without a formal system. Since those early days, education in Qatar has made great leaps and developed into a system of education reaching all the way to highest stages. Qatar follows a policy of compulsory and continuous education where all citizens receive free schooling reflecting the country's identity and providing equal opportunities to all.

BASIC EDUCATION

Qatar follows a policy of compulsory education until the end of the elementary stage and free education to all citizens. Basic education consists of the following stages,

Elementary Stage:	Six years
Preparatory Stage:	Three years
Secondary Stage:	Three years

The country has 113 elementary schools; 60 for boys and 53 for girls, 56 preparatory schools; 28 for boys and 28 for girls, and 41 secondary schools; 19 for boys and 22 for girls. Government schools provide free education for the children of non-Qatari residents who work for the public sector. Qatar also has private schools as well as schools for the different Arab communities like the Lebanese, Jordanian and Sudanese schools plus those for non-Arab communities like the Indian, American and other schools.

HIGHER EDUCATION

University education in Qatar started in the seventies when two colleges of education, one for male and one for female students, were established in 1973. The new campus for Qatar University was officially inaugurated in 1985. The university consists of the following seven faculties,

Faculty of Education

Faculty of Humanities and Social Sciences

Faculty of Science

Faculty of Islamic Studies

Faculty of Administration and Economics Faculty of Engineering

Faculty of Technology

All the above faculties have branches in the male and female student sections with the exception of the Faculty of Engineering, which is available to male students only. The academic staff have a large number of specialists from Qatar, all Arab countries and some foreign countries. The university has more than eight thousand students.

A large number of Qataris, particularly male students, attend universities outside the state. Universities in the USA and UK, in particular, have a large number of Qataris studying for higher degrees. The Ministry of Education and Culture grants a large number of scholarships to enable these students to obtain the highest degrees from the best universities.

Qatar also has a number of private colleges particularly for female students.

ELIMINATION OF ILLITERACY

The first centre for adult education and the elimination of illiteracy was established in 1954. Regular classes were started in 1956 when there were seven schools with 614 students. Two ladies centres were opened in 1976. Illiterate students were given four years of elementary schooling after which they were granted their literacy certificates. In the past such students were also given incentive allowances of QR150 per month. The Ministry of Education and Culture takes care to ensure the subjects studied are appropriate to the emotional needs of the students and that those given to female students are directly relevant to women's needs.
Latest statistics indicate that illiteracy in Qatar has declined in recent years. Statistics for 1997 show that illiteracy for Qataris over 10 years old is 13.6%, 8.6% for males and 18.4% for females.

ENGLISH LANGUAGE TEACHING

In Qatari schools and colleges, all subjects are taught in the Arabic language. English is taught as a foreign language in common use in the country. The Ministry of Education and Culture has decided to commence English language teaching from the start of the elementary stage.

Before oil was discovered, there was no formal education system in Qatar. Instead, some children in villages and towns memorized passages from the Quran and learned to read and write in a *kuttab*, an informal class taught in mosques or homes by literate men and women knowledgeable about Islam. Based on the custom of keeping women in a milieu shut off from the political, social, and economic opportunities afforded men, the development of education in Qatar focused mainly on the male population. From 1918 to 1938, for example, an Islamic school for adult males was run by Muhammad Abd al Aziz al Mana, an eminent scholar who had studied under Muhammad Abduh of Egypt and Al Alusi of Baghdad. According to a 1970 study, only 9 percent of the population born between 1895 and 1910 were literate, as were 15 percent of those born between 1910 and 1920 and 14 percent of those born between 1920 and 1930.

In 1949 Shaykh Hamad ibn Abd Allah opened a somewhat more modern school. The school, the Islah al Muhammadiyyah, had one teacher and fifty boys. In 1951 the school received funding from the ruling family, and the number of students and teachers increased. Subjects included Islamic religion and history, Arabic, arithmetic, geography, and English. By 1954 there were four such schools, with a total of 560 male students and twentysix teachers. The first girls' school funded by oil money was a small *kuttab* that had been run by Amina Mahmud since 1938. After it was reorganized in 1956 as the first public school for girls in Qatar, four teachers taught 122 students the Quran, Arabic, arithmetic, ethics, and health. In the same year, the Department of Education was established. The budget for education increased from QR1 million (for value of the Qatari riyal--see Glossary) in 1955 to QR25 million in 1960. Not only was all public schooling free, but between 1956 and 1962 students received a monthly stipend. Despite inequality during the 1950s between the number of boys and the number of girls attending school, attendance was almost equal by gender in the late 1970s, with girls outperforming boys academically.

In the early 1990s, the education system consisted of six years of primary school, three years of intermediate school, and three years of secondary school. The secondary education program includes schools specializing in religion, commerce, and technical studies in which only males are allowed. Females, however, might attend teacher-training institutions. Instruction throughout the system is in Arabic, but English is introduced in the last two years of primary school, and there are special language-training programs for government personnel. Private facilities are available for kindergarten instruction. In addition, many foreign communities have established schools for their children; the largest are the schools for the Indian community. Although the government offers assistance to private schools, they are funded mainly through tuition and private sources.

In the 1975-76 academic year, 21,402 children attended primary school; by the 1985-86 academic year, that number had risen to 31,844. Students continue to be segregated by gender. In 1986 approximately 5.6 percent of the gross national product (GNP--see Glossary) went toward public education. The state in the 1990s continued to cover education costs, including school supplies, clothing, meals, and transportation to and from school.

In the 1988-89 academic year, there were 48,097 students in ninety-seven primary schools taught by 2,589 teachers and 22,178 secondary students in seventy-eight schools taught by 2,115 teachers. At the three vocational schools, there were 924 students and 104 teachers. In the 1989-90 academic year, there were 5,637 students at the University of Qatar, which had 504 instructors, mostly Egyptians and non-Qatari Arabs.

The first institutions of higher education in Qatar were separate teacher-training colleges for men and women that opened in 1973. Before that, those wishing to pursue higher degrees either studied abroad (mainly in Egypt and Lebanon) or took correspondence courses. A decree establishing the University of Qatar was passed, and in 1977 faculties of humanities, social studies, Islamic studies, and science joined the education faculty of the teacher-training colleges. In the 1985-86 academic year, about 1,000 Qataris received government scholarships to pursue higher education abroad, mostly in other Arab countries and in the United States, Britain, and France.

HEALTH

Before oil was discovered, health care consisted of traditional medicine: barbers performed circumcisions and other minor procedures, and herbalists dispensed natural remedies. A one-doctor "hospital" opened in Doha in 1945. In 1951 Shaykh Ali ibn Abd Allah agreed to a British doctor and a small staff. The first state hospital, Rumailah Hospital, opened in 1959 with 170 beds. A 165-bed maternity hospital was established in 1965. The health budget was abused by Shaykh Ahmad ibn Ali's son and minister of health, Abd al Aziz ibn Ahmad Al Thani. He apparently sent thousands of Ahmad ibn Ali's supporters abroad for luxurious and, in many cases, unnecessary health care in the 1960s.

The development of social services, including health care, accelerated after the accession in 1972 of Shaykh Khalifa ibn Hamad, who dramatically altered the allocation of oil revenues. This included transferring the ruler's 25 percent of oil revenues to the state budget. But the health budget suffered because of the downturns in oil revenues. In 1986, for example, there were cuts of 10 percent in clinic staff.

There are three hospitals in Doha, with a total of about 1,100 beds. Hamad General Hospital, which opened in 1982, has modern facilities for emergency care, cardiovascular surgery, tomography, nuclear medicine, and plastic surgery. Rumailah Hospital, once the only general hospital, has become a center for geriatric, psychiatric, and rehabilitative care. It also has dental and dermatology departments and a burn unit. The Women's Hospital has 314 beds. In addition, dozens of clinics throughout the country ensure accessible primary care to most of the population. For example, 90 percent of births in the late 1980s were attended by a health professional. There are 752 government physicians and many other support staff. In the 1980s, several private clinics also opened in the capital.

Life expectancy at birth in 1986 was 65.2 years for males and 67.6 years for females. The infant mortality rate in 1989 was thirty-one per 1,000 live births. In the 1988-89 period, 81 percent of one- to three-year-olds were immunized. Major causes of death in 1989 were diseases of the circulatory system, injuries and poisonings, tumors, and perinatal conditions.

VOLUNTARY AND CHARITABLE ORGANIZATIONS

Qatar Charitable Society

For additional analytical, business and investment opportunities information, please contact Global Investment & Business Center, USA at (202) 546-2103. Fax: (202) 546-3275. E-mail: rusric@erols.com Global Business E-Books on Line: http://world.mirhouse.com

Telephone: 435 0202
General Secretary: Sheikh Abdalla Al Dabbagh
The oldest and largest charitable organisation in Qatar. It concentrates on collecting contributions from within Qatar for distributing to the needy inside and outside the country. It aims to support the needy, victims of war and natural disasters and orphans until the age of eighteen. The organisation, with an international outlook both in its aims and its operations, was established in 1992. It has seven offices outside Qatar that coordinate its activities in Asia, Africa and Europe.

Sheikh Eid bin Mohamed Al Thani Charitable Organisation

Telephone: 487 8051
Chairman of Board of Directors: Sheikh Dr Mohamed bin Eid Al Thani.
One of the largest charitable organisations in Qatar. It is at the forefront of providing large and significant amounts of aid to many Moslem nations suffering from disasters, natural and man-made. It also has many charitable activities within Qatar.

Qatar Red Crescent Society

Telephone: 443 5111 Zakat Fund
The Zakat Fund is a department of the Ministry of Endowments and Islamic Affairs
The fund operates under the direct supervision of the above ministry.

Organisation for Islamic Guidance

Telephone: 486 6340
General Secretary: Sheikh Suwar Al Thahab
This organisation is based in Sudan but has a permanent office in Doha. The organisation collects contributions in Qatar to distribute to the needy in the African continent.

There are also many committees and non-resident charitable organisations that are allowed to operate in Qatar without establishing permanent offices. Some of these are,

Guidance Committee, based in Kuwait
International Islamic Relief Organisation

GOVERNMENT AND POLITICS

Welfare, freedom, security and stability are the main features figured out by the Qatari local policy, while independence and rationality characterize its foreign policy.

Thanks to the wise and far-sighted leadership of HH the Emir Sheikh Hamad bin Khalifa Al-Thani, the State of Qatar enjoys an exemplary prosperity and occupies a deservedly prestigious position on the regional, Arab and international levels. The local Qatari policies are basically meant to ensure welfare for the citizens, while its foreign policy is based on noble principles to serve the best interest of the homeland, to consolidate the joint process of the GCC and to support Arab and Islamic causes.

The pioneering stances taken by small-sized Qatar have qualified it to become an effective player with a prestigious position.

Since assumption of authority in June 1995, HH the Emir has shown great keenness to lend more vigor and dimension to the foreign policy to serve the higher interests of the country, retaining thereby Qatar's independence of decision-making and keeping up the basic fundamentals featuring its Gulf and Arab characteristics.

HH Sheikh Hamad Bin Khalifa
Al Thani, Qatar's Amir

Within the context, the State of Qatar effectively supports the process of integration with fellow GCC member states and actively upgrades the standard of coordination maintained with them to materialize the legitimate aspirations of GCC peoples. The State of Qatar has sincerely endeavored to strengthen its close links with fellow GCC member states and unhesitatingly supports them, as it was the case with Kuwait during the Gulf crisis.

Now the State of Qatar cordially welcomes the upcoming 17th GCC summit which Doha will host this December 7 with a view that the summit would be a fresh start for further integration among GCC member states until joint action is fully maintained and a common strategy is mapped out.

The State of Qatar believes that any success by the GCC would bring about favorable fruits not only to member states but also to all Arab countries and would surely strengthen pan-Arab solidarity and unity of action.

For additional analytical, business and investment opportunities information, please contact Global Investment & Business Center, USA at (202) 546-2103. Fax: (202) 546-3275. E-mail: rusric@erols.com Global Business E-Books on Line: http://world.mirhouse.com

On the Arab level, the State of Qatar continuously call upon Arab countries to shun differences and restore effectively pan-Arab solidarity to serve the higher interests of the Arab nation. Hence, the State of Qatar has supported the Palestine question, backed the Yemeni unity, and showed deep keenness on Iraq's unity and sovereignty.

In harmony with these stances, the State of Qatar has decisively frozen normalization of relations with Israel unless the latter takes a positive move on the Modest peace process, especially on the Palestinian track of peace talks. This Qatari standpoint was widely welcomed by Arab countries because it urges Israel re-think its hardline stances.

In line with this tendency, the State of Qatar has called for a pan-Arab summit, where Arab leaders would draw realistic common strategies to secure welfare of Arab citizens and to set up an efficient and sustainable economic forum to safeguard pan-Arab economic interests and to activate common co-operation.

The State of Qatar seeks to maintain balanced and equitable relations with all world countries. It positively believes that disparity in viewpoints should not hinder constructive co-operation with sisterly and friendly countries. The State of Qatar also believes in the essential need for the adequate implementation of and the full abidance by the international agreements and conventions especially those calling for the settlement of disputes by peaceful means, including the resort to the International Court of Justice.

The State of Qatar carefully supports Islamic questions, foremost the just causes of the Bosnian and Chechen peoples.

The State of Qatar sides with Third World countries in their endeavours to overcome hardships and difficulties and in order to create a new world based on collective and constructive co-operation, of all nations to secure peace and welfare.

In this respect, the State of Qatar extends all forms of help and assistance and maintains effective co-operation with regional and international organizations, foremost the Arab League, the OIC (Organization of Islamic Conference), the OPEC (Organization of Petroleum Exporting Countries) the Non-Aligned Movement, as well as the United Nations and its specialized organizations.

In appreciation of Qatar's sound stances and effective regional and international role , the delegates to the Middle East and North Africa economic co-operation forums have unanimously agreed on Doha to be the host of their conference next year.

The State of Qatar believes that economic development slogans will never be realized unless equally effective efforts are exerted on human resources development and unless the advanced industrialized nations allow world countries on easy access to technology and remove the barriers to free flow of investment capitals to these countries.

Under the wise leadership of HH the Emir Sheikh Hamad bin Khalifa Al-Thani, the State of Qatar dedicates valuable efforts to develop national economy on scientific basis to cope up with international changes. Economic liberalization measures were taken, the local market was opened up for free investment and trading exchanges, and new plans were launched to make optimal use of natural and human resources to ensure prosperity in the country.

Hopes are pinned on natural gas sources as the most promising future income of the State, which perches on the world's largest single non-associated gas field, namely the North Gas Field the reserves of which are estimated at about 380 trillion cubic feet. Gas investments have so far totaled some US$ 30 billion, in an extremely ambitious programme expected to turn Qatar into a major supplier of gas on the international market.

With its estimate reserves of over 7.6 trillion cubic meters of natural gas, the State of Qatar has the world's third largest gas reserves.

In the meantime, the State of Qatar has increased its oil output to about half a million barrels per day. Oil production is planned to be further upgraded to some 700,000 barrels per day in the year 2000.

The State of Qatar offers huge viable investment opportunities in oil, gas, refining and petrochemical industries and offers countless incentives to attract foreign investments.

For this objective, huge capitals were invested in the development of an up to date reliable infrastructure. The Ras Laffan Sea Port, which is one of the world's largest jetties is just as example to cite. The jetty can handle 23 million tonnes of liquefied natural gas per annum, besides oil and petrochemical products.

The State of Qatar is deservedly qualified to be a great attraction to investors, thanks to its distinguished geographic position, its political and economic stability, over and above the long experience it has gained in projects management and execution.

Within weeks, the first shipment of Qatari LNG will go to Japan, which agreed to purchase six million tonnes of LNG per annum from Qatar for 25 years. Negotiations are also under way with Pakistan, Taiwan and Turkey for the signing of sale-and-purchase LNG contracts.

The International Monetary Fund expects Qatari gas and oil exports to raise the annual general income from three billion dollars at present to seven billion dollars in 2000. This increase would not only balance the deficit but also ensure a fair surplus that would allow Qatar retain its favourable standard as its GNP per capita is one of the world's highest.

The Qatari people have cordially welcomed the appointment by H.H. the Emir Sheikh Hamad Bin Khalifa Al Thani of H.H. Sheikh Jassem bin Hamad Al Thani as Heir Apparent.

In the context of creating the desired institutional state, H.H. the Emir appointed H.H. Sheikh Abdullah Bin Khalifa Al Thani as Prime Minister, separating for the first time in Qatar's history between Emiri and Premiership posts.

H.H. the Emir has always encouraged citizens to contribute to the all-round development process in the country. Observers agree that Qatar is on the threshold of a new era of development.

A landmark in Qatar's new policy is the expected democratic process in municipal elections which will be the first popular participation. It followed another step in the democratic process that is the election of members of the board of Qatar Chamber of Commerce and Industry.

And in order to expand popular participation in policy-making in the country, H.H. the Emir has increased the number of members of the Advisory Council to 35 from 30.

To give Qatari women a role in the government, H.H. the Emir has issued a decision appointing a Qatari woman to the post of Under Secretary of the Ministry of Education. This is in line with H.H.'s belief in the importance of women's role in advancing overall development in the country.

A long-term economic and financial plan calls for expanding the industrial base of the country to lessen dependence on oil as a sole earner of hard currency. Such a policy has reduced the State's deficit and curbed inflation to one of the lowest levels in the world. Qatar's development plan which also aims at harnessing the country's huge gas resources aims at providing best services to citizens. And according to a World Bank report of 1995, Qatar is one of the richest countries in the world.

An international conference on human rights held recently in Athens said there was no indication of the presence of any political prisoners in Qatar, neither was there any evidence of torture cases for citizens or residents.

Freedom is secured for all citizens in Qatar. Freedom of speech is upheld by H.H. the Emir who believes that such freedom is necessary for citizens participation in running the affairs of the country and an important bulwark for the success of thought and creativity. Hence, H.H. the Emir has decided to lift censorship on newspapers. H.H. has also dissolved the Ministry of Information to give way for expression of all persuasions of thought. Information organs have been created to keep abreast of international advancement in this sector. In this context, a news satellite channel has been set up for Qatar to beam Qatar's voice to the world.

Youths have been given a boost in various sectors, especially in sports where Qatari teams have been a source for pride in many sports events.

For additional analytical, business and investment opportunities information, please contact Global Investment & Business Center, USA at (202) 546-2103. Fax: (202) 546-3275. E-mail: rusric@erols.com Global Business E-Books on Line: http://world.mirhouse.com

POLITICAL ENVIRONMENT

NATURE OF POLITICAL RELATIONSHIP WITH THE U.S.:

Since he took over power in a bloodless coup in 1995, Sheikh Hamad bin Khalifa Al-Thani, the Emir of the State of Qatar has continued to support a strong U.S. Qatari relationship based on shared interests in promoting regional peace and stability as well as trade ties. The first of its kind since the U.S. and Qatar agreed to exchange diplomatic relations in 1974, the Emir's official visit to the U.S. in June 1997 established grounds for a steady and constant development of relations in various fields between the two countries. This includes education, trade, defense as well as oil and natural gas technology and partnership. A strong supporter of a just and durable peace and economic development in the Middle East, Qatar publicly opposes terrorism and extremism of any kind. Its policy calls for resolving all political and border issues through peaceful negotiations and international arbitration. It was in this spirit that Qatar hosted the Middle East/North Africa (MENA) Conference in 1997 and will host the Islamic Conference Organization (ICO) Summit in 2000. Future opportunities for further development of relations in various fields between the U.S. and Qatar exist.

POLITICAL SYSTEM: BASIC STRUCTURE

In a move towards democratization, the pragmatic Emir of Qatar, Sheikh Hamad bin Khalifa Al-Thani established a 32-member committee in mid-July, 1999, for drafting a permanent Constitution for this developing country.

The new Constitution will be tailored to call for establishing an elected Advisory Council (Parliament) to replace the current one which comprises 30 members appointed by the Emir. The current 30-year modified/provisional Constitution falls short of dealing with the aspirations of the Qatari people and provides little chance for them to play a role in the decision making process. It vests extensive powers in the Emir. He enjoys both executive and legislative powers and, as such, promulgates laws through consultations with the Council of Ministers (Cabinet) and Advisory Council. Laws are subject to the Emir's approval prior to taking effect.

Qatar has no political parties or political elections or labor unions and as such no opposition officially exists. Election of a Central Municipal Council was launched for the first time in March 1997. Although all successful candidates were men, women were given the right to nomination and election. Some women were appointed in leading government positions at the level of Undersecretary and Professor in the Ministry of Education and the State-owned Qatar University.

In his endeavor to decentralize powers vested in himself, the Emir has established a separate position of Prime Minister, currently occupied by his brother Sheikh Abdullah bin Khalifa Al-Thani. This position was traditionally invested in the Emir. He has also appointed Sheikh Jassim bin Hamad, one of his sons, as Heir Apparent, and Deputy Emir when the Emir is outside the country for any reason.

For additional analytical, business and investment opportunities information, please contact Global Investment & Business Center, USA at (202) 546-2103. Fax: (202) 546-3275. E-mail: rusric@erols.com Global Business E-Books on Line: http://world.mirhouse.com

There is no doubt that the monarchical political system will go through further democratization reforms and more social liberalization. In the meanwhile, however, the government will continue to pay heed to the country's cultural and traditional values.

Qatar is an emirate with a conventional hereditary system. It is ruled by the Al Thani family whose presence in the peninsula dates from the eighteenth century. The Al Thani are named after the doyen of the family Sheikh Thani bin Mohamed who is the father of Sheikh Mohamed bin Thani, the first ruler of the Qatar peninsula in the mid nineteenth century. Al Thani are a branch of the Arab tribe of Beni Tameem.

BASIC STATUTE

The amended provisional basic statute of rule in the country for 1972 declares that: Qatar is a sovereign and independent Arab state, Islam is the official religion of the country and the Shariah (Islamic Law) is the principal source of legislation. Democracy is the basis for the system of government. The official language is Arabic and the Qatari people are part of the Arab nation.

The state exercises sovereignty over all the territories and territorial waters, which fall within its international borders. It has no right to renounce sovereignty or withdraw from any part of those territories or waters. The State is responsible for maintaining the integrity, security and stability of the country as well as using all its resources to defend it against any act of aggression.

The state believes in and strives for the unity of Arab states: a necessity dictated by the common interests of our region and those of the Arab world. Similarly, the state supports all efforts to foster the spirit of fraternity and democracy.

The aim of Qatar's foreign policy is to strengthen bonds of friendship with all countries, especially with the Islamic peoples. The State accepts the principles contained in the United Nations Charter, which support the right of all peoples and nations to self-determination.

The State is legally entrusted with the control and supervision of the national economy to accomplish economic development in the country through sound planning and technical cooperation with specialized international agencies. Private ownership, capital and labour form the basic components of the social structure of the country. They are regarded as individual rights that serve a social function, and are organized by the law.

The state also guarantees all free enterprises, provided that it does not conflict with the interests of the state. In accordance with religious, moral and national principles, basic statute is fully concerned with the well being of the family, as it is the nucleus of the society. To that end, specific legislation have been enacted to protect the family and the young generation, and every effort is being made to provide equal opportunities for all citizens to practice their right of work on the basis of social justice protected by the law.

Civil Rights and liberties:
The citizens of Qatar enjoy equal civil rights and responsibilities without discrimination on grounds of race, origin or religion. Laws cannot be applied retroactively and no sentence may be passed except under the terms of an existing law. A suspect is innocent until proven guilty and is entitled to a fair trial.

The civil liberties guaranteed by the state include the right of residence, freedom of press and publication and private ownership. These rights cannot be circumscribed except where the practice of such rights contravenes the law or the public interest. The basic statute requires all those residing in the state to observe public order and respect public customs and morals.
On its part, the state is responsible for providing public jobs for all residents.

CONSTITUTIONAL AUTHORITIES

His Highness the Emir is the Head of the constitutional authorities, holding both legislative and executive powers. The Council of Ministers assists in implementing the general policies of the State and the Advisory Council gives recommendations and advice on public matters referred to it by the Council of Ministers.

RULING FAMILY

The Head of State of Qatar is the Emir (from the Arabic word for prince). All the rulers of the State of Qatar since its independence in 1971 belong to the traditional ruling family of the area - the Al-Thani.

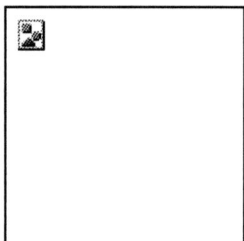

The Al-Thani have ruled in Qatar since the mid nineteenth century. Through a series of treaties with the British, the family became recognised as de facto rulers of the Qatar area, and were accorded continued official ruling status under independence.

In the early 1990's the family was comprised of three main branches - the Bani Hamad, the Bani Ali and the Bani Khalid. It was a very sizeable tribe, being composed of an estimated 20,000 members at the time.

For additional analytical, business and investment opportunities information, please contact Global Investment & Business Center, USA at (202) 546-2103. Fax: (202) 546-3275. E-mail: rusric@erols.com Global Business E-Books on Line: http://world.mirhouse.com

right to left : Sh. Abdullah Bin Qassim Al Thani, Sheikh Ali, and Sheikh Hamad, grandfather of present Emir

There were two official Al-Thani rulers before independence (plus four previous acknowledged rulers)- Sheikh Ali bin Abdullah (1949 - 1960), and Sheikh Ahmed bin Ali (1960 - 1972).

Neither took an active role in the running of the country. However this situation began to change in the 1950's when Sheikh Khalifa Bin Hamad, the cousin of Ahmed, became Heir Apparent and served not only as Prime Minister, but headed various other ministries such as Foreign Affairs, Finance and Petroleum and Education and Culture at different times. Sheikh Khalifa was effectively the first modern ruler of Qatar, taking a close interest in and a strong supervisory role over all aspects of the government and development of his country and people.

H.H. Sheikh Hamad bin Khalifa Al-Thani, Emir of the State Of Qatar

Sheikh Khalifa was succeeded by his son and Heir Apparent, H.H. Sheikh Hamad Bin Khalifa in 1995. Sheikh Hamad was born in Doha in 1950 and was educated both in Qatar and overseas. Prior to his accession, he also held the post of Defence Minister - a title which he has retained as Emir.

Since the accession of Sheikh Hamad, the country has made enormous strides forward in opening up its business and investment opportunities, in furthering the development of its hydrocarbon resources and in the expansion of foreign relations.

This is largely due to the influence of the Emir and to the implementation of policies that originated at the very highest level. Sheikh Hamad is enormously popular with his people, as was touchingly evidenced by the spontaneous displays of loyalty when he returned from extensive recuperation overseas, following a kidney transplant operation.

For additional analytical, business and investment opportunities information, please contact Global Investment & Business Center, USA at (202) 546-2103. Fax: (202) 546-3275. E-mail: rusric@erols.com Global Business E-Books on Line: http://world.mirhouse.com

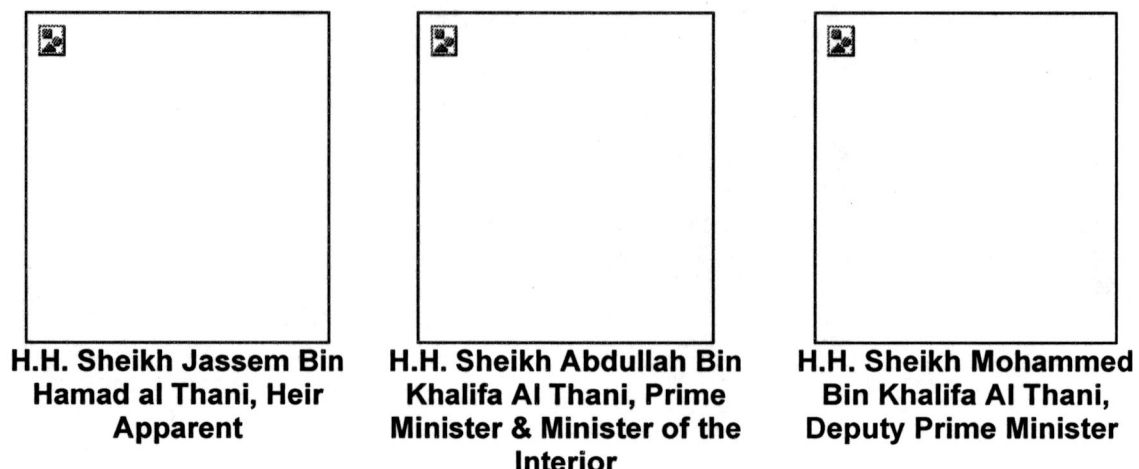

H.H. Sheikh Jassem Bin Hamad al Thani, Heir Apparent

H.H. Sheikh Abdullah Bin Khalifa Al Thani, Prime Minister & Minister of the Interior

H.H. Sheikh Mohammed Bin Khalifa Al Thani, Deputy Prime Minister

Sheikh Hamad is known as a great family man and takes a deep interest in the education and cultural development of his many children. In 1996, the Emir named his third son, H.H. Sheikh Jassim Bin Hamad, Heir Apparent of Qatar. Educated at Sandhurst in Britain and in Qatar, Sheikh Jassim is rapidly assuming increasing responsibility and has deputised for his father on a number of occasions. The younger brother of the Emir, H.H. Sheikh Abdullah Bin Khalifa was appointed to the post of Prime Minister in 1996, and another brother, HH Sheikh Mohammed Bin Khalifa became Deputy Prime Minister.

The Al-Thani are holders of absolute power in the State of Qatar, and have shown themselves to be benevolent, forward-thinking and wise rulers.

Qatar is governed by a traditional monarchy. The Al-Thani family have formally ruled the country since the nineteenth century. The monarch is hereditary (though it does not strictly follow the rules of primogeniture) and passes from one ruler to the next nominated family member, which is usually a son.

His Highness, Sheikh Hamad Bin Khalifa Al-Thani

The current Heir Apparent, **Sheikh Jassim Bin Hamad Al-Thani**, is the third son of the Emir, **Sheikh Hamad Bin Khalifa Al-Thani**, while the post of Prime Minister (titular head of government) is held by the brother of the Emir, **Sheikh Abdullah Bin Khalifa Al-Thani**. The current Emir also holds the posts of Minister of Defence and Commander-in-Chief of the armed forces.

Although there have been two changes in the monarchy since 1972 that have been brought about by family consensus, both have been completely peaceful. The Emir is an absolute ruler, deriving his formal power from the Basic Law of 1970, also known as the provisional Constitution. According to this law, the Emir is bound to rule according to the main principles of fairness, honesty, the Islamic religion, generosity and mutual respect. There are no central government elections and political parties are proscribed by law. The supreme legislative body - the Advisory Council, is appointed by the Emir and consists largely of Ministers (also appointed) who advise on policy matters in addition to formulating the laws of the country. There are currently 35 members of the Advisory Council.

The Emir is also advised by the Council of Ministers, which forms his cabinet. Most members of the Council of Ministers are also members of the Advisory Council. The judicial system comes under the provenance of Emiri rule, although individual matters are largely decided by Sharia, or Islamic, law, to which the Emir is subject. However, certain civil codes are in the process of implementation.

The country is divided into administrative divisions, known as municipalities, of which there are nine. The country is preparing for the first ever municipal elections , due to be held in early 1999, in which all eligible adult nationals will be able to vote.

FOREIGN RELATIONS

Qatar has a balanced history of foreign relations. Shortly after independence, the country joined the United Nations and several of its specialised agencies, such as the Food and Agriculture Organisation, the International Labour Organisation, the World Health Organisation and UNESCO.

Membership of these bodies has ensured that Qatar is always well briefed on world political situations and is able to make a positive and valuable contribution to issues of concern.
Despite the turbulence of the region in which Qatar is located, the country has managed to maintain equable, if not always excellent, relations with all its neighbours and with other Middle Eastern countries.

Qatar is an active member of the Gulf Cooperation Council and has twice hosted summits in Doha.

Frequent overseas visits by the Emir and the Foreign Minister, in addition to visits to Qatar by a host of international leaders and figures of importance have ensured that a high level of communication is maintained.

Diplomatic relations have been established with a large number of countries around the world, and these increase annually, with the opening of more embassies on both sides.

H.H. The Emir with US President, Bil Clinton

Relations with the major powers, the USA, Britain and France in particular, are cordial and are reflected by increasing political links, defence contracts and trade relations with these countries.

In addition, strong trade links exist between Qatar and Japan and Korea, the key markets for the country's hydrocarbon exports.

The Head of State of Qatar is the Emir (from the Arabic word for prince). All the rulers of the State of Qatar since its independence in 1971 belong to the traditional ruling family of the area - the Al-Thani.

The Al-Thani have ruled in Qatar since the mid nineteenth century. Through a series of treaties with the British, the family became recognised as de facto rulers of the Qatar area, and were accorded continued official ruling status under independence.

In the early 1990's the family was comprised of three main branches - the Bani Hamad, the Bani Ali and the Bani Khalid. It was a very sizeable tribe, being composed of an estimated 20,000 members at the time.

There were two official Al-Thani rulers before independence (plus four previous acknowledged rulers)- Sheikh Ali bin Abdullah (1949 - 1960), and Sheikh Ahmed bin Ali (1960 - 1972).

Neither took an active role in the running of the country. However this situation began to change in the 1950's when Sheikh Khalifa Bin Hamad, the cousin of Ahmed, became Heir Apparent and served not only as Prime Minister, but headed various other ministries such as Foreign Affairs, Finance and Petroleum and Education and Culture at different times. Sheikh Khalifa was effectively the first modern ruler of Qatar, taking a close interest in and a strong supervisory role over all aspects of the government and development of his country and people.

Sheikh Khalifa was succeeded by his son and Heir Apparent, H.H. Sheikh Hamad Bin Khalifa in 1995. Sheikh Hamad was born in Doha in 1950 and was educated both in Qatar and overseas. Prior to his accession, he also held the post of Defence Minister - a title which he has retained as Emir.

Since the accession of Sheikh Hamad, the country has made enormous strides forward in opening up its business and investment opportunities, in furthering the development of its hydrocarbon resources and in the expansion of foreign relations.

This is largely due to the influence of the Emir and to the implementation of policies that originated at the very highest level. Sheikh Hamad is enormously popular with his people, as was touchingly evidenced by the spontaneous displays of loyalty when he returned from extensive recuperation overseas, following a kidney transplant operation.

Sheikh Hamad is known as a great family man and takes a deep interest in the education and cultural development of his many children. In 1996, the Emir named his third son, H.H. Sheikh Jassim Bin Hamad, Heir Apparent of Qatar. Educated at Sandhurst in Britain and in Qatar, Sheikh Jassim is rapidly assuming increasing responsibility and has deputised for his father on a number of occasions. The younger brother of the Emir, H.H. Sheikh Abdullah Bin Khalifa was appointed to the post of Prime Minister in 1996, and another brother, HH Sheikh Mohammed Bin Khalifa became Deputy Prime Minister.

The Al-Thani are holders of absolute power in the State of Qatar, and have shown themselves to be benevolent, forward-thinking and wise rulers.

THE EMIR

Qatar is an emirate with a conventional hereditary system. It is ruled by the Al Thani family whose presence in the peninsula dates from the eighteenth century. The Al Thani are named after the doyen of the family Sheikh Thani bin Mohamed who is the father of Sheikh Mohamed bin Thani, the first ruler of the Qatar peninsula in the mid nineteenth century. Al Thani are a branch of the Arab tribe of Beni Tameem.

The Emir is the head of state. In accordance with the modified provisional constitution, the Emir decrees laws on the recommendation of the Council of Ministers and after consultation with the Advisory Council. The Council of Ministers, appointed by an Emiri decree, is the highest executive authority in the land. However, laws are not enacted until after Emiri consent.

For additional analytical, business and investment opportunities information,
please contact Global Investment & Business Center, USA
at (202) 546-2103. Fax: (202) 546-3275. E-mail: rusric@erols.com
Global Business E-Books on Line: http://world.mirhouse.com

ADVISORY COUNCIL

The Advisory Council first met on 15 May 1972. It was formed according to the Modified Provisional Constitution, which was enacted in 1972. The Council comprises 35 members who must be wise, sensible, and competent and represent one of the social sectors or the country's regions. The Council is the country's first democratic experiment since independence in 1971. It debates all issues of public interest submitted by the Government whether political, administrative, economic, legal or legislative. The Emir regularly takes consideration of the Council's views and recommendations before making his final decision.

PERMANENT COMMITTEES

The Advisory Council has the following five permanent committees,
· Legal and Legislative Affairs Committee
· Financial and Economic Affairs Committee
· Public Services Committee
· Internal and External Affairs Committee
· Cultural Affairs and Information Committee

COUNCIL OPERATION

The council debates matters that are referred to it by the Council of Ministers, like new legislation, amendments to existing legislation or other business. The Council also debates matters proposed by its own members. Often, members of the Council of Ministers participate in debates to effect an optimal level of transparency and clarity.

The Council also, through its various committees, addresses the country's internal affairs, the budgets of large Government projects, drafts of proposed legislation and the general policy of the state. The Advisory Council can request the Council of Ministers to submit data and information relating to any subject that falls under its jurisdiction. It can also request any Minister to submit detailed information regarding items handled by his Ministry. No Council member may face trial because of any views expressed by him in the Council, unless he has defamed or libelled another person.

COUNCIL OF MINISTERS

In accordance with the Amiri Order no. (1) of 1992 concerning re-formation of Cabinet, the Ministry of *Awqaf* and Islamic Affairs came into existence in place of Presidency of *Shari'ah Courts* and Religious Affairs in 4-3-1413 A.H. corresponding to 1-9-1992.

By then, a new extensive stage of development started when H.E. the Minister issued a number of decrees forming some committees to develop and re-organize action course at the Ministry.

As a result, the following laws and decrees were issued :

1- Law no, (9) of 1993 concerning organizing the Ministry and specifying its competencies and functions.

2- Ministerial decrees no (29) of 1994 and no.(7) of 1995 regarding the formation of sections at the Ministry Units and pointing out their competencies and functions .

3- Law no.(6) on forming *Hajj* Affairs Committee ,which takes care of *Hajjis* and makes its by-law.

4- Cabinet decree no. (1) of 1994 -amended by decree no. (5) on forming The *Hajj* Affairs Committee of eight members and a head. Then, the Committee made its by-law laid down in the Ministerial decree no. (37) of 1996.

5- Law no. (21) of 1994 amending some rules of law no. (8) of 1992 on establishing *Zakā h* Fund.

6- Ministerial decree no. (2) of 1996 which determined the formation of a Committee for *Awqaf* revenues development.

7- Law no. (20) of 1996 regarding the by-law of *Awqaf* estates .

8- Ministerial decree no. (20) of 1996 concerning wardship of Minors Affairs estates and the like.

9- A decree-law issued under no. (24) of 1995 on cancellation of the Ministry of Labor, Social Affairs and Housing and attaching Social Affairs Department to the Ministry of *Awqaf* and Islamic Affairs with its full competencies and functions.

To produce social development, a generation adhering to our values and good traditions, and a well-qualified Qatari woman; the Ministry amended the Social Affairs Department competencies and functions, and gave birth to Woman Affairs Department. Furthermore, Cabinet approved the above-named in decree no. (20) of 1996, and then, the Ministerial decree no.(5) of 1997 was issued on establishing sections in the new departments and specifying their competencies and functions.

The current Government consist of the following ministries,

Ministry of Defence

Ministry of Interior

www.mofa.gov.qa/government/ministries/moi/index-e.htm

Ministry of Foreign Affairs

www.mofa.gov

Ministry of Finance, Economy and Commerce

www.mofa.gov.qa/government/ministries/mofec/index-e.htm

Ministry of Endowments and Islamic Affairs

www.islam.gov.qa

Ministry of Municipal Affairs and Agriculture

www.mmaa.gov.qa

Ministry of Civil Service Affairs and Housing

www.mofa.gov.qa/government/ministries/mopah/index-a.htm

Ministry of Communications and Transport

www.mofa.gov.qa/government/ministries/moct/index-a.htm

Ministry of Education and Higher Education

www.mofa.gov.qa/government/ministries/moec/index-a.htm

Ministry of Energy, Industry, Electricity and Water

www.mofa.gov.qa/government/ministries/moei/index-a.htm

Ministry of Public Health

www.mofa.gov.qa/government/ministries/moph/index-a.htm

Ministry of Justice

www.mofa.gov.qa/government/ministries/moj/index-a.htm

The Council also includes, in addition to ministers of the above ministries, a number of ministers without portfolio.
www.mofa.gov.qa/government/ministries/ministers

The Council operates on the concept of ministerial joint accountability to HH the Emir. The ministers are concerned with executing the state's policies and achieving the maximum possible social, cultural and administrative development for the country.

The ministers propose draft laws, regulations and by-laws prepared by their respective ministries. They also monitor the application of the laws, regulations and legal judgments in addition to monitoring the state's expenditure. They also prepare the draft state budget and adopt the necessary measures to ensure the state security and public order. The ministers also, within their jurisdiction, safeguard the state's interest abroad including establishing international relations according to law.

CONSTITUTION

The 1970 provisional constitution (sometimes called the basic law) declares Qatar a sovereign Arab, Islamic state and vests sovereignty in the state. In fact, sovereignty is held by the amir, but, although he is supreme in relation to any other individual or institution, in practice his rule is not absolute. The constitution also provides for a partially elected consultative assembly, the Advisory Council. The first council's twenty members were selected from representatives chosen by limited suffrage. The size of the council was increased to thirty members in 1975. Among the council's constitutional prerogatives is the right to debate legislation drafted by the Council of Ministers before it is ratified and promulgated.

The amir is also obliged to rule in accordance with Islamic precepts, which include fairness, honesty, generosity, and mutual respect. Islamic religious and ethical values are applicable to both the ruler's personal life and his rule. Thus, the ruler must retain the support of the religious community, which often asserts itself in such areas as media censorship, education regulations, and the status of women.

The state political organs include the ruler, the Council of Ministers, and the Advisory Council. The ruler makes all major executive decisions and legislates by decree. The constitution institutionalizes the legislative and executive processes in the functions of the ruler, in effect formalizing his supremacy. Among the ruler's constitutional duties are convening the Council of Ministers, ratifying and promulgating laws and decrees, commanding the armed forces, and appointing and dismissing senior civil servants and military officers by decree. The constitution provides that the ruler possess "any other powers with which he is vested under this provisional constitution or with which he may be vested under the law." This means that the ruler may extend or modify his powers by personal decree.

The constitution also provides for a deputy ruler, who is to assume the post of prime minister. The prime minister is to formulate government programs and exercise final supervisory control over the financial and administrative affairs of the government. When the constitution was promulgated, Khalifa ibn Hamad was concurrently prime minister and heir apparent, but the constitution did not specify that the post of prime minister must be held by the heir apparent.

The Council of Ministers, which resembles similar bodies in the West, forms the amir's cabinet. A major government reshuffle in July 1989 reorganized several ministries, bringing in younger men loyal to Khalifa ibn Hamad's son, Shaykh Hamad ibn Khalifa. The Al Thani continued to dominate the government, with the most influential (after the amir and heir apparent) being Shaykh Abd Allah ibn Khalifa, minister of interior; Shaykh Ahmad ibn Hamad, minister of municipal affairs and agriculture; and Shaykh Muhammad ibn Khalifa, minister of finance, economy, and trade (see fig. 10). In October 1992, of the sixteen Council of Ministers posts, ten were occupied by the Al Thani and six by commoners.

The Council of Ministers is responsible collectively to the ruler, as is each minister individually. The ruler appoints and dismisses ministers (technically on the recommendation of the prime minister when that post is occupied by someone other than the ruler). Only native-born Qataris can become ministers, and the constitution prohibits the prime minister and other ministers from engaging in business or commercial activities while holding state office.

The Advisory Council debates laws proposed by the Council of Ministers before they are submitted to the ruler for ratification. If approved by the ruler, a law becomes effective on publication in the official gazette. In 1975 the amir empowered the Advisory Council to summon individuals to answer questions on legislation before promulgation. The Advisory Council also debates the draft budgets of public projects and general policy on political, economic, social, and administrative affairs referred to it by the prime minister. The Advisory Council can request from the Council of Ministers information pertaining to policies it is debating, direct written questions to a particular minister, and summon ministers to answer questions on proposed legislation. Ministers have the right to attend and address Advisory Council meetings in which policy matters within their purview are being discussed; in practice, no use has been made of this constitutional guarantee because members of the Council of Ministers are also members of the Advisory Council.

As the constitution stipulates, Qatar is divided into ten electoral districts for the purpose of forming the Advisory Council. Each district elects four candidates, of whom the ruler selects two, making a total of twenty; they constitute the relatively representative portion of the council. The members represent all Qataris, not just those in their districts. The Advisory Council was increased to thirty members in December 1975 and to thirty-five members in November 1988. Membership is limited to native-born citizens at least twenty years of age. The constitution states that members are to serve three-year terms, but in May 1975 members' terms were extended for an additional three years and then for additional four-year terms in 1978, in 1982, in 1986, and in 1990.

Before the implementation of the constitution, the ruler's legislative authority frequently overlapped or encompassed judicial functions because he personally adjudicated disputes and grievances brought before him. The constitution marks the beginning of an attempt to organize the judiciary. The secular courts include a higher and lower criminal court, a civil court, an appeals court, and a labor court. Civil and criminal codes, as well as a court of judicial procedure, were introduced in 1971. All civil and criminal law falls within the jurisdiction of these secular courts. A labor court was created in 1962, primarily because few of the country's existing judicial customs and codes were applicable to contemporary labor relations.

For additional analytical, business and investment opportunities information, please contact Global Investment & Business Center, USA at (202) 546-2103. Fax: (202) 546-3275. E-mail: rusric@erols.com Global Business E-Books on Line: http://world.mirhouse.com

The sharia court is the oldest element in Qatar's judiciary. The court's law is based on the Hanbali legal school of Islam, wherein judges (qadis) adhere to a strict interpretation of the Quran and sunna, or traditions of the Prophet Muhammad. Originally, the sharia court's jurisdiction covered all civil and criminal disputes between Qataris and between all other Muslims. Beginning in the 1960s, the court's jurisdiction was successively restricted by decree. In the early 1990s, its responsibilities were confined primarily to family matters, including property, inheritance, divorce, and Islamic ethics. Non-Muslims were tried in secular courts unless they were married to Muslims.

The constitution establishes the legal presumption of innocence and prohibits ex post facto laws. It also stipulates that "judges shall be independent in the exercise of their powers, and no party whatsoever may interfere in the administration of justice." The judiciary is nominally independent, not so much as a result of a constitutional guarantee but because its jurisdiction is unlikely to confront the ruler's exercise of power. Secular courts adjudicate on the basis of the ruler's past decrees, and religious courts are restricted to questions of personal status. No provision exists for judicial review of the constitutionality of legislation.

According to the preamble to the 1970 constitution, the government was undergoing a transitional stage of development. The constitution was thus provisional and was to be replaced with a new constitution after the transitional period ended. Shaykh Khalifa ibn Hamad has usually legitimated government changes that he decrees by reference to the constitution. As of early 1993, however, there had been no indication that the full implementation of the constitution was imminent (for example, the electoral aspects of selection to Advisory Council membership) or that the transitional period was ending and a new constitution forthcoming.

In addition to describing and delineating governmental authority, the constitution sets forth such protections as equality among Qataris regardless of race, sex, or religion; freedom of the press; sanctity of the home; and recognition of both private and collective ownership of property. Such guarantees, however, are limited by the public interest and must be in accordance with the law--which is determined by the ruler. In practice, freedom of the press means that incoming foreign publications are screened by a government office for potentially objectionable material, and the indigenous press exercises self- censorship and is subject to sanction if it fails to deal appropriately with political and religious issues

The constitution also includes a commitment to certain economic, social, and cultural principles, including state provision of health care, social security, and education. Housing, pension, education, and medical programs were begun in the 1960s and expanded by Shaykh Khalifa ibn Hamad as oil revenues permitted throughout the years. There were no state taxes on individuals, and the state subsidized the prices of basic commodities to minimize the effects of inflation. Although these programs appeared to reflect West European statism, they were manifestations of the ruler's sense of duty, based on obligations inherent in Islamic ethics.

THE AL THANI

For additional analytical, business and investment opportunities information,
please contact Global Investment & Business Center, USA
at (202) 546-2103. Fax: (202) 546-3275. E-mail: rusric@erols.com
Global Business E-Books on Line: http://world.mirhouse.com

In the early 1990s, the Al Thani ruling family comprised three main branches: the Bani Hamad, headed by Khalifa ibn Hamad (r. 1972-); the Bani Ali, headed by Ahmad ibn Ali; and the Bani Khalid, headed by Nasir ibn Khalid (minister of economy and commerce in 1984). The family had 20,000 members, according to one estimate.

The two preindependence rulers, Ali ibn Abd Allah (r. 1949- 60) and his son, Ahmad ibn Ali (r. 1960-72), had no particular interest in supervising daily government, content to hunt in Iran and Pakistan and spend time at their villa in Switzerland. Thus, somewhat by default, those duties were assumed, beginning in the 1950s, by Ahmad ibn Ali's cousin, Khalifa ibn Hamad, the heir apparent and deputy ruler. By 1971 Khalifa ibn Hamad not only had served as prime minister but also had headed the ministries or departments of foreign affairs, finance and petroleum, education and culture, and police and internal security.

On February 22, 1972, with the support of the Al Thani, Khalifa ibn Hamad assumed power as ruler of Qatar. Western sources frequently refer to the event as an overthrow. Qataris regarded Khalifa ibn Hamad's assumption of full power as a simple succession because leading members of the Al Thani had declared Khalifa ibn Hamad the heir apparent on October 24, 1960, and it was their consensus that Ahmad ibn Ali should be replaced.

The reasons for the transfer of power were not entirely clear. Khalifa ibn Hamad reportedly stated that his assumption of power was intended "to remove the elements that tried to hinder [Qatar's] progress and modernization." Khalifa ibn Hamad has consistently attempted to lead and to control the process of modernization caused by the petroleum industry boom and the concomitant influx of foreigners and foreign ideas so that traditional mores and values based on Islam can be preserved. He and other influential members of the ruling family are known to have been troubled by the financial excesses of many members of the Al Thani. Ahmad ibn Ali reportedly drew one-fourth, and the entire Al Thani between one-third and one-half, of Qatar's oil revenues in 1971. The new ruler severely limited the family's financial privileges soon after taking power.

Family intrigue may also have played a part in the change of rulers. Factionalism and rivalries are not uncommon, particularly in families as large as the Al Thani. Western observers have reported rumors that Khalifa ibn Hamad acted to assume power when he learned that Ahmad ibn Ali might be planning to substitute his son, Abd al Aziz, as heir apparent, a move that would have circumvented the declared consensus of the Al Thani.

THE MERCHANT FAMILIES

The merchant sector in Qatar differed from other gulf Arab countries before the exploitation of oil in its small size (Doha was an insignificant port compared with ports in Kuwait, Bahrain, or Dubayy), in the absence of foreigners (the Indians were forced out in the late 1800s, leaving Qatar the only gulf amirate without Indians until the 1950s), and in the dominant role of a single family, the Al Thani. Although there were merchants before oil, there was no merchant class as in Dubayy or Kuwait. Two important families before oil were the Darwish and the Al Mana, who made their living through trade, pearling, and smuggling and who competed for favor with the ruler. The Darwish and the Al Mana maintained their influence by trading loans and advice to the shaykh for monopolies and concessions.

With the arrival of Petroleum Development (Qatar), the Darwish reaped huge profits through their monopoly on supplying labor, housing, water, and goods to the oil company. This monopoly ended, however, when workers, small merchants, and antiBritish Qataris used Abd Allah Darwish, the patriarch of the Darwish family, as one of several convenient targets for an antiregime strike in 1956. By this time, however, with oil revenues growing, the shaykh could remove himself from financial dependence on the merchants, who lost a measure of political influence.

A series of citizenship and commercial laws promulgated in the 1960s helped to channel economic benefits in the direction of Qatari nationals in general and the merchants and ruling family in particular. Only Qataris were permitted to own land, for example, and companies were required to be at least 51 percent Qatari owned. In the 1970s, some laws were enacted that worked against merchant interests by limiting prices and profits.

As they had before the discovery of oil, the Al Thani continued engaging in trade and in other enterprises. Sometimes they used their family connections to win lucrative contracts for themselves or for firms in which they had more common business partners, such as the Jaidah, the Attiyah, and the Mannai families.

OPPOSITION

Because no public dissent is tolerated in Qatar, opposition usually manifests itself in royal family intrigue or behind-the- scenes grumbling by aggrieved parties. The apparent public tranquillity is cultivated by the amir and by the private but closely controlled media. Incidents in the 1980s, however, demonstrated that opposition to the regime existed.

In September 1983, for example, a conspiracy to assassinate the ruler or a GCC head of state was uncovered by Qatari authorities, and seventy people were arrested. Contradictory press reports said that either some military people were involved or that the plot reflected a squabble among members of the ruling family. Qatari security forces learned of the plot from Egyptian intelligence via the Saudi Arabians. Informed that the plotters were backed by Libya, Qatar declared the Libyan chargé d'affaires persona non grata. The target of the plot, according to conflicting reports, was either Shaykh Khalifa ibn Hamad or GCC heads of state who were coming to Doha for a November summit. Since then, there have been other reported assassination attempts.

In August 1985, it was reported that Shaykh Suhaym ibn Hamad Al Thani, one of the amir's brothers, disappointed that the position of crown prince was given to Shaykh Khalifa ibn Hamad's son, Hamad ibn Khalifa, plotted a coup and maintained a cadre of supporters and a cache of weapons in the north of the country. When Shaykh Suhaym ibn Hamad died suddenly, his sons blamed Minister of Information and Culture Ghanim al Kuwari for not responding promptly to the call for medical help. After supporters of

Suhaym ibn Hamad and his sons attempted to kill Ghanim al Kuwari, they were imprisoned.

Soon after the Iraqi invasion of Kuwait, Palestinians and Iraqis living in Qatar came under intense government scrutiny. Dozens were deported, and many more were forced to leave after their contracts were not renewed.

THE MEDIA

Qatar has no official censorship, but newspapers recognize the need for self-censorship in not publishing material critical of the ruling family, the government, or religious issues. The privately owned press consists of three Arabic dailies--*Ar Rayah* (The Banner), *Al Arab* (The Arab), and *Ash Sharq* (The East)--and an English daily, *Gulf Times*. The Ministry of Information and Culture operates the Qatar News Agency, the Qatar Broadcasting Service, and the Qatar Television Service.

GOVERNMENT STRUCTURE

PLANNING COUNCIL

On the 6th of June 1998 the Emiri decision to set up the Planning Council was issued, providing for the establishment of a planning and follow-up unit at each ministry, public corporation and government department as per the instructions of the concerned Minister or authorized official. In its first Article the Emiri Decision ordered the establishment of a legally and financially independent body named the Planning Council. The Article stipulated that the Council have a general secretariat headed by a secretary general, whose appointment is made in accordance to an Emiri Decision based on the nomination of the Council's president.

OBJECTIVES OF THE PLANNING COUNCIL:
1. To prepare the State's economic and social policies and plans in line with the basic principles and guidelines specified by the basic statute of the State and to follow up the implementation of these policies and plans after having been ratified by the Council of Ministers.
2. To express its views in the form of recommendations to be submitted to the Council of Ministers after having been ratified by H.H. the Emir.
3. To submit a detailed annual report to the Emir on various projects included in the State's economic and social plan, explaining the extent and scope of success and achievements realized through the application of the plan, as well as the impediments and difficulties the plan had to face in the course of implementation. The report also contains the Council's recommendations on the solutions and remedies to be done to resolve the difficulties. In preparation to take a decision in regard to this report, H.H. the Emir refers the report to the Council of Ministers for

study and recommendation.

THE ORGANIZATION OF THE COUNCIL:
1. The Council comprises the Minister of Energy and Industry, a President, a number of members that should include representatives from the Emiri Diwan, Ministry of Finance, Economy and Trade, Ministry of Civil Service Affairs and Housing, Ministry of Municipal Affairs and Agriculture and Ministry of Education.
2. The Council forms (from among technicians and experts within or outside its membership) units and committees, each specializing in a particular field of activity and headed by a member of the Council.

PROGRAMS AND PROJECTS OF THE PLANNING COUNCIL:
In the light of a far-reaching outlook, the Council is studying an administrative and economic reform program to determine the development trends and reform measures to be taken in all economic and social fields. Administrative reform include reviewing the organizational structures at the ministries and government bodies to decide which sections and departments to be incorporated, abolished or developed. Development of these units can take the form of raising efficiency standards, reducing operation cost and optimizing performance in order to attain the final goal of meeting the basic and demanding needs of the citizens. The economic reforms include introducing to the financial and monetary sector a number of procedures and policies that aim to sustain the process of economic growth as a whole.

The Council is in the process of implementing the national information network project, which is to provide accurate, updated and electronically processed information to support decision making process and extend developed services.

Workforce planning aims to optimize the utilization and productivity of the national workforce to include increasing work opportunities for women in suitable fields that conform to the teachings of Islam and the traditions, rationalizing the recruitment of expatriate workforce in line with distinct organizational standards and encouraging the employment of Gulf and Arab workforce in compatibility with the requirements of development, social stability and the uniformity of the society.

STATE AUDIT BUREAU

The State Audit Bureau was established on 28th April 1973 as an independent government body with legal entity, directly reporting to H.H. the Emir. Its budget is annexed to the budget of the Emiri Diwan. The president of the Bureau undertakes the responsibility to prepare the Bureau's annual draft budget and to submit thereof to H.H. the Emir or any other regularly authorized official for ratification. Unbound by other government regulations and laws, he issues the Bureau's personnel affairs regulating directives, which shall not come into force until they are ratified by the Council of Ministers and duly issued for application. Pending that, the Bureau's personnel service is subject to the provisions of the general civil service law and its executing orders and regulations. The audits and checks on the Bureau's accounts are ordered by H.H the Emir or whom he may authorize.

The State Audit Bureau scrutinizes the accounts of all ministries and their affiliated departments and bodies, alongside with the accounts of public corporations, national companies and other government bodies.

The Bureau functions under the provisions of its constituent law that defines its responsibilities and authorities, foremost of which is to ensure that financial actions and accounting procedures regarding funds collection and spending are done in an orderly manner, in conformity with the declared financial, accounting and administrative regulations and within the framework of the general rules of the budget.

The Bureau carries out preceding audit for projects, tenders and contracts before they are placed for consideration, put to tender or signed. The Bureau's representatives participate in the work of existing tender committees, which deal either with public sector establishments or the companies under the scrutiny jurisdiction of the Bureau. It also contributes in the work of other government committees charged with supervising compliance with the declared financial and accounting regulations. Its role is to call the attention of these committees towards possible discrepancies.

The State Audit Bureau is formed of the following bodies:
1. Government Sector Audit Department.
2. Economic Sector Audit Department.
3. Tenders and Contracts Audit Department.
4. Legal Affairs Department.
5. Administrative and Financial Affairs Department.

CENTRAL MUNICIPAL COUNCIL

The first municipal council in Qatar was formed in the early 1950s and it was reorganized in 1956. Doha municipality came into being in May 1963. The Ministry of Municipal Affairs was established in 1972 as a government body responsible for supervising the functions of municipalities.

Decree No 4 for 1963 organized, for the first time, the election and appointment of the members of the municipal council. Law No 11for 1963 followed. It stipulated that the municipal council is formed by a decree and that the appointment of the members is based on the nomination of the Minister of Municipal Affairs and Agriculture. The first joint meeting of municipal councils in the country was held in 1983. Most of the credit goes to this meeting in deciding to form a central municipal council to replace the numerous municipal councils.

The Central Municipal Council:
The idea to form the municipal council by direct elections was revived when H.H. the Emir of Qatar issued the Law No 12 for 1998 organizing the election law of the Central Municipal Council. H.H. also issued the Emiri Decree No 17 for 1998 on the election of the members of the Central Municipal Council. Several committees were subsequently formed. They included the legal, security, and information, technical, supply, and follow up committees. A preparatory committee was also formed under the patronage of Her Highness the wife of H.H. the Emir to carry out an awareness program for women, emphasizing the importance of their participation in the elections both as candidates and voters.

248 candidates including 6 women contested the 4-year term of 29 seats. Polling date was set for Monday the 8th of March 1999, and 21,995 eligible males and females registered to cast their votes in their respective constituencies.

The election experience was very well received publicly and officially and the response was overwhelming by all sectors of the Qatari society, males and females alike. The participation of women as voters and candidates invited a wide-range and favorable echo, locally and internationally. 35 Arab and foreign parliamentarians were hosted to oversee the conduct of the first elections in the country.

The Qatari democratic practice exceeded the surrounding experiences in four aspects: voting age was brought down to 18, which expands the scope of participation in the democratic process, the Qatari media was utilized in an unprecedented manner in the Gulf region by giving live coverage of the debates and discussions between candidates and voters, women were allowed to participate as voters and candidates for the first time and a headquarters was provided in each constituency, where the 29 members of the Council can hold discussions and meetings with their electorates.

Voting Regulations:
The Emiri Decree No 17 for 1998 specified the regulations governing the elections of the members of the Central Municipal Council. All Qatari males and females that fulfil the following conditions have the right to cast their votes:
1. They must be of Qatari origin, or have been naturalized citizens for a period of at least 15 years.
2. They must be 18 years of age.
3. They must not be indicted on a criminal charge of breach of trust or honesty. Otherwise they must have been rehabilitated.
4. The constituency must be the real place of residence for respective voters.
5. They must not be members of the armed forces or security forces.

The Council is formed of 29 members representing constituencies spreading over 230 regions in the State of Qatar. The membership term in the Council is 4 years.

The Council Sessions:

On the 4th of May 1999 H.H. Sheikh Hamad Bin Khalifa Al-Thani, the Emir of the State of Qatar issued a decree inviting the Central Municipal Council to hold its first meeting in full attendance to elect the Council's Chairman and Deputy Chairman from among its members by secret ballot.

H.H. Sheikh Jassim Bin Hamad Al-Thani, the Heir Apparent inaugurated the first session of the Central Municipal Council on the 15th of May 1999. The Council holds its ordinary meetings in Doha and in public once every two weeks. Extraordinary meetings must be requested by one third of the members. The meetings are considered regular only where the quorum of two thirds of the members is available. The maximum period for which a meeting can be put off for lack of quorum is three days, after which the meeting can be held with the attendance of one third of the members.

Work Mechanism of the Council:

The Council issues its resolutions by plurality of votes. Under the supervision of the Chairman, the Council forms a Secretariat General and appoint a Secretary General. The job of the Secretary General is to prepare the meetings' agenda and submit thereof to the Chairman, record the minutes of the meetings and the Council's recommendations and submit, to the Minister of Municipal Affairs and Agriculture, those parts of the recommendations that call for his or any higher authority's action.

The Council's Authorities:

The Central Municipal Council is an independent entity. The Ministry of Municipal Affairs and Agriculture has no authority over its functions. It is totally free to practice its responsibilities without any interference from the Ministry. The roles of the Ministry and the Council complement each other. The role of the Council is still one of advisory and monitoring. The Council has the right to discuss all matters and problems, and its agenda is not confined to what is raised by the Ministry. The Ministry approves the recommendations of the Council, whose members decide their own work program and budget without external interference.

Both the Ministry of Municipal Affairs and Agriculture and the Central Municipal Council coordinate their efforts to reach the common goal of serving the country and the citizens. The Minister of Municipal Affairs and Agriculture explains the different points of view to the Council through a specialized committee. In case the difference in opinion persists, subjects of discord, accompanied by the two different viewpoints, are raised to the Council of Ministers for consideration.

The 29 members of the Council focus their attention on providing the compelling needs of the society and securing the basic services with a view to rationalize spending. They do that through a well-defined plan and good coordination of time, effort and resources, and through giving priority to projects like road building, sanitary drainage, parks and recreation sites.

Members of the Central Municipal Council:

1. Miaizir...Hamad Abdullah Mohammad Al Nasheerah Al Marri... Chairman
2. Al Hilal...Ibrahim Abdulraheem Mahmoud Ahmed Al Haidoos... Deputy Chairman
3. Al Jasrah... Nasser Muhsin Mohammad Bu Kshaishah
4. Al Doha Al Hadeetha...Ahmed Abdullah Sultan Al Silaiti
5. Al Markhiyya...Ibrahim Abdullah Hassan Al Ibrahim
6. Madeenat Khalifa Al Shamaliyya... Nasser Mohammad Isa Faris Al kaabi
7. Madeenat Khalifa Al Janoobiyya...Isa Khalifa Umran Al bakr Al Kawari
8. Bin Umran... Mohammad Saif Ali Al Kawari
9. Al Salata Al Jadeeda...Ahmed Khalifa Mohammad Al Aseeri
10. Airport...Abdulrahman Mohammad Abdulrahman Al Jifairi
11. Al Wakra...Ahmed Jassim Abdulrahman Muftah Al Muftah
12. Mesaieed...Mohammad Ahamad Ali Al Shawi Al Marri
13. Abu Hamoor... Hamad Mubarak Saeed Noora Al Marri
14. Al Ghanim Al Jadeed... Ghanim Abdulrahman Ghanim Al Ghanim
15. Al Murra...Saleh Saeed Mohammad Saeed Malhiyya
16. Miraikh...Nasser Falah Abdullah Nasser Al Dousari
17. Miaizir Al Shamaliyya...Saoud Abdullah Hamad Hizab Al izba
18. Al Rayyan Al Jadeed...Mohammad Hamoud Shafi Al Shafi
19. Al Rayyan Al Gadeem... Mohammad Saleh Hamad Al Houl Al Marri
20. Al Nassiriyya...Mohammad Mansour Khaleel Al Khaleel Al Shahwani
21. Al Gharrafa... Ahmed Hussain Rashid Hussain Al Kibaisi
22. Um Silal Ali... Ahmed Ibrahim Sultan Al sheeb
23. Al Khraitiyyat ...Abdullah Abdulrahman Isa Al Mannai
24. Al Shahaniyya... Faleh Mubarak Fahad Al Ajlan Al Hajri
25. Dukhan... Hassan Misfir Hamad Al Abbadi Al Hajri
26. Al Khor... Rashid Jassim Darwish Al Miraikhi Al Muhannadi
27. Al Zakheera... Ali Hssan Jumaa Alhassan Al Muhannadi
28. Madeenat Al Shamal... Saad Ali Hassan Al Niaimi
29. Al Ghuwairiyya... Nasser Abdullah Saeed Al Kaabi

QATAR FOREIGN POLICY

H.H. Sheikh Hamad Bin Khalifa Al-Thani, Emir of the State of Qatar is considered a highly competent politician and a great contributor to the enrichment of international and regional political practice. The manifestations of that contribution are reflected in the boosting of economic and political cooperation between Qatar and the Gulf Arab States in particular, and between Qatar and the rest of the world in general. Such contributions emanate from a strategic vision, which is marked by courage, originality, objectivity and comprehensiveness.

The personalities Doha received during the last five years and the official visits paid by H.H. the Emir Sheikh Hamad Bin Khalifa Al Thani to the three old continents in addition to North America, all were positively reflected in Qatar's high standing amongst the states of the world which qualified it to play positive and influential role marked by transparency, realism, clarity of vision and the adoption of moderate political approach.

INTERNATIONAL RELATIONS

Qatar is very keen to participate actively in the efforts to deal with all the concerns and challenges that the Gulf region encounters. It places increasing emphasis on supporting the march of the Gulf Cooperation Council (GCC) spares no effort to bring about solidarity and strengthen ties of mutual trust and communication between Arab countries, propagates the wisdom of resorting to peaceful means in resolving all disputes among countries, approves the United Nations efforts to uphold peace and security and works to maintain good relations with all peace-loving peoples and countries.

Qatar rejects and denounces all forms and manifestations of terrorism, regardless of its causes, objectives and means. It, however, differentiates between terrorism and the peoples' struggle and legitimate rights of freedom and self- determination in accordance with the provisions of the international law. Qatar in all regional and international occasions expresses its grave concern over the escalation of conflicts, ethnic cleansing and denial of the rights of minorities in some countries in Asia, Eastern Europe, Africa and other continents. Qatar welcomes all the agreements concluded with a view to resolving such problems and pledges support for the efforts exerted by regional and international organizations to achieve peace and stability in many states and regions of the world.

REGIONAL ISSUES

The successive meetings of the Supreme Council of the GCC came out with a multitude of important strategic resolutions and protocols covering areas of political cooperation, military and defense cooperation and economic integration among member states. Qatar had actively participated in the efforts, which reached fruition with establishment of the GCC on the 25th of May 1981. Since then the council has been working very hard through the efforts of its members to serve the region's interests and aspirations towards stability, comprehensive development and progress.

Arab Issues:

Qatar has welcomed the efforts of the Arab League aiming to pave the way bring about reconciliation and restore solidarity between Arab countries on strong basis of openness and objectivity in service of the common Arab interests.

Qatar supports the Middle East peace process out of its firm believe in the necessity to achieve comprehensive and just peace for all the peoples of the region in order to attain the region's aspirations towards development and progress. Qatar also underlines the importance of reaching a solution on the Syrian and Lebanese tracks to result in the total withdrawal of Israeli troops from all Arab occupied territories including Jerusalem, Golan Heights and Southern Lebanon, and the restoration of all legitimate national rights of the Palestinian people to establish their own state with Jerusalem as capital.

In the context of humanitarian assistance Qatar has extended a great deal of financial, medical and other assistance to several poor Arab countries.

Qatar decided to donate 50 million dollars to Al-Aqsa Fund and the Intifada Support Fund, which were set up during the extra-ordinary session of the Arab Summit Conference convened in Cairo, in October 2000.

ISLAMIC ISSUES

Qatar works hard to strengthen ties of mutual cooperation and fraternity with Muslim states and peoples, and extends all possible material and moral support in service of the common causes of the Arab and Muslim nations.

H.H. the Emir participated with his brothers the leaders of Islamic states in the active deliberations of the 8th summit conference of the Organization of Islamic Conference (OIC), convened in Tehran from 9 to 11 December 1997.

H.H. the Emir addressed the 25th session of the Islamic foreign ministers' meeting held in Doha between 15 and 19 March 1998 in preparation for the OIC summit conference. In this comprehensive keynote speech, H.H. the Emir emphasized the economic dimension of Islamic solidarity. He believes that the Organization should attach great importance to this dimension in its incessant efforts to bring about solidarity between its members. H.H. the Emir also urged the OIC member states to open up for economic and commercial cooperation and develop their economic infrastructures as well as the interstate trade. These factors, according to H.H. the Emir, are considered to be the most decisive in bringing about closeness and cohesion between the member states and in securing their common interests in service of the prosperity and progress of their peoples.

For additional analytical, business and investment opportunities information, please contact Global Investment & Business Center, USA at (202) 546-2103. Fax: (202) 546-3275. E-mail: rusric@erols.com
Global Business E-Books on Line: http://world.mirhouse.com

Qatar expressed its deep sorrow over the decision adopted by the US Congress in June 1997 recognizing Al-Quds as the unified capital of Israel. The Qarari Ministry of Foreign Affairs reiterated that this decision is a blatant provocation to the sentiments of the Islamic and Arab nations and a violation of the Middle East peace process, the resolutions of the international legitimacy and the announced policy of the US administration in the Middle East.

In April 1996 an agreement has been reached to set up a committee for the salvation of Al-Quds. The committee comprises scholars, intellectuals and economists from Qatar and Palestine and it endeavors to stimulate all activities related to Al-Quds city, particularly in the political and financial fields, increase Arab investments, protect the Islamic holy places and rehabilitate the holy city.

Qatar participated with the donor countries in the meeting held in Ankara in March 1996 to support peace in Bosnia and Herzegovina. Qatar now provides political and financial support to the ongoing peace process.

In June 1997, His Highness the Emir took upon his shoulders the expenses of the reconciliation conference of the Somali warring factions, the first of its kind to be convened in Somalia.  On the 10th of November 1998, a Qatari initiative succeeded in bringing Sudan and Eritrea to sign, in Doha, an initial memorandum of understanding to improve their bilateral relations. Signing took place at the closing ceremony of the meeting, which was attended by the Sudanese foreign minister and his Eritrean counterpart.

IN THE INTERNATIONAL ARENA

Qatar works very hard to establish close ties of cooperation with all peace loving countries and peoples, extends generous financial aid to many developing countries in Asia and Africa and contributes to various regional and international aid funds to create the widest possible avenues of international cooperation.

Qatar has always been a staunch supporter of liberation movements and has constantly denounced all kinds of racial discrimination wherever it exists. In May 1994, Qatar hosted in Doha, the meetings of the Regional Security and Arms Limitation General Committee. Qatar adopts a set of principles as a basis for peace and security in the Middle East and the world at large. At the top of those principles comes the abstention from using or threatening to use force against territorial integrity of other countries, and seeking to resolve disputes by peaceful means such as regional or international arbitration, and dialogue. In recognition of Qatar's vital role and contribution in the efforts to uphold peace, the special work group of the Regional Security and Arms Limitation Committee for the Middle East decided in December 1994 to establish a regional center for the group in Doha to act as a front line dispute prevention facility.

And as an expression of appreciation from the international community of the policies

For additional analytical, business and investment opportunities information,
please contact Global Investment & Business Center, USA
at (202) 546-2103. Fax: (202) 546-3275. E-mail: rusric@erols.com
Global Business E-Books on Line: http://world.mirhouse.com

adopted by Qatar in the regional and the international spheres, Qatar was elected in March 1995 deputy chairman for the International Social Development Summit Conference, in the context of the UN regional groups representation.

FOREIGN RELATIONS

The Iraqi invasion and occupation of Kuwait and the resulting threat to other small gulf states forced Qatar to alter significantly its defense and foreign policy priorities. For example, whereas Qatar had supported Iraq financially in its 1980-88 war against Iran, Qatar quickly joined the anti-Iraq coalition after the invasion. Formerly a political and economic supporter of the Palestine Liberation Organization (PLO), Qatar bitterly condemned the alliance between the PLO and many Palestinians on the one hand and Saddam Husayn on the other hand. Moreover, Qatar's previous opposition to superpower naval presence in the gulf turned into an open willingness to permit the air forces of the United States, Canada, and France to operate from its territory.

The GCC, which for years had been aimed, in part, at dealing with a perceived Iranian threat (both external and, in the cases of Kuwait, Bahrain, and Saudi Arabia, internal), became a forum for condemnation of Iraq and a venue for building a concerted defense against further Iraqi advances. After the Iraqi defeat, Qatar and other GCC members focused their energies on improving cooperation and coordination on mutual defense issues while also continuing to work together in social, cultural, political, and economic spheres. Qatar, like Saudi Arabia, has been historically sensitive to outside military intervention in the gulf and was eager to bolster regional security measures.

The war also drew Qatar and other GCC members closer to Egypt and Syria, the two strongest Arab members of the anti-Iraq coalition. The Qatari-Egyptian rapprochement began in 1987 when the two countries resumed diplomatic relations after the League of Arab States (Arab League) summit that adopted the resolution allowing members to reestablish diplomatic links at their discretion. After the war, Egypt and Syria received large sums from the gulf states in appreciation for their roles. Qatar and Syria signed an agreement on trade and economic and technical cooperation in January 1991.

Even before August 1990, Qatar historically had close relations with its larger and more powerful neighbor, Saudi Arabia. Because of geopolitical realities and the religious affinity of the two ruling families (both adhere to the conservative Wahhabi interpretation of Islam), Qatar followed the Saudi lead in many regional and global issues. Qatar was one of the few Arab countries that observed the full forty-day mourning period after the assassination of Saudi Arabia's King Faisal ibn Abd al Aziz Al Saud in March 1975 and the death of King Khalid ibn Abd al Aziz Al Saud in 1982. The two countries signed a bilateral defense agreement in 1982, and on several occasions Saudi Arabia acted as mediator in territorial disputes between Qatar and Bahrain.

Qatar also has had cordial relations with Iran, despite Qatar's support of Iraq during the Iran-Iraq War. In 1991 Shaykh Hamad ibn Khalifa welcomed Iranian participation in gulf security arrangements. Iran was one of the first countries to recognize Shaykh Khalifa ibn Hamad in 1972. Relations were based partially on proximity (important trade links exist between the two countries, including a ferry service between Doha and Bushehr) and partly on mutual interests. Plans were being formulated in 1992 to pipe water from the Karun River in Iran to Qatar. The Iranian community in Qatar, although large, is well integrated and has not posed a threat to the regime. Iran's claim in May 1989 that one-third of Qatar's North Field gas reservoir lay under Iranian waters apparently was resolved by an agreement to exploit the field jointly.

Relations with Bahrain continue to fluctuate between correct and strained, with tensions rising regularly over territorial disputes dating back for decades. Most of the friction involves Hawar and the adjacent islands, which both countries claim. Tensions rose most recently in July 1991 when, according to reports, Qatari naval vessels violated Bahraini waters, and Bahraini jet fighters flew into Qatari airspace. The issue was referred in August to the International Court of Justice in The Hague to determine whether it had jurisdiction over the dispute. Other disputes have involved the abandoned town of Az Zubarah, on the northwest coast of Qatar. The most serious crisis took place in April-June 1986, when Qatari forces raided Fasht ad Dibal, a coral reef in the gulf north of Al Muharraq in Bahrain that had been artificially built up into a small island. They took into custody twenty-nine workers who were sent by Bahrain to build a coast guard station. The workers were released in May, and installations on the island were destroyed. Qatar submitted the dispute to the International Court of Justice at The Hague, but Bahrain refused the jurisdiction of the court in June 1992. The dispute was ongoing as of early 1993.

Britain's historical role in the gulf has guaranteed a special relationship with its former protectorates. Qatari- British relations are tempered by a complex blend of suspicion and cordiality. On the one hand, Qataris are wary of the former colonial power because they remember instances when they were ill-served by their "protector," especially regarding the exploitation of oil. On the other hand, the long-term British presence in the gulf has fostered many fruitful political, economic, and cultural ties between the two countries. The British Embassy in Doha, for example, is the only foreign mission that owns its land outright. In addition, many Britons advise or work for the Qatari government at high levels. British banks and other businesses are well represented in Doha. Many Qataris attend university in Britain, own homes there, and visit regularly.

Relations with the United States have been generally proper but took a sudden turn for the worse in March 1988 when United States-made Stinger missiles (obtained through unsanctioned channels) were observed at a military parade in Doha. When the Qatari government refused to relinquish the weapons to the United States or to allow an inspection, the United States instituted a policy of withholding military and economic cooperation. The Stinger issue was settled when Qatar destroyed the missiles in question in 1990. Furthermore, both sides acknowledged the need to cooperate militarily in the face of Iraq's invasion of Kuwait. Operation Desert Shield and Operation Desert Storm greatly improved Qatar's image of the United States as a desirable security partner and resulted in changed bilateral military relations. On June 23, 1992, Qatar and the United States signed a bilateral defense cooperation agreement that provided for United States access to Qatari bases, pre-positioning of United States matériel, and future combined military exercises.

Following Saudi Arabia's lead, Qatar refused for many years to have diplomatic relations with the Soviet Union. This changed in the summer of 1988, when Qatar announced the opening of relations at the ambassadorial level with the Soviet Union and with China. In the wake of the dissolution of the Soviet Union in 1991, Qatar established relations with the newly independent Russian Federation.

Qatar became a member of the United Nations in September 1971, soon after it proclaimed independence. It was a member of several of its specialized agencies, including the International Civil Aviation Organization, the Food and Agriculture Organization, the International Labour Organisation, the World Health Organization, the Universal Postal Union, and the United Nations Educational, Scientific, and Cultural Organization.

QATAR MEMBERSHIP IN ORGANIZATIONS

GULF ORGANIZATIONS:
- Gulf Cooperation Council (GCC)
  - Arab Centre for Educational Research
  - Higher Education Council
  - Arab Education Office for the Gulf States
  - Arab Gulf States' Joint Programme Production Organizations
  - Arab Gulf University
  - Gulf Organization for Industrial Investment
  - Gulf News Agency
  - Gulf States Labour & Social Affairs Minister's Follow-up Office
  - Gulf Television Board
  - Arab Gulf Programme For United Nations Development Organizations (AGFUN)
  - Gulf Cooperation Council Folklore Centre.
  - Gulf Air Company.
  - Gulf States Health Minister's Follow up Office.
  - Co-operation Council States Specifications and Standards Board.

Arab Organizations:
- League of Arab States
  - Organization of Arab Petroleum Exporting Countries (OAPEC)
  - Arab Academy for Maritime Transport
  - Arab States Civil Aviation Council
  - Arab Industrial Development Organization
  - Arab Health Ministers' Council
  - Arab Housing Ministers' Council
  - Arab Interior Ministers' Council
  - Arab Justice Ministers' Council
  - Arab Transport Ministers' Council
  - Arab Youth & Sports Ministers' Council

- Arab Social Affairs Ministers' Council
- Arab Labour Organization
- Arab Monetary Fund
- Arab Organization for Agricultural Development
- Arab Organization for Specifications & Standards
- Arab Planning Institute
- Arab Postal Union
- Arab States Broadcasting Union
- Arabsat
- Organization of Arab Cities
- Arab League Educational Cultural and Scientific Organization
- Arab Social Defence Organization Against Crime
- Arab Fund for Economic & Social Development

INTERNATIONAL ORGANIZATIONS

- United Nations Organization (UN).
- Organization of the Islamic Conference (OIC).
- Non-Aligned Movement.
- International Monetary Fund (IMF).
- World Health Organization (WHO).
- International Court of Justice (ICJ).
- International Labour Organization (ILO).
- Food and Agriculture Organization (FAO).
- UN Industrial Development Organization (UNIDO).
- United Nations Educational, Scientific and Cultural Organization (UNESCO).
- Organization of Petroleum Exporting Countries (OPEC).
- International Criminal Police Organization (INTERPOL).
- International Civil Aviation Organization.
- Universal Postal Union.
- World Meteorological Organization.
- World Trade Organization (WTO).
- Islamic Development Bank.
- Islamic International News Agency.
- Al-Quds Fund.
- Islamic Capitals' Organization.
- Islamic Education, Scientific and Cultural Organization (ISESCO).
- The International Atomic Energy Agency (IAEA).
- The World Intellectual Property Organization (WIPO).
- World Trade Organization (WTO).
- International Satellite Organization (INTELSAT).
- United Nations Environment Programme (UNEP).
- United Nations Development Programme (UNDP).

- International Fun for Agriculture Development (IFAD).
- International Maritime Organization (IMO).

QATAR CURRENT CHAIR OF OIC

QATAR, THE CURRENT CHAIR OF THE ORGANIZATION OF THE ISLAMIC CONFERENCE

Qatar was unanimously chosen as the venue for the 9th session of the Islamic Summit Conference during Tehran's 8th Islamic Summit of December 1997, in response to the proposal of H.H Sheikh Hamad Bin Khalifa Al-Thani, the Emir of the State of Qatar.

The 9th Islamic Summit Conference was convened in Qatar on the 13th of November 2000. Choosing Qatar as venue for this conference testifies to the high position of Qatar in the Islamic world. Qatar pledged to pursue with greater determination the efforts to revive the spirit of solidarity and strengthen the ties of cooperation among Islamic states. Qatar also reiterated its commitment to actively contribute to the promotion of the common causes of the Islamic Ummah by extending all possible financial or moral assistance. This is particularly important as the region has to face the challenges of the new developments in the international arena, where the concepts of globalization, trade exchange, free market policies, democracy and freedom of expression are the order of the day.

It was not a surprise that Qatar hosted this conference. It has a vast experience in the field of conference organization. In 1997 it hosted Doha Economic Conference and a year later it hosted the Islamic Foreign Ministers' conference, in addition to many Gulf summit conferences, and several meetings tackling the various themes of economy, security and petroleum.

THE ROLE OF QATAR AS THE CURRENT CHAIR OF THE OIC

H.H. Sheikh Hamad Bin Khalifa Al- Thani, Emir of the State of Qatar and the current Chairman of the Organization of Islamic Conference, recognizes the compelling need to take effective measures to bring about immediate halt of the Israeli aggression against the Palestinian people and provide the necessary international protection to the Palestinian people. After conducting consultations with the Arab Republic of Egypt, the chair of the Arab summit at the time, and the Kingdom of Morocco, the chairman of Al-Quds Committee, H.H. the Emir sent a delegation led by H.E. Sheik Hamad Bin Jassim Bin Jabr Al-Thani, the Qatari foreign Minister to New York on November 27th /2000 in order to initiate direct contacts with the UN Secretary General and the Security Council member states. It was agreed in those meetings that all forms of violence should stop and international peacekeeping forces should be sent immediately to the occupied territories. It was also agreed that a fact-finding committee should be sent there too to determine the parties responsible for committing war crimes against the Palestinians, in accordance with the Security Council Resolution No. 1322 of 2000.

Doha Summit Conference entrusted H.H. the Emir, in his capacity as Chairman of the 9th Session of the Islamic Summit Conference, to extend his good offices in consultation with Iraq and Kuwait to prepare the ground to resolve the differences between them in accordance with the principles and objectives of the United Nations, the relevant

Security Council resolutions, and the principles and objectives of the OIC.

Also a delegation representing the OIC arrived in Afghanistan from Doha in March 2001, in order to persuade Afghan officials not to demolish the statues and relics which existed in Afghanistan before the advent of Islam. The delegation comprised H.E. Ahmad Bin Abdulla Al-Mahmoud, the Minister of State for Foreign Affairs, Reverend scholar Dr. Yousif Al Qaradawi and a number of distinguished Muslim scholars.

DOHA CONFERENCE 2002

**Under the Patronage of
Her Highness Sheikha Mouza Bent Nasser Al-Misnad
Wife of H .H the Emir,
Board Chairperson of Qatar Foundation for Education, Science and community
Development,
President of the Supreme Council for Family Affairs**

**The Family Development Center In collaboration with,The Islamic Development
Bank, organizes
Doha Conference on:
The Complementary role of: NGOs, international and governmental organizations
in sustainable development.**

**March 4 to 6, 2002
Sheraton Doha Hotel**

Supported by:

Qatar national hotels- the formal transporter - the formal press Gulf publishing and printing - Qatar airways -al- rayyah-Qatar national bank - Qatar international Islamic bank - Qatar for cement co.

Welcome in Doha:

To explore broader horizons for a better future, to stimulate a more effective contribution by NGOs (non-governmental organizations) in Islamic countries, and to envisage a future-oriented concept for a concerted action between regional and international organizations to serve sustainable development and improve living standards,
The Family Development Center (FDC) is gratified to invite you to Doha conference 2002,
The Complementary Roles Of NGO'S, International And Governmental Organizations In Sustainable Development.

The idea:

The family development center, and the Islamic Development Bank (IDB), a key institution belong to the Organization of the Islamic Conference (OIC), was prompted by a sincere desire, to see what help and assistance NGOs and women organizations, might require from regional and international organizations, to re-shape their institutional structures, and turn them fit enough to play an effective role in social and economic development to serve the progress and welfare of societies.

The objectives:

1-To activate channels of cooperation between IDB and NGOs in OIC member-states. This includes communication of information about the contributions IDB might offer to upgrade NGOs performance through feedback.

2-To set up a database for accomplished projects and define ways of benefiting from IDB and other regional and international donors.

3-Presentation of IDB blueprint entitled: How IDB deals with NGOs?. Text of the presentation would be passed on to participants for discussion.

4-Open discussions to figure out which projects can be viable enough to improve the living standards of human communities and which projects would need technical and material assistance from donors.

5-Contribution to eradicate or curb poverty in OIC member states.

6-Extend help and assistance for the
fulfillment of this objective by rendering technical assistance to NGOs serving in social development areas, upgrade the qualifications of their cadres, exchange expertise and information, besides technology transfer through training courses or supply of trainers and experts.

7-Support small-scale ventures, which might be helpful to poorer communities in member states and define the training requirements for existing human resources.

8-Provide the opportunity for NGOs and women organizations to assemble and discuss possible future cooperation, coordination and exchange of expertise.

IDB!! What is it?

IDB is an international financial institution founded by the OIC Finance Ministers at their first meeting in Jeddah in Dhul Qaada, 1391 Hegira year, corresponding to December 1972.
It has 52 member countries, other than Nigeria, which will bring membership to

53 upon admission sometime this year.

Scopes of IDB's contribution:

IDB contributes to project financing and renders technical assistance:

Financing operations fall into three categories:
- Project financing and technical assistance
- Trade financing
- Special assistance
IDB provides long and medium-term investment financing in the shape of loans, leasing, credit sales, capital sharing, industrialization, profit sharing and technical assistance.

IDB's financing operations have so far amounted to US dollars 21,252 million.

IDB renders technical assistance as follows:
It renders technical expertise for project studies and implementation.
It prepares specialized studies; construct potentials and upgrades human resources at national institutions, NGOs and women organizations.
So,The conference is an international forum open to all NGOs of OIC member countries.

Why Doha? And why FDC?

Doha is the capital city of the State of Qatar, current chair of the OIC.
FDC is an NGO, which offers social development services in the State of Qatar.
FDC is a social and economic development organization affiliated to Qatar Foundation for Education, Science and Community Development.
It aims at fostering sustainable development for all members of the society and for all social layers by helping them improve their economic, social, and cultural standards.

The participant:

The conference addresses all active NGOs concerned with community development
Effective community developments NGOs in OIC member states are invited to take part in the conference.
The invitation is also extended to all people concerned, specialists, researchers, and scholars in the field of social development.

Main topics:

1- First topic: the role of international, regional, and developmental institutions in rendering financial and technical assistance to communal activities.

2- second topic: "NGOs contribution to the fight of poverty and to socio-economic development, meant to upgrade social and economic standards of the society".

The conference language:
Arabic is the official language of the conference. Interpretation into both English and French would be available.

Registration:

For registration, application forms can be
Faxed To: 00974-4366579. Or to 00974-4361110
Or can be mailed by post to the following address
Doha Conference
"The Complementary roles of NGOs, international, and governmental organizations in sustainable development"
P.O.Box 3509
Family Development Center
Doha-Qatar.
Before January 25,2001, as a latest deadline.

FDC bears all travel, accommodation and living expenses for one member of active social development NGOs nominated by OIC member countries.

The registration fees are $50 for free-lancer participants and $100 for delegates of various private or governmental organizations..

The organizers would offer them the following:
- supply them with the conference researches and publications.
-Facilitate hotel reservation at the conference venue at special rates.
-Facilitate discounts on Qatar airway flights.
-Facilitate Smoothen procedures to get entry visa into Qatar.

MINISTRY OF FOREIGN AFFAIRS

His Excellency Sheikh   Hamad Bin Jassim Bin Jabr Al-Thani

Minister of Foreign Affairs

Curriculum Vitae :

Date of Birth:
- 1959.

Political History:
- 1982-1989, Director of the Office of the Minister of Municipal Affairs and Agriculture.
- 18-7-1989, appointed Minister of Municipal Affairs and Agriculture.
- 14-5-1990, appointed Deputy Minister of Electricity and Water for two years alongside with his post as Minister of Municipal Affairs and Agriculture.
- Supervised several successful projects and developed the agricultural sector.
- Held the following posts in addition to his position as Minister of Municipal Affairs and Agriculture and Deputy Minister of Electricity and Water:
- Chairman of Qatar Electricity and Water Company.
- President of the Central Municipal Council.
- Director of the Special Emiri Projects Office.
- Member of QP Board of Directors.
- Member of the Supreme Council for Planning.
- 1-9-1992, appointed Minister of Foreign Affairs.
- Kept his position as Minister of Foreign Affairs in the subsequent ministerial reshuffles in July 1995, October 1996 and January 1999.

Other key positions:
- Member of the Supreme Defence Council, which was established in 1996.
- Head of Qatar's Permanent Committee for the Support of Al Quds, which was formed in 1998.
- Member of the Permanent Constitution Committee formed in 1999.
- Member of the Ruling Family Council established in 2000.
- Member of the Supreme Council for the Investment of the Reserves of the State, which was established in 2000.

For additional analytical, business and investment opportunities information,
please contact Global Investment & Business Center, USA
at (202) 546-2103. Fax: (202) 546-3275. E-mail: rusric@erols.com
Global Business E-Books on Line: http://world.mirhouse.com

His Excellency   Ahmad Bin Abdullah Al-Mahmoud

Minister of State for Foreign Affairs and Member of the Council of Ministers

Curriculum Vitae :

Date of Birth:
-Born in 1953.

Academic Qualifications:
-B.A. in Arabic Language and Islamic Studies, Cairo University (1976).
-M.A. in Economics, with honors, Central Michigan University (1981).

Political History:
-Started his career at the Ministry of Foreign Affairs at the rank of Third Secretary (1976).
-Head of the Economic Affairs Section and representative of the Ministry of Foreign Affairs on the Qatari National Committee of Education, Culture and Science (1983).
-Ambassador of the State of Qatar to the Sultanate of Oman (1984-1986).
-Resident Ambassador of the State of Qatar to the United States of America, as well as Non-Resident Ambassador to Mexico and Venezuela (1987-1989).
-Undersecretary of the Ministry of Foreign Affairs (1989-1995).
-Minister of State for Foreign Affairs (1995).
-Member of the Council of Ministers in 1999.

Sheikh   Jabr Bin Yousif Bin Jassim Al - Thani

Director of the Minister's Office

Curriculum Vitae :

For additional analytical, business and investment opportunities information, please contact Global Investment & Business Center, USA at (202) 546-2103. Fax: (202) 546-3275. E-mail: rusric@erols.com
Global Business E-Books on Line: http://world.mirhouse.com

Date of Birth:
-1967.

Academic Qualifications:
- Bachelor of Law.

Work Experience:
- 13 years at the Ministry of Interior.
- Attended several military courses.
- Joined the Ministry of Foreign Affairs in 2000.
- Director of International organizations, Conferences and Treaties Department. Holding the rank of a consultant.
- Director of His Excellency the Minister of Foreign Affairs office since June 2001.
- Attended several functions including the Millennium Summit Conference of the Ministry of Foreign Affairs and the 55th session of the UN General Assembly in New York in 2000.
- Documentations Committee Head at the Islamic Conference held in Doha.

Mr.   Khalid Rashid Al-Hamoudi Al-Mansouri

Director of Information and Research Department

Curriculum Vitae

Department's Sections and Tasks :

DEP. OF INFORMATION & RESEARCH

Tel 4334445
Fax 4353592

Subordinate Sections:
Electronic Data and Documentation, Information, Technology, Public Relations, Communications and Relations, Information Monitoring.

Responsibilities of Electronic Data and Documentation Section:
1. Receive and deliver all correspondence exchanged between various departments at

the Ministry and other government departments such as foreign diplomatic missions, ministries and government and private departments, register these correspondence, list them with reference numbers on special rolls and refer the rolls to the Electronic Data and Documentation Center. The General Receiving Unit does this job.

2. Receive all correspondence of the Ministry with all attachments and documents, pass them through a special electronic program i.e. electronic data and documentation program, which stores all correspondence electronically in the data base of the center, making it easy to restore when needed. This system replaces the traditional manual archives system, which was used in the past for storing the Ministry's correspondence and documents. Electronic Data and Documentation Center is responsible for this job.

3. Transport and exchange diplomatic bags between the Ministry and Qatari diplomatic missions abroad. Presently work is done through the electronic bag system, one of whose characteristics is storing contents of the bag and step by step following the movement of the bag through all stations. This is the responsibility of the Diplomatic Bag Unit.

Ambassador   Mahmoud Abdulaziz Al Sahlawi

Director of Administrative and Financial Affairs Department

Curriculum Vitae

Department's Sections and Tasks :

ADMINISTRATIVE & FINANCIAL AFFAIRS DEP.

Tel 4334400
Fax 4324131

Subordinate sections:
Administrative Affairs, Financial Affairs.

Responsibilities of Administrative Affairs Section:
1. Supervise the application of laws and administrative regulations organizing the activities of the Ministry, follow up amendments that come upon them and take necessary actions thereon.
2. Prepare data and estimates of the requirements of the Ministry and its workforce in all

categories, types, levels and titles, and prepare the draft of the first chapter budget of the Ministry in coordination with other affiliated departments.

3. Propose and apply administrative techniques aiming to control and simplify work procedures to include the usage of computer.

4. Estimate training requirements for the Ministry's workforce and coordinate therein with other departments of the Ministry.

5. Prepare responses to internal and external inspections on administrative actions at the Ministry.

6. Supervise and uphold the security of the Ministry's building.

7. Facilitate personal administrative requirements of the Ministry's workforce at other concerned departments.

Responsibilities of the Financial Affairs Section:

1. Supervise the application of financial laws and regulations organizing the activities of the Ministry, follow up amendments that come upon them and take necessary actions thereon.

2. Propose, apply and develop financial systems and techniques in coordination with other departments of the Ministry and follow up the endorsement and application of such systems and techniques.

3. Prepare and follow up the endorsement and application of the Ministry's annual budget draft in coordination with other departments of the Ministry.

4. Register all financial operations of the Ministry in accordance with declared financial and accounting principles and rules of practice.

5. Propose and supervise the application of financial systems in regard to the expenses of Qatar's diplomatic and consular missions abroad.

6. Prepare and analyze periodical and final accounts of the Ministry and of Qatar's diplomatic and consular missions abroad, deduce the general trends of performance level and prepare required reports thereon.

7. Prepare responses for the comments of internal and external inspections on financial operations in the Ministry.

8. Estimate and provide the requirements of the Ministry for material and services in coordination with other departments of the Ministry.

9. Supervise the stores of the Ministry.

Ambassador   Khalil Ibrahim Al Mulla Al Jufairi

Director of Financial and Administrative Inspection Office

Curriculum Vitae

Department's Sections and Tasks :

FINANCIAL & ADMINISTRATIVE INSPECTION OFFICE

Tel: 4334290
Fax: 4320775

Responsibilities:

1. Monitor accounts of various departments of the Ministry of Foreign Affairs including units belonging to the Ministry's headquarters and diplomatic and consular missions abroad, by means of checking, reviewing and inspecting documents, books, records of received, due or expended funds and verifying that financial actions and accounts records have been executed properly and according to financial and accounting regulations and general principles of the general budget of the State.
2. Expose cases of financial and administrative negligence, discrepancy and excess and investigate the reasons that caused them and propose remedy actions.
3. Review consular proceeds, carry out required stock taking of cash funds, consular stamps and any other external documents of financial value and verify their compliance with entries and records.
4. Check, study and review various financial, accounting and administrative regulations and systems in order to verify their adequacy, specify areas of deficiency therein and propose remedial actions that could bring about the best level of efficiency and accuracy.
5. Monitor order of financial and administrative actions and prepare periodical reports on inspection visits executed by the Office.
6. Carry out all other duties that fall within the responsibilities of the Office if commissioned by the Minister or the Minister of State for Foreign Affairs.

H.E. Ambassador   Ahmad Jassim Muhammad Al-Mulla

Director of Protocol Department

Curriculum Vitae

Department's Sections and Tasks :

DEP. OF PROTOCOL

Tel 4334277
Fax 4448327

Subordinate Sections:
Ceremonies and Receptions, Privileges and Immunities, Passports.

Responsibilities of Ceremonies and Receptions Section:
1. Coordinate with concerned officials at Ceremonies Department at the Ministry of Emiri Diwan Affairs in organizing and holding reception and farewell ceremonies, alongside with other official arrangements concerning heads of states, prime ministers and senior foreign officials.
2. Make required arrangements in regard to reception ceremonies held for heads of diplomatic missions at their arrival in the country for the first time to present their credentials, receive and keep credentials of heads of foreign diplomatic missions accredited to the State and prepare documents dealing with establishing diplomatic representation with countries and international and regional organizations, which the State decides to establish relations with or join.
3. Prepare for official banquets, receptions and ceremonies.
4. Coordinate with concerned parties in regard to arrangements, dates and timings of audience given by government officials to members of foreign diplomatic and consular corps accredited to the State and coordinate programs of official visits of foreign delegations.
5. Compile and update main data on official occasions in other countries in order to extent official courtesy.
6. Prepare and update lists of Qatari and foreign diplomatic and consular corps.
7. Supervise the car workshop of the Ministry and organize the use of cars for various purposes.

Responsibilities of Privileges and Immunities Section:
1. Manage the affairs of the members of foreign diplomatic and consular corps and

representatives of international and regional organizations accredited to the State.
2. Propose granting and organizing diplomatic privileges and immunities and handle and follow up matters dealing with their application in accordance with the principle of similar treatment.
3. Follow up matters related to belongings of diplomatic missions accredited to the State, their quarters and residences of their diplomatic staff.
4. Follow up the registration of the cars of accredited diplomatic missions and provide diplomatic registration plates in coordination with concerned government departments.

Responsibilities of Passports Section:
1. Issue and renew Qatari diplomatic, special and VIP passports and prepare lists thereof.
2. Supervise entry and transit visas issued by Qatari representative missions abroad on foreign diplomatic, special and VIP passports.
3. Issue identity cards for member of foreign diplomatic and consular corps and representatives of international and regional organizations accredited to the State.
4. Coordinate with concerned government bodies in regard to issuing identity cards for non-diplomatic foreign staff working at representative missions accredited to the State.

Mr. Adel Ali Al Khal

Director of International Organizations, Conferences and Treaties Department

Curriculum Vitae

Department's Sections and Tasks :

DEP. OF INTERNATIONAL ORG. CONFERENCES & TREATIES

Tel 4334311, 4324587
Fax 4424479

Subordinate Sections:
United Nations, International Organizations and Conferences, International Conventions and Agreements.

Responsibilities of UN Section:

1. Propose ways of strengthening the relations of the State of Qatar with the UN and its specialized agencies.
2. Study, analyze and evaluate researches and recommendations and resolutions referred from the UN and its specialized agencies, give opinion thereon and recommend suitable courses of action.
3. Follow up activities of the UN and its specialized agencies and study and recommend positions towards questions under consideration at the UN.
4. Prepare to attend the sessions of the UN General Assembly meetings and prepare Qatar's annual speech at the General Assembly.
5. Evaluate the recommendations and resolutions issued by the UN and its specialized agencies and endorsed by the State of Qatar, and follow up the implementation thereof.
6. Coordinate contact between the UN and its specialized agencies on one side and concerned government departments in the State of Qatar on the other.
7. Follow up and evaluate projects implemented by the UN Development Program in the State of Qatar.
8. Evaluate and follow up settlement of Qatar's contributions and donations to UN agencies.

Responsibilities of International Organizations and Conferences Section:
1. Propose ways of developing the relations of the State of Qatar with international organizations and conferences.
2. Follow up the activities of international organizations, conferences and meetings and evaluate the advantages of participating therein.
3. Coordinate with government concerned bodies on organizing the Department's participation in the activities of international organizations, conferences, meetings and exhibitions.
4. Study and analyze the recommendations and resolutions issued by international organizations and conferences and follow up the implementation of those endorsed by the State of Qatar.
5. Propose ways of benefiting from development and technical assistance and programs provided by international organizations and conferences.
6. Evaluate and follow up the settlement of contributions and donations pledged by the State of Qatar to international organizations and conferences.

Responsibilities of International Conventions and Agreements Section:
1. Follow up all developments pertaining to international agreements and conventions.
2. Coordinate with Legal Affairs Department and concerned government bodies on studying and preparing drafts of agreements and conventions, which the State of Qatar is considering to join, and give opinion on signing or joining them.
3. Take necessary actions to conclude international agreements and conventions in which Qatar is a party and prepare to issue and register them at specialized international bodies in coordination with Legal Affairs Department.
4. Follow up the international agreements and conventions in terms of renewal, termination and amendment, in coordination with Legal Affairs Department and concerned government bodies and in accordance with the decisions of higher authorities.

Ambassador   Jumaa Issa Jumaa Al-Hassan Al-Mohannadi

Director of Technical Office

Curriculum Vitae

Department's Sections and Tasks :

TECHNICAL OFFICE

Tel 4443566
Fax 4448475

Responsibilities:
1. Establish, purchase and maintain diplomatic missions quarters and diplomatic residential units in countries where there is diplomatic representation of the State.
2. Prepare agreements and contracts in regard of land exchange with other countries.
3. Assign building units for diplomatic missions of other countries situated in the capital Doha on similar treatment basis.
4. Coordinate with embassies of other countries and with concerned government bodies on technical matters where necessary.
5. Review initial designs and issue preliminary approval for the construction of any building belonging to any diplomatic mission based in the State.
6. Prepare technical aspects for conferences supervised by the Ministry.

Mr. Hadi Nasser Mansour Al- Hajiri

Director of Legal Affairs Department

Curriculum Vitae

Department's Sections and Tasks :

LEGAL AFFAIRS DEP.

Tel 4334302
Fax 4325759

Subordinate Sections:
Conventions and Agreements, Legal Council and Disputes.

Responsibilities of Conventions and Agreements Section:
1. Study projects of international and regional agreements and conventions, which the State of Qatar is considering to join and give opinion thereon in coordination with concerned departments at the Ministry and other government bodies.
2. Give legal opinion on draft legislation of bilateral conventions and agreements that the State decides to conclude with other countries, and coordinate therein with concerned departments at the Ministry and other government bodies.
3. Follow up the developments in international and regional bilateral conventions and agreements and give legal opinion thereon.
4. Coordinate with legal committees specializing in international and regional affairs, follow up the performance of these committees and give opinion on conformity or otherwise with the laws and interests of the State.

Responsibilities of Legal Council and Disputes:
1. Give legal advice to the Minister on all matters he refers to the department.
2. Give legal council on draft legislation and other forms of enactment referred to the Department.
3. Prepare and formulate drafts of various forms of legislative enactment and drafts of legal circulars, which the Ministry intends to issue.
4. Give legal council on questions and matters of legal nature, which are referred from Qatari diplomatic and consular missions abroad.
5. Study and prepare notes and reports on disputes, which involve the State of Qatar, with a view to preserve the rights and interests of the State.
6. Review, prepare and formulate drafts of contracts and commitments, which the

Ministry concludes with other parties and follow up the legal aspects of problems encountering the implementation thereof.

7. Investigate occurrences and discrepancies imputed to the employees of the Ministry and referred from the Minister or the two Undersecretaries, prepare notes on investigation findings supported by legal opinion and follow up the implementation of decisions taken on this regard.

Department's Sections and Tasks :

Consular Affairs Dep.

Tel 4424489
Fax 4426279

Subordinate Sections:
Nationals Affairs, Expatriates Affairs, Authentication and Visas.

Responsibilities of Nationals Affairs Section:
1. Sponsor the interests of Qatari nationals in other countries and follow up such interests in coordination with concerned bodies, regardless of the whereabouts of concerned persons at the time when the matter is being handled.
2. Consult with the Department of Legal Affairs in matters dealing with the rights of nationals outside the country in preparation to take necessary steps to safeguard those rights.
3. Handle legal paperwork and requests for interrogation deputation.
4. Prepare and follow up the implementation of consular affairs organizing directives, guidelines and regulations in line with declared laws and decisions.

Responsibilities of Expatriates Affairs Section:
1. Handle expatriate consular affairs that fall within the jurisdiction of the Department.
2. Coordinate with concerned bodies to practice the rights of the State of controlling and checking ships or the crew of ships that carry foreigners as well as Qatari-registered ships and airplanes that retain their original nationalities when on other territory.
3. Coordinate with concerned bodies to assist foreign ships and airplanes and their crews, receive notifications on their passage across territorial waters or space and advice opinion on issuing requested passage permits.

Responsibilities of Authentication and Visas Section:
1. Confirm, at the request of nationals and expatriates, the authenticity of all certificates and documents issued by ministries, government departments and diplomatic and consular missions accredited to the State of Qatar, by affixing the stamp of the Ministry on the documents in question.
2. Coordinate with concerned government bodies on visa requests submitted from Qatar's diplomatic missions abroad on behalf of foreigners with regular passports.

3. Issue passage clearance for non-commercial transportation across Qatari territorial waters and space, in coordination with concerned government bodies.

4. Propose, organize and decide consular fees and control levy thereof in coordination with the Administrative and Financial Affairs Department.

Ambassador   Yousuf Isa Mohammad Al Jabir

Director of GCC Affairs Department

Curriculum Vitae

Department's Sections and Tasks :

GCC AFFAIRS DEP.

Tel 4334205, 4334307
Fax 4444640

Subordinate Sections:
Secretariat General, Bilateral Cooperation.

Responsibilities of Secretariat General Section:
1. Receive, study, analyze, give opinion and take necessary actions on correspondence, reports, studies, recommendations and decisions submitted from the Secretariat General and subordinate bodies.
2. Follow up the implementation of decisions taken by the State on the recommendations of the Secretariat General and decisions and recommendations of standing committees, Council of Ministers, ministerial meetings and meetings of undersecretaries, technicians and experts.
3. Coordinate and consult with concerned government bodies to prepare required studies in the political, economic, social, cultural, technical, and environmental and other fields pertinent to the agenda and meetings of the Council of Ministers and specialized committees.
4. Coordinate with concerned section at the Department of Organizations, Conferences and International Agreements on the multilateral agreement projects of the GCC countries.
5. Prepare reports and studies required by the Secretariat General and coordinate with

concerned government bodies therein.
6. Prepare, as per the directives of the Director of the Department, for summit and ministerial meetings, organize the participation of the State of Qatar in these meetings and prepare studies, issues and reports required for the participation.

Responsibilities of Bilateral Cooperation Section:
1. Propose ways of developing bilateral relations between the State of Qatar and other GCC countries in all fields.
2. Prepare required studies, researches and reports to boost bilateral cooperation with GCC member countries in various fields.
3. Coordinate with concerned government bodies and concerned section at the Department of Organizations, Conferences and International Agreements and the Department of Legal Affairs to prepare the drafts of bilateral agreements that the government decides to conclude with GCC member countries.
4. Evaluate bilateral agreements concluded with any of the GCC member countries in all fields and Follow up the implementation thereof.

H.E. Ambassador   Saif Mugaddam Al Buainain

Director of Arab Affairs Department

Curriculum Vitae

Department's Sections and Tasks :

ARAB AFFAIRS DEP.

Tel 4334483
Fax 4324072

Subordinate Sections:
Middle East, North Africa, Arab League Affairs.

Responsibilities of Middle East and North Africa Sections:
1. Propose ways of developing bilateral relations between the State of Qatar and Arab countries in all political, economic, cultural and technical fields.
2. Coordinate with the Department of Organizations, Conferences and International

Agreements, the Department of Legal Affairs and concerned government bodies in regard to bilateral draft agreements between the State of Qatar and any Arab country in all fields, follow up the implementation and evaluate the outcome of those agreements.

3. Study and evaluate reports and researches submitted by Qatar's Diplomatic missions in Arab countries, give opinion thereon for the attention of the Director of the Department and follow up and coordinate the activities of those missions.

4. Study matters referred by the Director of the Department on conditions, developments in Arab countries and relations between the State of Qatar and Arab countries.

5. Coordinate, follow up and develop relations with diplomatic missions of Arab countries in Qatar, follow up publications and newsletters issued by these missions and give opinion thereon.

Responsibilities of Arab League Section:

1. Receive, study and evaluate reports, studies, recommendations and decisions of the Arab League and affiliated bodies and give opinion thereon.

2. Follow up the implementation of government decisions referred by the Director of the Department regarding the recommendations submitted by the Arab League.

3. Coordinate between the Arab League and concerned government departments in Qatar regarding the functions and meetings of the Council of Ministers and various committees and consult with these government bodies to prepare required studies in various fields.

4. Prepare for the meetings of Arab summits and Council of Ministers and coordinate with concerned government bodies to organize the participation of the State of Qatar in these meetings and to prepare studies, issues and reports required for the participation.

5. Study and evaluate the conditions of organizations, associations, committees and subordinate agencies of the Arab League.

6. Prepare, follow up and evaluate procedures of settlement of the financial commitments of Qatar towards the Arab League and subordinate agencies.

7. Follow up the implementation of the decisions issued by the Arab League and specialized subordinate organizations and which were approved by the State of Qatar and prepare reports on implementation progress of these decisions.

Ambassador   Abdulrahman Mohammad Sulaiman Al Khulaifi

Director of Asian and African Affairs Department

Curriculum Vitae

For additional analytical, business and investment opportunities information, please contact Global Investment & Business Center, USA at (202) 546-2103. Fax: (202) 546-3275. E-mail: rusric@erols.com Global Business E-Books on Line: http://world.mirhouse.com

Department's Sections and Tasks :

ASIAN & AFRICAN AFFAIRS DEP.

Tel: 4334320
Fax: 44262076

Subordinate Sections:
East Asia, West Asia, African Affairs.

Responsibilities:
1. Study and propose ways of developing bilateral relations between the State of Qatar and Asian and African countries in the political, economic, cultural and technical fields.
2. Coordinate with the Department of Organizations, Conferences and International Agreements and the Department of Legal Affairs on bilateral agreement projects between the State of Qatar and any Asian or African country in all fields, and follow up the implementation of those agreements and evaluate their outcome.
3. Study, analyze and evaluate the reports, researches and subjects dealing with developments and conditions in Asian and African countries and the relations of Qatar with these countries.
4. Follow up publications and press releases issued by Asian and African diplomatic missions in Qatar, and give opinion thereon when necessary.
5. Coordinate with the Department of Organizations, Conferences and International Agreements, the Department of Legal Affairs and other concerned government departments on one side, and with Asian and African organizations on the other side on matters relating to cooperation with those organizations and give opinion thereon.

Mr.   Khalid Rashid Al-Hamoudi Al-Mansouri

Director of European and American Affairs Department

Curriculum Vitae

Department's Sections and Tasks :

EUROPEAN & AMERICAN AFFAIRS DEP.

Tel: 4334422
Fax: 4427357

Subordinate sections:
Western Europe, Eastern Europe, America.

Responsibilities:
1. Study and recommend ways of strengthening and developing bilateral relations between the State of Qatar and West and East European countries and American countries in the political, economic, cultural and technical fields.
2. Coordinate with the Department of Organizations, Conferences and International Agreements, the Department of Legal Affairs and concerned government departments regarding projects of bilateral agreements between the State of Qatar and East and West European countries and American countries, follow up the implementation of such agreements and evaluate the results thereof.
3. Study, analyze and evaluate reports, researches and matters pertaining the conditions and developments in West and east European countries and American countries as well as the relations between these countries and the State of Qatar.
4. Follow up newsletters, press releases and publications issued by diplomatic missions accredited to Qatar and comment thereon when necessary.
5. Coordinate with the Department of Organizations, Conferences and International Agreements, the Department of Legal Affairs and concerned government organs on the one hand and with European organizations and American countries on the other in regard to all referred matters of cooperation involving those parties and comment on such matters when necessary.

Ambassador   Saeed Bin Khalifa Al Damn Al-Mohannadi

Director of Duty Office

Curriculum Vitae

Department's Sections and Tasks :

DUTY OFFICE

Operator: 4433433

Direct Phone: 4322800 - 4442300
Contact could be made through these phone numbers from midnight till 7 am.
Fax: 4327333 - 4327444

Duty Categories:
1. Full Duty:
In this shift, duty officer should be available in person in the office during the period from 1 pm to midnight, 7 days a week including public holidays.
2. Partial Duty:
In this shift, duty officer is not required to be present in the office in person. He should be in phone contact with the full duty officer during the period from midnight to 7 am.

Responsibilities of the Office:
1. Receiving communication, correspondence, information and articles dispatched to the Ministry during the duty hours and referring the same to the concerned bodies and vice versa.
2. Deputizing for the Ministry's departments and offices in circulating all the following documents immediately among the Qatari diplomatic and consular missions abroad and resident and non-resident foreign diplomatic missions accredited to the country:
- Speeches given inside or outside the country by H.H. the Emir and the government officials.
- Official comments and declarations by authorized officials from the Ministry of Foreign Affairs.
- Final communiques of the conferences held inside the country
- Circulars regarding holidays and other matters.
3. Acting as a contact link between government officials and international officials inside or outside the country.
4. Following-up the important issues concerning the duties of the Qatari officials abroad and securing all requirements as fast as possible for these officials.
5. Dispatching the special information leaflets for the officials while they are abroad.
6. Receiving and delivering official letters by hand from and to the heads of diplomatic missions accredited to Qatar.
7. Actively participating in all international conferences held inside the country and in which either the Ministry of Foreign Affairs or the other government departments are participating.
8. Following-up and finalizing the procedures of issuing flight landing or passage clearance in coordination with the concerned government bodies.
9. Following-up the affairs of the Qatari communities abroad and helping to solve their consular problems.
10. Opening the VIP lounge at the airport and issuing diplomatic visas at the airport.

The Duty Office handles all the above mentioned tasks during the duty shifts after official work hours in complete coordination with the concerned officials at all the departments of the Ministry.

REGIONAL AND NATIONAL SECURITY CONSIDERATIONS

ANY THREAT TO THE STABILITY of the Persian Gulf endangering the region's oil flow greatly concerns the rest of the world. The Iranian Revolution of 1979 was the opening stage in more than a decade of upheaval. The outbreak of war between Iran and Iraq in 1980, the expansion of the war to nonbelligerent shipping, and the presence of foreign naval flotillas in the gulf followed. When general hostilities eventually broke out, they arose from an unexpected quarter--Iraq's sweep into Kuwait in August 1990 and the possibility of Iraqi forces continuing down the gulf coast to seize other oil-rich Arab states. The smaller Arab regimes volunteered use of their ports and airfields as bases for the coalition of forces in Operation Desert Storm to defeat Iraq.

The overwhelming concentration of military power that enabled Iraq to swallow up Kuwait underscored the vulnerability of the territory and oil facilities of the other gulf states. To the extent that their military resources permitted, each of the Arab states participated in the coalition that defeated Iraq and drove it out of Kuwait. It was clear, nonetheless, that they played a subordinate role in the vast operation in which the United States, Britain, and France predominated, accompanied by Egypt and Syria.

After its sharp setback, Iraq in early 1993 remained a major regional power and a littoral state of the Persian Gulf, along with Iran and Saudi Arabia. None of the five other Persian Gulf littoral states--Kuwait, Bahrain, Qatar, the United Arab Emirates, or Oman-- is in a position to defend its borders or territorial waters alone. In the face of their fragility, these Persian Gulf states continue to take measures to reinforce their individual and collective security. Relative to size and population, they have been among the world's most lavish spenders on the needs of their armed forces. Nevertheless, their military potential is limited by small manpower pools, ethnic divisions, limited area, and little experience in the effective use of modern weaponry.

A few months after the start of the Iran-Iraq War in 1980, the six nonbelligerents--the five gulf states and Saudi Arabia-- in 1981 banded together in the Gulf Cooperation Council (GCC). Although the GCC had economic, social, and political aims, its main purpose was the creation of a defensive military alliance. The GCC leaders feared that a decisive Iranian military victory would fuel the drive of the radical Shia (see Glossary) Muslims of Iran to spread their form of Islam. Concurrently, the GCC states accelerated their individual military efforts by purchasing modern aircraft, armored vehicles, air defense systems, and missile-armed naval vessels.

The GCC members are determined to construct a collective self-defense system without the direct involvement of foreign powers. For both political and practical reasons, however, the military goals of the GCC--standardization of equipment, coordination of training, integration of forces, and joint planning--have been achieved only to a limited degree. The gulf states have also been forced to restrain their military purchases as a result of declining oil revenues.

In the immediate aftermath of the Persian Gulf War, agreement was reached with the GCC to station Egyptian and Syrian troops in Kuwait to ensure the military stability of the northern gulf. By 1993, however, this plan seemed to have been abandoned. Instead, Kuwait and most other gulf states turned to cooperation with the West to develop a new security framework. The United States concluded agreements to permit pre-positioning of United States equipment for combat units, port access, and joint exercises and training. Britain and France also negotiated military cooperation arrangements. The effect was to spread a Western strategic umbrella over the region without the permanent stationing of foreign forces, although a United States and British naval presence is expected to continue.

In early 1993, more than a year after the gulf war ended, the danger of renewed violence in the region had receded, although no reconciliation among the antagonists had occurred. Iraq had not fully recovered from its humiliating defeat; nevertheless, its reduced army and air force still overshadow the combined forces of the GCC. Iran's military strength was depleted during its eight-year struggle with Iraq, and recovery is proceeding slowly. Although it appears to have shifted to more moderate policies, Iran's ambition to be a factor in regional gulf security has been treated with suspicion.

Traditional rivalries and territorial disputes among the smaller gulf states still linger but have steadily diminished as sources of tension. Subversion and terrorist incidents, often linked to Iran, have abated, as has the potential for disruption by foreign workers manipulated by external forces. The police vigilantly control internal dissent that can threaten the stability of the existing regimes. Nevertheless, resistance to democratic reforms by some members of the conservative ruling families of the gulf increases the likelihood of future destabilization and upheaval.

HISTORICAL OVERVIEW

According to archaeologists, warfare was a common activity 5,000 years ago among the peoples of the area of the Middle East that in modern times became Iran, Iraq, Saudi Arabia, and the smaller gulf states. Intermittent hostilities, often based on rivalries between the Persians of the eastern coast of the gulf and the Arabs of the western coast, have occurred ever since. Sargon, Hammurabi, Nebuchadnezzar II, and Alexander the Great were among the best known kings who led warring armies in the 2,500 years before the birth of Christ. During the centuries of Greek and Roman domination, the gulf region was of limited interest to the major powers, but the area's importance as a strategic and trading center rose with the emergence of Islam in the seventh century A.D. The caliphate's military strength was concentrated at Hormuz. Strategically sited at the mouth of the gulf, its authority extended over ports and islands of the Arabian Sea and the Persian Gulf

The strategic importance of Hormuz, however, did not survive the appearance of Western powers, initially the Portuguese who came to the gulf in the late fifteenth century after Vasco da Gama's discovery of the route to India via the Cape of Good Hope. The Ottomans and the Iranians also tried to dominate the gulf but faced opposition from local tribes in Bahrain and Muscat, reluctant to cede authority over their territories, which by then were the most important areas on the coast. Increasing British involvement in India beginning in the late eighteenth century quickened British interest in the gulf region as a means of protecting the sea routes to India.

The principal challenge to Britain arose from the Qawasim tribal confederation originating in the area of the present-day United Arab Emirates (UAE). The Qawasim, who amassed a fleet of about 900 vessels, demanded tribute for the passage of merchant vessels and were regarded as pirates by the Europeans. Between 1809 and 1820, British sea power gradually brought about the destruction of the Qawasim fleet. This in turn led to the signing of agreements with Britain by the Qawasim and other shaykhs (see Treaties with the British , ch. 1). The amirates promised to have no direct dealings with other foreign states and to abstain from piracy. Britain in turn assumed responsibility for the foreign relations of the amirates and promised to protect them from all aggression by sea and to lend its support against any land attacks. Before the end of the century, Britain extended protection to Bahrain and Kuwait; Qatar entered the system after it repudiated Ottoman sovereignty in 1916.

Although Muscat was traditionally a center of the slave trade, its sultan agreed to abandon this activity in return for British help in building a navy. In the early nineteenth century, the sultan's efficient fleet of sloops, corvettes, and frigates enabled him to support a maritime empire extending from East Africa to the coast of present-day Pakistan. With the eventual decline of this empire, owing in part to its division into two states--Zanzibar and Oman--Britain's influence grew, and it signed a treaty in 1891 similar to those with the gulf amirates.

The strategic importance of the Persian Gulf became increasingly apparent as the oil industry developed in the twentieth century. Saudi Arabia, Iraq, and Iran all claimed some of the territory of the gulf states during the years between World War I and World War II, but Britain's firm resistance to these claims enabled the amirates to maintain their territorial integrity without resort to arms. Except for a small force of the British Indian Navy to ensure observance of the treaty conditions and maintain maritime peace in the gulf, Britain abstained from direct military involvement. As the wealth of the gulf's oil resources became clear, the size of the British military establishment expanded. By the end of the 1960s, Britain had about 9,000 men in Oman, Sharjah (an amirate of the UAE), and Bahrain, where British military headquarters was located. The Trucial Oman Scouts, a mobile force of mixed nationality that Britain supported and British officers commanded, became a symbol of public order in the UAE until Britain's withdrawal from the Persian Gulf in 1971.

IMPACT OF THE IRAN-IRAQ WAR, 1980-88

The first major threat to the security of the Persian Gulf states followed the outbreak of war between Iran and Iraq in 1980. The war began after a period of deteriorating relations between these two historic rivals, dating from the fall of Mohammad Reza Shah Pahlavi in 1979 and his replacement as Iranian leader by Ayatollah Sayyid Ruhollah Musavi Khomeini. Full-scale warfare erupted in September 1980 as Iraqi military units swept across the Shatt al Arab waterway--which forms the confluence of the Tigris and

Euphrates rivers--into the province of Khuzestan, Iran's richest oil-producing area. Iraqi president Saddam Husayn hoped to overthrow Khomeini, who had been overtly attempting to spread his Islamist (also seen as fundamentalist) revolution into Iraq, where the minority regime of Sunni (see Glossary) Muslims ruled over a majority population of Shia Muslims.

By November 1980, the Iraqi offensive had lost its momentum. Rejecting an Iraqi offer to negotiate, Khomeini launched a series of counteroffensives in 1982, in 1983, and in 1984 that resulted in the recapture of the Iranian cities of Khorramshahr and Abadan. The destruction of huge oil facilities caused both belligerents sharp declines in oil revenues. Iraq was able to obtain substantial financial aid from Saudi Arabia and other gulf states. In early 1986, an Iranian offensive across the Shatt al Arab resulted in the fall of the Iraqi oil-loading port of Faw and the occupation of much of the Faw Peninsula almost to the Kuwait border. But the Iranians could not break out of the peninsula to threaten Basra, and their last great offensive, which began in December 1986, was ultimately repelled with heavy losses. In the spring of 1988, the freshly equipped Iraqi ground and air forces succeeded in retaking the Faw Peninsula and, through a succession of frontal assaults, continued into Iran. Iranian battlefield losses, combined with Iraqi air and missile attacks on Iranian cities, forced Khomeini to accept a ceasefire , which took effect in August 1988.

Initially, the fighting between Iran and Iraq only peripherallyaffected the Persian Gulf states. In May 1981, Bahrain, Kuwait, Oman, Qatar, Saudi Arabia, and the UAE banded together in the GCC to protect their interests and, if necessary, to defend themselves In 1984 Iran reacted to Iraqi air attacks on Iran's main oil terminal on the island of Khark by attacking ships destined for ports in gulf countries that assisted Iraq's war effort. Iranian links with a coup attempt in Bahrain in 1981, Shia terrorist activity in Kuwait, and Iranianinspired violence in Mecca underscored the conviction of the Arab states of the gulf that Iran was the primary threat to their security.

Iran stepped up the tanker warfare in early 1987 by introducing high-speed small craft armed with Italian Sea Killer missiles. Kuwait had already sought the protection of United States naval escorts through the gulf for reflagged Kuwaiti vessels. Determined to protect the flow of oil, the United States approved and began tanker convoys in May 1987. Eleven Kuwaiti ships--one-half of the Kuwaiti tanker fleet--were placed under the United States flag. Other Kuwaiti tankers sailed under Soviet and British flags. Although United States escorts were involved in a number of clashes with Iranian forces and one tanker was damaged by a mine, Iran generally avoided interfering with Kuwaiti ships sailing under United States protection.

PERSIAN GULF WAR, 1991

Despite its huge losses in the Iran-Iraq War, Iraq was unchallenged as the most powerful military presence in the gulf area. Reviving Iraq's old territorial claims against Kuwait, Saddam Husayn called for the annexation of Bubiyan and Warbah islands at the mouth of the Shatt al Arab to give Iraq a clear passage to the gulf. He also accused Kuwait of illegally siphoning off oil from Ar Rumaylah field, one of the world's largest oil pools,

For additional analytical, business and investment opportunities information,
please contact Global Investment & Business Center, USA
at (202) 546-2103. Fax: (202) 546-3275. E-mail: rusric@erols.com
Global Business E-Books on Line: http://world.mirhouse.com

which the two countries shared. Saddam Husayn threatened to use force against Arab oil producers, including Kuwait and the UAE, that exceeded their oil quotas, charging them with colluding with the United States to strangle the Iraqi economy by flooding the market with low-priced oil.

Although Iraq had accompanied its threats by moving troops to the border area, the world was largely taken by surprise when, on August 2, 1990, the Iraqi army invaded and occupied Kuwait. A force of about 120,000 soldiers and approximately 2,000 tanks and other armored vehicles met little resistance. The Kuwaiti army was not on the alert, and those troops at their posts could not mount an effective defense. Some aircraft operating from southern Kuwait attacked Iraqi armored columns before their air base was overrun, and they sought refuge in Saudi Arabia. Of the 20,000 Kuwaiti troops, many were killed or captured, although up to 7,000 escaped into Saudi Arabia, along with about forty tanks.

Having completed the occupation of Kuwait, the Iraqi armored and mechanized divisions and the elite Republican Guard advanced south toward Kuwait's border with Saudi Arabia. Intelligence sources indicated that the Iraqis were positioning themselves for a subsequent drive toward the Saudi oil fields and shipping terminals, possibly continuing toward the other gulf states.

In the first of a series of resolutions condemning Iraq, the United Nations (UN) Security Council on August 2 called for Iraq's unconditional and immediate withdrawal from Kuwait. In the ensuing months, a coalition force of more than 600,000 ground, sea, and air force personnel deployed to defend Saudi Arabia and to drive the Iraqis out of Kuwait. Command of the force was divided: commander in chief of the United States Central Command, General H. Norman Schwarzkopf, headed United States, British, and French units; his Saudi counterpart, Lieutenant General Khalid ibn Sultan ibn Abd al Aziz Al Saud, commanded units from twentyfour non-Western countries, including troops from Saudi Arabia, Egypt, Syria, Kuwait, and the other gulf states. In addition to 20,000 Saudi troops and 7,000 Kuwaiti troops, an estimated 3,000 personnel from the other GCC states took part in the land forces of the coalition offensive, known as Operation Desert Storm.

When the massive coalition ground assault of Operation Desert Storm got under way on February 24, 1991, troops of the Persian Gulf states formed part of two Arab task forces. The first, Joint Forces Command North, consisting of Egyptian, Saudi, Syrian, and Kuwaiti troops, deployed on Kuwait's western border. Joint Forces Command East deployed along the gulf immediately south of Kuwait and consisted of about five brigades (each well below the strength of a regular Western brigade) from Saudi Arabia, Kuwait, Bahrain, and Qatar. The main attack was a sweeping movement by United States, British, and French forces in the west designed to cut the links between the Iraqi forces in Kuwait and their bases in Iraq. The Saudis and Kuwaitis on the western border of Kuwait, composed of about four brigades organized as the Khalid Division, together with an Egyptian regiment, breached Iraqi defenses after allied bombing and engineer operations blasted passages. Iraqi troops, although in strong positions, surrendered or streamed to the north. Units of Joint Forces Command East advanced up the coastal road, capturing the city of Kuwait on the third day of the offensive after light fighting and the surrender of thousands of Iraqi soldiers.

TERRITORIAL DISPUTES

Before the oil era, the gulf states made little effort to delineate their territories. Members of Arab tribes felt loyalty to their tribe or shaykh and tended to roam across the Arabian desert according to the needs of their flocks. Official boundaries meant little, and the concept of allegiance to a distinct political unit was absent. Organized authority was confined to ports and oases. The delineation of borders began with the signing of the first oil concessions in the 1930s. The national boundaries had been defined by the British, but many of these borders were never properly demarcated, leaving opportunities for contention, especially in areas of the most valuable oil deposits. Until 1971 British-led forces maintained peace and order in the gulf, and British officials arbitrated local quarrels. After the withdrawal of these forces and officials, old territorial claims and suppressed tribal animosities rose to the surface. The concept of the modern state- -introduced into the gulf region by the European powers--and the sudden importance of boundaries to define ownership of oil deposits kindled acute territorial disputes.

Iran has often laid claim to Bahrain, based on its seventeenth-century defeat of the Portuguese and its subsequent occupation of the Bahrain archipelago. The Arab clan of the Al Khalifa, which has been the ruling family of Bahrain since the eighteenth century, in turn pushed out the Iranians in 1780. The late shah, Mohammad Reza Pahlavi, raised the Bahrain question when the British withdrew from areas east of Suez, but he dropped his demand after a 1970 UN-sponsored plebiscite showed that Bahrainis overwhelmingly preferred independence to Iranian hegemony. The religious leaders of the Iranian Revolution revived the claim to Bahrain primarily on the grounds that the majority of Bahrainis were Shia Muslims. Iranian secular leaders subsequently renounced the claim in an attempt to establish better relations with Bahrain.

In 1971 Iranian forces occupied the islands of Abu Musa, Tunb al Kubra (Greater Tumb), and Tunb as Sughra (Lesser Tumb), located at the mouth of the gulf between Iran and the UAE. The Iranians reasserted their historic claims to the islands, although the Iranians had been dislodged by the British in the late nineteenth century. Iran continued to occupy the islands in 1993, and its action remained a source of contention with the UAE, which claimed authority by virtue of Britain's transfer of the islands to the amirates of Sharjah and Ras al Khaymah. By late 1992, Sharjah and Iran had reached agreement with regard to Abu Musa, but Ras al Khaymah had not reached a settlement with Iran concerning Greater Tumb and Lesser Tumb.

Another point of contention in the gulf is the Bahraini claim to Az Zubarah on the northwest coast of Qatar and to Hawar and the adjacent islands forty kilometers south of Az Zubarah, claims that stem from former tribal areas and dynastic struggles. The Al Khalifa had settled at Az Zubarah before driving the Iranians out of Bahrain in the eighteenth century. The Al Thani ruling family of Qatar vigorously dispute the Al Khalifa claim to the old settlement area now in Qatari hands as well as laying claim to the

For additional analytical, business and investment opportunities information, please contact Global Investment & Business Center, USA at (202) 546-2103. Fax: (202) 546-3275. E-mail: rusric@erols.com Global Business E-Books on Line: http://world.mirhouse.com

Bahraini-occupied Hawar and adjacent islands, a stone's throw from the mainland of Qatar but more than twenty kilometers from Bahrain. The simmering quarrel reignited in the spring of 1986 when Qatari helicopters removed and "kidnapped" workmen constructing a Bahraini coast guard station on Fasht ad Dibal, a reef off the coast of Qatar. Through Saudi mediation, the parties reached a fragile truce, whereby the Bahrainis agreed to remove their installations. However, in 1991 the dispute flared up again after Qatar instituted proceedings to let the International Court of Justice in The Hague decide whether it had jurisdiction. (Bahrain refused the jurisdiction of the court, and as of early 1993 the dispute was unresolved.) The two countries exchanged complaints that their respective naval vessels had harassed the other's shipping in disputed waters.

As one pretext for his invasion of Kuwait in 1990, Saddam Husayn revived a long-standing Iraqi claim to the whole of Kuwait based on Ottoman boundaries. Ottoman Turkey exercised a tenuous sovereignty over Kuwait in the late nineteenth century, but the area passed under British protection in 1899. In 1932 Iraq informally confirmed its border with Kuwait, which had previously been demarcated by the British. In 1961, after Kuwait's independence and the withdrawal of British troops, Iraq reasserted its claim to the amirate based on the Ottomans' having attached it to Basra Province. British troops and aircraft were rushed back to Kuwait. A Saudi-led force of 3,000 from the League of Arab States (Arab League) that supported Kuwait against Iraqi pressure soon replaced them.

The boundary issue again arose when the Baath (Arab Socialist Resurrection) Party came to power in Iraq after a 1963 revolution. The new government officially recognized the independence of Kuwait and the boundaries Iraq had accepted in 1932. Iraq nevertheless reinstated its claims to Bubiyan and Warbah in 1973, massing troops at the border. During the 1980-88 war with Iran, Iraq pressed for a long-term lease to the islands in order to improve its access to the gulf and its strategic position. Although Kuwait rebuffed Iraq, relations continued to be strained by boundary issues and inconclusive negotiations over the status of the islands.

In August 1991, Kuwait charged that a force of Iraqis, backed by gunboats, had attacked Bubiyan but had been repulsed and many of the invaders captured. UN investigators found that the Iraqis had come from fishing boats and had probably been scavenging for military supplies abandoned after the Persian Gulf War. Kuwait was suspected of having exaggerated the incident to underscore its need for international support against ongoing Iraqi hostility.

A particularly long and acrimonious disagreement involved claims over the Al Buraymi Oasis, disputed since the nineteenth century among tribes from Saudi Arabia, Abu Dhabi, and Oman. Although the tribes residing in the several settlements of the oasis were from Oman and Abu Dhabi, followers of the Wahhabi (see Glossary) religious movement that originated in Saudi Arabia had periodically occupied and exacted tribute from the area. Oil prospecting began on behalf of Saudi oil interests, and in 1952 the Saudis sent a small constabulary force to assert control of the oasis. When arbitration efforts broke down in 1955, the British dispatched the Trucial Oman Scouts to expel the Saudi contingent. After a new round of negotiations, a settlement was reached whereby

Saudi Arabia recognized claims of Abu Dhabi and Oman to the oasis. In return, Abu Dhabi agreed to grant Saudi Arabia a land corridor to the gulf and a share of a disputed oil field. Other disagreements over boundaries and water rights remained, however.

The border between Oman and Yemen remained only partially defined, and, as of early 1993, border clashes had not occurred since 1988. Improving relations between Oman and the People's Democratic Republic of Yemen (PDRY, also seen as South Yemen)--which was reunited with the Yemen Arab Republic (YAR, also seen as North Yemen) in 1990--offered some hope that the border would be demarcated. Earlier, the physical separation of the southeern portion of Oman from its territory on the Musandam Peninsula (Ras Musandam) was a source of friction between Oman and the various neighboring amirates that became the UAE in 1971. Differences over the disputed territory appeared to have subsided after the onset of the Iran-Iraq War in 1980.

REGIONAL SECURITY PROBLEMS

The Persian Gulf is a relatively constricted geographic area of great existing or potential volatility. The smaller states of the gulf are particularly vulnerable, having limited indigenous populations and, in most cases, armed forces with little more than symbolic value to defend their countries against aggression. All of them lack strategic depth, and their economies and oil industries depend on access to the sea. Conflicts involving the air forces and navies of the larger gulf powers inevitably endanger their critical transportation links. Closure of the Strait of Hormuz--which was threatened but which never actually occurred during the Iran-Iraq War--would have a catastrophic effect on regular ship movements.

The oil drilling, processing, and loading facilities of the gulf states, some of them on offshore platforms, are vital to their economies. In an era of highly accurate missiles and highperformance aircraft, the protection of these exposed resources against surprise attack presents enormous difficulties. Even those states that can afford the sophisticated weaponry to defend their installations can ensure their effectiveness only through proper training, manning, and maintenance.

Most of the Arab gulf states, although vulnerable by air and by sea, are relatively immune from ground attack. Because of their geographic position on the Arabian Peninsula, they are exposed on their landward side only to vast desert tracts controlled by Saudi Arabia, with which they are linked by security treaties. Potential aggressors in the region, although heavily armed, lack the equipment or experience to project their forces over long distances. The only realistic possibility of overland attack seems to be in the north, where Kuwait has no natural line of defense and its oil facilities are near both Iran and Iraq. In early 1992, Kuwaiti officials disclosed plans to construct an electronic fence stretching more than 200 kilometers along the Kuwait-Iraq border. Although some obstacles might be emplaced to obstruct an Iraqi crossing, the main purpose of the fence is to prevent infiltration. Border guards of Kuwait's Ministry of Interior are to patrol the fence area.

In the south, reunited Yemen had inherited large stocks of military equipment from the Soviet Union's earlier support of the PDRY. The PDRY's political support of Iraq in the Kuwaiti crisis caused the GCC states to regard it as a potentially hostile neighbor. Although offensive operations against Oman or Saudi Arabia, with which it shared long, undefined borders, seem unlikely, the encouragement of border infiltration by all three countries cannot be ruled out.

The Iranian Revolution of 1979 introduced a new threat to stability in the gulf. Shia form a majority of the population of Bahrain and an important part of the foreign labor force in Kuwait and are considered potential dissidents in any future hostilities. Numerous terrorist actions in Kuwait during the 1980s were attributed to domestic Shia instigated by Iran Iran is one of the strongest military powers of the region and has historically sought to extend its influence to the Arab shore of the gulf. Nevertheless, fears of military confrontation subsided after the Iran-Iraq War ended. The influence of the more extremist elements within the Iranian government appears to have declined; Iran also had opposed Iraq's invasion of Kuwait.

In spite of Iraq's defeat in 1991, Kuwait remains the most vulnerable of the gulf states. Despite the crippling of Iraq's offensive military capabilities, it continues to be a formidable military power in the region. Its postwar manpower strength is estimated at 380,000, including at least three intact divisions of the elite Republican Guard, as well as large stocks of armor, artillery, and combat aircraft. Only with the assurance of outside support can the GCC states be confident that they can successfully resist renewed Iraqi aggression.

The gulf Arabs believe that a settlement of the Arab-Israeli conflict will enhance gulf security. Direct conflict with Israel was a remote contingency in early 1993, although Israel's doctrine of preemptive attack and its demonstrated ability to hit distant targets must be reckoned with in their strategic planning. Because the northwestern areas of Saudi Arabia are well within range of Israeli attack, air defense units that would otherwise be available to the GCC for gulf defense must be positioned there. Efforts of the Arab gulf states to upgrade their air defense systems have often been viewed by the United States Congress and by the public as hostile to Israeli interests.

In early 1993, one year after Saddam Husayn's defeat in the Persian Gulf War, the region's security appeared more stable than in many years. The fear of a communist encroachment or of a superpower confrontation has evaporated. Iran seems to be seeking greater accommodation with its gulf neighbors, although the Tehran government is continuing its military buildup and insists that it has a role in regional mutual security. Iraq, although still hostile, does not present a significant military threat. The United States and other Western powers have indicated that they will act against any new instability in the gulf that endangers their interests.

COLLECTIVE SECURITY UNDER THE GULF COOPERATION COUNCIL

For additional analytical, business and investment opportunities information, please contact Global Investment & Business Center, USA at (202) 546-2103. Fax: (202) 546-3275. E-mail: rusric@erols.com Global Business E-Books on Line: http://world.mirhouse.com

The six Persian Gulf states of the Arabian Peninsula-- Bahrain, Kuwait, Oman, Qatar, Saudi Arabia, and the UAE--formed the GCC in May 1981 with the aim of "co-ordination, integration, and co-operation among the member-states in all fields." Although none of the committees initially established dealt with security, the final communiqué of the first meeting affirmed the will and the intention of the signatories to defend their security and independence and to keep the region free of international conflicts. Four months later, the chiefs of staff of the armed forces of the six member states met to discuss regional military cooperation. The immediate objective was to protect themselves from the dangers posed by the Iran-Iraq War and the political violence associated with revolutionary Islamism. In a series of meetings over the years, the defense ministers and chiefs of staff devoted numerous sessions to the improvement of military cooperation and the creation of a joint command and joint air defense mechanisms. Managing their common security challenges collectively has made progress in some areas, but little in others. Creation of a fully integrated air defense system was far from a reality as of early 1993. The GCC states have not realized plans to develop an arms production capacity, although they have launched a new effort to revive an earlier arrangement with Egypt to create a pan-Arab weapons industry.

Political differences among GCC members have been the main obstacles to placing gulf defense on a collective rather than on a bilateral basis, even in such matters as achieving interoperability of equipment and cooperating in training, logistics, and infrastructure. The GCC experienced delays in reaching agreement to cooperate in internal security matters because Kuwait, the chief target of terrorism, feared that its relatively liberal domestic security regime might be impaired. Until Kuwait agreed to a GCC agreement in late 1987, Saudi Arabia and several other members of the GCC coordinated their efforts bilaterally, including the exchange of equipment, expertise, and training; the extradition of criminals; and the interception of border infiltrators. GCC members have adopted parallel policies on deportation and travel restrictions and share information on suspected terrorists and plots.

Ground and air units of the six member states have carried out small-scale combined training exercises. Military assistance, provided mainly by Saudi Arabia and Kuwait under GCC auspices, has enabled Bahrain to modernize its stock of combat aircraft and Oman to improve its air and sea defenses around the Strait of Hormuz. In 1984 GCC defense ministers agreed to create the Peninsula Shield force and base it at Hafar al Batin in Saudi Arabia, about sixty kilometers south of the Kuwaiti border. Under the command of a Saudi general, the unit consists of one Saudi brigade and a composite brigade with token personnel from the other states.

The limited reaction of the GCC to the August 2 Iraqi invasion of Kuwait exposed its weakness when faced with direct aggression against a member of the alliance by a much stronger power. The GCC immediately condemned the Iraqi action, but when GCC defense ministers met three weeks later, they could only agree on strengthening the Peninsula Shield force. During the Persian Gulf War, national contingents deployed separately as units of Arab task forces.

For additional analytical, business and investment opportunities information,
please contact Global Investment & Business Center, USA
at (202) 546-2103. Fax: (202) 546-3275. E-mail: rusric@erols.com
Global Business E-Books on Line: http://world.mirhouse.com

At the conclusion of the war on March 3, 1991, the six members of the GCC, along with Syria and Egypt, met in Damascus to agree on the establishment of a permanent security force to protect Kuwait against future aggression. Syria and Egypt were to contribute troop contingents on a reimbursable basis. The Damascus Agreement soon unraveled when differences emerged over the desirability of a long-term Egyptian and Syrian presence in the gulf. However, Egypt and Syria remain committed under the agreement to send military aid to Kuwait and the other gulf states if a threat arises.

Kuwait subsequently negotiated defense cooperation agreements with the United States, Britain, and France as an additional form of security if its borders were again threatened At a GCC meeting in late 1991, Oman proposed that the six GCC members develop a 100,000-strong joint security force under a unified military command. The Omani plan was set aside after other defense ministers questioned whether the manpower target was attainable and whether administrative and procedural problems could be overcome. The consensus of the ministers was that the Peninsula Shield force should be the nucleus of a unified army, the realization of which might be many years in the future.

MILITARY CAPABILITIES OF THE PERSIAN GULF STATES

During the decade after the outbreak of the Iran-Iraq War, all the gulf states set out to strengthen their armed forces by converting to the most modern weapons they could obtain and assimilate. By 1993 each state had at least a modest inventory of tanks and other armored equipment, air defense missiles, combat aircraft, armed helicopters, and missile-armed naval craft with which to deter an intruder. Kuwait is less prepared than the others, not having recovered from the losses it suffered in personnel and equipment during the Persian Gulf War. A fundamental constraint for all the gulf states has been the limited pool of qualified manpower and, in most countries, the problem of attracting recruits when better employment opportunities exist in the civilian sector. The emphasis on advanced weaponry is part of an effort to minimize the need for personnel. As stated by a senior Kuwaiti officer, the object is to obtain the best equipment technologically, "easy to maintain, understand, and operate . . . the greatest firepower for the smallest human effort." But integrating modern weapons into the gulf armies and ensuring their effective operation create other problems. Such problems include the necessity of continued reliance on foreign officers and foreign maintenance and training staffs at a time when all gulf states are trying to achieve greater self-sufficiency. Dependence on foreign personnel, moreover, implies a degree of loyalty and trustworthiness that may not be forthcoming in times of crisis.

Although in every case the gulf armies are much larger than the air forces and navies, the ground forces have traditionally been oriented toward counterinsurgency actions and the protection of the ruling families. Most of the armies are organized into one or more combat brigades; actual fighting strengths are generally lower than the brigade structure implies. Except for the officers and men who were briefly exposed to modern military operations during the Persian Gulf War--and in the late 1960s and first half of the 1970s during Oman's war with Dhofari guerrillas and their supporters in the PDRY--most have not faced actual combat situations.

For additional analytical, business and investment opportunities information,
please contact Global Investment & Business Center, USA
at (202) 546-2103. Fax: (202) 546-3275. E-mail: rusric@erols.com
Global Business E-Books on Line: http://world.mirhouse.com

In recognition of the great strategic importance of their air and sea defenses, the gulf states have all introduced modern combat aircraft and air defense missile systems, such as the United States Hawk surface-to-air missile (SAM). Several of the states have in their inventories or on order attack helicopters to help protect their oil facilities and oil drilling platforms in the gulf. All the gulf states have communications, control, and warning systems for the effective use of their fighter aircraft and antiaircraft missiles. But each air force is small, and, unless integrated with others, the overall effectiveness of the GCC in air defense is marginal. In spite of the attention the problem has received, there is no common network linking all air defense squadrons and SAMs to the Saudi Arabian air defense system and to the Saudi airborne warning and control system (AWACS) aircraft. Technical difficulties, including the incompatibility of national communications systems and the reluctance to turn control of national air defense over to a unified command structure, account for this weakness.

Fast-missile attack craft acquired by all of the gulf navies with small but well-trained crews could inflict damaging blows to heavier fleets and discourage hostile amphibious operations. The sixty-two-meter corvettes belonging to Bahrain and the UAE are the largest vessels among the gulf navies. As the tanker war demonstrated, the navies lack minesweeping capability, and their shipboard defense weapons against air attack are also weak. Only Oman has available larger amphibious transports to convey troops and vehicles for defending islands or remote coastal areas.

Defense expenditures of the gulf states are among the highest in the world relative to population. According to an analysis covering 1989, prepared by the United States Arms Control and Disarmament Agency, Qatar recorded the highest per capita military expenditures of any country in the world, followed by Israel and the United States. Oman ranked fourth and Kuwait sixth. The UAE was eleventh highest; Bahrain, listed in twentyseventh place worldwide, had the lowest outlays relatively of the gulf states. Military spending as a percentage of central government expenditures also is high, amounting to more than 40 percent in Oman and the UAE, for example. In contrast, military spending in Bahrain is 13 percent of central government expenditure. Military expenditures as a percentage of the gross national product (GNP--see Glossary) are more moderate except for Oman, whose military outlays were more than 20 percent of GNP in 1989. Force ratios are also high in Oman and the UAE; both countries had about twenty men in uniform per 1,000 population in 1989. Their respective rankings were eleventh and twelfth highest in the world. Bahrain and Kuwait had manpower levels of about ten per 1,000 population, whereas the level for Qatar was fifteen per 1,000 in 1989.

In spite of the small personnel pools and the desire of all the gulf governments to train nationals to replace foreigners as quickly as possible, constraints found in traditional Islamic societies prevent the widespread recruitment of women to serve in the armed forces. Oman and Bahrain have allowed a few women to enlist. They receive combat-style training and learn how to operate small arms. In Bahrain, however, almost all the women have been assigned to hospital staffs. In 1990 the UAE introduced a five-month training course for female recruits with the assistance of a team of female soldiers from the United States. About 1,200 women applied; only seventy-four were accepted. Two top members of the first class were selected to continue with officer training at the Royal

Military Academy at Sandhurst, in Britain. The other graduates of the first class were assigned as bodyguards of female members of the ruling families and as specialists in such fields as military intelligence.

Before the Persian Gulf War, some women served in support departments of the Kuwaiti armed forces, including engineering, military establishments, moral guidance, and public relations. In July 1991, noting that a large number of women had volunteered for service in the postwar military, the minister of defense said that some would be accepted for a training period of three to six months but would initially be unsalaried. A role would then be found for them. The minister cautioned that acceptance by Kuwaiti society was essential for the government to move ahead with this plan.

QATAR

In company with other gulf amirates, Qatar had long-standing ties with Britain but had remained under nominal Ottoman hegemony until 1916, when the British took over the foreign affairs and defense of Qatar. During the next five decades, Britain also exercised considerable influence in the internal affairs of the amirate. When the announcement came that it would withdraw its military forces from the gulf by 1971, Qatari leaders were forced to consider how to survive without British protection. Unable to support a large military establishment, Qatar has placed its reliance on small but mobile forces that can deter border incursions. Nevertheless, the Iran-Iraq War brought attacks on shipping just beyond its territorial waters, underscoring its vulnerability to interference with oil shipments and vital imports. In addition to seeking collective security through the GCC, Qatar has turned to close ties with Saudi Arabia, entering into a bilateral defense agreement in 1982.

The ruler in 1992, Shaykh Khalifa ibn Hamad Al Thani, had taken control of the country twenty years earlier, when the leading members of the ruling family decided that Khalifa's cousin, Ahmad ibn Ali Al Thani, should be replaced because of his many shortcomings as amir. As supreme commander of the armed forces, Khalifa ibn Hamad issued a decree in 1977 appointing his son and heir apparent, Hamad ibn Khalifa Al Thani, to the post of commander in chief. The same decree created the Ministry of Defense and named Hamad ibn Khalifa as minister. Hamad ibn Khalifa was a graduate of Sandhurst and had attained the rank of major general.

At the time of independence on September 3, 1971, the armed forces consisted of little more than the Royal Guard Regiment and some scattered units equipped with a few armored cars and four aircraft. By 1992 it had grown to a force of 7,500, including an army of 6,000, a navy of 700, and an air force of 800. In addition to the Royal Guard Regiment, the army had expanded to include a tank battalion, three mechanized infantry battalions, a special forces company, a field artillery regiment, and a SAM battery. The combined combat strength of these units, however, is estimated to be no more than that of a reinforced regiment in a Western army.

Initially outfitted with British weaponry, Qatar shifted much of its procurement to France during the 1980s in response to French efforts to develop closer relations. The tank battalion is equipped with French-built AMX-30 main battle tanks. Other armored vehicles include French AMX-10P APCs and the French VAB, which has been adopted as the standard wheeled combat vehicle. The artillery unit has a few French 155mm self-propelled howitzers (see table 40, Appendix). The principal antitank weapons are French Milan and HOT wire-guided missiles. Qatar had also illicitly acquired a few Stinger shoulder-fired SAMs, possibly from Afghan rebel groups, at a time when the United States was trying to maintain tight controls on Stingers in the Middle East. When Qatar refused to turn over the missiles, the United States Senate in 1988 imposed a ban on the sale of all weapons to Qatar. The ban was repealed in late 1990 when Qatar satisfactorily accounted for its disposition of the Stingers.

Three French-built La Combattante III missile boats, which entered service in 1983, form the core of the navy. The boats supplement six older Vosper Thornycroft large patrol boats. A variety of smaller craft are operated by the marine police.

The air force is equipped with combat aircraft and armed helicopters. Its fighter aircraft include Alpha Jets with a fighter-ground attack capability and one air defense squadron of Mirage F1s, all purchased from France. All of the aircraft are based at Doha International Airport. The planned purchase from the United States of Hawk and Patriot missile systems will give Qatar a modern ground-based air defense. British pilots on detail in Oman remain on duty with the air force, and French specialists are employed in a maintenance capacity. Nevertheless, an increasing number of young Qataris have been trained as pilots and technicians.

The lack of sufficient indigenous manpower to staff the armed forces is a continuing problem. By one estimate, Qatari citizens constitute only 30 percent of the army, in which more than twenty nationalities are represented. Many of the officers are of the royal family or members of leading tribes. Enlisted personnel are recruited from beduin tribes that move between Qatar and Saudi Arabia and from other Arab groups. Many Pakistanis serve in combat units. In 1992 there were still a number of British officers, as well as Britons, French, Jordanians, and Pakistanis in advisory or technical positions. More young Qataris are being recruited, and the number of trained and competent Qatari officers is steadily increasing.

Although official data on military expenditures are not published, the defense budget estimate of US$500 million for 1989 was 8 percent of the gross domestic product (GDP--see Glossary). The estimate of US$934 million for 1991, an increase of 80 percent over 1989, was presumably attributable to the costs of the Persian Gulf War. During the hostilities, the Qatari tank battalion was deployed to the Saudi-Iraqi border as part of Joint Forces Command East. Saudi and Qatari forces that had dug in to defend the road leading south from the border town of Ras al Khafji were forced to withdraw when the Iraqis made their only incursion onto Saudi territory on January 29, 1991. The three Saudi battalions and the one tank battalion from Qatar maintained contact with the Iraqi forces and participated in the coalition counterattack two days later that drove the Iraqis out of the town with considerable losses. The Qatari contingent, composed mostly of Pakistani recruits, acquitted itself well. The Qatari battalion also formed part of the Arab forces that advanced across Iraqi positions toward the city of Kuwait during the general coalition offensive on February 24, 1991. Beginning on January 22, 1991, Qatari aircraft joined other countries in carrying out strikes against Iraqi forces. United States, Canadian, and French fighter squadrons flew daily missions from Doha during the gulf war. One Qatari tank was lost in the engagement, and a number of Arab soldiers were killed or wounded. No Qatari combat deaths were reported during the war.

Although the amirate has experienced little internal unrest, the large number of foreigners--forming 80 percent of the work force--are regarded as possible sources of instability. Qatar is determined to maintain control over their activities and limit their influence. A significant number of resident Palestinians, some of whom included prominent businessmen and civil servants, were expelled after the Iraqi invasion of Kuwait. Iranian Shia have not been the source of problems but are nevertheless looked on as potential subversives. Foreigners are liable to face arbitrary police action and harassment and often complain of mistreatment after their arrest.

The Ministry of Interior has controlled the police force of about 2,500 members since 1990. The local police enforces laws and arrests violators. The General Administration of Public Security, which in 1991 replaced the Criminal Investigation Department, is a separate unit of the ministry charged with investigation of crimes. The Mubahathat (secret police office), a nearly independent branch of the Ministry of Interior, deals with sedition and espionage. The army's mission does not include internal security, although the army can be called on in the event of serious civil disturbances. Nevertheless, a separate agency, the Mukhabarat (intelligence service), is under armed forces jurisdiction. Its function is to intercept and arrest terrorists and to keep surveillance over political dissidents.

Qatar has both civil and sharia courts, but only sharia courts have jurisdiction in criminal matters. Lacking permanent security courts, security cases are tried by specially established military courts, but such cases have been rare. In sharia criminal cases, the proceedings are closed, and lawyers play no formal role except to prepare the accused for trial. After the parties state their cases and after witnesses are examined by the judge, the verdict is usually delivered with little delay. No bail is set, but in minor cases, charged persons may be released to a Qatari sponsor. Most of the floggings prescribed by sharia law are administered, but physical mutilation is not allowed, and no executions have occurred since the 1980s.

The police routinely monitor the communications of suspects and security risks. Although warrants are usually required for searches, this does not apply in cases involving national security. The security forces reportedly have applied severe force and torture in investigating political and security-related cases. Suspects can be incarcerated without charge, although this is infrequent. The United States Department of State noted that standards of police conduct have improved in spite of a 1991 incident in which a group of Qataris were detained without charge for two months in connection with the unauthorized publication of tracts and letters critical of the government; at least one member of the group, which included several members of the ruling family, is said to have been beaten.

BACKGROUND

As a regional commercial power in the nineteenth century, Oman held territories on the island of Zanzibar off the coast of East Africa, in Mombasa along the coast of East Africa, and until 1958 in Gwadar (in present-day Pakistan) on the coast of the Arabian Sea. When its East African possessions were lost, Oman withdrew into isolationism in the southeast corner of the Arabian Peninsula. Another of the gulf states with long-standing ties to the British, Oman became important in the British-French rivalry at the end of the eighteenth century, when Napoleonic France challenged the British Empire for control of the trade routes to the East. Although nominally a fully independent sultanate, Oman enjoyed the protection of the empire without being, de jure, in the category of a colony or a protected state. With its external defenses guaranteed and its overseas territories lost, the sultanate had no need for armed forces other than mercenaries to safeguard the personal position of the sultan.

In 1952, when the Saudis occupied Omani territory near the Al Buraymi Oasis, a British-led force from the Trucial Coast fought the incursion and retook the territory for the sultan. Later in the same decade, the sultan again called on British troops to aid in putting down a rebellion led by the former imam (see Glossary) of Oman, who attempted to establish a separate state free of rule from Muscat. British ground and air forces dispatched to aid the Muscat and Oman Field Force succeeded in overcoming the rebels in early 1959. Nevertheless, instead of a minor intertribal affair in Oman's hinterland, the rebellion became an international incident, attracting wide sympathy and support among members of the League of Arab States (Arab League) and the UN.

An agreement between Sultan Said ibn Taimur Al Said and the British government in 1958 led to the creation of the Sultan's Armed Forces (SAF) and the promise of British assistance in military development. The agreement included the detailing of British officers and confirmed the existing rights of Britain's Royal Air Force to use facilities at Salalah in Dhofar region and at Masirah, an island off the Omani coast in the Arabian Sea.

Sultan Said ibn Taimur was ultraconservative and opposed to change of any kind. Kindled by Arab nationalism, a rebellion broke out in 1964 in Dhofar, the most backward and exploited area of Oman. Although begun as a tribal separatist movement against a reactionary ruler, the rebellion was backed by leftist elements in the PDRY. Its original aim was the overthrow of Said ibn Taimur, but, by 1967, under the name of the Popular Front for the Liberation of the Occupied Arabian Gulf--which in 1974 was changed to the Popular Front for the Liberation of Oman (PFLO)-- it adopted much wider goals. Supported by the Soviet Union through the PDRY, it hoped to spread revolution throughout the conservative regimes of the Arabian Peninsula.

Said ibn Taimur's reprisals against the Dhofari people tended to drive them into the rebel camp. In 1970, as the Dhofari guerrilla attacks expanded, Said ibn Taimur's son, Qabus ibn Said Al Said, replaced his father in a coup carried out with the assistance of British officers. Qabus ibn Said, a Sandhurst graduate and veteran of British army service, began a program to modernize the country and to develop the armed forces. In addition to British troops and advisers, the new sultan was assisted by troops sent by the shah of Iran. Aid also came from India, Jordan, Pakistan, Saudi Arabia, and the Trucial Coast, all interested in ensuring that Oman did not become a "people's republic." An Iranian brigade, along with artillery and helicopters, arrived in Dhofar in 1973. After the arrival of the Iranians, the combined forces consolidated their positions on the coastal plain and moved against the guerrillas' mountain stronghold. By stages, the Omanis and Iranians gradually subdued the guerrilla forces, pressing their remnants closer and closer to the PDRY border. In December 1975, having driven the PFLO from Omani territory, the sultan declared that the war had been won. Total Omani, British, and Iranian casualties during the final two-and-one-half years of the conflict were about 500.

OMANI ROLE IN THE PERSIAN GULF WAR, 1991

Oman's perceptions of the strategic problems in the gulf diverge somewhat from those of the other Arab gulf states. Geographically, it faces outward to the Gulf of Oman and the Arabian Sea, and only a few kilometers of its territory--the western coast of the Musandam Peninsula--border the Persian Gulf. Nevertheless, sharing the guardianship of the Strait of Hormuz with Iran, Oman's position makes it of key importance to the security of the entire gulf. In its willingness to enter into strategic cooperation with the United States and Britain, Oman has always stood somewhat apart from the other gulf states. In 1980 Muscat and Washington concluded a ten-year "facilities access" agreement granting the United States limited access to the air bases on Masirah and at Thamarit and As Sib and to the naval bases at Muscat, Salalah, and Al Khasab. The agreement was renewed for a further ten-year period in December 1990. Although some Arab governments initially expressed their disapproval for granting the United States basing privileges, the agreement permitted use of these bases only on advance notice and for specified purposes. During the Iran-Iraq War, the United States flew maritime patrols from Omani airfields and based tanker aircraft to refuel United States carrier aircraft. The United States Army Corps of Engineers carried out considerable construction at the Masirah and As Sib air bases, making it possible to pre-position supplies, vehicles, and ammunition. Hardened aircraft shelters were built at As Sib and Thamarit for use of the ROAF.

Oman's traditionally good relations with Iran were strained by Iran's attacks on tanker movements in the gulf and Iran's emplacement of Chinese Silkworm antiship missile launchers near the Strait of Hormuz. The sultanate reinforced its military position on the Musandam Peninsula, which is only about sixty kilometers from Iranian territory.

After the Iraqi invasion of Kuwait, Oman declared its support for the multinational coalition ranged against Iraq. The facilities on Masirah became an important staging area for the movement of coalition forces to the area of conflict. Oman also contributed troops to Operation Desert Storm as part of the Arab contingent of Joint Forces Command East. A reinforced Omani brigade, along with Saudi, UAE, Kuwaiti, and other forces, participated in the ground assault paralleling the gulf coast that converged on the city of Kuwait. No Omani combat deaths were reported.

DEMOCRACY AND HUMAN RIGHTS

DEMOCRACY

Qatar is one of the more stable countries in the Middle East. While it follows a hereditary system of government, its people enjoy many freedoms, the most noteworthy is freedom of expression for which Qatar is renowned both regionally and on a global scale. The current Emir, Sheikh Hamad bin Khalifa Al Thani, has followed a clear democratic path since he assumed power in 1995. His Highness declared on 16 November 1998 his decision to amend the provisional constitution, establish an elected Central Municipal Council and work towards the formation of an elected Advisory Council within the framework of a new and permanent constitution.

MUNICIPAL COUNCIL

The Central Municipal Council was formed after the general election in March 1999. This was a direct result of HH the Emir, Sheikh Hamad bin Khalifa Al Thani, decision to direct the country towards democracy. With regional and international attention, all members of the council, the first of its kind, were elected by direct and secret ballot. All male and female citizens could equally stand for election. The participation of Qatari women as candidates and voters generated huge interest as a courageous and pioneering step for Qatar. Even though no women were elected, the step was nevertheless a great success. The council, which has advisory status, comprises twenty-nine members who meet regularly to debate all issues relevant to the operation of the various municipalities in the state. The council reports directly to the Ministry of Municipal Affairs and Agriculture.

PARLIAMENT PROJECT

In July 1999, HH the Emir, Sheikh Hamad bin Khalifa Al Thani, established a special high committee to draft a new permanent constitution. The formation of the Central Municipal Council is a first step towards an elected parliament where Qatari women are expected to be able to stand and to vote, a first for the counties of the Arabian Gulf. The committee, which comprises thirty-two members, will prepare a draft within three years of its formation.

HUMAN RIGHTS

Qatar, an Arab state on the Persian Gulf, is a monarchy with no constitution or political parties. Qatar is governed by the ruling Al-Thani family through its head, the Amir. The current Amir, Sheikh Hamad bin Khalifa Al-Thani, took power from his father in June 1995 with the support of leading branches of the Al-Thani family, and in consultation with other leading Qatari families. This transition of authority did not represent a change in the basic governing order. The Amir holds absolute power, the exercise of which is influenced by religious law, consultation with leading citizens, rule by consensus, and the right of any citizen to gain access to the Amir to appeal government decisions. The Amir

For additional analytical, business and investment opportunities information,
please contact Global Investment & Business Center, USA
at (202) 546-2103. Fax: (202) 546-3275. E-mail: rusric@erols.com
Global Business E-Books on Line: http://world.mirhouse.com

generally legislates after consultation with leading citizens, an arrangement institutionalized in an appointed advisory council that assists the Amir in formulating policy. In March citizens were permitted to participate in the election of a national body, the Central Municipal Council, for the first time. The judiciary is nominally independent, but most judges hold their positions at the Government's pleasure.

The country has efficient police and security services. The civilian security force, controlled by the Interior Ministry, comprises two sections: The police and the General Administration of Public Security and the investigatory police (Mubahathat), which is responsible for sedition and espionage cases. The Interior Ministry has a special state security investigative unit (Mubahith) that performs internal security investigations and gathers intelligence. In addition, there is an independent civilian intelligence service (Mukhabarat).

The State owns most basic industries and services, but the retail and construction industries are in private hands. Oil is the principal natural resource, but the country's extensive natural gas resources are playing an increasingly important role. Rapid development in the 1970's and 1980's created an economy in which foreign workers, mostly South Asian and Arab, outnumber citizens by a ratio of 4 or 5 to 1. The Government has embarked upon a program of " Qatarization, " which is aimed at reducing the number of foreign workers. Many government jobs are offered only to citizens and private sector businesses are encouraged to recruit citizens as well.

The Government restricts citizens' rights; however, there was substantial progress in a few areas. Citizens do not have the right to change their government; however, the Government's program of gradual democratic initiatives provided citizens with the opportunity to elect officials to the Central Municipal Council. Both male and female citizens were permitted to vote and to run for a seat on the Council. In addition a constitutional committee was convened in July to draft a permanent constitution that would provide for parliamentary elections. Arbitrary detention in security cases, and restrictions on the freedoms of speech, press, assembly, association, religion, and on workers' rights, continued to be problems. However, the Government continued to take some steps to ease restrictions on the practice of non-Muslim religions. Despite female suffrage, in practice women's rights are restricted by social customs. Noncitizen workers, who make up a majority of the residents of the country, face discrimination in the workplace.

RESPECT FOR HUMAN RIGHTS

RESPECT FOR THE INTEGRITY OF THE PERSON, INCLUDING FREEDOM FROM:

POLITICAL AND OTHER EXTRAJUDICIAL KILLING

There were no reports of political or other extrajudicial killings.

For additional analytical, business and investment opportunities information, please contact Global Investment & Business Center, USA at (202) 546-2103. Fax: (202) 546-3275. E-mail: rusric@erols.com Global Business E-Books on Line: http://world.mirhouse.com

DISAPPEARANCE

There were no reports of politically motivated disappearances.

C. TORTURE AND OTHER CRUEL, INHUMAN, OR DEGRADING TREATMENT OR PUNISHMENT

There have been no reported instances of torture for several years. The Government administers most corporal punishment prescribed by Islamic law but does not allow amputation.

Prison conditions generally meet minimum international standards.

The Government does not permit domestic human rights groups to exist, and no international human rights organization has asked to visit the country or its prisons.

D. ARBITRARY ARREST, DETENTION, OR EXILE

The law prohibits arbitrary arrest; however, the police have the discretion to arrest persons based on a low level of suspicion, and arbitrary detention in security cases remains a problem. The authorities generally charge suspects within 48 hours. Suspects generally are presented to the Attorney General within 24 hours of arrest. The Attorney General decides whether to hold the suspect up to a maximum of 4 days, after which time the suspect is presented before the judge, who may order the suspect released or remanded to custody to await trial. The accused is entitled to legal representation throughout this process. Suspects who are detained in security cases generally are afforded access to counsel; however, they may be detained indefinitely while under investigation. There were no known recent cases of incommunicado detention.

In June 1998, the Amir ordered the arrest of Abdulrahman Al-Nuaimi, a Ministry of Education official who distributed a letter to the press critical the Amir's decision to allow women to vote and run for office in the Municipal Council elections. Contrary to reports that he was released in 1998, Al-Nuaimi remains in custody.

The public trial of persons arrested for involvement in the February 1996 coup attempt continued. Sheikh Hamad Bin Jassim Bin Hamad Al-Thani, who was named as the prime suspect in the coup bid, was arrested under mysterious circumstances on or about July 23. He remains in custody following his appearance before the trial judge to answer charges of plotting to destabilize the regime and revealing military secrets to foreign powers. Prosecutors have called for the death penalty for all those accused, including Hamad Bin Jassim Bin Hammad. A verdict was expected in early December; however, the arrest of Hamad Bin Jassim Bin Hamad delayed proceedings into 2000.

Involuntary exile has occurred but is rare. There were no reported cases this year.

E. DENIAL OF FAIR PUBLIC TRIAL

The judiciary is nominally independent; however, most judges are foreign nationals who hold residence permits granted by the civil authorities, and thus hold their positions at the Government's pleasure. The number of citizen judges is increasing.

The judiciary deals with the bureaucracies of three ministries. Civil (or Adlea) courts are subordinate to the Ministry of Justice, and Shari'a (Islamic law) courts fall under the Ministry of Endowments and Islamic Affairs. The prosecutors fall under the Ministry of Interior.

There are two types of courts: The civil courts, which have jurisdiction in civil and commercial matters, and the Shari'a Court, which has jurisdiction in family and criminal cases. There are no permanent state security courts; however, although there have been no cases before these courts since the Amir assumed power, they have not been abolished formally by law and remain an option. Defendants tried by all courts have the right to appeal. The original case and the appeal in Shari'a Court are no longer heard by the same judge, and procedural loopholes that permitted this practice in the past are to be closed as part of a pending judicial reform package.

The legal system is biased in favor of citizens and the Government. A Muslim litigant may request the Shari'a Court to assume jurisdiction in commercial or civil cases. Non-Muslims are not allowed to bring suits as plaintiffs in the Shari'a Court; however, they may file suit in the civil courts. This practice prevents non-Muslim residents from obtaining full legal recourse. Trials in the civil courts are public, but in the Shari'a Court only the disputing parties, their relatives, associates, and witnesses are allowed in the courtroom. Lawyers do not play a formal role except to prepare litigants for their cases. Although non-Arabic speakers are provided with interpreters, foreigners are disadvantaged, especially in cases involving the performance of contracts.

Defendants appear before a judge for a preliminary hearing within 7 days of their arrest. Judges may extend pretrial detention for 1 week at a time to allow the authorities to conduct investigations. Defendants in the civil courts have the right to be represented by defense attorneys but are not always permitted to be represented by counsel in the Shari'a court.

Shari'a trials are usually brief. Shari'a family law trials are often held without counsel. After both parties have stated their cases and examined witnesses, judges are likely to deliver a verdict after a short deliberation. Criminal cases are normally tried within 2 to 3 months after suspects are detained. Suspects are entitled to bail, except in some instances, such as in cases of violent crime. Bail may be provided by citizens or noncitizens. Foreigners who are charged with minor crimes may be released to a citizen sponsor. They are prohibited from departing the country until the case is resolved.

There were no reports of political prisoners.

F. Arbitrary Interference with Privacy, Family, Home, or Correspondence

Traditional attitudes of respect for the sanctity of the home and the privacy of women provide a great deal of protection against arbitrary intrusion for most citizens and residents. A warrant must be obtained before police may search a residence or business, except in cases involving national security or emergencies. Search warrants are issued by judicial authorities. There were no reports of unauthorized searches of homes during the year. The police and security forces are believed to monitor the communications of suspected criminals, of those considered to be security risks, and of selected foreigners.

With prior permission, which is usually granted, citizens may marry foreigners of any nationality and apply for residence permits or citizenship for their spouses.

RESPECT FOR CIVIL LIBERTIES

A. Freedom of Speech and Press

Although the Government reduced restrictions on freedom of speech and of the press in 1996 and permitted a significant expansion of press freedom, some restrictions still remain. The Government formally lifted censorship of the media in 1995, and since then the press has been essentially free of government interference. However, journalists continue to practice self-censorship, due to real or perceived social and political pressures. Some journalists reportedly were subjected to pressure by the Government during the year after they published articles critical of it. No instance of explicit criticism of any citizen, whether of their public or private affairs, has been noted in local newspapers. Television and radio are state-owned, but the privately owned satellite television channel Al-Jazeera operates freely.

There were no reports of instances of political censorship of foreign news media or broadcasts of foreign programs on local television over the past year. The Censorship Office in the Ministry of Information was abolished (together with the Ministry) in 1996, but censors still work at broadcast media under the overall supervision of the Ministry of Religious Endowments. Pornography and expressions deemed hostile to Islam are subject to censorship, but in practice censorship is applied irregularly.

In July radio and television call-in programs addressed the sensitive subject of cash entitlements paid to members of the ruling Al-Thani family. Citizens expressed disagreement with the system in public forums, with no evidence of subsequent reprisals. However, one person did write a letter of retraction to a local newspaper a few days after her comments.

A Ministry of Education official who wrote a letter critical of the Amir's decision to allow women to vote and run for office in the Municipal Council elections remains in custody (see Section 1.d.).

For additional analytical, business and investment opportunities information, please contact Global Investment & Business Center, USA at (202) 546-2103. Fax: (202) 546-3275. E-mail: rusric@erols.com Global Business E-Books on Line: http://world.mirhouse.com

Customs officials screen imported print media, videocassettes, and other such items for pornography, but have stopped blocking the importation of non-Muslim religious items.

A growing number of citizens and residents have access to the Internet, which is provided through the state-owned telecommunications monopoly. Internet service is censored for pornographic content through a proxy server, which blocks those web sites containing certain key words and phrases. A user who believes that a site is censored mistakenly may submit the web address to the Internet service provider to have the site reviewed for suitability. The Government is responsive to these submissions.

Citizens enjoy broad freedom of speech, but are restricted by the social and family restraints of a very traditional society. There is no apparent fear of government monitoring of private speech. However, the larger foreign population does not believe it enjoys the same freedoms and acts accordingly.

There is no legal provision for academic freedom. Most instructors at the University of Qatar exercise self-censorship.

B. FREEDOM OF PEACEFUL ASSEMBLY AND ASSOCIATION

The Government severely limits freedom of assembly. The Government does not allow political demonstrations.

The Government severely limits freedom of association. The Government does not allow political parties or membership in international professional organizations critical of the Government or of any other Arab government. Private social, sports, trade, professional, and cultural societies must be registered with the Government. Security forces monitor the activities of such groups.

C. FREEDOM OF RELIGION

The state religion is the conservative Hanbali school of the Sunni branch of Islam, as interpreted by Muhammad Ibn Abd Al-Wahab, an 18th century religious reformer who emphasized the strict observance of religious duties. The Government officially prohibits public worship by non-Muslims; however, it tolerates and protects private services conducted in private with prior notification to the authorities. The Government has indicated, through foreign diplomats and in meetings with Christian leaders, its long-range intention to identify and lease parcels of land to the recognized Catholic, Anglican, and Orthodox communities upon which they would be permitted to erect churches, albeit without bells or the external display of crosses. In the meantime, the Government has indicated its support for the lease of existing villas for use in worship services by such groups, provided that they obtain the Qatari landlord's approval.

The community of the Church of Jesus Christ of Latter-Day Saints (Mormons) now meets in a villa leased for the express purpose of worship. The police provide traffic control for authorized Catholic services, which may be attended by up to 1,000 or more persons at times. The Government recently began to issue visas to Christian clergy under foreign embassy sponsorship. There are no restrictions on non-Muslims providing religious instruction to their children. However, non-Muslims may not proselytize and conversion from Islam is theoretically a capital offense. However, there is no record of an execution for such a conversion since independence.

The Government allows Shi'a Muslims to practice their faith freely; however, community leaders have agreed to refrain from certain public practices such as self-flagellation.

D. FREEDOM OF MOVEMENT WITHIN THE COUNTRY, FOREIGN TRAVEL, EMIGRATION, AND REPATRIATION

There are no restrictions on internal travel, except around sensitive military and oil installations. In general, women do not require permission from male guardians to travel. However, men may prevent female relatives from leaving the country by providing their names to immigration officers at ports of departure. Technically, women employed by the Government must obtain official permission to travel abroad when requesting leave, but it is not known to what extent this regulation is enforced. Citizens critical of the Government face restrictions on their right to travel abroad.

All citizens have the right to return. Foreigners are subject to immigration restrictions designed to control the size of the local labor pool. Foreign workers must have the permission of their sponsor (usually their employer) to enter and depart the country, but their dependents may leave the country without restriction. Foreign women who are married to citizens are granted residence permits and may apply for citizenship; however, they are expected to relinquish their foreign citizenship.

The Government has not formulated a formal policy regarding refugees, asylees, or first asylum. Those attempting to enter illegally, including persons seeking asylum from nearby countries, are refused entry. Asylum seekers who are able to obtain local sponsorship or employment are allowed to enter and may remain as long as they are employed. A Bahraini Air Force pilot defected to Qatar in 1996, and the Government stated that he was free to stay, calling him a refugee and offering him its full protection.

RESPECT FOR POLITICAL RIGHTS

THE RIGHT OF CITIZENS TO CHANGE THEIR GOVERNMENT

Citizens do not have the right to change their government or the political system peacefully. The political institutions blend the characteristics of a traditional Bedouin tribal state and a modern bureaucracy. There are no political parties or organized opposition groups. However, in March citizens had the opportunity to choose officials to the Central Municipal Council in free and fair elections.

The Amir exercises most executive and legislative powers, including appointment of cabinet members. On March 8, citizens elected a 29-member Central Municipal Council.

For the first time, men and women age 18 and older were permitted both to vote and to run as candidates. The Council is a nonpartisan body that addresses issues such as street repair, green space, trash collection, and public works projects. Its role is to advise the Minister of Municipalities and Agriculture. The Council cannot change policy on its own.

Under the amended Provisional Constitution, the Amir must be chosen from and by the adult males of the Al-Thani family.

In November 1998, the Amir announced his intention to form a constitutional committee to draft a permanent constitution that would provide for democratic parliamentary elections. The constitutional committee was inaugurated on July 13 and includes a number of government officials, academics, and prominent business leaders. The Amir reiterated in his remarks to the committee members that he expects their efforts to lead to the establishment of an elected parliamentary body.

Women have the right to vote and some ran as candidates for the Central Municipal Council, but none were elected.

GOVERNMENTAL ATTITUDE REGARDING INTERNATIONAL AND NONGOVERNMENTAL INVESTIGATION OF ALLEGED VIOLATIONS OF HUMAN RIGHTS

The Government does not permit local human rights organizations to exist. No international human rights organizations are known to have asked to investigate conditions in the country. However, Amnesty International and foreign embassies were invited to send observers to sessions of the public trial of those accused in the 1996 coup attempt. Foreign observers attended the trial sessions held during the year.

DISCRIMINATION BASED ON RACE, SEX, RELIGION, DISABILITY, LANGUAGE, OR SOCIAL STATUS

Institutional, cultural, and legal discrimination based on gender, race, religion, social status, and disability exists. Women

Violence against women and spousal abuse occur but are not believed to be widespread. Some foreign domestic servants, especially those from South Asia and the Philippines, have been mistreated by employers. According to Shari'a (Islamic law), all forms of physical abuse are illegal. The maximum penalty for rape is death. The police actively investigate reports of violence against women. In the last few years, the Government demonstrated an increased willingness to arrest and punish offenders, whether citizens or foreigners. Offenders who are citizens usually receive lighter punishments than do foreigners. Abused domestic workers usually do not press charges for fear of losing their jobs.

The legal system allows leniency for a man found guilty of committing a " crime of honor, " a euphemism that refers to a violent assault against a female by a male relative for alleged sexual misconduct; however, such honor killings are rare. In September a former minister, Ali Saeed Al-Khayareen, killed his two half-sisters for their alleged sexual misconduct. Al-Khayareen was being held at the Al-Rayyan detention center, but reportedly was released late in the year.

The activities of women are restricted closely both by law and tradition. For example, a woman is prohibited from applying for a driver's license unless she has permission from a male guardian. This restriction does not apply to noncitizen women. The Government adheres to Shari'a in matters of inheritance and child custody. While Muslim wives have the right to inherit from their husbands, non-Muslim wives do not, unless a special exception is arranged. In cases of divorce, Shari'a prevails; younger children remain with the mother and older children with the father. Both parents retain permanent rights of visitation. However, local authorities do not allow a noncitizen parent to take his or her child out of the country without permission of the citizen parent. There has been a steady increase in the number and severity of complaints of spousal abuse by the foreign wives of local and foreign men. Women may attend court proceedings but generally are represented by a male relative; however, women may represent themselves.

Women largely are relegated to the roles of mother and homemaker, but some women are now finding jobs in education, medicine, and the news media. Women appear to receive equal pay for equal work; however, they often do not receive equal allowances. These allowances generally cover transportation and housing costs. Increasingly, women are receiving government scholarships to pursue degrees at universities overseas. The Amir has entrusted his second wife, who is the mother of the Heir Apparent, with the high-profile task of establishing a university in Doha.

In 1996 the Government appointed its first female undersecretary, in the Ministry of Education. Although women legally are able to travel abroad alone (see Section 2.d.), tradition and social pressures cause most to travel with male escorts. There also have been complaints that Qatari husbands take their foreign spouses' passports and, without prior approval, turn them in for Qatari citizenship documents. The husbands then inform their wives that the wives have lost their former citizenship. In other cases, foreign wives report being forbidden by their Qatari husbands or in-laws to visit or to contact foreign embassies.

There is no independent women's rights organization, nor has the Government permitted the establishment of one.

CHILDREN

The Government demonstrates its commitment to children's rights through a well-funded, free public education system (elementary through university) and a complete medical protection program for Qatari children. However, children of most foreigners are denied free education and have only limited medical coverage.

Very young children, usually of African or South Asian background, have been used as jockeys in camel races. Little information is available on wages and working conditions for these children (see Sections 6.c. and 6.d.).

There is no societal pattern of abuse of children.

PEOPLE WITH DISABILITIES

The Government has not enacted legislation or otherwise mandated provision of accessibility for the disabled, who also face social discrimination. The Government maintains a hospital and schools that provide high-quality, free services to the mentally and physically disabled.

RELIGIOUS MINORITIES

Shi'a Muslims fill many positions in the bureaucracy and are prominent in business. However, they experience discrimination in employment in some sensitive areas, such as security.

NATIONAL/RACIAL/ETHNIC MINORITIES

The Government discriminates against some citizens of non-Qatari origin. In the private sector, many citizens of Iranian origin occupy some of the highest positions. However, they rarely are found in senior decisionmaking positions in government.

WORKER RIGHTS

A. THE RIGHT OF ASSOCIATION

The right of association is strictly limited, and all workers, including foreigners, are prohibited from forming labor unions. Despite this restriction, almost all workers have the right to strike after their case has been presented to the Labor Conciliation Board and ruled upon. Employers may close a place of work or dismiss employees once the Conciliation Board has heard the case. The right to strike does not exist for government employees, domestic workers, or members of the employer's family. No worker in a public utility or health or security service may strike if such a strike would harm the public or lead to property damage. Strikes are rare.

The Labor Law provides for the establishment of joint consultative committees composed of representatives of the employer and workers. The committees do not discuss wages but may consider issues such as organization and productivity, conditions of employment, training of workers, and safety measures and their implementation.

Since 1995, Qatar has been suspended from the U.S. Overseas Private Investment Corporation (OPIC) insurance programs because of the Government's lack of compliance with internationally recognized worker rights standards.

B. THE RIGHT TO ORGANIZE AND BARGAIN COLLECTIVELY

Workers are prohibited from engaging in collective bargaining. In general wages are set unilaterally by employers without government involvement. Local courts handle disputes between workers and employers.

There are no export processing zones.

C. PROHIBITION OF FORCED OR COMPULSORY LABOR

The law prohibits forced or compulsory labor. Three-quarters of the work force are foreign workers, who are dependent on a single employer for residency rights. This leaves them vulnerable to abuse. For instance, employers must give consent before exit permits are issued to any foreign employee seeking to leave the country. Some employers temporarily withhold this consent to force foreign employees to work for longer periods than they wish. The Government prohibits forced and bonded labor by children and generally enforces this prohibition effectively; however, some very young children work as jockeys in camel races (see Sections 5 and 6.d.).

D. STATUS OF CHILD LABOR PRACTICES AND MINIMUM AGE FOR EMPLOYMENT

Minors between the ages of 15 and 18 may be employed with the approval of their parents or guardians and some children may work in small, family-owned businesses. However, child labor is rare. Education is compulsory through the age of 15. Very young children, usually of African or South Asian background, are used as jockeys in camel races (see Sections 5 and 6.c.) and 6.f.). Little information is available on wages and working conditions for these children. The Government prohibits forced and bonded labor by children and generally enforces this prohibition effectively (see Section 6.c.).

Minors may not work more than 6 hours a day or more than 36 hours a week. Employers must provide the Ministry of Labor with the names and occupations of their minor employees. The Ministry may prohibit the employment of minors in jobs that are judged dangerous to the health, safety, or morals of minors. Employers also must obtain permission from the Ministry of Education to hire a minor.

E. ACCEPTABLE CONDITIONS OF WORK

There is no minimum wage, although a 1962 law gives the Amir authority to set one. The 48-hour workweek with a 24-hour rest period is prescribed by law, although most government offices follow a 36-hours-per-week work schedule. Employees who work more than 48 hours per week, or 36 hours per week during the Muslim month of Ramadan, are entitled to overtime pay. This law is adhered to in government offices and major private sector companies. It is not observed with respect to domestic and personal employees. Domestic servants frequently work 7 days per week, more than 12 hours per day, with few or no holidays, and have no effective way to redress grievances against their employers.

The Government has enacted regulations concerning worker safety and health, but enforcement, which is the responsibility of the Ministry of Energy and Industry, is lax. The Department of Public Safety oversees safety training and conditions, and the state-run petroleum company has its own set of safety standards and procedures. The Labor Law of 1964, as amended in 1984, lists partial and permanent disabilities for which compensation may be awarded, some connected with handling chemicals and petroleum products or construction injuries. The law does not specifically set rates of payment and compensation.

Foreign workers must be sponsored by a citizen or a legally recognized organization to obtain an entry visa and must have their sponsor's permission to depart the country. Any worker may seek legal relief from onerous work conditions, but domestic workers generally accept their situations in order to avoid repatriation. The Government also penalizes Qatari employers who violate residence and sponsorship laws. Some foreign domestics have been mistreated by their employers (see Section 5).

F. TRAFFICKING IN PERSONS

The law prohibits trafficking in persons, and there were no confirmed reports that persons were trafficked in, to, or from the country during the year.

For additional analytical, business and investment opportunities information,
please contact Global Investment & Business Center, USA
at (202) 546-2103. Fax: (202) 546-3275. E-mail: rusric@erols.com
Global Business E-Books on Line: http://world.mirhouse.com

STRATEGIC INFORMATION FOR CONDUCTING BUSINESS

OIL AND NATURAL GAS

OIL

In 1935, after years of behind-the-scenes wrangling involving the shaykh, British and United States oil companies, the British, and the Saudis, an onshore concession was granted to the AngloPersian Oil Company, which transferred the concession to Petroleum Development (Qatar), an affiliate of the Iraq Petroleum Company (IPC). British, French, and United States oil companies held shares in IPC. Petroleum Development (Qatar) was renamed the Qatar Petroleum Company (QPC) in 1953.

As a result of adequate crude oil supplies at the time, exploratory drilling in Qatar did not begin until 1938. Oil was discovered in Dukhan, on the west coast, in 1939. By 1940 about 4,000 barrels per day (bpd--see Glossary) were being produced. World War II and its aftermath brought development to a halt between 1942 and 1947, and exports did not begin until 1949. The Dukhan field extends south from Dukhan along the west coast and has three oil reservoirs layered progressively deeper between limestone formations and a natural gas field underlying them all. Dukhan crude has an American Petroleum Institute (API) rating of 40 and a sulfur content of 1.2 percent. A pipeline carries crude from the Dukhan fields to storage, refining, and terminal facilities on the east side of the peninsula at Umm Said.

In 1952 a Royal Dutch Shell subsidiary, Shell Company of Qatar (SCQ), obtained a concession for offshore exploration on the continental shelf. Most offshore discoveries centered on the island of Halul, about ninety kilometers east of Doha. The major offshore fields and the dates they were discovered are Idd ash Sharqi (1960) and Maydan Mahzam (1963). Offshore production began in 1964. Because Qatar and Abu Dhabi claimed the Al Bunduq field, the two parties agreed to exploit it jointly starting in 1969. Another offshore field was discovered in the summer of 1991 by Elf Aquitaine Qatar. Offshore crude had an API rating of 36 and a sulfur content of 1.4 percent. Offshore crude is stored at facilities on the island of Halul, which also has pumping stations and two single-buoy moorings for loading tankers. Combined offshore and onshore reserves as of January 1990 were 4.5 billion barrels, offering thirty-two years of production at 1989 levels.

Both concessions were for seventy-five years and gave the oil companies the right to explore, produce, refine, transport, and market all oil found in the stipulated area. In addition, the concessionaire companies were exempt from taxes and duties on imports and exports but were required to hire local labor where possible. The Anglo-Persian Oil Company (after a down payment of 400,000 rupees in 1935) was required to pay Shaykh Abd Allah ibn Qasim 150,000 rupees annually thereafter . (During World War II, when oil operations were suspended, the annual payment was 300,000 rupees.) Before commercial production could begin, an industry had to be assembled. The company built

For additional analytical, business and investment opportunities information, please contact Global Investment & Business Center, USA at (202) 546-2103. Fax: (202) 546-3275. E-mail: rusric@erols.com Global Business E-Books on Line: http://world.mirhouse.com

a jetty at Bir Zikrit and shipped in water, foodstuffs, and almost 100,000 tons of equipment and supplies from Bahrain before the first drop of oil was pumped. Once exports began, oil became extremely profitable in Qatar and in the rest of the Persian Gulf as a result of favorable concession terms, cheap labor, relatively inexpensive drilling and pumping costs, and easy access to transportation.

In 1952 the 1935 concession agreement was revised (in line with others in the region) to split profits fifty-fifty between the company and the ruler. Shaykh Ali ibn Abd Allah's share rose from about US$1 million in 1950 to US$61 million in 1958, after which his profits dipped to US$53 million in 1959 and did not rise to the 1958 level until 1963. Some money reached the local economy, but the initial impact of oil exports consisted mainly of high incomes for the Al Thani and high inflation on basic commodities.

From its initial concession in 1935, QPC kept aloof from the shaykh and was seen by the ruler and workers as high-handed and inept; for example, it triggered strikes by forgetting to issue workers' coffee rations or inadvertently forcing them to work during Muslim holidays. In the 1950s, the company had its own infrastructure (power, water, communications, and housing) and provided health care to workers and police protection to its facilities.

To gain some leverage over the oil company with regard to revenues, pricing, and production, Qatar joined the Organization of the Petroleum Exporting Countries (OPEC) in 1961, one year after it was formed. Qatar has stayed close to its OPEC production quota when it has been in its economic interest but has often exceeded its quota to compensate for soft markets or to take advantage of the price increases that resulted from the Iraqi invasion of Kuwait in August 1990.

Between 1960 and 1970, annual oil production more than doubled, from 60.4 million barrels (165,000 bpd) to 132.5 million barrels (363,000 bpd). Production peaked in 1973 at 208.2 million barrels (570,000 bpd). Between 1974 and 1980, production leveled off in the range of 410,000 bpd to 520,000 bpd. The early 1980s saw a steady decline, apart from a small recovery in 1984, with an annual production of 151.5 million barrels (415,000 bpd). After another flat period in the mid 1980s, production levels rose once again in the late 1980s and early 1990s, with 146.7 million barrels (402,000 bpd) produced in 1990 (see table 20, Appendix). The 395,000 bpd production levels of 1989 and the first eight months of 1990 exceeded OPEC quotas.

After independence in 1971, the Qatar National Petroleum Company was created in 1972 to handle oil operations. In 1973 the government held 25 percent each of QPC and SCQ. Two years later, the Qatar General Petroleum Corporation (QGPC) was established, and the government signed new agreements with the oil companies giving QGPC 60 percent ownership. By 1977 onshore and offshore operations were fully nationalized, and service contracts were given to former concessionaires.

Production of petroleum products began in 1953 when a QPCowned refinery started up with a capacity of 600 bpd. By 1975 refining capacity had expanded to 6,000 bpd, and by the early 1980s another 4,000-bpd-capacity had been added. A refinery opened in

1983 and added 50,000 bpd in capacity, bringing the national total to more than 60,000 bpd. The National Oil Distribution Company refined an average of 62,000 bpd in 1990; 75 percent of production was exported. As a result of the jump in prices caused by the Iraqi invasion of Kuwait, 1990 profits were 40 percent higher (US$1 billion) than in 1989. Most of the refined products are consumed locally.

NATURAL GAS

The Qatari government celebrated twenty years of independence in September 1991 with the inauguration of Phase One of the North Field development project. The gas project, in a 6,000-squarekilometer field off Qatar's northeast coast, is supervised by Bechtel of the United States and by Technip Geoproduction of France. The project marks a major step in Qatar's switch from a reliance on oil to gas for most of its revenues. The North Field is the world's largest natural gas field, and its exploitation will place Qatar in the top ranks of the world's gas producers. Natural gas from other fields provides fuel for power generation and raw materials for fertilizers, petrochemicals, and steel plants. With the expected depletion of oil reserves by about 2023, planners hope natural gas from the North Field will provide a significant underpinning for the country's economic development.

In the early 1970s, Qatar flared about 80 percent of the 16.8 million cubic meters of natural gas produced daily in association with crude oil liftings. In that decade, the country made progress in using its natural gas resources despite several setbacks. Whereas nearly 66 percent of onshore gas was flared in 1974, by 1979 that proportion had fallen to less than 5 percent.

Two natural gas liquids (NGL) plants began operation in Umm Said in 1981. NGL-1 used gas produced from the Dukhan field, and NGL-2 processed gas associated with offshore fields. The combined daily capacities were 2,378 tons of propane, 1,840 tons of butane, 1,480 tons of condensate, and 2,495 tons of ethane-rich gas. However, repeated difficulties prevented the plants from coming on-line as scheduled and operating at full capacity. A massive explosion at the precursor of NGL-1 in 1977 killed six people and caused US$500 million in damage. NGL-2 had problems with the pipelines that connected the plant with offshore fields. The sharp drop in oil production in the 1980s meant that lack of feedstock caused plant shutdowns and underproduction. As a result, downstream (see Glossary) users suffered as well. In 1982 the two plants produced 500,000 tons of propane and butane-- slightly more than one-half of plant capacity. Condensate production lagged even further at 138,000 tons, or 40 percent of capacity.

This gloomy outlook is mitigated to some degree by hope for development of the massive natural gas reserves in the North Field. Discovered in 1972 by SCQ, its proven reserves of 4.6 million cubic meters (as of 1989) will be productive well into the twenty-first century. The Qatar Liquefied Gas Company (Qatargas) was established in 1984 as a joint venture with QGPC and foreign partners to market and export liquefied natural gas (LNG) from the North Field.

For additional analytical, business and investment opportunities information, please contact Global Investment & Business Center, USA at (202) 546-2103. Fax: (202) 546-3275. E-mail: rusric@erols.com Global Business E-Books on Line: http://world.mirhouse.com

Phase One of the US$1.3 billion project was officially inaugurated on September 3, 1991. By the end of the month, it was pumping 23 million cubic meters of gas per day from sixteen wells. This is expected to meet an estimated 17 million cubic meters per day of domestic demand.

QGPC plans a massive development at Ras Laffan in association with the North Field project. In addition to a new port with LNG, petroleum products, and container loading berths, project plans include a 2,500-ton per year methanol plant and a 450,000-ton per year petrochemical complex. The development is scheduled for completion in the late 1990s.

In line with its desire to diversify the firms engaged in developing its resources, Qatar signed a letter of intent in February 1991 with Chubu Electrical Power Company of Japan to supply 4 million tons per year of North Field gas for twenty-five years, starting in 1997. This amount represents two-thirds of Qatargas's expected capacity of about 6 million tons per year.

ECONOMIC AND SOCIAL DEVELOPMENT

Gross National Product (GNP) US$12 billion
GNP per capita: US$21,000
Growth rate: 3%
Inflation: 1%

Major industries: Oil production and refining, fertilisers, petrochemicals, steel, cement

Main trading partners: Japan, Italy, Germany, and UK

The main focus of the state's efforts is the development of the Qatari people and the national economy. It is natural that the oil and gas sectors should be the main concern of the government who are continuing to develop Qatar's petroleum resources in an optimal way.

Qatar General Petroleum Corporation (QGPC) have put in place a strategy to develop the North Field gas reservoir, discovered in 1971, and use this resource to obtain new income streams. There are plans to export gas via pipelines and as liquefied natural gas (LNG). New industries will also be built.

The state is striving to diversify its income sources by establishing basic industries such as petrochemicals, steel, chemical fertilisers and cement. It also provides incentives to the private sector to build light and medium industries, provides opportunities for investments and encourages all kinds of trade.

The state also encourages the agriculture, animal and fishing industries, in spite of difficult circumstances, as it recognises these to be important elements in the developmental process. Great attention is given to the optimal use of land, capital, water and animal resources.

At the forefront of the state's priorities is providing the highest levels of social stability and prosperity to its citizens and all residents. Education is available at all levels and specialities up to university level. There are also a number of private schools for the different communities.

The state also pays particular attention to youth affairs and sports activities. Sport programs were first established in 1961, followed by the establishment of sporting associations in the late seventies and then the Higher Council of Youth Affairs and the Olympic Committee.

The Youth and Sports General Authority oversees 40 youth establishments, 16 sports associations and more than 9 sporting clubs, a cultural club and a scientific one.

In addition, the state provides advanced social services to its low-income citizens, the disabled and the elderly. Housing and other necessary assistance is provided.

A health care umbrella covers the whole country and provides integrated services of prevention, cure and rehabilitation through a linked chain of basic care centres to major hospitals.

The communications and transport network has made huge strides in the area of telecommunications. Qatar now enjoys direct dialling to more than 200 countries, while the domestic network has more than 122,000 lines. The postal service operates on the most modern scientific methods.

The country's ports have been developed, expanded and provided with the necessary infrastructure to enable them to keep up with economic development. The important ports in Qatar are Doha, Mesaieed and Ras Laffan.

The state provides water and electricity to consumers through the many projects completed to meet expanding demand and the requirements of gas and major industries. Three power stations provide electric energy to the country, Ras Abu Fontas, Ras Abu Aboud and Al Arish.

ENERGY SECTOR[3]

---

[3] *Qatar contains the third largest natural gas reserves and the largest non-associated gas field in the world. Qatar is also emerging as a major exporter of liquefied natural gas. An OPEC member, Qatar exports over 600,000 barrels of oil per day.*

Since 1995, Qatar has been ruled by Sheikh Hamad bin Khalifa al-Thani, who took power in a palace coup against his father. Sheikh Hamad has implemented several changes in policy, including a limited political liberalization creating an elected council and giving women the right to vote. In the economic sphere, Qatar has suffered from many of the same problems as other oil-dependent Persian Gulf states, especially the need to diversify economic development beyond crude oil exports and scale back the generous state subsidies for consumers, which date from the oil boom of the 1970s and early 1980s.

Qatar's real gross domestic product (GDP) grew at an annual rate of 3.3% in 1999, after posting growth of only 0.3% in 1998 due to low oil prices. The projected real GDP growth rate for 2000 is 4.6%, and around 5% after 2000, based mainly on rising production and sales of natural gas. Inflation in Qatar remains low, at 2.2% for 1999 and projected at 2.3% for 2000.

Qatar's policy of economic diversification has led to a surge in investment in projects for the export of liquefied natural gas (LNG) and petrochemicals. The government expects that it will be able to earn more per barrel of crude oil produced if it can export refined products and petrochemicals, as well as create private sector jobs - in a country which has been heavily dependent on government ministries to provide employment for the population.

The main short-term economic problem for Qatar is servicing its debt, which rose from under $5 billion to over $10 billion between 1994 and 1996, and surged to nearly $12 billion in 1999. Qatar accumulated this debt largely for infrastructure investment in oil and gas projects, which sharply increased Qatar's oil production capacity, construction of facilities for the export of LNG, and petrochemical plants. The increase in revenues which was expected, however, was interrupted by low crude oil prices in 1998 and early 1999, and by the Asian financial crisis. The recovery in prices for crude oil, as well as the start of deliveries from the RasGas LNG project, have greatly eased Qatar's debt payment burden.

Qatar recorded a budget surplus for the 1999/2000 fiscal year, which ended in March 2000. This was the first budget surplus in several years. The budget for the 2000/2001 fiscal year will be in surplus if Qatar's crude oil continues to sell for an average of at least $15 per barrel.

OIL

Qatar has proven, recoverable oil reserves of 3.7 billion barrels, of which about 2.2 billion barrels are located in the Dukhan field, Qatar's only onshore field. The remaining proven 1.5 billion barrels are held in six offshore fields Bul Hanine, Maydan Mahzam, Id al-Shargi North Dome, al-Shaheen, al-Rayyan, and al-Khalij. Qatar contains crude oil with gravities in the 24°-41° API range. The country's two primary export streams are Dukhan (41° API) and Marine (36° API) blend. Despite the country's significant oil

For additional analytical, business and investment opportunities information, please contact Global Investment & Business Center, USA at (202) 546-2103. Fax: (202) 546-3275. E-mail: rusric@erols.com Global Business E-Books on Line: http://world.mirhouse.com

production and reserves, oil accounts for less than 15% of domestic energy consumption. Qatar exports almost all of its oil production to Asia, with Japan its largest customer. In 1999, net oil exports totaled 760,000 barrels per day (bbl/d), and production has risen in mid-2000 as a result of OPEC's decision to increase production quotas at its March 2000 meeting.

In 1999, Qatar produced 806,000 bbl/d of liquids, up from 782,000 bbl/d in 1998, and only 466,000 bbl/d as recently as 1994, before Qatar began its rapid expansion of production capacity. As of May 2000, Qatar's monthly crude oil production was averaging 680,000 bbl/d. The country also produces a significant amount of lease condensate and other natural gas liquids (NGLs), both of which fall outside Qatar's OPEC crude production quota of 658,000 bbl/d, which became effective July 1, 2000.

Following the coup in 1995, Qatar initiated a number of new policies aimed at increasing oil production, locating additional oil reserves before existing reserves become too expensive to recover, and investing in advanced oil recovery systems to extend the life of existing fields. To accomplish this, the government, in recent years, has improved the terms of exploration and production contracts and production sharing agreements (PSA). The improved terms are designed to encourage foreign oil companies to improve oil recovery in producing fields and to explore for new oil deposits.

Onshore Development
In March 1998, Qatar signed an onshore oil exploration agreement with Chevron Corporation. It is a five-year PSA and exploration agreement, covering a 4,209 square-mile area known as Block-2. Block-2 covers virtually all of the Qatari peninsula except for the Dukhan field. Seismic surveys were conducted in 1998, and drilling commenced in 1999. Chevron also holds offshore Block-1 jointly with Hungary's MOL.

OFFSHORE DEVELOPMENT

One of Qatar's newer oil fields is al-Rayyan, operated by BP Amoco, which recently acquired Atlantic Richfield Corporation (Arco). Arco took over as operator from Wintershall and began exploration in September 1995. Wintershall, British Gas, and Gulfstream Petroleum also own significant shares. The field came on stream in November 1996, producing 20,000 bbl/d of heavy oil from four wells. It lies in offshore Block-11 at the southern edge of the North Field near Ras Laffan. The PSA for the field was signed on July 16, 1997. Al-Rayyan has been producing about 25,000 bbl/d in recent months, and BP Amoco and its consortium partners are investing in further development of the field which will bring its production capacity up to 60,000 barrels per day. The field eventually will have five production wells to tap most of the reserves in place, as well as one delineation well.

Qatar's latest offshore oil field to come onstream is al-Khalij. Production began in March 1997, after five years of exploration and appraisal work, at an initial rate of 6,000 bbl/d. Al-Khalij is located in Block-6, along Qatar's maritime border with Iran, and to the east of the North Field. Development of the field had been delayed since 1991 as Elf Aquitaine Qatar, the field's operator, sought improved production sharing terms from Qatar

General Petroleum Corporation (QGPC). In October 1997, Elf increased production to 20,000 bbl/d. Production in early 2000 was running at 32,000 bbl/d. Elf expects to eventually raise production further to 50,000-60,000 bbl/d. Al-Khalij produces a medium/sweet (28° API) oil with about 1% sulphur. The oil is piped to Halul Island for processing and transportation. Elf holds a 55% interest in the 25-year PSA, with an option for a five-year extension. The remaining 45% interest is held by Italy's Agip.

Maydan Mahzam became operational in 1965, and its production is currently about 75,000 bbl/d, which is down significantly from its peak. However, QGPC is currently undertaking a renovation intended to extend the life of the field. This work includes plans for 37 new wells over the next decade.

Bul Hanine came on line in 1973, producing well over 100,000 bbl/d, but production began falling off in the early 1990s. Output fell to 120,000 bbl/d in 1991, 90,000 bbl/d in 1993, and 70,000-80,000 bbl/d currently. Development plans to boost production include drilling 86 new wells, and QGPC recently announced a tender for work related to gas-reinjection to maintain pressure in the field. Bul Hanine holds approximately 700 million barrels of recoverable reserves.

Al-Shaheen, operated by Maersk Oil Qatar of Denmark, has become one of Qatar's productive oil fields, with production of around 150,000 bbl/d. Located in Block-5 about 43 miles off Qatar's northeastern coast, al-Shaheen produces a sour (29°-33° API) oil with 1.7%-2% sulphur. The field is thought to be linked to a section of the North Field.

Id al-Shargi North Dome (ISND), first discovered by Shell in 1960 and now operated by Occidental Petroleum (Oxy), lies 59 miles east of Qatar's northern tip. In 1994, the field was producing 12,000 bbl/d when Occidental signed a 25-year PSA with QGPC, agreeing to invest $700 million in field development, reservoir repairs, gas and water injection systems, and further exploration. Recent output from ISND has reached 135,000 bbl/d. Production is expected to surpass 150,000 barrels per day in 2001.

In December 1997, Occidental signed another PSA with QGPC to develop the Id al-Shargi South Dome (ISSD) oil field. ISSD is located 15 miles from ISND, and Oxy will operate ISSD as a satellite of ISND, keeping overall per-unit operating costs lower. The field came onstream in November 1999, and is expected to reach production of 50,000 bbl/d by the end of 2000. Occidental's ownership interest in ISSD is 44%, and the company plans to invest $450 million during the life of the project, with $400 million to be spent over the first five years. ISSD is estimated to contain recoverable reserves of 200 million-300 million barrels.

A longtime dispute has existed between Qatar and Bahrain over their rights to waters between them in the Persian Gulf and ownership of the Hawar Islands. The dispute has been submitted to the International Court of Justice (ICJ) in the Hague, and oral arguments in the case took place in June 2000. A decision is expected before the end of 2000. Some analysts suspect that the oil deposits of Qatar's onshore Dukhan field may extend northward to the Hawar Islands and waters offshore.

For additional analytical, business and investment opportunities information, please contact Global Investment & Business Center, USA at (202) 546-2103. Fax: (202) 546-3275. E-mail: rusric@erols.com Global Business E-Books on Line: http://world.mirhouse.com

DOWNSTREAM

Qatar's National Oil Distribution Company (Nodco) is upgrading its refinery at Umm Said. The upgrade will increase capacity from 57,500 bbl/d to 83,000 bbl/d. A 30,000 bbl/d condensate refining unit also is being built on the same site. The projects are expected to be completed by the end of 2001.

In March 1997, QGPC signed a memorandum of understanding (MOU) with the foreign partners of Qatar Liquefied Natural Gas Company (Qatargas) and Ras Laffan Liquefied Natural Gas Company (Rasgas), providing for construction of a $400-million, 80,000-bbl/d condensate refinery at Ras Laffan. After its proposed completion in 2002, the plant will process condensate from the two companies' North Field developments. Condensate streams from the North Field contain high levels of mercaptan sulfur compounds and consequently are unable to be processed at most refineries.

In November 1997, Phillips Petroleum Company signed an $1.1-billion deal with QGPC to build a petrochemical plant, Q-Chem. The plant will have the capacity to produce 500,000 tons per year of ethylene and 467,000 tons per year of polyethylene, including high-density and linear low-density polyethylene. QGPC holds a majority 51% stake in the project, and Phillips holds the remaining 49% stake. Bank financing for the project was secured in mid-1999. The plant is expected to begin exports in 2002.

NATURAL GAS

With proven reserves of 300 trillion cubic feet (Tcf), Qatar's natural gas resources ranks third in size behind Russia's and Iran's. Most of Qatar's gas is located in the North Field, which contains 380 Tcf of in-place and 239 Tcf of recoverable reserves, making it the largest known non-associated gas field in the world. In addition, the Dukhan field contains an estimated 5 Tcf of associated and 0.5 Tcf of non-associated gas. Smaller associated gas reserves also are contained in the Id al-Shargi, Maydan Mahzam, Bul Hanine, and al-Rayyan oil fields. The Qatari government believes that the country's economic future lies in developing this vast gas potential. Currently, Qatar has two liquefied natural gas (LNG) exporters: Qatar LNG Company (Qatargas); and Ras Laffan LNG Company (Rasgas).

The Qatargas downstream consortium comprises QGPC (65%), Total (10%), Mobil (10%), Mitsui (7.5%), and Marubeni (7.5%). In December 1996, the Qatargas venture delivered its first shipment of LNG to Japan. The Qatargas LNG plant consists of three, 2-million-ton-per-year (Mmt/y) (97 billion cubic feet - Bcf) trains. The third train was completed in 1999. Qatargas has plans to add a fourth train by 2002.

Rasgas is Qatar's second LNG project. The two major shareholders in the project are QGPC and Mobil. Rasgas consists of two 2.5-Mmt/y (122 Bcf) trains. The first train was completed in early 1999, and loaded its first cargo in August 1999 for South Korea's Kogas, which has a supply contract. The second train came onstream in April 2000. A tender for planned third and fourth trains is planned for late summer 2000.

For additional analytical, business and investment opportunities information, please contact Global Investment & Business Center, USA at (202) 546-2103. Fax: (202) 546-3275. E-mail: rusric@erols.com Global Business E-Books on Line: http://world.mirhouse.com

In May 2000, ExxonMobil and QGPC signed a final development and production sharing agreement for the North Field. The Enhanced Gas Utilization (EGU) project will develop upstream infrastructure in a portion of the field for domestic use, export to neighboring Persian Gulf states, and use as a feedstock for petrochemical projects. The initial phase of the project will produce 500 million cubic feet per day (Mmcfd), with eventual capacity slated to rise to 1.75 Bcf/d.

Qatar's original markets for its LNG exports were Japan and South Korea, the world's two largest LNG importers. India also has become a major market for Qatari LNG. While Enron cancelled its LNG plant, which was to supply its Dabhol power plant in India, RasGas signed an agreement in July 1999 to supply 7.5 Mmt/y (365 Bcf/y) of LNG to Petronet, a gas distribution consortium in India, beginning in mid-2003. CMS Energy of the United States also has purchased some spot cargoes of Qatari LNG.

Another significant proposed project will tie Qatar into the United Arab Emirates (UAE) Dolphin Project, an integrated gas pipeline grid for Qatar, UAE, and Oman, with a possible subsea connection linking Oman to Pakistan. The United Offsets Group (UOG), a UAE state owned corporation backing the project, signed preliminary memorandums of understanding with Qatar, Oman, and Pakistan in June 1999. Mobil also signed a preliminary agreement in June 1999 for the gas supply from Mobil's production capacity in the North Field. The total project is expected to cost $10 billion, including costs associated with the development of more extensive gas distribution networks in the UAE and Oman. Qatar initially will sell around 800 Bcf/y of North Field gas, starting in 2002, transported through a pipeline linking the North Field to Abu Dhabi in the UAE. Construction is to start in 2001, and links between Abu Dhabi, Dubai, and Oman should be completed by 2003. UOG announced in March 2000 that TotalFinaElf and Enron had been selected to implement the project, and each will have an equity stake of 24.5%. TotalFinaElf will develop its concession in the North Field to provide gas, while Enron will focus on pipeline development. The Dolphin Project has been driven in part by the desire of UAE and Oman to use more natural gas for power generation and industrial use, and the decline in their own production of associated natural gas due to OPEC crude oil production cuts. Pakistan's participation is doubtful, due to its financial condition and the possibility of imports from Iran.

Kuwait also has held discussions with Qatar about the purchase of Qatari gas. A preliminary agreement was signed for gas sales in May 2000, which would source the gas from ExxonMobil's North Field holdings. Details of the project and volumes are still being discussed.

ELECTRICITY

Qatar currently has an electric generation capacity of 1,445 megawatts (MW), and produces 6.7 billion kilowatthours of electricity per year. Most of the country's power plants are gas-fired. The residential sector accounts for 80% of Qatar's electricity consumption. In response to recent financial pressures, the Qatari government announced in 1999 that it would limit the provision of free electricity to Qatari-citizen households, with payment required for consumption above a set threshold.

For additional analytical, business and investment opportunities information, please contact Global Investment & Business Center, USA at (202) 546-2103. Fax: (202) 546-3275. E-mail: rusric@erols.com Global Business E-Books on Line: http://world.mirhouse.com

In May 2000, the Qatari government took a major step towards privatization of its power sector. Assets owned by the Ministry of Electricity and Water (MEW) were transferred to the Qatar General Electricity and Water Corporation (QEWC). QEWC is 57% controlled by local investors and 43% controlled by the government.

The Ras Abu Fontas B-plant is the country's largest and newest power and water desalination plant. It has an electric generation capacity of 650 MW and water output of 33 million gallons per day. QEWC has solicited bids for a planned 400 MW expansion of the plant, and an award is pending.

QEWC issued a tender in May 2000 for the proposed Ras Laffan Independent Power and Water Project ("Ras Laffan IWPP"), which will be co-located with the Ras Laffan gas and industrial complex. The plant will have a generating capacity of 750 MW when completed, with the first 400 MW scheduled to be operational by 2003. The successful bidder will take a 55% stake in the project, with QEWC holding 25%.

Sources for this report include: CIA World Factbook 1999; Dow Jones News Wire service; Economist Intelligence Unit ViewsWire; Gulf News; Hart's Middle East Oil and Gas; International Market Insight Reports; Oil and Gas Journal; Petroleum Economist; Petroleum Intelligence Weekly; U.S. Energy Information Administration; WEFA Middle East Economic Outlook.

INDUSTRY

The government has established heavy industry to diversify Qatar's economy. The pattern has been to allow foreign firms to provide expertise in planning, construction, management, and marketing in return for minority shares in the companies. Oil revenues have funded the construction of plants and the development of infrastructure; natural gas has been used as a source of power and as feedstock. The country's main power generation and water desalination plants are at Ras Abu Abbud and Ras Abu Fintas. Electrical generating capacity in 1990 was 1,095 megawatts, and there were plans to add an additional 234 megawatts in the early 1990s. Power consumption in 1990 stood at 4,818 million kilowatt-hours and peak demand at 987 megawatts. Bureaucratic delays stalled many projects, and poor market conditions and technical problems doomed others to unprofitability. Major construction projects such as factories are seldom completed on schedule.

The Industrial Development Technical Centre (IDTC), formed in 1973, directs much of Qatar's industrialization, apart from petroleum extraction. The IDTC identifies industries to meet Qatar's medium- and long-term needs and coordinates industrial planning. In addition, the IDTC monitors the performance of all industries on a monthly basis. In the early 1980s, the center began assessing the environmental impact of industrial plants and production. The IDTC has also been involved in pilot manufacturing programs: in 1989 it announced the formation of the Qatar Industrial Manufacturing Company, owned partly by the government and designed to establish small- and medium-sized enterprises and to buy shares in existing companies.

The country's center for heavy industry is Umm Said. Smaller industries and businesses are concentrated in the As Salwa Industrial Area. The government encourages business and industry by offering, among other things, low-interest loans; free road, water, and electrical hookups; subsidized electricity and water; land leases at minimal cost; and protective tariffs and tax incentives.

The three largest enterprises are the Qatar Fertilizer Company (Qafco), Qatar Steel Company (Qasco), and Qatar Petrochemical Company (Qapco). Qafco was established in 1969 and since 1975 has been owned by OGPC (75 percent) and Norsk Hydro of Norway (25 percent). The government took over Qafco's management in 1991. The Qafco facility, which uses methane-rich natural gas from the Dukhan field as feedstock to produce ammonia and urea, has been less affected by periodic drops in oil production than plants relying on offshore natural gas. Production increased steadily in the 1970s, and a second plant opened in 1979. Nonetheless, because of a steep decline in world fertilizer prices, in 1986 Qafco faced its first operating losses since 1977, despite record levels of production (660,000 tons of ammonia and 744,000 tons of urea). In 1990 Qafco produced 710,000 tons of ammonia (down from 714,000 tons in 1989) and 760,000 tons of urea (down from 778,561 tons in 1989). It had profits of US$40 million in that year. India and China are Qafco's main customers.

Qasco was established in 1974 with 70 percent state ownership. Kobe Steel Company (20 percent) and Tokyo Boeki (10 percent) of Japan hold the remaining shares. Japanese companies initially handled construction, production, marketing, and export. The Qasco plant, which began producing in 1978, has consistently outproduced its 330,000-ton per year design capacity. Its main products are steel bars used to reinforce structural concrete. The plant uses imported iron ore and local scrap; its direct reduction and rolling stages are rated as highly efficient. Despite high levels of output, lack of demand and low prices have contributed to millions of dollars in losses.

Production levels have risen steadily from the outset, with 1979 production at 378,544 tons of steel bars. Because of declines in world steel prices, in 1982 the plant registered its first losses despite a 485,000-ton production level. The mid1980s saw a sharp decline in demand and increased foreign competition. The company registered a loss of US$13.7 million in 1985. In response to cheaper Japanese and Korean imports, the government imposed a 20 percent tariff on bars similar to those produced domestically. The plant returned to profitability in 1988. Qasco took over management of the plant in 1989; Kobe Steel Company remained as consultant. In 1990 Qasco produced a record 565,000 tons of steel bars, up from 556,538 tons in 1989. Plans to expand the plant were approved. Saudi Arabia has been the principal customer, followed by the UAE and other gulf countries.

Qapco's petrochemical complex in Umm Said started production in 1981 with an annual output of 132,679 tons of ethylene, well below its 280,000-ton capacity. The plant also has a capacity to produce 140,000 tons of linear low-density polyethylene (LLDPE) and small amounts of sulfur and propylene. QGPC holds 84 percent of the company, and ORKEM of France holds the remaining 16 percent.

Shortages in feedstock caused by troubles in 1982 with gas pipelines from the offshore fields caused production to drop by one-half. Such difficulties, combined with sluggish sales in the early and mid-1980s, contributed to large operating losses: QR69 million in 1984; QR156 million in 1985; and QR57 million in 1986. The end of the decade, however, saw significant improvement, with profits of around QR420 million in 1989 and production of ethylene at 295,000 tons, LLDPE at 181,000 tons, and sulfur at 52,000 tons.

As a result of the 1989 cabinet reshuffle, the Supreme Council for Planning (SCP) was formed to coordinate the diversification of Qatar's economy by, among other things, encouraging industries linked to the North Field gas project . There are plans for a US$500 million petrochemical complex and also a 240,000-ton per year aluminum smelter at Umm Said that will use North Field gas.

Some industries that are smaller but important suppliers of the domestic market include a flour mill and several cement companies. The Qatar Flour Mills Company processes flour and bran from wheat. It began production in 1969, and output in the 1980s was 700 tons per day. The Qatar National Cement Company (QNCC), owned jointly by the government and private shareholders, uses local gypsum in cement production. QNCC was established in 1965 with a production capacity of 100,000 tons per year. By 1982 the plant had a capacity of 330,000 tons per year. Annual production varied as a result of the competition of cheap imports, and after achieving an output of 319,740 tons in 1985, production declined steadily. Following a low of 160,000 tons in 1988, in 1990 the plant produced 327,000 tons of cement in 1990.

LABOR

The discovery of oil brought wage labor to Qatar, removing many pearl divers, fishermen, and herders from reliance on a subsistence economy that was plagued with privation, debt, and other hardships and setting them in a new system of relatively steady labor for cash. But the work force did not consist entirely of free males. In the early 1950s, there were about 3,000 slaves, brought from Africa, in the peninsula. The 250 slaves who were working for Petroleum Development (Qatar) in 1949 turned over 80 to 95 percent of their wages to their owners. (After the British political agent expressed his disapproval of the practice to the shaykh, the ruler decreed reluctantly that slaves could keep 50 percent of their wages.)

Because there were no labor regulations in the 1940s and 1950s, hours, conditions, and wages varied widely. Some workers were paid less than one rupee per day, others received as much as four rupees per day. (In contrast, a man working on a pearl boat might earn only sixty rupees in six months.) Sometimes overtime was compensated; at other times it was not. In the late 1930s and into the 1940s, workers put in seven-day weeks, with only one day off per month. Workers were often dismissed for minor infractions and endured humiliating treatment and difficult, dangerous conditions to hold their jobs.

For additional analytical, business and investment opportunities information, please contact Global Investment & Business Center, USA at (202) 546-2103. Fax: (202) 546-3275. E-mail: rusric@erols.com Global Business E-Books on Line: http://world.mirhouse.com

The special skills of the pearl divers were used to help set up offshore rigs. Other workers were employed as drivers, cooks, and houseboys for British personnel, and still others were employed as roustabouts. There were four levels of salaries and amenities in Petroleum Development (Qatar). At the top were the British engineers and foremen, next the clerks (mostly Indians), then the drivers, and then the laborers at the bottom of the pay and accommodation scale. Local merchants acted as representatives of the oil company and collected one rupee from Qataris and forty to fifty rupees from foreigners for work certificates.

At the outset, the unskilled laborers were Qataris and other gulf Arabs. They had frequent disagreements with the oil company's management, most of whom were non-Qataris, and some disagreements flared into strikes. Early strikes focused on wages, conditions, and benefits. In addition, the shaykh often encouraged strikes to pressure concessions from the oil company at the times he was negotiating new contracts.

During one strike in 1951, Qatari workers opposed those from Dhofar (in present-day Oman). To resolve the matter, the Dhofaris were deported (a solution to labor disputes that, along with imprisonment, continued to be used in the early 1990s). Shaykh Ali ibn Abd Allah freed the slaves in 1952 and paid 1,500 rupees each to 660 of them. A major strike in 1955 by Qatari workers induced the shaykh to form a Qatari riot squad to be used against them. In 1956 well-organized oil workers joined opposition forces in demonstrations against the regime and against the British. In response, the government inserted clauses in labor contracts banning political activity.

In 1959 a labor department was established to deal with oil workers. In 1962 a labor law was enacted that gave preference in hiring first to Qataris, then to other Arabs, and finally to other foreigners. Strict controls existed on foreign workers, whose visas stipulated that they must work for a specific Qatari sponsor at a specific job. In practice, there was some fluidity in employment. Trade unions were banned, but Qatari workers had workplace-based organizations, known as workers' committees, that dealt with grievances. The country's labor court was the first in the gulf. The government has sought to encourage Qataris to take jobs in the industrial work force (the process of "Qatarization"). In 1993, however, the majority of laborers and middle-level employees, were foreigners.

All foreign workers require sponsorship by a Qatari, some of whom illegally charge their employees high fees for renewing sponsorship. Other abuses include breach of contract and physical or sexual abuse.

Regulations govern safety in the workplace, but these are unevenly enforced. The labor force represents 42 percent of the population, with 7 percent of the force made up of women. Those women who work outside the home are often teachers, nurses, clerks, or domestic servants. In-service industries absorb 69 percent of the work force, industry 28 percent, and agriculture 3 percent.

AGRICULTURE AND FISHING

Small-scale farming, nomadic herding, pearling, and fishing were the predominant means of subsistence in the region for the centuries before the discovery of oil. Although the relative importance of these activities has declined as a means of livelihood (with commercial pearling disappearing completely), the government has attempted to encourage agriculture and fishing to provide a degree of self-sufficiency in food.

Between 1960 and 1970 agriculture grew. The number of farms, for example, increased fourfold to 411. Qataris who own agricultural land or properties generally hold government jobs and hire Iranians, Pakistanis, or non-Qatari Arabs to manage their farms. The government operates one experimental farm. Of land under cultivation in 1990, about 48 percent was used for vegetables (23,000 tons produced), 33 percent for fruit and date production (8,000 tons), 11 percent for fodder (70,000 tons), and 8 percent for grains (3,000 tons). In 1990 the country had approximately 128,000 head of sheep, 78,000 goats, 24,000 camels, 10,000 cattle, and 1,000 horses. There are also dairy farms and about 2,000 chickens for poultry. All but 20 percent of local demand for eggs is met domestically. Despite the encouragement of agriculture and fishing, these two elements of the economy together produced only about 1 percent of the gross domestic product (GDP--see Glossary) in 1989

Severe conditions, such as extremely high temperatures and lack of water and fertile soil, hinder increased agricultural production. The limited groundwater that permits agriculture in some areas is being depleted so rapidly that saltwater is encroaching and making the soil inhospitable to all but the most salt-resistant crops. According to estimates, groundwater will be depleted about the year 2000. As a partial solution, the government plans to expand its program of using treated sewage effluent for agriculture. Parkland and public gardens in Doha are already watered in this way.

The Qatar National Fishing Company was incorporated in 1966 to fish for shrimp in territorial waters and to process catches in a refrigerated factory. Japan is a large market for Doha's commercial fish. The total catch of fish and other aquatic animals for 1989 was 4,374 tons.

TRANSPORTATION AND TELECOMMUNICATIONS

In 1993 Qatar had 1,500 kilometers of roads, 1,000 of which were paved and the rest gravel. Most paved highways are centered in the Doha area or radiate from the capital to the northern end of the peninsula, to Dukhan on the west coast, or southwest to the border with Saudi Arabia to connect with the Saudi highway system. Outside the capital and the principal highways, however, large stretches of country are accessible only by vehicles with four-wheel drive.

Facilities for air and water transportation are located in or near the capital. Doha is the main port, having four berths capable of handling ships up to nine meters in draught and five additional berths that can accommodate ships requiring 7.5 meters of water. Forty kilometers south of Doha, Umm Said handles petroleum exports. Doha International Airport, with a 4,500-meter runway, accommodates all types of airplanes. Qatar is part owner of Gulf Air, the flag carrier for Qatar, Bahrain, the UAE, and Oman. Most

For additional analytical, business and investment opportunities information, please contact Global Investment & Business Center, USA at (202) 546-2103. Fax: (202) 546-3275. E-mail: rusric@erols.com Global Business E-Books on Line: http://world.mirhouse.com

international air traffic to and from Qatar is shunted through Bahrain, but Gulf Air and a few international carriers offer nonstop service from Doha to other points in the Middle East, South Asia, the Philippines, and France.

Domestic and international telecommunications are excellent. In 1992 Qatar had 110,000 telephones, or twenty-three per 100 inhabitants, a per capita figure higher than many European nations. Radio-relay and submarine cables link Qatar with all the Arab states around the Persian Gulf. Three satellite ground stations, one operating with the International Telecommunications Satellite Organization's (Intelsat) Atlantic Ocean satellite, one operating with Intelsat's Indian Ocean satellite, and one operating as part of the Arab Satellite Communication Organization (Arabsat) system, provide excellent international telephone and data links and live television broadcasts. Seven AM and three FM radio stations have programs in Arabic, French, Urdu, and English. A powerful shortwave station with broadcasts in Arabic and English is heard worldwide.

MONEY AND BANKING

The Indian rupee was the principal currency until 1959, when the government replaced it with a special gulf rupee in an effort to halt gold smuggling into India. In 1966 Qatar and Dubayy jointly established a currency board to issue a Qatar-Dubayy riyal. In 1973 Qatar introduced its own riyal, which was pegged to the International Monetary Fund's (IMF-- see Glossary) special drawing rights (SDR--see Glossary). The exchange rate is tied to the United States dollar at a rate of QR3.64 per US$1.00.

The Qatar Monetary Agency (QMA), established in 1973, has most of the traditional powers and prerogatives of a central bank. The QMA regulates banking, credit, and finances; issues currency; and manages the foreign reserves necessary to support the Qatari riyal. Unlike many central banks, the agency shares control over the country's reserves with what was in 1973 the Ministry of Finance and Petroleum. QMA does not act as the state's banker, which is the preserve of the Qatar National Bank (QNB).

QMA's long-time governor, Majid Muhammad al Majid as Saad, was replaced in January 1990 by Abd Allah Khalid al Attiyah, who had been general manager of QNB. The position of governor was upgraded to ministerial level, signaling a more assertive future role for QMA in the country's banking sector.

Banks give loans at rates between 7 and 9 percent, and they pay 7 percent on deposits. About fifteen local and foreign banks operate in Qatar. Two banks--Qatar Islamic Bank, licensed in 1989, and Qatar International Islamic Bank, licensed in 1990-- reflect a trend toward Islamic banking that started in Saudi Arabia.

Banking in the gulf has been vulnerable to the shaky regional security situation. As a result of the Iraqi invasion of Kuwait, banks in Qatar lost an estimated 15 to 30 percent of deposits in late 1990.

BUDGET

For additional analytical, business and investment opportunities information,
please contact Global Investment & Business Center, USA
at (202) 546-2103. Fax: (202) 546-3275. E-mail: rusric@erols.com
Global Business E-Books on Line: http://world.mirhouse.com

Oil and gas revenues make up 90 percent of government revenue, and government spending is the primary means of injecting these earnings into the economy. Given the small size of the local market, government spending generates most of the economic activity. Because of increased involvement in the international economic scene, in April 1989 Qatar's fiscal year was changed from the Islamic to the Gregorian calendar.

Large budget surpluses in the 1970s funded major development projects, with government spending leveling off and dropping in the 1980s, years of more modest oil revenues. After years of surpluses, the government had a deficit of nearly QR8 billion in 1983. The government has attempted to keep deficits down by reducing the number of new projects and delaying those under way. In addition, the fiscal situation of the regime can often be gauged by the amount of time required to pay contractors.

Budgets offer only a rough estimate of actual government spending. Many significant items, such as military and amirate expenses, do not appear. Projections are consistently conservative, and deficits often are lower than predicted. In the 1986-87 period, when oil prices plummeted, the government did not even announce a budget. Restrained spending in recent years has meant frustration for contractors relying on government contracts, but the policy has also led to ever-shrinking deficits. The budget continued to show a deficit in the early 1990s

Overseas assets are estimated at between US$10 and US$14 billion. These assets have been periodically tapped to make up for shortfalls in oil revenues.

TRADE

The main export and source of revenue is oil, although the government's efforts to diversify Qatar's industrial base have resulted in the growth of other exports. Crude oil, petroleum products, and LNG accounted for 82 percent of exports in 1989, chemicals (ammonia and urea) accounted for 12.4 percent, and manufactures (mainly steel) accounted for 5.1 percent. Total earnings for the year were QR9.7 billion. Japan was the largest customer at 54.4 percent of purchases, followed by Thailand (5.0 percent) and Singapore (4.0 percent)

Because imports are financed by oil revenues, the level of goods coming into the country rises and falls with the oil economy. Between 1969 and 1979, for example, the value of imports grew an average of 40 percent annually. Imports declined in the early to mid-1980s, sinking to a low of QR4.0 billion in 1986, then rising gradually until they reached QR4.8 billion in 1989.

Machinery and transportation equipment accounted for 37.0 percent of imports in 1989, manufactured goods for 23.9 percent, food and live animals for 15.1 percent, and chemicals and chemical products for 6.0 percent. The main import sources were Japan (18.8 percent), Britain (11.6 percent), the United States (8.8 percent), Italy (7.8 percent), and the Federal Republic of Germany (West Germany) (7.3 percent).

For additional analytical, business and investment opportunities information, please contact Global Investment & Business Center, USA at (202) 546-2103. Fax: (202) 546-3275. E-mail: rusric@erols.com Global Business E-Books on Line: http://world.mirhouse.com

In keeping with a Gulf Cooperation Council (GCC) agreement, Qatar raised tariffs from 2.5 to 4.0 percent in 1984. In addition, there is a 20 percent duty on steel products similar to those produced by Qasco. Qatar plays a small role in the regional entrepôt trade. Most imports arrive by sea and are for local use, with only a small percentage reexported to Saudi Arabia and the UAE.

CURRENCY

Legal tender in Qatar is the Qatari Riyal. This came into being in 1973, the former currencies being the Indian Rupee and, briefly, the Qatar and Dubai Riyal (from 1996 to 1973). All currency is issued in the name of the Qatar Central Bank and the notes bear the signatures of the Minister of Finance, Economy and Trade, along with the Governor of the Central Bank. The Riyal is divided into 100 dirhams. Notes exist for 1, 5, 10, 50, 100 and 500 Riyals, and coins for 25 and 50 dirhams. Apparently there are still some smaller denomination coins in existence, but these have not been minted since the 1970s! In line with other modern currencies, Riyal notes are protected by security devices such as serial numbers and water marks. The currency is pegged at a fixed rate to the US dollar at 1 $US = 3.65 Qatari Riyals and is freely convertible into other currencies.

QATARI RIYAL NOTES:

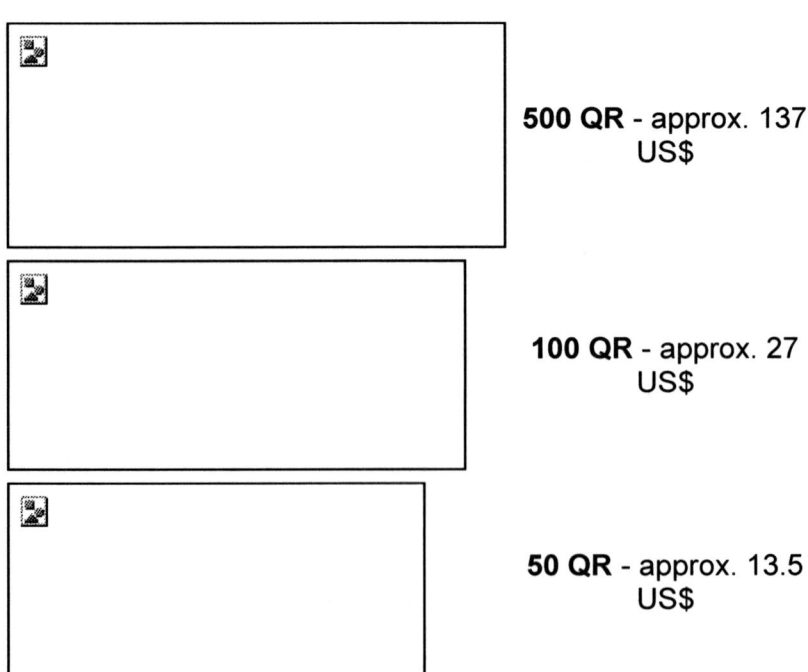

500 QR - approx. 137 US$

100 QR - approx. 27 US$

50 QR - approx. 13.5 US$

For additional analytical, business and investment opportunities information, please contact Global Investment & Business Center, USA at (202) 546-2103. Fax: (202) 546-3275. E-mail: rusric@erols.com Global Business E-Books on Line: http://world.mirhouse.com

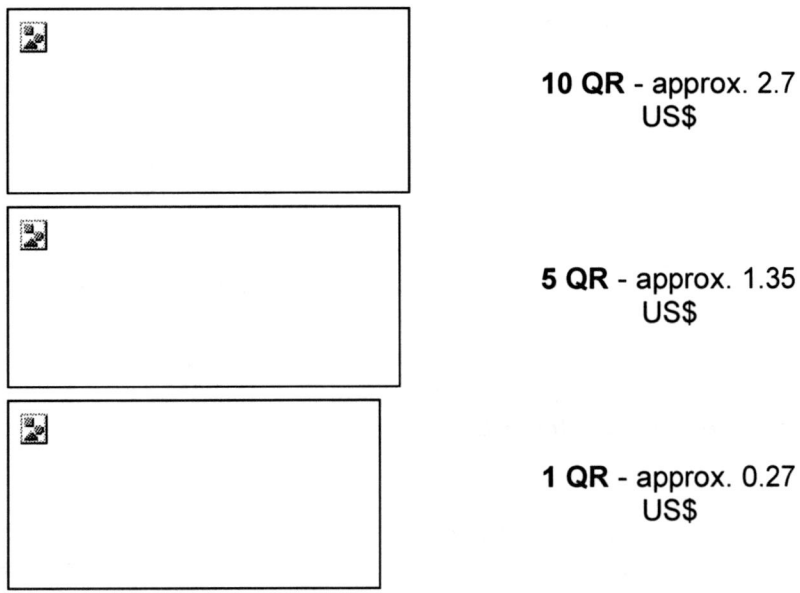

10 QR - approx. 2.7 US$

5 QR - approx. 1.35 US$

1 QR - approx. 0.27 US$

BANKING

The Commercial Bank of Qatar was established in1975,as the first wholly owned private Commercial Bank in Qatar. Initially capitalised at QR 10 million is has grown and prospered over the years to become an important regional bank with Capital and Reserves of over QR500 million and a total Assets boom of QR 4.6 billion as at 31.12.99. It has been profitable in every year since its foundation and has paid dividends annually.

It is CBQs ultimate objective to become the Bank of Choice in Qatar for Retail, Investment and Corporate Banking Services and to expand offshore where suitable opportunities arise

The Bank dominates the Retail sector. Its customers issue over 17% or 1 in every 6 cheques in the system. It issues over 50% of all credit cards in Qatar and handles over 95% of the merchant card acquiring business. It is the only bank to deal with all major international cards – Visa, MasterCard, Diners, American Express and J.C.B and it handles over 30% of the vehicle finance business in the country. According to Moody's the rating agency, CBQ has " a Strong and Defensible franchise especially in Retail banking".

Corporate banking also remains very much at the centre of the of the Bank's activities and will continue to do so. With the vast and sustainable improvement in export revenues, new opportunities for project and syndicated banking will present themselves locally and internationally. Excluding Government and quasi Government business it is probably placed second amongst banks in Qatar and has a strong and loyal corporate business base which can be developed.

In 1999 we launched the Visa Platinum Card and we introduced the first reward programme for our Diners Club members and premier Visa Card Brands. In essence these reward programmes offer airline miles and hotel accommodation for all eligible card expenditure. Partners include Gulf Air through their Falcon Frequent Flyer Programme for Visa cardholders and American Airlines, United Airlines, Bass hotels, Best Western , Starwood Group of Hotels are just some of the partners for Diners Club ACCOLADES members.
At the start in the new millennium, we introduced a special service for our most valuable customers; the Platinum Service which is designed to take banking to a new level offering exclusive privileges to the members.

CBQ's Investment Division has been no less active in developing and offering new products. A new Islamic fund is now available to our customers and we have recently launched the third in our series of Tejari Guaranteed Funds (TGF3). As before, TGF3 gives its Banks clients the ability to achieve stock market level performance with the assurance that the principle sum invested will be completely protected.

QATAR INDUSTRIAL BANK (QIB)

With a view to encouraging private sector participation in industrial development through small and medium-scale industries, the Government of Qatar founded the Qatar Industrial Bank in 1997 through the participation of local commercial banks. QIB provides soft loans to deserving private sector industries with easy terms of repayment.

THE DOHA SECURITIES MARKET

The opening of the Doha Securities Market or Stock Exchange in 1997 has given a major boost to the financial sector in the country. At present trading is limited to Qatari investors, although there are plans to open the market to foreign investors through mutual funds and other trading instruments. Currently, 18 different shareholding companies are listed on the market, with around Nine Billion QR market capitalisation. Seven firms, including three national banks, have been accredited to act as brokers at the stock market. It is expected that the opening of the Doha Securities Market will fuel economic growth, facilitate privatisation in the country, limit potential out-flow of capital, encourage and attract investors, and will ultimately promote the image of the State of Qatar. The Government also has plans to licence the operation of offshore banking facilities in Qatar to create new financial centres and generally boost financial activities in the country. In general, Qatar enjoys a traditional, liberal banking service. The proposed changes, designed to open up the market to encourage foreign investors, will give more impetus to growth in the financial sector that will complement and underline the concurrent development of the industrial base of the country.

USING BANKS IN QATAR

All foreign residents may open a bank account in Qatar, provided they earn a minimum salary (the varying levels of which are specificied by the individual banks), hold a current resident's permit and have the written permission of their sponsors. The banks offer a range of different types of accounts and the potential account holder is advised to look into this and select the one most appropriate to their needs, before commencing the process. Interest rates on accounts are attractive, and there are all sorts of offers in the market place.

All the main banks offer ATM facilities, with the appropriate bank cards, in addition to credit card services etc. The system of ATM's has recently been modified in Qatar, such that the banks are linked through the machines, and you do not therefore have to go to your own branch to get cash. ATM machines are to be found all over the country, and many are located in shopping centres in addition to outside bank banches.

Another new system in the country is NAPS, through which you can pay for purchases in certain retail outlets using your bank card, and the money is deducted directly from your account (like the Switch system in the UK). All banks also offer cheque books, although many retail outlets in Qatar will not accept cheques in payment of purchases! The banks in Qatar all offer facilities for sending money overseas; a system which is much used by expatriates! Considerable experience in this area ensures that links with a huge variety of banks all over the world have been established and that this system works efficiently. The large majority of such transactions are conducted by electronic transfer of funds, although cheques can also be issued in a variety of currencies.

A variety of currencies are held by the major banks in Qatar, enabling the purchase of foreign currency and of various travellers cheques to be carried out with ease. Certain banks offer investment advisory services and can give up-to-date information on local and global money markets. Loan facilities are usually available to expatriates (generally for car purchases) and these can be arranged with relative ease (and the usual array of paperwork). Personal loans can also be arranged, if required, as can overdraft facilities. Commercial Bank of Qatar in particular operates its own vehicle financing section, which is popular with many borrowers. In general, the banking system in Qatar is modern and wholly up-to-date with relevant technological developments. The full range of services provided in any western country is available and expatriates can have every confidence in the system.

Banking hours in Qatar are generally 7.30am - 12.00, Saturday through Wednesday and 7.30am through 11am on Thursdays. All banks are closed on Fridays.

For additional analytical, business and investment opportunities information, please contact Global Investment & Business Center, USA at (202) 546-2103. Fax: (202) 546-3275. E-mail: rusric@erols.com Global Business E-Books on Line: http://world.mirhouse.com

LIST OF MAJOR BANKS IN QATAR

- *Al Ahli Bank of Qatar* Tel : 4326611
- *ANZ Grindlays Bank* Tel : 4473700
- *Arab Bank Ltd.* Tel: 4437979
- *Bank Saderat Iran* Tel: 4414646
- *Banque Paribas* Tel: 4433844
- *British Bank* Tel:4335222
- *The Commercial Bank of Qatar* Tel: 4490222
- *Doha Bank Ltd.* Tel: 4456600
- *Mashreq Bank* Tel: 4413213
- *Qatar Islamic Bank* Tel: 4409409
- *Qatar National Bank* Tel: 4362449
- *Standard Chartered Bank* Tel: 4414252
- *United Bank Ltd.* Tel: 4438666

TRADE

The export and import of goods and services play a major role in the structure of Qatar's Gross Domestic product. Export revenues are the main source of public spending and development financing, while imports are the only means of obtaining various required commodities.

FOREIGN TRADE IS THEREFORE CRUCIAL TO THE ECONOMY.

Qatar is fully integrated into the world's free trade economic system and became the 121st member of GATT (General Agreement on Trade and Tariffs), now known as WTO (World Trade Organisation) in 1994. The country is also a prominent member of the GCC (Gulf Co-operation Council), OPEC (Organisation of Petroleum Exporting Countries), the IMF (International Monetary Fund), OAPEC (Organisation of Arab Petroleum Exporting Countries), the Arab League and the United Nations.

Excellent foreign relations with a variety of key countries world-wide combined with tolerant and prudent domestic policies have proved conducive to the development of foreign trade.

With the substantial increase in industrial activity over the past few years, largely due to the development of natural gas production, there has been a corresponding increase in import and export activities.

With regard to the rest of the world, Qatar's main export market is currently Asia, in particular Japan which buys most of the exported crude oil, plus China and India, which import substantial quantities of fertilisers and petrochemicals. The chief buyers of LNG are currently Japan and Korea, although this situation may change in future, in light of the recent economic crisis in the Far Eastern countries.

The main sources of imports are USA, Japan and the UK. The picture has altered dramatically since the development of LNG projects, as a major percentage of imports are currently related to these.

COMMERCIAL EXPORTS

At the present time, crude oil continues to dominate the pattern of exports. In 1996, for example, oil export revenues constituted over 90% of the country's total export earnings.

New LNG export earnings, which began to generate significant revenue in 1997, were projected to earn US$374 million in that year alone and are set to rise over the 25 year contracted sales period.

At present Japan and Korea are the main contracted customers for LNG, through their Sales and Purchase Agreements with Qatargas and Rasgas respectively.

Although hydrocarbons will dominate the export pattern for years to come, the increase in production and sales of chemical and manufactured industrial goods from downstream activities will assist in the desired diversification of the economy.

All the associated oil and gas industries in Qatar successfully export their products to various countries. For example QAPCO sells petrochemicals within the GCC in addition to India, Pakistan and Australia, QAFCO's fertilisers largely go to India and China while the steel produced by QASCO is largely sold to other countries in the GCC.

COMMERCIAL IMPORTS

The USA, Japan, Britain, Germany, Italy and France are Qatar's main trading partners and have dominated the import market over the last few years. In 1996, these countries accounted for 64% of estimated total imports. Additionally, GCC countries are a significant factor in the equation. Imports are currently dominated by capital relevant goods for the two major LNG projects. In addition, significant imports include vehicles, foodstuffs, luxury items, electronic equipment and a whole host of manufactured goods required to support the population and industries of the country.

Goods vital to the development of the industrial infrastructure are eligible for tariff-free import conditions, as are food products and personal effects. However a low import duty rate of 4% applies to most other commodities.

Protection is applied to products competing with locally produced items, resulting in tarrifs of 20% on imported steel and cement and 30% on urea. Tobacco is subject to 50% import duty, while records and musical instruments incur 15% duty.

However, an exemption from customs duties exists for goods manufactured in GCC countries.

For additional analytical, business and investment opportunities information,
please contact Global Investment & Business Center, USA
at (202) 546-2103. Fax: (202) 546-3275. E-mail: rusric@erols.com
Global Business E-Books on Line: http://world.mirhouse.com

PRACTICAL INFORMATION FOR LIVING AND TRAVELING IN QATAR

GENERAL

Police, Fire, Ambulance 999
Hamad Medical Corporation 4392222
Hamad Medical Corporation-Emergency 4393507
Women's (Rumaillah) 4393333
Veterinary 4653083
Water Emergency 4325959
Electricity Emergency 4435704
Airport Arrival/Departure 4351550
Flight Inquiries 4622999
Doha Seaport 4457457
Telephone Directory 180
Telegrams 130
Speaking Clock (Arabic) 141
Speaking Clock (English) 140
Q.Tel- General Inquiries 4400400
Qatar Cablevision 177
Internet Qatar 4329999

AIRLINES AND TRAVEL AGENCIES

Aeroflot 4437186
Air China 4412100
Air France 4320802
Air India 4418423
Air Lanka 4441217
Alitalia 4441161
American Airlines 4436600
Austrian Airlines 4441161
Biman (Bangladesh) 4413422
British Airways 4321434
British Caledonian 4428043
Cathay Pacific 4328934
China Airlines 4441161
Cubana Airlines 4441161
Cyprus Airways 4418666
Egypt Air 4458458
Emirates 4418877
Gulf Air 4455444
Indian Airlines 4356020
Iran Air 4323666
Iran Asseman Airlines 4445160
KLM 4321208

Kuwait Airways 4435340
Lufthansa 4428008
MEA 4422288
Olympic Airways 4416700
Oman Air 4320509
PIA 4426290
Philippine Airlines 4438585
Qantas 4418666
Qatar Airways 4333777
Royal Jordanian 4431431
Saudia 4432200
Scandinavian Airlines 4428002
Singapore Airlines 4441161
Sudan Airways 4320877
Swissair 4428008
Syrian Arab Airlines 4412911
Thai Airways 4328381
Turkish Airlines 4412911
TWA 4328381
UTA 4321427
Yemen Airways 4412911
Ali Bin Ali Travel Bureau 4441161
Darwish Travel & Tourism 4422411
Darwish Travel Bureau 4427111
Mannai Travel 4442402
Overseas Travel 4435999
Qatar Travels 4428001
Qatar Tours 4424112
Skyline Travel 4621880

CAR RENTAL

Avis 4447766
Budget 4419500
Euro Dollar 4321313
Europcar 4438404
Hertz 4416891

COURIER SERVICES

Aramex Int 4426101
DHL 4621202
Federal Express 4434409
TNT Express Worldwide 4622262
UPS (United Parcel Service) 4322444

For additional analytical, business and investment opportunities information,
please contact Global Investment & Business Center, USA
at (202) 546-2103. Fax: (202) 546-3275. E-mail: rusric@erols.com
Global Business E-Books on Line: http://world.mirhouse.com

EMBASSIES

Algeria 4662900
Bangladesh 4671927
Bosnia & Herzegovina 4670194
Cuba 4672072
China 4884200
Egypt 4832555
Eritrea 4417934
France 4832283
Germany 4876959
India 4672025
Iran 4835300
Iraq 4672237
Italy 4436842
Japan 4831224
Jordan 4832203
Kuwait 4832111
Lebanon 4477773
Mauritanian Islamic Republic 4836003
Morocco 4831885
Nicaragua 4867260
Oman 4670744
Pakistan 4832525
Palestine 4422531
Philippines 4831585
Romania 4444348
Russian Federation 4329117
Saudi Arabia 4832030
Somalia 4832200
South Korea 4832238
Sri Lanka 4861980
Sudan 4423007
Syria 4831844
Tunisia 4832645
Turkey 4835553
United Kingdom 4421991
UAE 4885111
USA 4864701
Yemen 4432555

HEALTH CENTRES

Khalifa Town 4862 655
Al Montaza 4435784
Abu Hamour 4674261

For additional analytical, business and investment opportunities information,
please contact Global Investment & Business Center, USA
at (202) 546-2103. Fax: (202) 546-3275. E-mail: rusric@erols.com
Global Business E-Books on Line: http://world.mirhouse.com

Abu Baker Alsiddiq 4681795
Umm Ghuwalina 4433892
Khor 4722401
Al Gharafa 4869970
Omer Bin Al Khatab 4415353
Al Rayyan 4803461
Airport 4663741
Al Khaleej (West Bay) 4837788
Umm Salat 4789889
Al Khor 4720222
Al Shamal 4731320
Al Ghuwariyah 4728267
Al Jumaillyah 4781562
Dukhan 4711334
Al Shahaniya 4718053
Umm Said 4770701
Outpatient Clinic 4420444
Al Jazira Polyclinc 4351155
Al Mansoura Polyclinc 4883377
Doha Clinic 4327300

MEDICAL SERVICES

Dr. John Heap (Medical) 4477475
Dr. Amal Badi (Gynecologist) 4324349
Dr. M. Kayyali (pediatric consultant) 4478555

Dental:
Dr. Odd Overoyen 4675225
Dr. Deborah Overoyen 4675995
Family Dental Clinic 4442924
Dr. Sarah Aalders 4477175
Dr. John Heap (Medical) 4477475
Dr. Amal Badi (Gynecologist) 4324349
Dr. M. Kayyali (pediatric consultant) 4478555

LIFE IN QATAR

By and large, Qatar is a very pleasant place to live and work. As the infrastructure of the country is constantly developing and improving, standards of living become higher all the time.

Expatriates reside in Qatar by virtue of their work, so unemployment is a virtually unknown phenomenon, and all the benefits of a secure working and living environment can be enjoyed.

For most residents, accommodation, utilities and travel to and from their home country once a year are assured by their employers, leaving expatriates free to save money, and to enjoy the benefits of life in a relatively low-cost location.

Above all, it should be stressed that life in Qatar is comfortable. In line with other Gulf countries, Qatar is a very safe place, with low crime rates.

This makes it an ideal family location. Expatriate schools exist to serve all the major ethnic communities to high school level and high standards of education are achieved.

State of the art facilities ensure that Qatar residents can benefit from up-to-date technology in terms of telecommunications, radio, TV and computers. This also ensures that business can be easily conducted with any other country in the world.

There is plenty to do in Qatar, with entertainment and leisure facilities in abundance. From the wealth of available sports to a good choice of restaurants, to various hobby and interest groups, residents have the opportunity to spend their leisure time profitably.

Shops are reasonably well stocked, and a wide variety of goods from all around the world is available.

Naturally, there are drawbacks. The country is very small, and the atmosphere can be somewhat "village" like. Those used to sophisticated urban life in other countries may miss theatre, cinema, concerts of all kinds and other cultural events. As most socialising is done in peoples homes rather than in public places, it is important to develop a network of friends, or life can be a bit lonely. Many younger people complain that it is not an easy place to be single in, as social life tends to revolve around married couples and families. All of these drawbacks can be overcome however, and a tolerable, if not wholly exciting, life can be forged here.

The climate is one of the main potential drawbacks to life in Qatar. However, as everywhere is air-conditioned, it is possible to survive the rigours of the climate in summer by staying indoors as much as possible. The very worst weather tends to be in July and August in any case, when many expatriates take their annual leave.

Provided the customs and habits of a Muslim society are adhered to in public, it is not hard for Westerners to live under Islam. Modesty in dress and behaviour are expected of residents, as are certain other tenets. This is no more than the respect deserved by a host country and must be accepted by expatriates.
In summary, if you enjoy a relatively peaceful, safe existence, and are content to make the most of the facilities available, in addition to enjoying the usual benefits of expatriate life, Qatar will suit you fine!

For additional analytical, business and investment opportunities information,
please contact Global Investment & Business Center, USA
at (202) 546-2103. Fax: (202) 546-3275. E-mail: rusric@erols.com
Global Business E-Books on Line: http://world.mirhouse.com

LOCAL CUSTOMS

People coming to the Gulf for the first time hold many misconceptions about life here, and about how to behave in a traditional Arab society.

The most important point to stress is that there are very few actual rules and regulations and behaviour should be guided by a sense of being a visitor in a host country and therefore respecting local customs and mores.

There are however, many features of life in Qatar with which first time visitors and residents will be unfamiliar.

These include :

DRESS CODES

Qatar is an Islamic country and Muslims have strong codes on dress habits for men and women. While it should be stressed that no-one is expected to dress in the same way as a National (indeed it is expressly forbidden for non-Qataris to do so), foreigners must display a degree of decency and modesty in their clothing. For men, this means not dressing in short shorts in public places, or prancing around in tiny, tight sports vests. Although one does see men wearing shorts at weekends, they are generally of the baggy, down-to-the-knees variety, but even these are a bit risque in certain places, especially outside Doha. Women should avoid shorts at all times (except when going to the beach or playing sports), mini skirts, crop tops and plunging necklines. This means dressing sensibly, preferably with the knees covered, yet still means that one can look fashionable and even alluring (if you feel you have to) without causing undue offence.

On the beach, in sports or health clubs and at all private functions you can wear what you like, but bear in mind that you have to travel by car or taxi to get there, so always take a covering garment, in case you have to get out of the car or in case you upset the taxi driver.

WOMEN

Women in traditional Arab society remain largely unseen by the population at large, and most Qatari women, especially older ones, wear the full abayah and the veil. However, Western women are accorded a reasonable amount of liberty in Qatar, with regard to dress and freedoms. Women may, of course, drive here and undergo the same procedures for obtaining licences as men (see our section on Transport). Women may also work pretty well anywhere (except on rigs offshore, where there are almost none), and wives under their husbands' sponsorship are in demand as cheap, local hire labour (see Employment). There are several single women, mostly teachers, who work in Qatar and who hold full resident's permits. There is no particular restriction imposed upon them, over and above those that apply to every expatriate here.

RAMADHAN

The Holy Month of Ramadhan is a key part of the Muslim calendar. This period of about 30 days (by the lunar calendar) occurs every year and is a time of fasting, contemplation and spiritual activity for Muslims. One of the tenets of Ramadhan is that no Muslim may eat, drink or smoke during daylight hours. This rule is extended to expatriates, at least in public. In practice, this means that, in the workplace, there must be no eating, drinking or smoking in open spaces. Many companies provide private, enclosed rooms where you can have a hot or cold drink, eat your lunch or puff away, and you must limit these activities to these desginated places. If your company does not provide such a facility, tough luck, you must simply abide by the rules. You cannot indulge in any of these oral activiities in your car, in a park, on the beach, or anywhere other than behind closed doors during this period.

Schoolchildren are generally exempt from these rules, and all expatriate schools ensure that the non-fasting (i.e. non Muslim) children are able to have a snack and a drink.

POLITICS AND CULTURE

Politics is basically a subject to avoid in Qatar. The system is one of absolute monarchy, and, although there are gradual steps towards a more participatory form of government (see our Political System section), there are no opposition parties and a dim view is taken of any form of dissent. It is best to keep ones views entirely to oneself on this issue.

Similarly, open criticism of Qatar, Qataris, Islam and any local custom, habit or way of life is not a good idea. Qataris are mostly very friendly people who welcome the majority of expatriates into their country and into their world, and do not expect to tolerate abuse of this welcome.

RELATIONSHIPS

Newcomers to Qatar must be aware that all physical relationships between people of the opposite gender who are not married to one another, or between people of the same gender are seriously frowned upon under Islam. Constraints do not permit us to go into detail on this subject, but the above should always be borne in mind. However, you can have an excellent social life in every sense of the word, provided great discretion is exercised.

For additional analytical, business and investment opportunities information, please contact Global Investment & Business Center, USA at (202) 546-2103. Fax: (202) 546-3275. E-mail: rusric@erols.com Global Business E-Books on Line: http://world.mirhouse.com

ALCOHOL AND DRUGS

Muslims are expressly forbidden to consume alcohol. Non-Muslim expatriates with a valid resident's permit can obtain liquor permits through the British Embassy and may purchase a limited quantity of alcohol once a month from a designated location. This is to be consumed only within the person's home. Under no circumstances should alcohol be sold or given to anyone else. Breaking this rule constitutes a serious offence and can result in a prison sentence and deportation.

There are refreshment facilities and discos available in the main hotels for non-Muslims, and these are lively, well-attended places frequented by the young, the not-so-young and those in pursuit of a fun evening out.

All drugs (other than strictly medicinal ones) are banned and their use, purchase and sale is harshly dealt with.

In no way do we wish to convey the impression, however, that this is a hard place to live. Provided sensitivity, prudence and discretion are exercised, in addition to an awareness that expatriates have limited rights, one can live freely and happily in the State of Qatar.

ACCOMODATION

Before making the serious decision of moving abroad, families and individuals usually contemplate several factors. After determining that a career opportunity warrants a move, the next consideration is lifestyle.

Travel opportunities, leisure activities, schooling, shopping and accommodation are important to a good standard of living. Fortunately all of these can be found in Qatar

Knowing what to expect when you arrive to Qatar will make the transition much easier. Expats enjoy a good standard of living and plenty of comfortable accommodation is available.

The system for finding your new home is probably quite different than what you have been used to, so being prepared will make the experience a lot simpler.

COMPANY PROVIDED ACCOMMODATION

Some sponsoring companies arrange housing for their personnel before they arrive to Doha. The quality and type of accommodation can vary tremendously so obtaining specific details on the provided housing is advised. If your recruiter has provided you with pictures and descriptions – ask if YOU will be living in that specific property. Sometimes the information becomes outdated and things change.

Considering that the personnel base in Qatar originates from various continents, housing expectations can vary. If you can convince your employer that you want to ensure the standard is up to the mark upon inspection you may have some recourse if you are disappointed.

Not to worry, many companies provide accommodation which is exceptionally comfortable if not luxurious while others offer an allowance.

This affords you the flexibility to find a residence which suits your personal lifestyle and needs.

FINDING ACCOMMODATION ON YOUR OWN

Housing is generally available only on a rental basis for expats, although there are exceptions.

Like in other parts of the world, there are different types of landlords. There are landlords with both great and small interests in the property market. They also differ by the level of service offered by the landlord.

A word of caution, the Qatar rent law does not protect the tenant to the same extent that you might be used to at home. So read your rental agreement carefully and remember – a verbal agreement isn't worth the paper it is written on. There are various interpretations on the word maintenance. We recommend that you rent with an established property owner. Check to ensure the owner is not in the habit of selling his property as this can cause great inconvenience to the tenant.

There are a number of ways you can go about renting your new home. More established property owners and real estate agents are listed in the Yellow Pages and in the State of Qatar Business Directory available in your hotel room. You can also find agents through the newspaper. Currently there is no license requirement for real estate agents in Doha, so you will find that levels of professional knowledge do vary. Qatar does not have a real estate board and a computerized, multiple listing system is not available.

LOCATION

Unlike other Gulf countries, Qatar does not have expat areas per se. Rental accommodation can be found throughout Doha.

Like most towns, however location is still important. Generally Doha is a small town so you are always only 20 minutes away from anything. As life isn't as convenient as home, many expats choose to live in optimally located compounds, villas and apartments.

When considering location many expats place importance on proximity to schools, shopping, private clubs, and access to taxis. Proximity to schools is more important when school bussing is not provided (British System). Accommodation located on secondary roads provides a quieter environment. For some, proximity to mosques can have relevance. Generally a preferred central location will affect the rental price.

ACCOMMODATION TYPES

Accommodation is available for all income levels and lifestyles with varying quality and service levels. Compared to other Middle Eastern countries, a high proportion of villa accommodation is available.
Independent villas usually offer spacious floor plans, gardens and privacy. Although the benefit of compound facilities are not available, many Doha residents prefer to attend one of several luxurious private clubs for their social and leisure activities.

Compound villas are plentiful and offer a variety of facilities. Newcomers find the neighbourhood atmosphere a comfort during the first few months settling in.
There are a variety of apartment complexes available at different rental rates within Doha. Plenty of new accommodation is available and some buildings offer more facilities than others.

CAUTION – inquire if the landlord will ensure that common areas of the complex are cleaned regularly.

LINGO

Unfurnished, semi furnished, fully furnished

These are important terms for evaluating property value!
A villa with a rental rate of QR 5,000 unfurnished might appear as a bargain beside a villa with a QR 6000 rental rate. But if the QR 6000 villa is semi furnished – think again. In Qatar an unfurnished villa can be merely a shell. Any combination of air conditioners, carpets, light fixtures, curtains, wardrobes and appliances are included in a semi-furnished standard.

To semi-furnish an average 3 bedroom villa with air conditioners, carpets, curtains, and appliances will cost between QR 27,000 – 40,000. Hence if you are planning to stay for 1 year, cost divided over the months of the contract would be between QR2,200 and QR 3,300.

The value of the semi furnished villa looks pretty good!

There are varying levels of Fully Furnished accommodation as well. Depending on your needs, apartments, studios and villas can be fully furnished up to and including your dishes if you so desire. Some property owners will furnish your property to suit your own tastes – ie you can select the furnishing you prefer.

In the 2000 Qatar market, the average rental increase for a three bedroom villa, from semi furnished to fully furnished would be QR2,000 monthly. This would be to furnish a living room suite, coffee and end tables, dining table and chairs, china cabinet, three

For additional analytical, business and investment opportunities information, please contact Global Investment & Business Center, USA at (202) 546-2103. Fax: (202) 546-3275. E-mail: rusric@erols.com Global Business E-Books on Line: http://world.mirhouse.com

beds, dressers and end tables. This rate can change depending on quality of furnishings and lease duration.

If a villa has been previously furnished their may be a reduction in rental rate.
To furnish an average 3 bedroom villa costs about QR 50,000 for reasonable quality furnishings.

Maintenance

Maintenance is not a standard service with rental property and when it is provided the standard and level of maintenance varies. Should you decide to "do it yourself", keep in mind sourcing material and skilled labour is difficult and time consuming in Doha. Providing for maintenance yourself also adds to your expenses.

Utilities/Other

Water and electricity fees are usually charged separate to the rent The Water and Electricity Department requires a deposit of QR 2,000 to open an account. The deposit is returned once you vacate the property and have cleared the balance of your account with them.
The average charge for a family of four living in a three bedroom villa is QR 300 monthly. Of course billing depends upon consumption levels.

TELEPHONE AND INTERNET CONNECTIONS

Qtel, the local telephone company, also requires a deposit to open an account. Quarterly line charges are approximately QR 100 for a standard telephone. Long distance rates are expensive, hence most expats rely heavily on the internet for email service and to stay connected with the world. The deposit required for a phone line is QR 1,000. A similar amount is required for the internet, however there is a new system in place whereby the user can be charged directly to his phone line, without setting up an account.

CABLE TV

An antenna system is used to feed the cable TV signal into properties. Some accommodation has the antennae provided, and the decoder box is provided with some furnished accommodation. To purchase an antenna and decoder costs approximately QR 1,800. A monthly rate for cable is from QR 60to QR 120.
Note: Some property owners will bypass the cumbersome line-ups and hassles and process the above paperwork on your behalf.

PEST CONTROL

Securing a contract with a local pest control company is simple and highly recommended. For an average 3 bedroom villa this will cost about QR 125 monthly.
Rental Rates

TRANSPORTATION

If you're into trainspotting, Qatar will disappoint you, as the two sole means of transport are air (for entering and leaving the country) and road (for getting about). Of course, you could try travelling by camel, but it's not recommended unless you have loads of time to spare!

AIR TRAVEL

Qatar has had its own national carrier Qatar Airways since 1994

The airline has recently undergone a complete revamp; increasing and upgrading its aircraft, adding new routes and bringing its services in line with those of a top-grade company.

In the early days, the airline built its reputation on value for money, offering basic services in return for fares that undercut competitors on major routes. This is no longer the case, and the prices are firmly in line with those of other competing airlines, while the service and quality have improved greatly.
Qatar Airways offers daily non-stop flights to a number of useful destinations - notably London (carefully timed to meet connections both within Britain and overseas), Munich (with strong central European connections), Bangkok and Kathmandu. Additionally, several flights are operated daily to other Gulf destinations, such as Dubai and Abu Dhabi. All in all, around 80 flights per week operate to and from Doha to about 20 destinations.

A number of other airlines operate to and from Doha, and 1998 has seen the welcome return of both British Airways and KLM, both of whom suspended flights to Qatar for a while. This is a reflection of the increased volume of passenger travel, boosted by the influx of expatriates working in the oil and gas industry.

Both airlines offer excellent connections to the USA, in addition to a host of British and European destinations. Gulf Air has been operating successfully in Qatar for a number of years (Qatar is still a co-owner of the airline) and offers an alternative for routes to Europe, in addition to many Far Eastern destinations.

Apart from the major carriers listed above, there are a whole host of airlines that list Doha as a destination - everything from Air Malta to Balkan Airlines.Should you not be able to fly directly from Doha to your preferred destination, Dubai, Bahrain and Abu Dhabi (easily reached from Doha) offer a wealth of options in this regard.

For additional analytical, business and investment opportunities information, please contact Global Investment & Business Center, USA at (202) 546-2103. Fax: (202) 546-3275. E-mail: rusric@erols.com Global Business E-Books on Line: http://world.mirhouse.com

Prices tend to be very similar between the major airlines, although various "special offers" crop up from time to time, especially in off-peak seasons. Airlines promote these heavily, and it is worth taking advantage of them as they are considerably cheaper than standard fares. For the adventurous, with time to spare, flights to Europe can be obtained at rock bottom prices, if you don't mind going via places like Sofia or Valetta.

There are plenty of travel agents in Doha, most of whom are competent, and some of whom are actually knowlegeable and helpful. A list of the major ones is given below.

If intending to travel at peak times, you will have to book early. Trying to leave Doha the week that the schools break up in the summer is a nightmare, as is trying to return the day before schools start. Apart from these times, and public holidays, like Eid, it is not usually difficult to get the seats and flights you want with about one week's notice.

ROAD TRAVEL

The only public transport in Doha is taxis. There are two main types - orange and white painted saloon cars and limousines.

Orange and white taxis are an omnipresent feature of Doha roads. They hurtle around, touting for business by hooting at pedestrians and will stop just about anywhere (in the middle of a roundabout is a favorite place). These taxis are outrageously cheap - an average fare inside Doha is about QR 9.00 (less than $3.00) and metering ensures that you pay the correct fare.

The major exception to this is taxis at the airport, who have a profound aversion to switching on their meters, and charge around QR 30 to just about everywhere. Even if you are a seasoned resident, it is difficult to reduce this amount. The way round it (if you don't have much luggage) is to walk to the main road and hail a taxi there, otherwise be prepared to pay their inflated prices.

Taxi drivers know Doha well, but their English language skills vary considerably. However, if you can direct them to your destination in monosyllables, you stand a reasonable chance of arriving where you want to go. Their driving is erratic and eccentric but mostly safe, as are the vehicles (though many of them have seen better days and are past the first flush of youth). Air conditioning can be a bit dodgy, so be prepared to sweat, and expect the radio to be playing at ear-splitting volume. Apart from these minor drawbacks, they are a wonderful form of transport, and great value for money.

Limousines are considerably more expensive (around QR 25.00 for an average trip) and have to be pre-booked. These are clean, comfortable, air conditioned and well driven by uniformed chauffeurs. They are to be recommended for transport to the airport, and for late night returns from parties. Limousines operate 24 hours per day, and the waiting time if, you ring on spec, can be anything from 20 minutes to 2 hours, depending on how busy they are. It is best to book about one day in advance ensure punctuality.

Most expatriates in Qatar own their own cars. This is almost a necessity, as not having one is very restrictive, given the lack of public transport.

DRIVING IN QATAR - LICENCES

You will need some form of driving licence in order to drive a vehicle in Qatar. If staying for less than a week, a valid Western licence will suffice. For those in possession of a residents permit, it is necessary to obtain a Qatari driving licence. These can be obtained easily by holders of US, Canadian, Australian and European Union driving licences and a driving road test is not necessary.

You will have to undergo an eye test (of the read the numbers on the board type) and will have to prove your familiarity with some basic road signs. Other nationalities are required to take a road test with an examiner. The whole business of arranging a licence is best arranged by your sponsor and can thus be quite easily undertaken. You are not advised to go it alone. Driving licences are usually valid for five years and are easily renewable with a further eye and road signs test.

BUYING A CAR - NEW

Practically every major make of vehicle is represented in Qatar. Various local companies hold agency agreements with one or more car manufacturer and new cars are offered at prices considerably lower than those in Europe and the USA. New models tend to arrive in Qatar about half a season behind their country of origin, offering customers a pretty up to date range. Manufacturers customise vehicles for the Middle East, with features such as stronger than usual air conditioning, bleepers at speeds over 120km/hr and tinted glass. Cars are all left hand drive and seat belts are now compulsory in Qatar on roads outside the major towns.

Four wheel drive vehicles are especially popular, both for those who indulge in off-road driving and those who simply like large, powerful family cars. Toyota Land Cruisers are the market leaders, with other popular makes being Nissan, Jeep, Mitsubishi and a whole host of others. Saloon cars are also widely sold here, with just about every major type represented.

There is no purchase tax on cars in Qatar, and this fact, plus healthy competition between sales agents, plus very low running costs makes private cars highly affordable for just about everyone. Expatriates can easily obtain bank loans in Qatar for vehicle purchases, provided they are on fixed contracts with a reasonable income. Repayment rates are competitive and generally loans run for the length of the employment contract.

BUYING A CAR - SECOND HAND

There is a thriving second-hand car market in Qatar. Daily newspapers carry extensive advertisements for these, as do most supermarket notice boards. Prices are generally very reasonable (especially towards summer, when departing expatriates are more desperate to sell) and a huge variety is on offer.

In general, the advice on buying second hand cars is the same throughout the world. In Qatar, it is particularly advisable to buy a vehicle that hasn¹t been flogged to death in the desert. Insist on seeing a service record, and check with the garage concerned (if possible). There is a high vehicle accident rate in this country and purchasers should be especially vigilant in checking this out.

An excellent service exists for those wishing to purchase a second hand four wheel drive. Tony Porter is a fine gentleman who offers a sales and advisory service, guiding buyers through this potential minefield. If you're not an expert in second hand cars, especially in this type of vehicle, you'd be well advised to contact him.

IMPORTING YOUR OWN CAR

This is generally not advisable unless you are especially attached to your car. Shipping is a lengthy and complex procedure and involves reams of paperwork. The car must not be more than two years old, must have the windscreen tinted and must not have a catalytic converter. A tax of 4% is levied on imported cars.

REGISTERING AND INSURING YOUR CAR

Whether you buy a new or second hand car, you will need to register the vehicle with the traffic police. This involves filling in a lot of forms and going to the traffic police office in Medinat Khalifa, where you may have difficulty in communicating with the relevant personnel. In general, you should take someone with you who is competent at dealing with these matters, and most companies have a specialist lurking around somewhere. Once registered, you must carry the car papers with you at all times in the vehicle. Vehicle insurance is compulsory in Qatar, and can be either fully comprehensive or third party. Prices range from about QR 300 to QR 2,000 depending on the usual factor. You will need to obtain insurance before registering the vehicle.

RENTING CARS

All the major rental agencies exist in Qatar. Renting is an excellent solution for the short-term visitor and anything from a compact saloon to a top of the range four wheel drive can be obtained at reasonable rates. Some rental companies offer preferential prices for long-term hire. Additionally, car rentals in other countries can be arranged and paid for in Doha, often at cheaper rates than those offered in the country concerned! Rental cars can be delivered to you just about anywhere, and can be dropped off at the airport, if preferred.

RUNNING COSTS

For additional analytical, business and investment opportunities information, please contact Global Investment & Business Center, USA at (202) 546-2103. Fax: (202) 546-3275. E-mail: rusric@erols.com Global Business E-Books on Line: http://world.mirhouse.com

Qatar residents enjoy some of the cheapest petrol in the world currently super grade is QR 0.70 per litre (QR 2.653 per gallon), meaning that you can fill your tank for as little as QR 25.00 for a compact saloon and QR 50.00 for a large four wheel drive. This makes owning a large gas guzzler positively viable and enables expatriates to drive the cars of their dreams, without undue loss of sleep over fuel costs. In addition, although the major service garages are expensive, there are excellent small repair and service workshops scattered throughout the country who can lash cars together for very reasonable prices.

As car theft in Qatar is virtually an unknown phenomenon, you can leave your car just about anywhere, and even leave it unlocked (although it would be a trifle foolish to leave valuables lying around). Car vandalism is also very rare, as is theft of car radios, CD players etc.

ACCIDENTS

Driving in Qatar is erratic to put it politely, and vehicle accidents are a frequent occurrence. Should you be unfortunate enough to get involved in an incident, the first thing to note is that **you must not move your vehicle** from the point of impact until the police have arrived and verified the situation. Even if you're blocking traffic on a three lane highway, you must stay put. The police will write an incident report and you will be required to visit the relevant police station to obtain this report before you can proceed any further. Without a police report, you cannot get your vehicle repaired.

Sorting out insurance for vehicle accidents is a thorny problem and is best solved by mutual consent with the other party, if this is possible. It is vital to take an Arabic speaker with you to the police station (preferably someone from your company) as many of the police do not speak English, and you will need someone to represent your interests and to ensure you are as fairly treated as possible.

Should the accident be serious and require hospitalisation of either party, the same rules still apply, and as soon as you are able to talk, you will have to give a police report.

Accidents should, of course, be avoided if at all possible and extremely careful driving at all times is highly recommended. Stick to reasonable speeds, watch other drivers like a hawk, expect the worst constantly and you should be OK. Driving in Qatar is actually good fun in a way, and it certainly hones your skills!

MOTOR BIKES

A few adventurous people in Qatar swear by motor bikes and there are some pretty powerful models available. However, this is only to be recommended if you're a very confident and competent biker. The flat roads afford the temptation to go for it in a major way, but it's by no means a good idea. Bikes don't like sand very much.

For additional analytical, business and investment opportunities information, please contact Global Investment & Business Center, USA at (202) 546-2103. Fax: (202) 546-3275. E-mail: rusric@erols.com Global Business E-Books on Line: http://world.mirhouse.com

BICYCLES

Again, only for the fit and adventurous. There are people who swear by desert cycling (they are most French and into that sort of thing) as a form of recreation. Casual cycling on public roads, especially by children, is emphatically not recommended.

TELECOM SERVICES

All telecommunications in Qatar are provided by
QATAR PUBLIC TELECOMMUNICATIONS CORPORATION (QTEL)

QTEL is one of the most forward thinking and technologically advanced telecommunications companies in the Middle East. They were the first to introduce the digital mobile network to the region and maintain relatively high standards of all branches of their operations.

TELEPHONES

It is virtually impossible to survive in Qatar without a telephone, and given that it is easy and cheap to obtain this service, which functions very well on the whole, there is no reason not to do so. Telephone lines both within Qatar and to and from overseas are of a high quality, in line with Western services. They are clear and suffer from minimal interference.

Local calls are free (which accounts for the inordinate amount of time that people spend on the phone in Qatar), while overseas calls, although more expensive than those in the USA or Western Europe, are still reasonable.

For example, calls to the USA and the UK are charged at QR 6.60 per minute at peak times and at QR 4.60 at off-peak times (7pm 7am daily and all day Fridays and public holidays). There are, of course, various options in the type of service that you can get. Installing a fixed line in your home is the most popular.

New residents wishing to establish a line will need to fill in the required forms, supply a letter of guarantee from their sponsor (or a refundable deposit of QR 1000), full photocopy of title pages of your passport and resident's visa, and provide a host of information to QTEL along the lines of exactly where they live and exactly what they want. Once all this has been completed, it takes about three or four days for the engineer to visit your home and install the line. A basic telephone unit is supplied free of charge for each line, although you will have to pay for the fancier models or supply your own (obtainable from various outlets).

Once installed, the line will function instantly and will continue to do so unless you fail to pay your monthly bills! There are various types of lines that can be provided. The basic service (no calls to mobile phones or overseas) costs QR 75 per quarter, and there are no charges for local calls. You can also opt for a line that covers local calls plus those to mobile phones (QR 75 per quarter, plus the cost of calls to GSM's), and finally, a line that provides direct access to the above plus overseas calls (charged at cost). All the above charges are applicable to individuals, while charges to companies are slightly higher (QR 100 per quarter for rental). There is no limit to the number of lines you may have in your home (many people opt to give telephone crazy teenagers their own lines) or to the number of extensions to each line. QTEL offers a host of other services, for example call waiting, conference calls, call transferring etc. and full details of these can be obtained from QTEL.

FACSIMILES

When installing a fax machine your home or office, it is necessary to inform QTEL that the line will be used exclusively for faxing. Obtaining a fax line involves the same procedures as above, and once again, works efficiently and well. Fax machines are available for purchase from QTEL for from various retailers around Doha (see shopping section electronic goods for details) and there is no problem in obtaining supplies (toner, paper etc.).

MOBILE TELEPHONES

Qatar uses the Global System for Mobiles (GSM), which is a digital system used throughout most of Europe and Asia, and which has recently been introduced in the USA. This gives a very high standard of reception. Mobile phones are extremely prevalent in Qatar, and can be seen in use at all times of the day and night just about everywhere! Mobile phone units can be purchased from the agents of the various manufacturers in Doha. The most popular brands are Motorola, Philipps, Ericsson, Nokia and Alcatel.

Prices vary from QR 1200 for basic models to about QR 3000 for snazzy, up to date units. There is also a thriving market for second hand models, although as the technology improves almost monthly, people generally prefer to have the latest "toys" . Once a unit has been purchased, it is necessary to obtain a SIM card from QTEL. This entails following the same procedure outlined above for obtaining a domestic telephone line.

There is an initial charge and monthly rental is charged at a fixed rate. Calls made from mobile phones are charged as well. Provided the mobile is used judiciously, the cost of running one in Qatar is, by comparison with the USA and Europe, very reasonable, although the initial cost of purchasing the unit is substantially higher. All mobile phone numbers in Qatar begin with the digit 5.

QTEL operates a number of ROAMING agreements with other countries, enabling Qatar-based mobile phones to be used in these places. They include most of the European countries, several Asian countries and most of the Middle East. For precise details, contact QTEL directly.

PAGERS

Pagers (commonly known as bleeps) are obtainable from QTEL and a rental of QR 70 per quarter. The procedure for getting hold of one is the same as for telephones and QTEL supply the pager unit. The service is limited to a basic number display. All bleep numbers in Qatar begin with the number 2.

INTERNET

Individuals or companies in Qatar can subscribe to a basic dial-up internet service, provided by QTEL. It is limited to a speed of 28.8 kbp/sec, and during peak hours, e.g. weekends and evenings, it can take time to obtain a line. At other times, however, it is quick and easy to log on. Larger companies can rent their own lease lines, which costs QR 8,000 per month, giving constant access to users. You do not need to rent a dedicated telephone line for the internet, although many individuals and companies prefer to do so.

To apply for an internet connection, you follow the same procedure as above and again, it will take about three or four days to get hooked up. To browse the world wide web from Qatar using QTEL's internet service, you will need to log on through Qatar's proxy server. This server, in addition to preventing pornographic and anti-Islamic sites from being accessed, also speeds up access to all other sites. Use of the internet is charged on a time basis of QR6 per hour, in addition to a basic subscription charge of QR 50 per month. This differs from the flat fee basis charged in the USA and in Europe, and users are therefore advised to use the service carefully, to avoid huge monthly bills!

There are also several Internet Caffes arround Doha, and they run on faster leased lines.

OTHER SERVICES

QTEL, in addition to the services outlined above, provides various other services for large companies in the area of data connections and satellite links. It is also responsible for satellite cable TV connections and billings in Qatar. For information on the latter, see our CINEMA/TV/RADIO section and for information on the former, contact QTEL directly.

EDUCATION

Universal education is a relatively new phenomenon in Qatar. Before the discovery of oil, there were a very few religious schools, for boys only, scattered throughout the country. However, it has been an important goal of the recent rulers of Qatar to introduce a comprehensive primary and secondary education system for every national child.

The system consists of six years of primary school, three years of intermediate school and three years of secondary school.
Public schooling is free for Qatari and expatriate Arab children, and all classes are conducted in Arabic. Many children go on to receive further vocational education in the areas of technical studies and teacher training.

Qatar University first opened its doors to students in 1973, and has grown considerably, offering degree courses in humanities, social studies, Islamic studies, science, engineering and education.

Several Qataris receive assistance to study abroad, mainly in the Arab World, UK and USA.

EXPATRIATE EDUCATION

All the major ethnic communities in Qatar have their own schools. Some of these cover Kindergarten through to High School graduation level (or end of secondary school), while others only go as far as primary level. In general, the standards of education achieved by these schools is high, and all of them maintain regular contact with educational authorities in their home countries. State examinations can be taken in Qatar, and the results are well above average.
Most of the schools are very well equipped, with extensive academic classroom and laboratory facilities, in addition to sports and recreation amenities. Many companies pay the cost of schooling for their employees' children. However, those who do not receive this benefit should be advised that the fees are relatively high. See listing below for prices of the various schools.

Al Hilal Kindergarten: 4672623

Choueifat School: 4650053
School fees: Kg1 - 8500 ; Kg2 - 11,500 ; Grades 1-6 12,500 ; Grades 7-9 14,500 (All fees are per year). Reg. Fee - 1,000 per family
School Secretary: Zeena Hamoudi

For additional analytical, business and investment opportunities information, please contact Global Investment & Business Center, USA at (202) 546-2103. Fax: (202) 546-3275. E-mail: rusric@erols.com
Global Business E-Books on Line: http://world.mirhouse.com

Head Teacher: Mr. Collins
Capacity: approx. 300 pupils

American School: 4421377
School fees: Elementary 5-10 years old (up to grade 5) 24.828 QR per year. Middle 11-13 years old (grade 6-8) 34.640QR per year. High 14-18 years old (grade 9-12) 36.508 per year. Reg. Fee : 3,650 per child
Public Relation: Debbie Abu Jabara
Admin Ass.: Prudie Fernandez
School Director: Dr. Shultz
Capacity: approx. 515 students

Bright Future Pakistani School: 4683250
School fees: Kindergarten 150QR. From Class 1- 150QR to Class 8 220QR, price increases by 10QR per class. Class 9- 290QR, Class 10- 300QR, Class 11- 320QR, Class 12- 350QR.
Headmaster: Dr Allah Bakhsh Malik
Capacity: approx. 4600 students

Central English Speaking Kindergarten: 4672570
Owner: Sara Louise Al Jaidah
Administrator: Helen Bolton
e-mail: cesk@iname.com
Fees: QR 2,300 per term QR 150 registration fee per child
(Fees for part time (2, 3 & 4 days also available)
Discounts for 2nd and subsequent siblings attending full time.
Capacity approx 120 children
CESK's programme offers children the opportunity to learn and develop in a secure, creative and stimulating environment. Our focus is on activity-based learning planned around the growing child's need for learning while doing. Working to a thematic progrmme. It is important to us that your child receives the very best education, care and attention possible. Our philosophy is based on personalised instruction that offers your child developmentally appropriate learning activities. The result is the opportunity for children of all ages to develop a strong foundation in learning, positive self-esteem and emotional well being.

Other goals of CESK are as follows:

To provide an atmosphere that will ensure self-esteem and a feeling of autonomy in each child.
To provide opportunities for physical, mental and social development in a nurturing, caring environment.
To provide age-appropriate activities that stimulates social and cognitive interaction.
To provide materials that will encourage creativity and learning.
To provide an atmosphere of acceptance, praise and love.

CESK admits children of any race, religion, colour & nationality. A multi-cultural, anti-biased curriculum is offered.

While we employ an 'open door' policy here at CESK we do advise parents to telephone in advance for an appointment, to ensure that someone will be available to answer all your questions and show you around.

We endeavour to provide a balance of individual, small-group and large-group activities. With a mix of spontaneous as well as teacher generated activities.

We have a spacious outdoor area, grassed, paved & shaded, as well as a soft playroom for safe, vigorous physical activities.

Children are supervised at all times during their session at the kindergarten.

The kindergarten is open Saturday - Wednesday from 7:30 am until 1:15 pm. Although children may be dropped off and collected anytime between these hours.

Our staff are experienced, the majority of whom hold qualifications in early childhood education, or are undergoing a correspondence course through the Pre-school Learning Alliance (PLA) in the United Kingdom leading to the Diploma in Playgroup Practice. All our staff under go yearly CPR and First Aid training.

The Kindergarten has regular field trips (aquarium, zoo etc.) and visits from people in our community to give talks to the children (dentist etc.)

There is a regular afternoon tea for parents, relatives and friends to get together in an informal way to see the Kindergarten, meet the staff and other parents. We are located beside the Oman Embassy at Al Hilal.

Under the supervision of the Ministry of Education.

Doha College: 4687379
School fees: Years 7-11 7.090QR per term. Years 12 and 13 7.800QR per term. Registration fee 2000QR per family
School Secretary: Mai Fisher
Principal: Alastair Baldwin
Capacity: approx.700 students

Doha English Speaking School: 4870170, 4862530, Fax. 4875921
School fees: Nursery 3,050QR per term + registration fee 150QR. Reception up to year 6 5,050QR per term + registration fee 1.500QR per child.
New admissions: Contact Mrs. Bradley
Principal: Ralph Thackray
Capacity: approx. 600 students
email: dess@qatar.net.qa
DESS is the largest British Embassy sponsored primary school in Qatar, and the longest established. It is a school for children who speak English, and all teaching is carried out in English.

We teach the National Curriculum for England and Wales, equipping British children to reintegrate seamlessly into U.K. schools. Our standardised test results are high, reflecting a solid academic approach, but we also value the development of the whole person.

If you have English speaking primary age children (3-11) and are moving to Qatar come to see us first.

Doha Independent School: Tel. 4684495, Fax. 4687897
School fees: Nursery 1.800QR per term. Reception up to year 6 3,800QR per term.
School Secretary: Mr D Young
Headmistress: Mrs. S.J. Williams
Capacity: 260 students
The Doha Independent School is a British Embassy sponsored, non- profit making organisation, under the direction of a Board of Governors.
The School is located just off the Salwa Road and occupies the same campus as the Doha College (for secondary aged pupils). The School has been in existence since 1978 and has occupied its present site since September 1987. The National Curriculum of England and Wales is followed. Current enrolment is 260 (3+ years to 11+ years). The school community is made up of many nationalities. Low pupil/ teacher ratios (an average of 20 pupils per class) enables the formation of a close relationship between staff and children.
The teaching staff are British nationals holding U.K. teaching qualifications. Specialist teaching of Special Needs, Music, P.E. and French is also offered. Class Teachers are assisted by experienced auxiliaries.
You would be very welcome to visit our School. For appointments please contact the School Secretary.

Doha Montessori: Tel: 4691635; Fax. 4691633
School fees: Nursery 2-4 years old 3000 QR per term. Elementary 5-12 years old 3500QR per term.
School Secretary: Henriette de Boer
Principal: Anna Thomsen
Capacity: approx. 1015 students
Doha Montessori School is committed to individualised education, catering to the unique learning rhythms of each child, allowing children the freedom to develop at their own pace.
With careful guidance and mentoring, we encourage a child's need to know, to achieve and belong, feel safe and esteemed in their learning process. We teach the British Curriculum, with instruction in French, Arabic, Q'uran, computers, etc.
Taking pride in what we do, we offer every child a strong and unique learning foundation, to be built upon for life!

French school: 4835800
School fees: Primary (6-11 years old) 10.047QR per year. College (11-18 years old) 11.253QR per year. Registration fee 1600 QR + deposit 1000QR .
School Secretary: Mrs. Moules
Headmaster: Guy Lelann
Capacity: approx. 330 children

Gulf English School: 4873865
School fees: Pre-School and Reception 6,900QR per year + 500QR registration. Years 1-6 10.500QR per year + 1000QR registration .Year 7 13,800QR per year + 1000QR

registration
School Secretary: Ghada Quffa
Headmistress: Dorothy Jones
Capacity: 280 students

Ideal Indian School: 4684929
School fees: Kindergarten 155QR. Class 1-4 180QR, class 5-10 240QR, class 11-12 350QR- all prices per month.
Headmaster: Ainsley L. Edgar
Capacity: 3.341 children

Jordanian School: 4358897
School fees: Kindergarten 2.475QR, Grade1-2 3.000QR, grade 3-4 3.150QR, grade 5-6 3.450QR , grade 7-9 4.950QR, grade 10-11 6.000QR-all prices per year.
Contact: Maha Al Mareh
Capacity: 750 students.

Middle East International School: 4449892
School fees: Nursery (3-4 years old) 430QR. Kindergarten (5 years old) 420QR. Grade 1-2 475QR, grade 3-4 500QR, grade 5-7 525QR, grade 8 600QR, grade 9 700QR, grade10 800QR, grade 11 900QR all prices per month.
School Secretary: Shirin Kabasi
Headmaster: Zaki El-Kahloud
Capacity: approx.300 children

Mulberry Bush- Nursery:4665427
Scholl fees- Registration fee 150QR. Five days a week - 770 QR per month. Four days a week - 605 QR per month. Three days a week - 510QR per month.
Owners: Anne Ferreri and Louise Al Jaidah
Capacity: approx. 80 children (max. class size 12)
We have a spacious paved and grassed outdoor area part of which is astroturfed & shaded, as well as a soft play room for safe, vigorous physical activities.

Children are supervised at all times during their session at the nursery.

The nursery is open Saturday - Wednesday from 6:30am until 2:00pm. Thursday from 7:00am until 1:00 pm. Children may be dropped off and collected anytime during these times. The main part of the day being from 8:30 am until 12:30 pm. Extra hours are available upon request.

Our staff are mature & experienced, the majority of whom are undergoing a correspondence course through the Pre-school Learning Alliance (PLA) in the United Kingdom leading to the Diploma in Playgroup Practice. We have excellent child:adult ratios.

The children participate in regular field trips, for example, the zoo & the aquarium.
We are open year round with the exception of Eid Al Adha, Eid Al Fitr, Christmas Day & New Years day, other days declared by government.

For additional analytical, business and investment opportunities information, please contact Global Investment & Business Center, USA at (202) 546-2103. Fax: (202) 546-3275. E-mail: rusric@erols.com
Global Business E-Books on Line: http://world.mirhouse.com

We run a full summer programme for children up to the age of seven years. With loads of fun activities, arts & craft, mini sports day, field trips etc.

Fees: Creche (birth – 16 months approx) QR 1,100 per month
16 months and above QR 770 per month

(Fees are for Sat – Wed) Thursdays and extra hours additional
Registration fee QR 150 per child
Discounts for 2nd and subsequent siblings and for 3 months advance payment

Park House English School: Tel/Fax. 4423343
School fees: Nursery 1.850QR per term. Reception to year 6 3.850QR per term. Registration fee 500QR
School Secretary: Debbie Ridley
Headmistress: Heather Brennan
Capacity: 350 students.
Park House English School aims to provide an excellent all round education for each child in its care.
A wide range of academic and extra curricular activities are offered to the children to allow them to develop fully, to build self-confidence and self- esteem and to respect others. The school follows the English NaTional Curriculum and caters for boys and girls aged 3-12 years. It is staffed by British teachers holding U.K. qualifications. All subjects are taught in English, and children also learn Arabic and French.
The school is situated in a leafy suburb near the town. It occupies two buildings surrounded by gardens: Acorns for 3-7 years olds and Oaks for 7-12 years olds. The school has its own swimming pool, multi-purpose sports pitch, and hall suitable for indoor games and concerts. The children enjoy variety of sports throughout a year and there is a strong emphasis on music and drama. We aim to enable all our pupils to make the most of their abilities.

Through excellent teaching and a positive approach to learning, we encourage our pupils to aim high, and also to enjoy their studies. Great emphasis is laid upon close consultation with parents throughout the pupils time in the school. The Headmistress and Form Teachers are always happy to be consulted. Throughout the school a high standard of discipline and dress is expected, and there is great emphasis on moral training. We aim to provide a happy, healthy educational establishment.

Philippine School: 4364148
School fees: Pre-School (3-5 years old) 350QR. Levels 1-3 (6-8 years old) 400QR, levels 4-6 (10-12 years old) 450QR, levels 7-10 (13-16 years old) 500QR- all prices per month.
School Secretary: Nancy Punu

Headmaster: Alberto Dorado
Capacity: approx. 350 students

Qatar Academy: 4803434
School fees: Pre-School 8.800QR , Reception 11.000QR, Grades 1-6 14,300QR, grades 7-11 10,900QR - all prices per year. 6th form 25,000 QR. Reg. Fee 2,000 per child
School Secretary: Jackie Hooper
Headmaster: David Cook
Capacity: approx. 450 students.

Qatar International School: Tel. 4690552, Fax. 4690557
School fees: Pre-School 2.200QR, Reception to Year 6 4,000QR Year 7 9 5.200QR, Year 10 and over 6.200QR-all prices per term (based on three terms per year). Registration fee: (once only) 1000QR per family.
Principal: Joyce Griffin
Deputy Principal: Lyn Webster
Secretary: Isobel Cruckshank
Capacity: 950 students
E-mail: info@qis.org

The Qatar International School is a private English medium school following the British National Curriculum.
Since its foundation in 1977, the school has grown to include 950 students between 3 and 16 years of age, drawn from a diverse range of nationalities. All subjects are taught in English, by experienced UK qualified teachers, with specialist teaching of French, Arabic and computer studies available throughout the school.

The whole school operates from a new, purpose built complex in the Mamoura area of Doha, benefiting from good facilities such as multi-purpose courts, football pitch, hall, music room and science laboratories. Class sizes are small, ensuring individual encouragement and attention at all times.
Organisationally, the school operates as three semi-autonomous sections; Pre-school, Primary and Secondary. Each section has its own staff, timetable and routine but co-ordinated by a centralised administration. This provides a consistent and integrated approach, ensuring a smooth transition as children move from one stage of their schooling to the next, and assists parents who would otherwise have children in several different schools around Doha.

Qafco Norwegian School: Tel. 4771323, Fax. 4770435
Headmaster: Rune Solberg
E-mail: norwschl.home.ml.org
Qafco Norwegian school started in 1971 and had up to 125 students in 1978/79. All students are Norwegians. We follow the Norwegian Curriculum and all lessons are in the Norwegian language, except for lessons in English and German.

There are three main stages: the initial stage (grades 1-4), the intermediate stage(grades 5-7) and the lower secondary stage (grades 8-10). The students start in grade 1 when they are six years old. The subjects taught are: christianity, other religions and moral education; Norwegian; mathematics; civics/social studies; arts and crafts; natural sciences and environmental subjects; English; music; home economics/cooking; physical education; additional subjects (theatre, Arabic, German, computers / information-technology, photography, practical project workŠ..)
The students made their own web page during the first part of this academic year. The web page is in the Norwegian language because it is made for giving students in Norway information about Qatar and our school. But it is still worth visiting to see layout and options. The adress is: norwschl.home.ml.org

Tinkerbell Nursery: 4684729

Shaqab College of Design Arts: Tel. 4805602, Fax. 4805432
E-mail: scoda@qatar.net.qa
Shaqab College of Design Arts (S-CODA) is a campus of Virginia Commonwealth University, School of the Arts located in Doha.

It offers professional design education to citizens of the Gulf region. Upon successful completion of their program graduates will earn the Virginia Commonwealth University Bachelor of Fine Arts degree in Communication Arts and Design (Graphic Design), Fashion Design and Merchandising, or Interior Design.

The comprehensive four-year curriculum, taught by experienced VCU instructors, nourishes creativityand innovation while developing the technical and business skills necessary for contemporary professional practice. Beginning in the Fall semester 1999, the college will occupy a new state of the art building providing students with the latest technology. Please visit our web site at www.vcu.edu/artweb/scoda.

Parents wishing to obtain further information on any of these schools are advised to contact the School Secretary directly on the above listed numbers.

Places are often limited, so early enrollment is advised.

HEALTH CARE

One of the major concerns of incoming residents to Qatar must surely be the quality and quantity of health care available. They will be reassured to know that the state operates a competent and comprehensive health care system, in line with government policy of providing full and free medical care to all Qataris, and, by extension, to all residents (although the latter now pay for all medical treatment both through payment for health cards - see below - and for certain additional treatments). In addition to state health care, a number of private doctors and dentists practise in Qatar.

STATE HEALTH CARE

The first hospital to be built in Qatar was the Rumaillah, which opened in 1959. The hospital still operates, but as a departmental wing of the large Hamad Hospital in Doha, the country's main medical facility. This was opened in 1982 and offers full emergency care, cardiovascular surgery, tomography, nuclear medicine and plastic surgery.

In addition there is a women's hospital, focussing on obstetrics and gynaecology, along with a successful fertility clinic. The psychiatric, geriatric and rehabilitation units are housed in the Rumailah Hospital. There are individual units for many specialisms, for example dialysis, and new departments are constantly being planned and implemented. The latest projected addition is a large new oncology unit, to be built at Rumailah Hospital.

A new hospital is underway in the North of the country, to serve the needs of the burgeoning population in Al Khor and Ras Laffan. This will cover most areas of general medicine and surgery and it is hoped that the facility will be opened in 2000.

In addition to the main hospitals, there are several primary health clinics throughout the country, the majority, of course, being in Doha. These are recognisable by the three tall green hexagonal signs mounted on long poles outside the clinic. These should be visited for non-urgent matters, and you can be referred to the Hamad by any of these clinics. In addition there is a paediatric emergency unit (red hexagons) at the roundabout joining Al Sadd St. with the C Ring Road. For procedures on getting registered, see the section on Health Cards below.

HAMAD HOSPITAL - WHAT TO EXPECT

Staffed mainly by foreign doctors (although there is an increasing number of qualiified Qatari doctors), this hospital is an extremely busy place, coping with a large volume of accident and emergency cases (mainly from traffic accidents) in addition to routine medical and surgical patient care. The hospital has both out and in-patient facilities, and the entrance area is well served with flower shops, bookshops (Arabic content only) cafeteria and ATM machines. There is also a central cashier's office where immediate payments must be made for non-free treatment.

The hospital is designed in a rectangular shape around courtyards with the wards fanning out from a central lift and services area. Most of the wards consist of four beds and each has a small private bathroom and at least two telephones. Private facilities (single rooms) are available for VIPs and for expatriates in the maternity wards only.

Westerners who need to go directly to Accident and Emergency at the Hamad will find the service reasonably quick. During normal working hours - i.e. from 8 to 2 daily, accident and emergency tends to be crowded with seemingly non-urgent cases, and the large number of accompanying family members makes the place look busier than it really is.

If you need an ambulance, this can be done by dialling 999. You should be able to give a clear coherent account of where you are and what the problem is. The emergency services operators do speak English and the service is very fast and efficient (if you're in Doha). For offshore and remote accidents, it is possible to arrange helicopter transportation to the hospital (most companies especially in the oil and gas business have efficient safety procedures that will organise this service very quickly).

Once your problem has been diagnosed by the physician on duty, you can expect rapid treatment - especially if surgery is required.

The standard of surgery is on the whole extremely good and the doctors are sympathetic. The nurses are mainly Filipinas and Indians.

Westerners used to limited visiting hours in hospitals in their home countries will be surprised by the constant stream of family and friends of patients who lurk around in the hospital during most hours of the day and night. It is not uncommon for wealthy patients to bring their maids into the hospital and at least one parent of most child patients tends to move in to the ward for the duration. A fold up bed and minimal bedding are provided for the parent in the children's wards (bring your own pillows and sheets if you can).

Tea and coffee are not served at all, so if you need this, bring your own and get the nurses to let you have hot water from their kitchenettes.

Like any stay in hospital, it's very boring being in the Hamad, so get as much reading material as possible and ensure that your friends come to see you as often as they can.

USEFUL NUMBERS:
*AMBULANCE **999***
*HAMAD HOSPITAL **4392222***

HEALTH CARDS

In order to receive clinic or hospital treatment anywhere in Qatar, all expatriates must hold a valid health card. This is the first thing that will be demanded upon arrival at hospital, even in accident and emergency. These cards can only be applied for by Qatar residents, and are obtainable from the nearest health clinic to your home. Upon payment of a fee (for each family member this is currently QR 200 for the initial card, valid for one year, and QR 100 for a renewal) you will be issued with a receipt, which will cover your needs until you receive the actual card (which can take up to a month). This card entitles the bearer to medical treatment, which is free for most items; although certain more expensive forms of treatment (like dialysis) are now subject to payment of additional fees. However, these fees are very reasonable compared to those in Western countries and should not cause any hardship to most Westerners. All prescriptions filled by hospital or clinic pharmacies are also subject to a nominal charge.

DENTAL

For dental emergencies and surgery, the Hamad has a dental department. However, most expatriates use private dental facilities (see below).

PRIVATE MEDICAL FACILITIES

There are oodles of private doctors operating in Qatar. Some are general practitioners, while others hold specialist qualifications. One can see their signs dotted all over Doha and other towns. However, most Westerners limit their visits to a very few of these, listed below :

Doctor John Heap - a fully registered British doctor, qualified to carry out various types of routine examinations for companies and for professional certification (e.g. pilots etc.). Dr Heap is also highly experienced in paediatric general practice, and offers a high standard of Well-Woman service, including most of the required tests. All samples are sent to UK for analysis and results are obtained within a week. He offers invaluable advice on drugs and medicines available from pharmacies in Qatar. Surgery hours are 8am - 12 noon and 3.30pm - 6pm. A general consultation is QR 150 upwards. Appointments can easily be made by telephone.
TELEPHONE 4477475

Doha Clinic - a general practice on Al Merghab St. Well thought of, clean and efficient place for general problems and certain specialisms such as gynaecology, opthalmology, dermatology and paediatrics. The doctors are mostly from Arab countries though English is spoken. The Clinic is open daily from 8am-12noon and 4pm-8pm and all day Fridays (general practitioner only). Appointments are advisable. Each consultation costs QR 100.
TELEPHONE 4327300

Al-Mansoor Polyclinic - Mainly Arabic and Indian doctors, but they also have a highly competent Yugoslav gynecologist, Dr. Iva. The Clinic is open daily from 8am-12noon and 4pm-8pm Monday to Thursday. Consultations cost from QR 150 upwards.
TELEPHONE 4823377

There are a few excellent private dental practices in Doha. The main ones are :

Family Dental Clinic - This practice is headed by Dr. Richard Stallard, who has been in Doha for years. It is staffed by Americans and, although expensive, offers the latest techniques in general, preventive, pediatric, orthodontic and cosmetic dentistry. Appointments generally necessary at least a week in advance.
TELEPHONE 4442924

Dr Odd Overoyen - a gentle, sympathetic Norwegian dentist, with an impressive array of Norwegian qualifications and a superb knowledge of paediatric orthodontics, Dr. Odd is one of the best in town. This practice has its own British technician (shared with Dr. Debbie), and offers excellent all-round dental care. Children tend to like Dr. Odd and he makes a point of being especially unthreatening with them. Appointments necessary but he will try to squeeze in emergencies as quickly as possible
TELEPHONE 4675225

Dr. Debbie Overoyen - Dr. Odd's wife, an American who runs a separate practice upstairs from her husband.
TELEPHONE 4675995

Dr. Sarah Aalders - Dr. Sarah is a very efficient British woman with a general practice just off the C Ring Road. She is gentle, does great salt scrubs but doesn't get involved with braces. Somewhat cheaper than the others, her practice offers excelent value for money.
TELEPHONE 4478885

QUEEN DENTAL CLINIC - 3 floors and 11 dentists working. American, Egyptian, British and Swedish educated doctors. *TELEPHONE 4860024*

VETERINARY

There is a sad lack of private veterinarians in Qatar. The government does operate a couple of veterinary clinics as follows :

Al Rayyan Tel : **4805911**
Al Shamal Tel : **4728577**

Due to the problems obtaining correct vaccinations for your pets, you are advised not to bring them to Qatar, unless you are willing to take the risk.

EMPLOYMENT

Employment is the raison d'etre for being in Qatar. With a few exceptions, expatriates do not come to the country on spec, seeking jobs (unless they happen to look for work while visiting family or friends already resident). A resident's visa for the head of household in Qatar, is, effectively therefore, a work visa.

Most Western expatriates are recruited from overseas, often through contacts, recruitment agencies or newspaper advertisements. Once in Qatar, they are not able to work for any company or organisation other than that sponsoring them, even in a part-time capacity.

The laws on this issue are strictly applied and have recently been tightened, to prevent any "casual" labour from remaining in the country.

Once a resident has been has in Qatar for a period of two years, and provided there is no objection from his or her sponsor, they are allowed to change jobs (and, of course sponsors) upon payment of a considerable fee, plus compliance with the necessary documentation that this entails. It is often a problem obtaining a release from the original sponsor, but this is purely an individual decision and no legal means exists to force the sponsor to comply. After the initial two year period, expatriates may change jobs more frequently, but, given the expense and hassle of doing so, very few are inclined to "job-hop".

Once employment ceases, whether due to expiration and non-renewal of the contract, or due to either party's wish, the right to remain in Qatar is no longer valid. Some sponsors may allow their former employees to stay for a while to get their affairs in order, or even to seek other work, but this is entirely at the discretion of the sponsor.

People who wish to work in a free-lance capacity or set up an independent business in Qatar must still have a sponsor, and whatever financial arrangement they then make with this sponsor is an individual decision. It is not possible to set up a business in Qatar without a Qatari partner

LOCAL WORK FOR SPOUSES AND OLDER CHILDREN

Spouses of expatriates (in practice usually wives - there are very few husbands in the country under their wife's sponsorship) are legally allowed to work as locally hired employees. Sons under 18 and unmarried daughters are also permitted to work in this manner, but these are the only category of people who can be hired by companies other than their sponsors. As a result, there is a reasonable demand for working wives and daughters (as they are cheap to hire - not requiring accommodation, air fares or other benefits usually accorded to overseas hired expatriates).

Having said this, the range of employment is limited to secretaries, administrators, school and university teachers, nurses (although salaries in this field are poor for Westerners), airline staff, bank clerks etc. Spouses with high qualifications in specialist areas will probably find it hard to obtain work on the same level as they enjoyed in their home country.

Salaries for local hire people are quite low (average secretarial salary in a high-profile company e.g. oil company is QR 5,000 per month). This is because applicants for these local hire jobs will be competing with nationals from the Indian subcontinent and others with low salary expectations. As a result, many spouses either opt to work in a routine low-paid job just to have something to do, or opt not to work at all, prefering not to compromise themselves in this manner. There is little part-time work available in Qatar (apart from helping with small children in schools and nurseries) and many spouses cannot fit their family obligations to suit the long working hours demanded by many employers.

TEMPORARY WORK

A number of women with families, who do not wish to work during school holidays, or spouses who do not wish to take up full employment can find work as temporary staff. Large companies in Qatar often have vacancies for temps, to cover the long holidays that are often taken by permanent staff. Temping can be a useful solution for those wishing to earn a little extra money, and to keep themselves occupied. It is also a good way to begin looking for a permanent job, as good temps are frequently offered posts by the companies that hire them.

If you want to consider temping, the best agency to contact is :
Key Resources Tel 353301 Contact : Jill McCarthy or Jane Bloom

WORKING HOURS

Working hours vary considerably from company to company. Government offices (including QGPC, the national oil company) work from 6.30 or 7.00am to 2.30pm.

Most private companies either work a straight shift from around 8am to 4pm or do split shifts from 8am to 1pm and 4pm to 7pm. Working hours are usually a minimum of 40 per week, and it is quite normal to work on Thursday mornings (i.e. at the weekend) without any overtime benefits. Precise working hours should be defined in the contract of employment for both overseas and locally hired expatriates.

QATAR LABOUR LAW

All employers and employees in Qatar are bound by Qatar Labour Law. This is a highly complex document, which sets out to define and protect the rights of workers in the country. Some of the more important points it contains include :

- All expatriate workers should have their initial air fares to Qatar and their final repatriation fares paid for by the sponsor (in practice the fares for vacations to and from the home country are usually paid by the sponsor according to the contract of employment).

- Paid leave must be granted to employees at least once every two years (most Westerners receive at least one leave per annum and sometimes more, especially if hired on bachelor status).
- All employees are entitled to a gratuity when they leave the company, of 3 weeks pay per year for the first five years of service, 4 weeks for the second five years and 6 weeks thereafter.
- All employees must be given a contract of employment, stating the terms and conditions of their hire.

There are many other parts to the law concerning working conditions, contracts, workers' rights etc., but all major companies are aware of these and comply scrupulously with the law when issuing contracts of employment and in their working conditions. If the employee wishes to take issue on any matter of the law with their employer, they are advised to do this through a lawyer, and there are a few who are used to dealing with labour cases, speak English and are to be recommended, listed below.

NAME OF LAW FIRM	TELEPHONE No.
Hassan A. Al-Khater	4437770
Abdulla Essa Al-Ansari	4351418 / 9
Khalid Bin Mohammad Al-Attiya	4364447 / 8
Law office of Gebran Majdalany	4428899

EMPLOYMENT OF OTHERS (E.G. DOMESTIC SERVANTS)

It is possible for residents in Qatar to sponsor one (or occasionally more) domestic servants to work exclusively for them and their family. However, this requires the Qatari sponsor's permission, and usually entails bringing someone in (via an agency) from India, Sri Lanka, the Philippines or wherever their country of origin may be. The process is lengthy, time-consuming and expensive. According to the labour laws, the expatriate employer is responsible for all their employee's air fares, repatriation, granting leave etc. in addition to paying large agency fees. It is also possible to sponsor a servant who is already in Qatar and has obtained a release letter from their original sponsor. However, apart from having a domestic servant who is sponsored by yourself, it is illegal to hire casual domestic labour, except through an agency, as this contravenes the law.

Once a domestic servant is hired, the employer is responsible for their behavior while in Qatar. As relations between unmarried couples are strictly illegal, it is very important to warn all servants to obey the law at all times, especially in this regard.

Salaries for domestic staff are low by Western standards, and the average pay for a housemaid is around QR 700 per month, although many Westerners choose to pay more. The terms of employment vary, with some employers paying for food for their servants, while others incorporate this cost into the salary. Leave must be granted at least every two years.

While employing a housemaid or nanny may prove expensive and arduous to initiate, it is very useful for working mothers and, provided the Qatari sponsor is helpful and supportive, not impossible to achieve.

Should you be unable to sponsor a maid or cleaner yourselves, they can be hired on a short-term basis through certain cleaning agencies. A list of these follows :

NAME OF AGENCY	TELEPHONE No.
Al-Quds Cleaning Co.	4663661
Luzan Cleaning Est.	4652304
Qatar Cleaning Co.	4870083

For additional analytical, business and investment opportunities information, please contact Global Investment & Business Center, USA at (202) 546-2103. Fax: (202) 546-3275. E-mail: rusric@erols.com Global Business E-Books on Line: http://world.mirhouse.com

CINEMA AND MASS MEDIA

Until quite recently, cinema going was an activity limited largely to the Asian and Arab populations of Qatar, as the cinemas almost exclusively showed films from these countries. However, all the public cinemas in Doha have recently taken to providing a bit more of a mixture, and the albeit infrequent English language movies are proving popular.

Public cinemas in Qatar are all owned and operated by the Qatar Cinema and Distribution Company.

There are three outlets. The Gulf Cinema and Doha Cinema, both situated on the C Road are somewhat old, cavernous and slightly tatty buildings with large screens. Entry prices are reasonable (well below those in Europe and the USA), and while the choice of films focuses largely on Indian or Arabic movies, the occasional Western family style blockbuster (about a year old) is screened.

Listings are obtainable from the newspapers or by telephoning the cinemas.
DOHA CINEMA / GULF CINEMA .671811

A new cinema opened in The Mall in 1998, owned and operated by QCD. This has five showings daily, concentrates on Western movies, and is clean, comfortable and pleasant to visit. The small, intimate size (93 seats, plus wheelchair facilities) brings it in line with modern cinema trends. One show daily is reserved for families, while the four others are open to the general public. Thankfully, mobile phones and pagers are banned in the cinema, which also boasts full-time video security cameras. For precise timings and prices, contact the *Mall Cinema* on 678666.

Details of films are given in the newspapers. As one would expect, serious nudity and scenes of what is described as " an adult nature" are censored. Violence and swearing however, are not. In addition to public cinemas, a number of clubs and cultural centres hold screenings of films.

The Doha Club has a full-sized cinema, and organises weekly showings of popular movies, open to the general public. Contact the Doha Club on 418822 for details.

The French Cultural Centre (671037) and the *British Council* (426193) frequently organise film showings. Contact them for details. In addition, various embassies arrange cultural weeks which include films. These will be listed in Qatar Info monthly magazine, and in the local press.

TV

Qatar Television (the State TV broadcasting corporation - now a commercial corporation) has one English language channel - Channel 37. This shows the films, has some documentaries (e.g. Beyond 2000), daily news in English (usually read by native English speakers, but not always) and a lot of local football.

There is an Indian movie shown every Thursday night, which is riveting if you don¹t speak Hindi (subtitles are in Arabic). There are two popular channels in Arabic QTV's own, plus the local satellite station - Al Jazeera. The latter is very popular with Arabs and is deemed interesting, up to date and topical.

Practically all accommodation in Qatar has a TV connection point and you simply have to organise an aerial. Modern compounds come with these in situ.

Taking the above information into account, you will doubtless wish to broaden your viewing options, and this can be done by subscribing to cable TV. In Qatar, this is provided by a microwave wireless system, obtainable from various dealers and operated by QTEL, to whom the subscriptions are paid. You will need to purchase an antenna and a receiver from the dealer in order to run cable TV and the same dealer will organise all the paperwork with QTEL for you.

Star Times, a publication giving a guide to a month's viewing on cable is available from supermarkets. It is fairly accurate, although not entirely (especially with movie times). The two English language newspapers (Gulf Times and Peninisula) both give exhaustive daily TV listings.

VIDEO

An alternative to watching the somewhat tired movies on cable TV is to rent videos. There are several video rental outlets in Qatar, some of which are to be found in useful places like supermarkets (notably the Centre and Q-Mart in the Mall).

Before the enforcement of copyright laws in Qatar in 1996, it was possible to rent videos very cheaply, but the quality was, frankly, lousy.

Nowadays, rental rates are around QR 10 for rental, with approximately QR 75 deposit and the time limit is roughly 2 3 days. A range of up-to-date films is available (with duly censored fruity bits) and it is thereby possible to keep in touch with the world of the movies. Don't expect to find the more arty type of films however, as the market is driven largely by best sellers.

RADIO

All radio in Qatar is state owned, although the corporation QBS (Qatar Broadcasting Service) has recently become commercial, allowing advertising. There is one English language station, known locally simply as QBS, that can be found on 97.5 and 102.6FM.

This charming little gem of the airwaves attempts to provide a fully comprehensive service, catering to the widest of tastes! In practice, there are several live music shows, hosted by DJ's of astoundingly variable competence and musical savvy, lots of bought in programmes from Europe and the USA (some of which are actually worth listening to - although the best of them are mystifyingly broadcast when everyone is at work) and eight daily news broadcasts, ranging from brief summaries to full 10 minute bulletins.

Judging by the strong opinions held by just about every English speaking expatriate on the subject of QBS, it would seem that lots of people listen to it, although few appear to actually like it. QBS also operates a French service, on 100.8FM from 4pm to 7pm daily. This covers news, items of local interest and a few music shows. There is also an Urdu service on 999MW from 4pm to 9pm daily and an Arabic channel.

Those who can't handle QBS's music will be delighted to know that, in good weather, you can easily access stations in Dubai, Abu Dhabi, Sharjah and Bahrain, some of which play excellent music. Fiddle with your dial till you get them. The BBC World Service is also obtainable on 15304SW.

There are no offshore pirate radio stations operating in the Gulf.

NEWSPAPERS

There are two main English language newspapers - the Gulf Times and The Peninsula, both of which are published in broadsheet format, contain roughly 24 - 26 pages, are published daily except Fridays and cost QR 2 (as do all newspapers in Qatar).

The Gulf Times is owned, along with its sister paper in Arabic Arrayah, by Gulf Publishing and Printing Organisation, and owns its own press in a purpose built facility on the C Ring Road, near the airport. The newspaper is very well established, and, until the arrival of the Peninsula in 1996, was the only English language paper in Qatar.

As one would expect, there is ample coverage of local events in addition to sports news from all over the world, business news, international coverage and full TV guide, including cable.

The Peninsula was founded in 1996. It is owned by the Al-Sharq Printing organisation, and has a sister Arabic newspaper Al-Sharq. The paper has a rather different layout from the Gulf Times, with clean, unfussy pages, although in many other ways is very similar in its mix of contents. Like the Gulf Times the Peninsula has a weekend section on Thursdays with features slanted towards leisure time and general interest.

Both newspapers are delivered to a large number of both government and private company offices on a daily basis. Those who wish to purchase a copy of either paper will find that nearly every roundabout or traffic light is crawling with newspaper vendors every morning at peak travel hours (6am - 9am) and you can buy a copy from your car! Otherwise, the main supermarkets carry stock.

MAGAZINES

QATAR TODAY is a rather newer magazine, in glossy A4 format, published by the Darwish group. It appears about 4 times per year and also features articles of local interest, company features, in addition to a small information section. The magazine is distributed through large companies and residential compounds, in addition to supermarkets.

The magazine can be reached on Tel: 674586, Fax : 673795 or e-mail : teleqat@qatar.net.qa.

FOREIGN NEWSPAPERS AND MAGAZINES

A selection of foreign daily and weekly papers, in addition to magazines of several types can be obtained in Qatar through supermarkets, or Family Bookshop. These come from one to three days after initial publication (depending on where they're coming from) and the concentration is heavily on material from the UK. Copies are censored for excessive revelations of bodily parts and occasionally for political content, so don't be surprised to find large swathes of black magic marker over photos. Seriously offensive pages are sometimes ripped out altogether, which can be frustrating!

All imported newspapers and magazines are expensive, but this is not surprising, given air freight costs. Copies of newspapers and the more serious magazines can be read for free at various embassies and cultural centres, so if you can't find what you want, or can't or won't afford it, try the relevant embassy.

The British Council has a good selection of British papers, as do the American and French Cultural Centres for their own country's material.

Some other Gulf English language publications are available in Qatar, for example the highly readable Khaleej Times from Dubai, or Emirates Woman - a glossy women's mag that is fast gaining credibility in the region.

BUSINESS CUSTOMS

The procedures for the establishment of a new business entity in Qatar are clearly defined in the commercial regulations governing business activity in the country.

The regulations allow for the establishment of various types of companies. All private and public companies are governed by the Commercial Companies Law No. 11 of 1981.

You can obtain full help and advice on establishing the appropriate business structure from the various Ministries involved in business activities.

These include:

- The Ministry of Finance, Economy and Commerce, Department of Commerce
- The Ministry of Energy and Industry, Department of Industrial Development
- The Ministry of Municipal Affairs and Agriculture The Ministry of Social Affairs and Accommodation
- The Qatar Chamber of Commerce and Industry also provides advice and information on the initial set-up of business in the State of Qatar.

TRAVEL

The best kept secret of the Gulf

Qatar, best described as "The best kept secret of the Gulf" geographically depicted as a peninsula from its northern tip to its southern border.

Not surprisingly, the adage that "small is beautiful" epitomizes the state of Qatar where it has strong historical & cultural ties to the surrounding crystal water sea.

Qatar, is situated between Europe & the Far East, thus has stopovers with all major airlines, hosting visitors, business visitors & transit passengers.

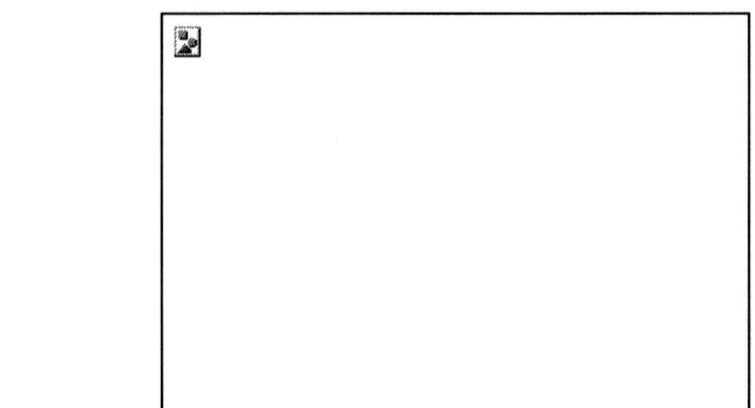

Five star hotels, seaside resorts, & first class amenities cater to varying needs & palates. Gastronomic fare is both exquisitely traditional & delightfully international & those with an appetite for shopping will find themselves in a veritable shopper's paradise where east truly meets west in Qatar.

Mother Nature, too, provides amply in Qatar. An abundance of sun, sea, & sand makes it tourist's nirvana.

Qatar is ideal choice for those seeking pristine beaches that stretches for miles, expanses of desert & breath taking sand dunes, and intimate acquaintance with the pleasures of traditional Bedouin life.

SELECTED HOTELS

Doha has four main hotels, in addition to a number of smaller ones. However, with the anticipated arrival of more foreign companies in Qatar, plus various forthcoming conferences, plans are underway to construct more high class hotels in the West Bay area, which should appear on the scene around the year 2000. The present total room capacity in Doha is just over 1,500.

Many companies house their incoming employees in hotels upon arrival, while they are sorting out and furnishing permanent accommodation for them. Additionally, employees who come to Qatar on "rotation" packages are usually lodged in hotels, as, of course, are short-term business visitors.

Over the last few years, the main hotels have also welcomed a few tourists to Qatar, on a package basis. Hotels in the Gulf provide more than simply accommodation. For local residents they are a focus of leisure and entertainment facilities.

All the main hotels in Qatar have a good selection of restaurants (see our Restaurants section), and a sports and leisure club attached (see Health Clubs). In addition to hosting various shows and concerts, private dinner dances etc., the hotels also provide outside catering services, which are frequently in demand for various functions.

In our listing we give approximate prices for rooms; however large companies tend to have preferential rates in operation, and tourists often pay a special price through the tour company. These prices are therefore only intended as a guide. For further information, contact the hotels directly.

Hotel Inter-Continental Doha

TEL. 4844444
FAX 4839555

The latest luxury hotel in Qatar opened late October 2000 - a welcome addition to the five-star hotel scene after a long wait of 18 years.

Poised by the sea, the 9-storey hotel's architecture reflects a harmonious integration between modern style and traditional Arabic elements. The ingenious design ensures that all 300 rooms have views over the Arabian Gulf and the extensive landscaped gardens. The hotel's location is ideal for both the business and leisure traveller, being a short distance to the diplomatic district, the university, the championship golf course and an easy drive to the business areas and international airport.

An arcade of 14 shops complements the superb range of facilities on offer in the hotel. Keen shoppers can choose from souvenirs, postcards, jewellery, books, and oriental carpets to take home. Bureau de Change, car rental and a bank are also available.

Leisure Facilities:

Large temperature controlled swimming poolPrivate 400 m2 sandy beachFive gazebos to provide shade during the hottest hoursTwo championship standard squash courts Two floodlit outdoor tennis courts· Beach volleyball courtLuxurious health club with modern fully equipped gymnasiumWater-sportsChildren's paddling pool and play area· Barber shopBeauticianSteam roomSaunaPlunge poolMassage

SHERATON DOHA HOTEL AND RESORT

TEL. 4854444
FAX 4832323

Owned by Qatar National Hotels and operated by Sheraton, this hotel is located in the West Bay area, where it dominates the skyline with its remarkable pyramidal shape. Designed and built by an American company in the mid 1970's (opened in 1979), the hotel boasts several facilities, including :

- 371 rooms (singles, doubles and suites) arranged over ten floors
- selection of restaurants, coffee shops, patisserie etc.
- bar and nightly disco
- large leisure centre and beach facilities

- dedicated conference centre with seating capacity of over 1,000
- private banqueting halls
- selection of shops and boutiques
- in-house tour operators who can organise many trips and expeditions on request
- car-hire
- business centre
- airport pick-up

Prices are QR 900 for a single room and QR 1000 for a double plus 17% tax. Suite prices on request. This hotel often acts as the host hotel for major meetings and conferences held in Doha. As a result, there are certain times when there is no room availability (e.g. during GCC conferences), and you are advised to book well in advance if possible.

DOHA MARRIOTT GULF HOTEL

TEL. 4432432
FAX 4418784

Situated on the opposite side of Doha bay from the Doha Sheraton, the Gulf is an older hotel that has recently undergone a number of refurbishments. It is also owned by Qatar National Hotels. The hotel boasts a large number of facilities, including the following :

- 294 rooms, including singles, doubles and suites,
- selection of restaurants, coffee shops and patisserie
- bar and nightly disco
- good leisure centre with extensive facilities, including boating and beach areas
- private banqueting halls
- small selection of shops and boutiques
- in-house tour operators who can organise many trips and expeditions on request
- car-hire
- business centre
- airport pick-up

A standard room costs QR 650 per night, a deluxe (in a new wing)QR 750, deluxe with sea view QR 850 (all plus 17% tax). The Marriott Gulf is a more cost-effective alternative to the Doha Sheraton. Although some of the facilities are in need of cosmetic attention, this is presently underway with an extensive refurbishment scheme. The hotel makes a great effort to organise sporting and leisure events in addition to constantly updating their menus and doing special theme nights. As a result, the hotel is lively, usually full and a pleasant place to visit.

RAMADA

TEL. 4417417
FAX 4410941

The Ramada Hotel is conveniently located in the centre of town, on the C Ring Road. The hotel is owned by a local company and is reasonably priced. Housed in a large bronze glazed rectangular building, the Ramada is currently undergoing extensive refurbishment of the interiors, and, so far this has resulted in a number of the bedrooms being redesigned and renovated. The public areas are also due for a renovation over the coming year or two. Facilities include :

- 302 rooms, which will expand to 328 after renovations, including singles, doubles and suites,
- selection of restaurants, coffee shops and patisserie
- bar and disco
- leisure centre with pool and tennis courts
- private banqueting halls
- small selection of shops and boutiques
- in-house tour operators who can organise many trips and expeditions on request
- car-hire
- business centre
- airport pick-up

Room rates are standard QR 450, single (newly designed/renovated) - QR 650 and double (standard) QR 650 plus 17% tax. Many local functions are held at the Ramada and they have a thriving outside catering business. The eminently reasonable room rates ensure that the hotel is frequently used by business visitors.

SOFITEL

TEL. 4435222
FAX 4439186

Hotel Sofitel Doha Palace is an international chain hotel of the ACCOR Group, France with over 3,000 properties worlwide. The hotel is located in the heart of the city centre just 10 minutes drive from the airport and within walking distance to the business district and shopping areas. The room rates are very reasonable and the hotel is very popular with the residents of Qatar for functions and dining out. The outside catering facilities of this hotel are excellent and so are the restaurants, thanks to the culinary abilities of the French Chef. The Sofitelís facilities include:
175 rooms including singles, doubles and suites
Selection of restaurants
Bar
Disco (Thursday and Friday)
Swimming Pool, Gymnasium and Sauna
Private Banqueting Halls

Car Hire
Airport pick-up on request
Can organise many trips and expeditions on request

Room rates are Single Qrs. 350, Double Qrs. 460, Service charges included. The Sofitel is ideally located for business or leisure visitors and is reasonably priced in comparison with the others.

SEALINE BEACH RESORT

TEL. 4772722
FAX 4772733

This new hotel opened a couple of years ago near Messaieed, in the south east of the country. It is designed as a beach resort, and is becoming a popular weekend and holiday destination for residents and nationals, as it benefits from beautiful beaches and access to the limitless sands of the Inland Sea area.

The resort offers self-catering accommodation from small rooms to three-bedroom chalets, although there is also a restaurant on-site. Various sporting and leisure facilities are included in the resort, although many of these are charged at an extra rate. Prices depend on whether you visit at the weekend or during the week (which is to be recommended, as it's much less crowded). Family chalets can be shared by more than one family, which makes it quite economical, especially during the week. You will need to take your passport if you book in. You can also visit on a day basis, which gives access to the pool and leisure facilities.

Double room Thursday / Friday - QR 457 (including tax). Any other day QR 314. Small chalet (includes bedroom, lounge, bathroom & kitchen with cooker, fridge & freezer). Weekdays QR 325, weekends/public holidays QR 662. Large 3 bedroom chalet weekdays QR 662, weekends/public holidays QR 903.

OTHER HOTELS
There are a few other hotels in Doha, of a two to three star standard. They include:

OASIS:
A large hotel on the bay, near the Sheraton Gulf Tel 4424424. 170 rooms. Room rates Single - QR 350, Double - QR 450 (tax included).

SHEZAN:
A small Asian run hotel on the C Ring Road near TV roundabout Tel : 4865225. Room rates : Single - QR 150, Double - QR 200.

DOHA PALACE:
A small Asian run hotel downtown in the Souq area. Tel : 4360101. 80 rooms. Rates :
Single - QR 250, Double - QR 350 (including tax).

REGENCY:
A new hotel downtown in the Souq area, near Arab Bank Roundabout.. Tel 4363363. 56
rooms. Rates : Single : QR 200 + 15% tax, Double - QR 250 + 15% tax.

US STATE DEPARTMENT SUGGESTIONS

COUNTRY DESCRIPTION: Qatar, a traditional emirate, is a modern, developed
country, and tourist facilities are widely available. Islamic ideals and beliefs provide the
conservative foundation of the country's customs, laws and practices. Qatar is not a
signatory to the Vienna Convention on Consular Relations nor to any other bilateral or
multilateral consular accord. The capital is Doha.

ENTRY REQUIREMENTS: Passports and visas are required. For further information,
travelers may contact the Embassy of the State of Qatar, 4200 Wisconsin Avenue, N.W.,
Suite 200, Washington, D.C. 20016, telephone (202) 274-1600, fax (202) 237-0053, or
the Consulate General of the State of Qatar, 4265 San Felipe Street, Suite 1100,
Houston, TX 77027, telephone (713) 968-9840, fax (713) 968-9841.

DUAL NATIONALITY: Qatari law does not recognize dual nationality. Persons who
possess Qatari citizenship in addition to U.S. citizenship are considered Qatari citizens
by the State of Qatar and are subject to Qatar's laws. Qatari citizenship imposes special
obligations, particularly with regard to child custody and exiting or entering the country.
For additional information, please see the Consular Affairs home page on the Internet at
http://travel.state.gov for our flyer on dual nationality or contact the U.S. Embassy in
Doha.

CRIME INFORMATION: Crime is generally not a problem for travelers in Qatar. The
loss or theft of a U.S. passport abroad should be reported immediately to the local police
and the nearest U.S. embassy or consulate. U.S. citizens can refer to the Department of
State's pamphlet, *A Safe Trip Abroad*, for ways to promote a more trouble-free journey.
The pamphlet is available by mail from the Superintendent of Documents, U.S.
Government Printing Office, Washington, D.C. 20402, via the Internet at
http://www.access.gpo.gov/su_docs, or via the Bureau of Consular Affairs home page at
http://travel.state.gov.

MEDICAL FACILITIES: Basic modern medical care and medicines are available in the
government-run Hamad General Hospital in Qatar. Serious medical problems requiring
hospitalization and/or medical evacuation to the United States can cost thousands of

dollars or more. Doctors and hospitals often expect immediate cash payments for health services, and U.S. medical insurance is not always valid outside the United States. U.S. Medicare and Medicaid programs do not provide payment for medical services outside the United States.

MEDICAL INSURANCE: Uninsured travelers who require medical care overseas may face extreme difficulties. Please check with your own insurance company to confirm whether your policy applies overseas, including provision for medical evacuation. Please ascertain whether payment will be made to the overseas hospital or doctor or whether you will be reimbursed later for expenses that you incur. Some insurance policies also include coverage for psychiatric treatment and for disposition of remains in the event of death. Useful information on medical emergencies abroad, including overseas insurance programs, is provided in the Department of State's Bureau of Consular Affairs brochure, *Medical Information for Americans Traveling Abroad*, available via the Bureau of Consular Affairs home page or autofax: (202) 647-3000.

OTHER HEALTH INFORMATION: Information on vaccinations and other health precautions may be obtained from the Centers for Disease Control and Prevention's hotline for international travelers at 1-877-FYI-TRIP (1-877-394-8747); fax 1-888-CDC-FAXX (1-888-232-3299), or via the CDC's Internet site at http://www.cdc.gov.

TRAFFIC SAFETY AND ROAD CONDITIONS: While in a foreign country, U.S. citizens may encounter road conditions that differ significantly from those in the United States. The information below concerning Qatar is provided for general reference only, and may not be totally accurate in a particular location or circumstance.

Safety of Public Transportation: Good
Urban Road Conditions/Maintenance: Good
Rural Road Conditions/Maintenance: Good
Availability of Roadside Assistance: Poor

Travel by road in Qatar is generally safe, although safety regulations in Qatar are not consistent with U.S. standards. Roads in Doha and Qatar's highway system are well planned and engineered. Informal rules of the road and local customs, however, may prove frustrating for first-time visitors. The rate of automobile accidents due to driver error is higher than in the United States. In rural areas, poor lighting, wandering camels and horses, and high-speed driving are other areas of concern.

For specific information concerning Qatari driver's permits, vehicle inspection, road tax and mandatory insurance, please contact either the Embassy of the State of Qatar in Washington, D.C. or the Consulate General of the State of Qatar in Houston, TX.

AVIATION OVERSIGHT: As there is no direct commercial service by local carriers at present between the United States and Qatar, nor economic authority to operate such service, the U.S. Federal Aviation Administration (FAA) has not assessed Qatar's civil aviation authority for compliance with international aviation safety standards for oversight of Qatar's air carrier operations. For further information, travelers may contact the

Department of Transportation within the U.S. at tel. 1-800-322-7873, or visit the FAA Internet web site at http://www.faa.gov/avr/iasa/.

The U.S. Department of Defense (DOD) separately assesses some foreign air carriers for suitability as official providers of air services. As a result of the August 23, 2000 crash of a Gulf Air flight in the Persian Gulf, DOD has recommended that military commands use air carriers other than Gulf Air for DOD official travel, at least until investigation of the crash is complete. For information regarding the DOD policy on specific carriers, travelers may contact DOD at (618) 229-4801.

CUSTOMS REGULATIONS: Qatari customs authorities enforce strict regulations concerning importation into Qatar of items such as alcohol, drugs, pork products, firearms, or anything deemed pornographic by Qatari authorities. While importation of religious material for personal use is acceptable, importation of religious material for the purpose of proselytizing is not. It is advisable to contact the Embassy of the State of Qatar in Washington, D.C., or the Consulate General of the State of Qatar in Houston for specific information regarding customs requirements.

CRIMINAL PENALTIES: While in a foreign country, a U.S. citizen is subject to that country's laws and regulations, which sometimes differ significantly from those in the United States and may not afford the protections available to the individual under U.S. law. Penalties for breaking the law can be more severe than in the United States for similar offenses. Persons violating Qatari laws, even unknowingly, may be expelled, arrested, or imprisoned. Penalties for possession, use, or trafficking in illegal drugs in Qatar are strict, and convicted offenders can expect jail sentences and heavy fines. Penalties for drunk driving and other alcohol-related offenses are treated with severity in Qatar and may result in heavy fines, imprisonment, or expulsion from the country.

CONSULAR ACCESS: U.S. citizens, particularly those of Arab descent, are encouraged to carry a copy of their U.S. passports with them at all times, so that, if questioned by local officials, proof of identity and U.S. citizenship are readily available.

SPECIAL CIRCUMSTANCES: Qatari employers/sponsors have customarily held on to the passports of their foreign (i.e., non-Qatari) employees during the term of their employment in Qatar. Foreign nationals, including U.S. citizens, may not leave Qatar without the permission of their employer/sponsor.

CHILDREN'S ISSUES: For information on international adoption and international parental child abduction, please refer to our Internet site at http://travel.state.gov/children's_issues.html or telephone (202) 736-7000. Qatar is not a party to any international or bilateral treaty regarding international child abduction, adoption or child support enforcement issues.

REGISTRATION AND EMBASSY LOCATION: U.S. citizens living in or visiting Qatar are encouraged to register at the Consular Section of the U.S. Embassy in Qatar and obtain updated information on travel and security within Qatar. The U.S. Embassy is located at the Al-Luqta District on 22nd February Street, P.O. Box 2399, Doha, phone

(974) 884-101, fax (974) 884-176. For after-hours emergencies, American citizens may contact the duty officer at (974) 5-531-085. On the Internet, you may reach the Embassy web site at http://qatar.net.qa/usisdoha. The workweek in Qatar and for the Embassy is Saturday through Wednesday.

Travel to Qatar is no longer restricted to business purposes - winter tourism has become an attraction in recent years. Arabic is the official language of Qatar, but English is widely spoken and is generally acceptable in private and public sectors. U.S. business representatives will find it very useful to bring promotional material and brochures in English and/or Arabic when traveling to Qatar.

ENTRY VISA REQUIREMENTS:

All travelers to Qatar should have passports valid for the next six months at least, and should hold valid entry visas. Qatari visas may be obtained through the Qatari Embassy in Washington, DC, the Qatari Consulate in Houston, Texas, and the Qatari Mission to the United Nations in New York. Four passport-sized photographs, a visa application and a letter from the sponsor in Qatar should be submitted for this purpose. However, a sponsorship letter is not always a basic requirement.

This procedure will usually take four working days or more. The U.S. and the Qatari Governments have a reciprocal arrangement by which Qatar issues U.S. businessman a multiple-entry visa for 10 years. U.S. businessmen are advised to obtain this visa prior to traveling to Qatar from the Qatari Embassy in Washington, or one of the other two Government of Qatar offices stated above. Moreover, the Qatari embassies in other countries are also authorized to provide this service. This type of entry visa does not entitle visitors and/or businessmen to work in Qatar, unless it is exchanged for a residence permit.

During the last few years, the Government of Qatar has eased restrictions on entry visas issued upon arrival at Doha International Airport. This procedure enables business representatives to have a seven-day visa if the local sponsor submits a special request to the Immigration Department three days ahead of the visitor's arrival at the airport. While no photographs are required, visitors should provide the local sponsor/agent, well in advance of the proposed visit, with passport details, religion, date/time of arrival, as well as name and flight number of the carrier airline. If approved, the entry visa is issued upon arrival against a fee of USD 30.00. This fee may be waived if the visitor is sponsored by an official Government department.

WORK WEEK:

The Government of Qatar's official working hours are 7:00 AM to 12:30 PM, Saturday through Thursday. Banking hours are 8:00 AM to 12:30 PM, while private sector hours are generally 8:00 AM to 12:30 PM and 3:00 PM to 6:30 PM, Saturday through Thursday. Friday is a day of rest for all sectors, including all embassies. The U.S. Embassy hours are 7:30 AM to 4:00 PM, Saturday through Wednesday.

For additional analytical, business and investment opportunities information, please contact Global Investment & Business Center, USA at (202) 546-2103. Fax: (202) 546-3275. E-mail: rusric@erols.com Global Business E-Books on Line: http://world.mirhouse.com

HOLIDAYS:

Officially, Qatar uses the Gregorian calendar year for all purposes. The Hijra (Islamic) calendar is also widely used. Religious holidays vary from year to year. Eid Al-Fitr (four days) marks the end of the fasting month of Ramadan and Eid Al-Adha marks the conclusion of the pilgrimage (Hajj) to Mecca. The only fixed holiday is: Independence Day - September 3.

The months from October through April are generally considered the best period for foreign business representatives to visit Qatar. The summer months are very hot and humid. Decision makers in both public and private sectors can be expected to be absent from the country during some part of the period June to September.

The U.S. Embassy closes for all Qatari and American Holidays.

TRANSPORTATION:

Road Transportation: Qatar has developed a good highway system which connects all the main points of the peninsula. Qatar's only foreign road connection is with Saudi Arabia. There are over 1000 miles of roads, most of which are hard-surfaced. Qatar is now connected with Europe via the Trans-Arabia Highway in Saudi Arabia and with the United Arab Emirates and Oman via a hard surfaced route, also through Saudi Arabia. A very large portion of Qatar's imports are now brought in overland by trucks with increasing amounts coming from container facilities at the ports of Dubai and Sharjah in the United Arab Emirates (U.A.E.).

Port Facilities: Qatar is currently serviced by two ports capable of handling cargo. General cargo usually enters through the eleven berths at the Doha port. Having already completed dredging operations to widen and deepen the port's main channel, the Government is constructing a new container service facility at the Doha port. Dredging operations to establish an adjacent smaller port facility for Qatar Flour Mill Company to handle wheat imports to the country have been completed already.

Bulk shipments are handled at the nine-berth Umm Said port, 30 miles south of Doha. General cargo is usually unloaded at Umm Said and brought by barge or trucks to Doha by the Qatar National Navigation and Transportation Company.

The Ras Laffan port facility (USD 1 billion), about 50 miles north of Doha on Qatar's East coast is meant for exporting Liquefied Natural Gas (LNG) to world markets. Actual shipments of LNG from this port started from December 1996. The port also is used for exports of sulfur and gas condensates, and has the ability to receive general cargo for use in LNG development projects.

Air Transport: In addition to the recently established Qatar Airways, Gulf Air is the country's national carrier. Doha International Airport is served by 20 international passenger airlines, including Gulf Air. The only one of its kind in Qatar, the airport is capable of handling large amounts of air freight.

To cope with the increasing passenger and freight traffic (25 percent increase in 1995/96) the Government plans to construct a new large airport facility on the area adjacent to the premises of the present one. The construction contract (USD 120 million), is due to be awarded by the end of 1998.

Laptop Computers and Software: Allowed entry for personal use.

Exhibition Materials: Allowed entry. If sold during or shortly after the exhibition, such materials are generally subject to 4 percent customs duty.

COMMUNICATIONS:

Qatar enjoys excellent local and international telecommunications facilities. A second earth satellite station was completed in 1988 and mobile telephone services (using the GSM system) were inaugurated in February 1994. Automatic telephone and fax dialing is available to more than 150 countries worldwide. The cost of international phone calls and fax from Doha to the United States are 25 percent higher than prevailing rates in the United States. Internal calls, however, are free of charge if conducted through regular telephones. There are charges for all calls made through mobile phones.

HOUSING:

Doha is the capital of the State of Qatar. It is simultaneously the country's commercial, marketing and banking center. More than 80 percent of Qatar's population lives in Doha and its suburbs. To meet the growing demand for houses, the Government and the private sector have resorted to establishing housing complexes of various traditional and western designs.

It has been a common practice in Qatar for employers in both the Government and the private sector to provide furnished accommodation for their expatriate employees. Alternatively, some employers provide housing allowances.

Contrary to the 1970s and the early 1980s when a small apartment fetched a rent of USD 5000 a month, houses are now available at about half or less of this rate. This depends, of course, upon locality, type of house and facilities. At the most recent housing complexes, three-bedroom villas are available at a monthly rent of USD 2200, and four-bedroom villas at USD 2,700.

Qatari landlords usually require a one year lease with advance payment of six months' rent, although exceptions exist. However, such arrangements, as well as the above rates, do not apply to larger single villas and palaces built for the use of higher management, bankers and leading businessmen. Electricity, water and gardens represent additional costs. In recent years, the lease contract in some cases has included a provision for the Qatari landlord to meet the cost of basic maintenance. House rents have witnessed a sharp increase (30 percent) in 1996-98, due to strong demand from foreign oil/gas companies. In general, housing cost/rent in Qatar may be about 50 percent above U.S. levels.

HEALTH:

All residents of Qatar have enjoyed free State-provided medical care ranging from outpatient clinics to hospitalization. However, due to declining oil production and revenues in the late 1980's and early 1990's, the Government has instituted an austerity program in recent years. According to recently issued regulations, expatriates have to pay fees for certain medical reports and for birth registration. While medicines are mostly dispersed free of charge for Qatari patients, the expatriate communities have to pay a nominal charge for all medicines.

A visitor to Qatar holding no residence permit has to pay for all medical services required throughout his/her visit to the country. Recently, a new form of payment has evolved: prior to undergoing surgery, a resident expatriate patient is required to donate blood. Import of all blood groups to Qatar has been suspended after discovery of some infected shipments of blood.

Apart from a few private clinics, medical care is provided by the State through the Ministry of Public Health. The nation's hospital needs were largely met in 1982, when the 660-bed Hamad General Hospital was inaugurated. Operating under Hamad General Hospital is the 300-bed Maternity Hospital, the only one of its kind in this country. The Government owns and operates two other hospitals. One, the Rumaillah Hospital, is meant to handle geriatric and disability cases and the other provides basic treatment for psychological diseases.

In recent years, Qatar has eased restrictions on private medical institutions. In addition to the State-owned and State-operated 20 health care centers, the Government has licensed about 20 private clinics including some advanced dental centers.

Future plans include charging all expatriates in Qatar for all medical services. A private children's hospital is already licensed and more private clinics are under consideration. In addition, visiting medical and surgical consultants from various countries provide treatment on difficult cases to supplement local medical services. It should be noted that health insurance is not a common practice in Qatar.

FOOD:

Makhbous (rice with roast sheep) is the most common food in the Gulf area. Qatar is no exception. Mutton figures prominently in the fare of most Qataris. Fish is also widely available and popular. Dishes prepared with grouper ("hammour") and sea bass are common. Chicken and beef are given second and third on their list of meats.

In recent years, Qataris have been giving up their age-old tradition of hosting ceremonial dinners at home. Instead, they have started hosting large, elaborate parties at one of the four five-star hotels in Doha which have international standards.

A wide variety of foodstuffs is imported to the country throughout the year in order to cater to the tastes of the large expatriate community drawn from several different countries. Several supermarkets in Doha have a wide range of foodstuffs readily available at all times. In general, foodstuffs and other basic commodities are 50 percent above prevailing prices in the U.S.

U.S. business representatives visiting Qatar should not turn down an invitation to lunch or dinner at home extended by their trade partners. Reciprocity is expected when the host visits the United States.

Alcoholic drinks are served only to visitors residing at the major hotels. Only holders of a special permit from the British Embassy may serve alcoholic drinks at home. In accordance with Islamic laws and regulations, pork and pork derivatives are not allowed to be brought into the country.

U.S. business travelers are encouraged to obtain a copy of the "Key Officers of Foreign Service Posts: Guide for Business Representatives" available for sale by the Superintendent of Documents, U.S. Government Printing Office, Washington, D.C. 20402; Phone: (202) 512-1800; Fax: (202) 512-2250. Business travelers to Qatar seeking appointments with U.S. Embassy Doha officials should contact the Commercial Section in advance. The Commercial Section can be reached by telephone at (974) 884-101 or (974) 884-165, or by fax at (974) 884-298 or (974) 884-163, or e-mail at: bfif97@qatar.net.qa

SUPPLEMENT

LAWYERS IN QATAR

A list maintained by the American Embassy in Doha

Arab Law Bureau P.O. Box 6607 Doha Ph: (974) 4830-202 Fax: (974) 4830-101 Areas of Practice: Banking & Finance, Company Law, Agency and Distribution, Joint Venture, Construction Contracts and Insurance Law	Law Office of Ali Abdulla Jaffar P.O. Box 11176 Doha Ph (974) 4432-188/ 4431-024 Fax: (974) 4430-373 Areas of Practice: General
Law Office of Abdul Latif Hoseni P.O. Box 3960 Doha Phone: (974) 4322-691 Fax: N/A Areas of Practice: General	Law Office of Ali bin Nasser Al-Naimi P.O. Box 2457 Doha Ph: (974) 4432-959/4432-747 Fax: (974) 4432-595 Areas of Practice: General
Law Office of Abdul Rab Al-Malki P.O. Box 1850 Doha Ph: (974) 4424-856 Fax: (974) 4434-336 Areas of Practice: Attorneys and legal consultants	Law Office of Behzad Y. Behzad P.O. Box 869 Doha Ph: (974) 4660-332 Fax: (974) 4664-888 Areas of Practice: Commercial, Banking, Company, Insurance, Trademarks, Industrial, Civil
Law Office of Abdulla Al-Khulaifi & Ali P.O. Box 22034 Doha Ph: (974) 4417-885 Fax: (974) 4418-170 Areas of Practice: General	Law Office of Dr. Najeeb bin Mohamed Ahmed Al-Nuaimi P.O. Box 9952 Doha Ph: (974) 4311-124 Fax: (974) 4310-314 Areas of Practice: Commercial, Banking, Insurance, Trademarks, Industrial, Civil
Law Office of Abdullah Essa al-Ausari P.O. Box 23399 Doha Ph: (974) 4351-418 Fax: (974) 4351-421 Areas of Practice: Lawyers and legal consultants	Law Office of Hassan A. al-Khater P.O. Box 1737 Doha Ph: (974) 4437-770 Fax: (974) 4437-772 Areas of Practice: Full range of legal services. UK educated.
Law Office of Hassan Satti al-Sayed P.O. Box 6780 Doha	Law Office of Rashid Jassim al-Businin P.O. Box 9393 Doha

Ph: (974) 4444-749 Fax: (974) 4444-750 Areas of Practice: General	Ph: (974) 4477-651 Fax: (974) 4477-427 Areas of Practice: Attorneys and legal consultants
Law Office of Khalid bin Mohammed al-Attiya P.O. Box 9228 Doha Ph: (974) 4364-447 Fax: (974) 4364-449 Areas of Practice: Litigation, civil law, commercial law, criminal law, marital law	Law Office of Rouhani and Partners P.O. Box 8747 Doha Ph: (974) 4425-815 Fax: (974) 4
Law Office of Majed Nasser al-Badr P.O. Box 17197 Doha Ph: (974) 4449-596 Fax: (974) 4370-814 Area of Practice: General	Law Office of Sayel Daher P.O. Box 5684 Doha Ph: (974) 4415-080 Fax: (974) 4443-930 Areas of Practice: General. Associated with Walker Martineau, London, UK

ECONOMIC AND TRADE STATISTICS

COUNTRY DATA:

Population: 522,000 (1997 census).

Population Growth Rate: 3.8 percent per year.

Religion(s): Mainly Islam. Minority Christian, Hindu, Sikh and Buddhist expatriate communities.

Government System: Monarchy.

Language(s): Mainly Arabic. English widely spoken.

Work Week: Saturday-Thursday.

DOMESTIC ECONOMY:

GDP: USD 9.2 billion (1997); USD 9.3 billion (1998, estimated); USD 9.4 billion (1999, estimated)

GDP Growth Rate: 1.5 percent (1996-97), 1.1 percent (1997-98, estimated), 0.5 percent (1998-99, estimated).

GDP per capita: USD 17,562 (1997); USD 17,875 (1998, estimated); USD 17,964 (1999, estimated)

Government spending as a percent of GDP: 40.4 percent (1996-97), 44.4 percent (1997-98, estimated), 48.9 percent (1998-99, estimated).

Inflation (Consumer Price Index, base year 1988 = 100): 2.8 percent (1997); 5.00 (1998, estimated); 7.00 (1999, estimated)

Foreign Exchange Reserves: Foreign currency: USD 677 million, gold reserves: USD 41.5 million.

Exchange rate for USD 1.00= QR 3.64 (as set by the Government of Qatar in 1980 and unchanged since then).

Foreign Debt: Not officially available. Estimated at USD 11 billion.

Debt Service Ratio (Ratio of principal and interest on foreign debt to foreign income): Not available.

U.S. Economic Military/economic assistance: Not applicable.

Trade:

Qatar's Imports:
From all countries: USD 3,322 million (1997); USD 3,348 million (1998); USD 2,678 million (1999, estimated).
From USA: USD 470 million (1997); USD 475 million (1998); USD 380 million (estimated).

Qatar's Exports:
To all countries: USD 3,791 million (1997); USD 3,500 million (1998, estimated); USD 3,231 million (1999, estimated).
To USA: USD 62 million (1997); USD 57 million (1998, estimated); USD 53 million (1998, estimated).

INVESTMENT STATISTICS:

U.S. investment is currently estimated at around USD 6 billion. Other information not available. For further information, please see Chapter VII: Investment Climate, of this report.

U.S. AND COUNTRY CONTACTS

U.S. AND COUNTRY CONTACTS:

Note: The country code for Qatar is 974 for all telephone and fax numbers. There are no area codes within Qatar.

U.S. EMBASSY TRADE RELATED CONTACTS:

Embassy of the United States of America
Ambassador: Elizabeth McKune
Deputy Chief of Mission: Matthew Tueller
Economic Commercial Officer: Darrin Hink
Economic Commercial Advisor: Jiryis H. Khoury
Commercial Clerk: Sima Carri
P.O. Box 2399
Doha, State of Qatar
Phone: (Comm): (974) 884-165 or (Embassy): (974) 884-101
Fax: (Comm): (974) 884-163 or (Embassy): (974) 884-298
E-mail: bfif97@qatar.net.qa

Agricultural Trade Office
Ron Verdonk, Regional Director
P.O. Box 9343
Dubai, U.A.E.
Phone: (971-4) 314-063
Fax: (971-4) 314-998
E-mail: atodubai@emirates.net.ae
(Covers: Qatar, Bahrain, Kuwait, Oman and U.A.E.)

AMCHAM AND/OR BILATERAL BUSINESS COUNCILS:

U.S. Qatar Business Council
Gordon S. Brown, President
5335 Wisconsin Ave., Suite 440
Washington, DC 20015-2034
U.S.A.
Phone: (202) 895-1712
Fax: (202) 244-8257
E-mail: qatarbiz@erols.com

National U.S.-Arab Chamber of Commerce
1100 New York Ave., N.W., East Tower, Suite 500
Washington, DC 20005
U.S.A.
Phone: (202) 289-5920
Fax: (202) 289-5938
Internet: http://www.nusacc.org
Affiliate Office:
U.S. Arab Chamber of Commerce (Pacific), Inc.
P.O. Box 422218
San Francisco, CA 94141-2218
U.S.A.

Phone: (415) 398-9200
Fax: (415) 398-7111

American Business Council
c/o Mr. Dan Siekkinen, President
P.O. Box 8388, Doha, State of Qatar
Phone: (974) 436-600
Fax: (974) 436-061

COUNTRY TRADE OR INDUSTRY ASSOCIATIONS IN KEY SECTORS:

Qatar Chamber of Commerce and Industry:
H.E. Sheikh Hamad bin Jassim bin Mohammed Al-Thani, President
Mr. Saleh Mubarak Al-Khuleifi, Vice President
P.O. Box 402, Doha, State of Qatar
Phone: (974) 621-491
Fax: (974) 621-131

Management:
Dr. Majid Al-Malki, Director-General
Mr. Nasser Al-Fayhanni, Office Director
Mr. Nasser Al-Dulaimi, Public Relations Manager [Phone: (974) 423-677]

Country Government Offices Relating to Key Sectors and/or Significant Trade Related Activities:

Office of H.H. the Emir:
H.H. Sheikh Hamad bin Khalifa Al-Thani, Emir of the State of Qatar
H.E. Abdullah Al-Attiyah, Head of the Emiri Diwan and Office Director
H.H. Sheikh Jassim bin Hamad bin Khalifa Al-Thani, Heir Apparent
P.O. Box 923, Doha, State of Qatar
Phone: (974) 423-939; (974) 416-664; (974) 462-262
Fax: (974) 437-660

Economic Studies Department:
Dr. Nasser Abdulghani
Mr. Bashir Yousef Al-Kahlout, Economic Researcher
Phone: (974) 462-320
Phone: (974) 412-942; (974) 416-964; (974) 427-370

Legal Affairs Department:
Mr. Adel Ahmed Al-Sharbini, Legal Advisor
Phone: (974) 462-328; (974) 412-849
Fax: (974) 462-172

Emiri Protocol Department:
Sheikh Mohammed bin Fahd bin Mohammed Al-Thani, Director
Mr. Ibrahim Ahmed Al-Malki, Assistant Director
Mr. Abdul Aziz Mohammed Khaled Al-Rabban, Assistant Director
Phone: (974) 422-322; (974) 415-299; (974) 361-639
Fax: (974) 437-660

Ministry of Electricity and Water:
Office of the Minister:
H.E. Abdullah bin Hamad Al-Attiyah, Minister
Mr. Mohammed Al-Muttawa, Office Director
Phone: (974) 410-613; (974) 423-251
Fax: (974) 440-048
P.O. Box 41, Doha, State of Qatar

Programs and Projects Department:
Mr. Jassim Al-Kuwari, Director
Phone: (974) 443-222; (974) 432-237 Fax: (974) 326-096

Consumer Affairs Department:
Phone: (974) 326-622; (974) 351-182
Fax: (974) 326-748
Mr. Mohammed Yousuf Al-Kawari, Director

Electricity Networks Department:
Mr. Mohammed Al-Khouri, Director
Phone: (974) 326-622; (974) 419-825
Fax: (974) 326-075

Water Networks Department:
Mr. Ali Al-Muhannadi, Director
Phone: (974) 494-444; (974) 494-265
Fax: (974) 327-230

Ministry of Energy and Industry:
Office of the Minister:
H.E. Abdullah bin Hamad Al-Attiyah, Minister
Mr. Hassan bin Ali Al-Saad, Office Director
Mr. Sabri Kazim, Technical Advisor [Phone: (974) 491-381, Fax: (974) 836-94]
P.O. Box 3212, Doha, State of Qatar
Phone: (974) 491-491; (974) 491-444
Fax: (974) 836-999

Department of Industrial Affairs:
Mr. Saleh Ali Al-Mannai, Director
P.O. Box 2599, Doha, State of Qatar

Phone: (974) 832-121/2/3/4
Fax: (974) 832-024

Qatar General Petroleum Corporation:
Chairman and Managing Director: The Minister of Energy and Industry (above)
P.O. Box 3212, Doha, State of Qatar
Phone: (974) 491-491
Fax: (974) 836-999

Public Relations Department:
Mr. Abdulaziz Al-Malki, Director
P.O. Box 3212, Doha, State of Qatar
Phone: (974) 491-391
Fax: (974) 831-484

Marketing Department:
Mr. Jassim Naame, Director, Crude Oil/Natural Gas
Sheikh Mohammed bin Ahmed Al-Thani, Manager, Refined Products
P.O. Box 3212, Doha, State of Qatar
Phone: (974) 491-348

Exploration and Development of New Ventures Department:
P.O. Box 3212, Doha, State of Qatar
Phone: (974) 491-288; (974) 833-091
Fax: (974) 831-850
Mr. Nasser K. Jaidah, Director
Mr. Rashid Ahmed Al-Sulaiti, Manager, Exploration and Joint Ventures Phone: (974) 831-286]
Mr. Ismail Nasralla, Manager, Downstream Joint Ventures
[Phone: (974) 491-448]

Corporate Planning Department:
Mr. Issa Al-Ghanim, Director
P.O. Box 3212, Doha, State of Qatar
Phone: (974) 491-390
Fax: (974) 831-257

Operations Department:
Mr. Saied Al-Mohannadi, Director
P.O. Box 47, Doha, State of Qatar
Phone: (974) 402-400
Fax: (974) 402-900

Legal Affairs and Contracts Department:
Mr. Mohammed Nasser Al-Fuhaid, Acting Director
Dr. Hassan Omar, Advisor
P.O. Box 3212, Doha, State of Qatar

Phone: (974) 308-266
Fax: (974) 478-175

Information and Computer Services Department:
Mr. Abdullah Talib, Director
P.O. Box 47, Doha, State of Qatar
Phone: (974) 402-240
Fax: (974) 413-629

Production Department:

A. Offshore Production:
Mr. Eid Al-Mohannadi, Director
P.O. Box 47, Doha, State of Qatar
Phone: (974) 402-655
Fax: (974) 402-752

B. Onshore Production:
Mr. Ali Salem Al-Marri, Director
P.O. Box 71, Doha, State of Qatar
Phone: (974) 716-339
Fax: (974) 711-790

Materials Department:
Mr. Ghanim Al-Kubaisi, Director
P.O. Box 47, Doha, State of Qatar
Phone: (974) 332-222
Fax: (974) 422-498

Technical Department:
Dr. Mohammed Al-Saada, Director
P.O. Box 47, Doha, State of Qatar
Phone: (974) 402-697
Fax: (974) 402-897

Umm Said Operation Department:
Mr. Ahmed Al-Najjar, Director
P.O. Box 50070, Umm Said, State of Qatar
Phone: (974) 774-300
Fax: (974) 770-433

Gas Processing and Distribution Department:
Mr. Abdulrahman Al-Sowaidi, Director
P.O. Box 50070, Umm Said, State of Qatar
Phone: (974) 774-237
Fax: (974) 770-420

Ministry of Communications and Transport:
Minister's Office:
H.E. Sheikh Ahmed bin Nasser Al-Thani, Minister
Mr. Tariq Al-Sulaiti, Office Director
P.O. Box 22228, Doha, State of Qatar
Phone: (974) 835-353; (974) 835-522
Fax: (974) 885-101

Office of the Undersecretary:
Mr. Salem Butti Al-Noaimy, Undersecretary
Phone: (974) 835-500
Fax: (974) 835-888

Department of Post:
Mr. Abdulrahman Jaber Al-Muftah, Director
P.O. Box 713, Doha, State of Qatar
Phone: (974) 835-555
Fax: (974) 837-777

Department of Ports:
Mr. Ghulam Abdullah Genkeer, Director
Phone: (974) 414-763
Fax: (974) 413-563

Department of Civil Aviation:
Mr. Abdulaziz Al-Noaimi, Director
P.O. Box 3000, Doha, State of Qatar
Phone: (974) 426-262
Fax: (974) 429-070

Qatar Public Telecommunications Corporation (Q-Tel):
Ambassador Mohammed I. Al-Emadi, General Manager
P.O. Box 217, Doha, State of Qatar
Phone: (974) 400-333
Fax: (974) 830-008

Public Relations Department:
Mr. Abdulwahid Fakhroo, Director
Phone: (974) 400-678
Fax: (974) 414-514

Commercial and Marketing Department:
Mr. Hamad Al-Attiyah, Director
Phone: (974) 400-456
Fax: (974) 426-000

Procurement Department:
Mr. Ibrahim Al-Obaidly, Director
Phone: (974) 400-363
Fax: (974) 440-111

Ministry of Municipal Affairs and Agriculture:
P.O. Box 2727, Doha, State of Qatar
Phone: (974) 336-336
Fax: (974) 414-868; (974) 437-630

Minister's Office:
H.E. Ali Al-Khater, Minister
Mr. Jaber Al-Shahwani, Office Director [Phone: (974) 413-580]
Mr. Mohammed Fahad Al-Faihani, Assistant Undersecretary for Agricultural Affairs [Phone: (974) 336-336]
Mr. Abdulrahman Al-Buainain, Assistant Undersecretary for Municipal Affairs [Phone: (974) 414-352]
Mr. Ahmed Al-Dosari, Assistant Undersecretary for Town Planning [Phone: (974) 336-336]
Mr. Issa Abdullah Al-Kubaisi, Assistant Undersecretary for Engineering Affairs [Phone: (974) 336-336]

Civil Engineering Department:
Sheikh Ali bin Nasser Al-Thani, Director
Mr. Nasser Al-Nasr, Office Director
P.O. Box 22188, Doha, State of Qatar
Phone: (974) 337-337
Fax: (974) 439-104

Building Engineering Department:
Mr. Abdulla BuHumid,Director
P.O. Box 22306, Doha, State of Qatar
Phone: (974) 427-140
Fax: (974) 418-620; (974) 430-475

Mechanical Equipment Department:
Mr. Hassan Sultan Al-Kawari, Director
Mr. Atif Al-Batal [Phone: (974) 444-633; (974) 444-634]
P.O. Box 39, Doha, State of Qatar
Phone: (974) 328-241
Fax: (974) 365-937

Environmental Affairs Department:
Mr. Khalid Al-Ghanim, Director
P.O. Box 7634, Doha, State of Qatar
Phone: (974) 320-825
Fax: (974) 415-246

Agricultural Development Department:
Mr. Ahmed Jaber Sarour, Director
P.O. Box 1966
Doha, State of Qatar
Phone: (974) 492-666
Fax: (974) 322-002

Dr. Majid R. Al-Kuwary, Asst. Director for Animal Health Affairs
P.O. Box 1966
Doha, State of Qatar
Phone: (974) 653-083
Fax: (974) 663-163

Ministry of Finance, Economy and Commerce:
P.O. Box 1968, Doha, State of Qatar
Phone: (974) 461-444
Fax: (974) 413-617

Minister's Office:
H.E. Yousuf Kamal, Minister
Mr. Abdulrahman Al-Dashti, Office Director
Phone: (974) 413-366; (974) 414-914

Department of Economic Affairs:
Mr. Ali Al-Khalaf, Director
Mr. Saud Al-Jufairi, Assistant [Phone: (974) 413-566, Fax: (974) 413-682]
P.O. Box 1968, Doha, State of Qatar
Phone: (974) 416-234
Fax: (974) 415-731

Department of Commercial Affairs:
Mr. Abdulaziz Al-Khulaifi, Director
Mr. Abdulrazzak Al-Kawari, Office Manager
P.O. Box 22355, Doha, State of Qatar
Phone: (974) 432-103
Fax: (974) 431-412

Commercial Registration:
Mr. Mohammed Al-Saadi, Manager
Phone: (974) 430-772

Commercial Agencies:
Mr. Abdullah Sultan Al-Asiri, Manager
Phone: (974) 416-884

Trademarks:
Mr. Ahmed Al-Jufairi, Manager
Phone: (974) 434-281

Intellectual Property Rights Department:
P.O. Box 5147, Doha, State of Qatar
Mr. Abdullah Qayid, Director
Tel: (974) 434-323
Fax: (974) 431-412

Exhibitions Department:
Mr. Ali Ibrahim, Director
Mr. Yousuf Al-Zaini, Head of International Affairs
P.O. Box 1968, Doha, State of Qatar
Phone: (974) 834-450
Fax: (974) 834-480

Central Tenders Committee:
Mr. Khalifa Al-Hitmi, Director
P.O. Box 1968, Doha, State of Qatar
Phone: (974) 413-089

Standards, Measurements & Consumer Protection:
H.E. Sheikh Abdullah bin Saud Al-Thani, Director
P.O. Box 1968, Doha, State of Qatar
Phone: (974) 408-500
Fax: (974) 478-849

Customs Department:
Sheikh Abdullah Bin Jassim Bin Fahd Al-Thani, Director
Mr. Miqbil Al-Hitmi, Assistant Director
Mr. Hijji Al-Malki, Office Director
P.O. Box 81, Doha, State of Qatar
Phone: (974) 414-333
Fax: (974) 414-959

Ministry of Public Health:
P.O. Box 42, Doha, State of Qatar
Phone: (974) 440-146; (974) 414-777
Fax: (974) 429-786

Office of the Minister:
Dr. Hajar Ahmed Hajar [Also Chairman of Hamad Medical Corporation (HMC)]
Mr. Hitmi Mubarak Al-Hitmi, Office Manager
Phone: (974) 355-370
Fax: (974) 350-012

Dr. Khalifa Al-Jaber, Assistant Undersecretary/Technical
Phone: (974) 417-022
Fax: (974) 442-722

Pharmaceuticals and Medicines Control Department:
Dr. Mohammed Ibrahim Al-Hail, Director
Dr. Aisha Al-Malki, Drug Registration [Phone: (974) 493-187]
P.O. Box 1919, Doha, State of Qatar
Phone: (974) 447-828
Fax: (974) 425-399

Hamad Medical Corporation (HMC):
Hamad General Hospital (HGH):
H.E. Dr. Hajar A. Hajar, Chairman
Dr. Mohammed Al-Abbadi, Medical Director
P.O. Box 3050, Doha, State of Qatar
Phone: (974) 392-222
Fax: (974) 443-099

Public Relations Department:
Mr. Salem Al-Mohannadi, Director
Phone: (974) 392-012
Fax: (974) 392-263

Materials Management Department:
Mr. Mahmoud Al-Mahmoud, Director
Phone: (974) 392-262
Fax: (974) 423-399

Central Laboratories
Mr. Jassim Jaidah, Director
Ministry of Public Health
P.O. Box 9374
Phone: (974) 417-676
Fax: (974) 353-769
(Inspection and analysis of imported food products)

Dr. Ahmed Mohammed Al-Mulla
Deputy Director of Preventive Health
Ministry of Public Health
P.O. Box 9374, Doha, State of Qatar
Phone: (974) 325-005
Fax: (974) 433-019

Dr. Ahmed Abdul Karim Al-Mulla
Deputy Director of Preventive Medicine
Ministry of Public Health

P.O. Box 9374
Doha, State of Qatar
Phone: (974) 325-005
Fax: (974) 429-786

Ministry of Interior:
P.O. Box 2433, Doha, State of Qatar .
Phone: (974) 330-000
Fax: (974) 443-750

Logistics Department:
Captain Omair Mohammed Al-Ramzani, Director
P.O. Box 4020, Doha, State of Qatar
Phone: (974) 426-633
Fax: (974) 449-228

Ministry of Defense:
Qatar Armed Forces
Procurement Department, General Headquarters
Brigadier Mohammed Khalil, Director
P.O. Box 37
Doha, State of Qatar
Phone: (974) 404-270; (974) 436-920
Fax: (974) 433-464

Country Commercial Banks:
Central Bank of Qatar
H.E. Abdullah Bin Khalid Al-Attiyah, Governor
P.O. Box 1234, Doha, State of Qatar
Phone: (974) 456-456
Fax: (974) 415-587

Al-Ahli Bank of Qatar
Mr. Izzat Mohammed Al-Rashid, General Manager
P. O. Box 2309, Doha, State of Qatar
Phone: (974) 326-611
Fax: (974) 444-652

Mashreq Bank PSC
Mr. Assad Abdo Koshaish, General Manager
P. O. Box 173, Doha, State of Qatar
Phone: (974) 413-213/7
Fax: (974) 413-880

Arab Bank Ltd.
Mr. Ghassan Ahmed Bundakji, Senior Manager

P. O. Box 172, Doha, State of Qatar
Phone: (974) 437-979
Fax: (974) 410-774

Bank Saderat Iran
Mr. Mohammed Zamani, Manager
P. O. Box 2256, Doha, State of Qatar
Phone: (974) 414-646
Fax: (974) 430-121

Banque Paribas
Mr. Christian de la Touche, General Manager
P. O. Box 2636, Doha, State of Qatar
Phone: (974) 433-844/7
Fax: (974) 410-861

British Bank of The Middle East (Now known as HSBC)
Mr. Chris Meares, Chief Executive Officer
P. O. Box 57, Doha, State of Qatar
Phone: (974) 423-124; (974) 422-646
Fax: (974) 416-353; (974) 436-794 (CEO)

Commercial Bank of Qatar Ltd.
Mr. T. P. Nunan, General Manager
P. O. Box 3232, Doha, State of Qatar
Phone: (974) 490-222
Fax: (974) 443-807; (974) 320-716 (GM)

Doha Bank Ltd.
Mr. Mohammad Mustafa Jamjoum, General Manager
P. O. Box 3818, Doha, State of Qatar
Phone: (974) 456-709; (974) 456-710 (GM)
Fax: (974) 416-631; (974) 310-416 (GM)

Grindlays Bank Plc
Mr. John Fleming Murray, General Manager
P. O. Box 2001, Doha, State of Qatar
Phone: (974) 473-700
Fax: (974) 473-710

Qatar Industrial Development Bank
Mr. Maqbool Habib Khalfan, General Manager
P. O. Box 22789, Doha, State of Qatar
Phone: (974) 421-600
Fax: (974) 350-433

Qatar International Islamic Bank
Mr. Abdulbasit Al-Sheibi, Acting General Manager
P. O. Box 664, Doha, State of Qatar
Phone: (974) 332-600
Fax: (974) 444-101

Qatar Islamic Bank
Mr. Marwan Awad, General Manager
P. O. Box 559, Doha, State of Qatar
Phone: (974) 438-000; (974) 439-498
Fax: (974) 412-700

Qatar National Bank
Mr. John Finigan, General Manager
P. O. Box 1002, Doha, State of Qatar
Phone: (974) 407-407
Fax: (974) 413-753

Standard Chartered Bank Plc
Mr. Nick Ellison, General Manager
P. O. Box 29, Doha, State of Qatar
Phone: (974) 414-251
Fax: (974) 413-739

United Bank Ltd.
Mr. Mohammed Abdul Raouf, General Manager
P. O. Box 242, Doha, State of Qatar
Phone: (974) 438-666
Fax: (974) 424-600

Multilateral Development Bank Offices in Country:
Not available

TPCC Trade Information Center in Washington:
Phone: 1-800-USA-TRAD(E)
Fax: (202) 482-4473.

U.S. Department of State Office of Business Affairs:
Phone (202) 746-1625
Fax: (202) 647-3953

U.S. Department of Commerce Country Desk Officer:
(For market access and regulatory problems only)

Qatar Desk Officer: Cherie Loustaunau
Office of the Near East, Room 2039
U.S. Department of Commerce
14th St. & Constitution Ave. N.W.
Washington, DC 20230
Phone: (202) 482-1860
Fax: (202) 482-0878

Country Desk Officer: State Department:
Mr. Harry Kamian
NEA/ARP, Room 4224
Department of State
Washington, DC 20520-6258
Phone: (202) 647-6572
Fax: (202) 736-4459

U.S. DEPARTMENT OF AGRICULTURE, FOREIGN AGRICULTURAL SERVICE, TRADE ASSISTANCE AND PROMOTION OFFICE:

Trade Assistance and Promotion Office (TAPO)
Foreign Agricultural Service (FAS)
U.S. Department of Agriculture
Ag Box 1052
Washington, DC 20250-1052
Phone: (202) 720-7420
Fax: (202) 690-4374

Overseas Private Investment Corporation (OPIC):
Phone: (202) 336-8799

LEADING QATARI FIRMS:

Al-Bassem Group
Mr. Issa Kopti, General Manager
P.O. Box 17877, Doha, State of Qatar
Phone: (974) 441-040
Fax: (974) 441-588

Al-Fardan Group
Mr. Hussain Al-Fardan, Managing Director
P.O. Box 63, Doha, State of Qatar
Phone: (974) 408-408
Fax: (974) 351-885

Al-Jabor Group Holdings
H.E. Sheikh Jabor bin Mohammed Al-Thani, Managing Director
P.O. Box 295, Doha, State of Qatar
Phone: (974) 328-500
Fax: (974) 445-543; (974) 449-411

Ali bin Ali Group
Mr. Adel Ali bin Ali, Chairman; Nabil Ali bin Ali, Managing Director
P.O. Box 3331, Doha, State of Qatar
Phone: (974) 421-915; (974) 426-201
Fax: (974) 433-778

Almana Group
Mr. Omar Hamad Almana, Managing Director; Mr. Saud Almana, General Manager
P.O. Box 491, Doha, State of Qatar
Phone: (974) 621-222
Fax: (974) 622-420

Al-Muftah Group
Mr. Abdulrahman Muftah, Chairman; Mr. Abdulrahman Muftah Al-Muftah, Managing
Director; Mr. P.A. Abu Bakker, General Manager; Mr. Said Gul, Head of Projects
Development
P.O. Box 875, Doha, State of Qatar
Phone: (974) 446-868
Fax: (974) 441-415

Al-Mukhtar Trading & Contracting Co.
Mr. Abdulrahman Abdullah Abdulghani, General Manager [Phone: 621-000; Fax: (974)
621-830]
P.O. Box 5536, Doha, State of Qatar
Phone: (974) 478-454
Fax: (974) 478-226

Arabian Construction Engineering Co. (ACEC)
H.E. Sheikh Hamad bin Jassim Al-Thani, Chairman; Mr. Ghalib Shoush'a, Managing
Director
P.O. Box 1277, Doha, State of Qatar
Phone: (974) 417-521; (974) 417-522
Fax: (974) 430-112

Faisal bin Jassim Group
Sheikh Faisal bin Jassim Al-Thani, Chairman; Mr. Ibrahim Naameh, General Manager
P.O. Box 3288, Doha, State of Qatar
Phone: (974) 440-244
Fax: (974) 447-189

GEMCO (Gulf Electrical Materials Co.)
Mr. Ahmed Saleh Al-Obaidley, Owner
P.O. Box 157, Doha, State of Qatar
Phone: (974) 329-480; (974) 321-753
Fax: (974) 321-752

Ghanim Al-Thani Holdings
Sheikh Ghanim bin Ali Al-Thani, Owner
P.O. Box 5319, Doha, State of Qatar
Phone: (974) 428-201
Fax: (974) 445-248

Hamad bin Khalid (HBK)
Mr. Amal Azzi, General Manager
P.O. Box 1362, Doha, State of Qatar
Phone: (974) 433-644
Fax: (974) 438-729

Hassan Ali Bin Ali Establishment (HABA)
Mr. Hassan Ali Bin Ali, Chairman
P.O. Box 3331, Doha, State of Qatar
Phone: (974) 418-181
Fax: (974) 423-484

International Project Development Company
Mr. Ahmed Hussain Khalaf, Managing Director
P.O. Box 19613, Doha, State of Qatar
Phone: (974) 363-840
Fax: (974) 361-925

Jaidah Motors & Trading Co.
Mr. Jassim Jaidah, Chairman
P.O. Box 150, Doha, State of Qatar
Phone: (974) 426-161
Fax: (974) 414-100; (974) 415-400

KABAS
Mr. Mahmoud Abu Errub, Managing Director
P.O. Box 1760, Doha, State of Qatar
Phone: (974) 683-203
Fax: (974) 684-033

Kassem Darwish Fakhroo & Sons (KDS)
P.O. Box 350, Doha, State of Qatar
Mr. Hassan Darwish, Managing Director
Phone: (974) 423-463
Fax: (974) 426-378

Mannai Corporation
Mr. Ahmed Mannai, Managing Director
P.O. Box 76, Doha, State of Qatar
Phone: (974) 412-555; (974) 412-800
Fax: (974) 411-982

Nabina Trading Establishment
Mr. Ibrahim Nabina, General Manager
P.O. Box 130, Doha, State of Qatar
Phone: (974) 652-345
Fax: (974) 652-386

Nasir bin Abdullah and Sons Trading Co.
Sheikh Abdullah bin Nasser Al-Thani, General Manager
P.O. Box 329, Doha, State of Qatar
Phone: (974) 417-575
Fax: (974) 440-203

Nasser bin Khalid (NBK) Group
Sheikh Nawaf bin Nasser bin Khalid Al-Thani, Chairman
P.O. Box 82, Doha, State of Qatar
Phone: (974) 443-838
Fax: (974) 425-181; (974) 328-412

Salam Group
Mr. Issa Abu Issa, Chairman; Mr. Hussam Abu Issa, General Manager
P.O. Box 121, Doha, State of Qatar
Phone: (974) 832-050
Fax: (974) 832-180

Teyseer Trading & Contracting Co.
Mr. Abdulrahman Mannai, General Manager
P.O. Box 1555, Doha, State of Qatar
Phone: (974) 622-226
Fax: (974) 622-225

Chapter XII: Market Research and Trade Events

Appendix F: Market Research: List of Agricultural Reports:

- Agricultural Export Opportunities Update Reports
- American Food Directory in the GCC-5
- Annual Marketing Plan
- GCC-5 Dry Pulses Market Brief
- GCC-5 Food Industry Report
- GCC-5 Food Retail Sector Report

- GCC-5 Ice Cream Production
- Guide for Doing Business in the Gulf
- Hotels and Restaurants Sector in the Gulf Region
- Qatar Food Import Regulations and Standards
- Update of U.S. Agricultural Exports to the GCC-5

Note: Agricultural Reports are available from the Reports Office, USDA/FAS, Ag Box 1052, Washington, D.C. 20250-1052 and from the FAS Home Page on the Internet at the following URL:
http://www.fas.USDa.gov

LARGEST BANKS

Central Bank of Qatar
H.E. Abdullah Bin Khalid Al-Attiyah, Governor
P.O. Box 1234, Doha, State of Qatar
Phone: (974)456-456
Fax: (974)415-587

Al-Ahli Bank of Qatar
Mr. Izzat Mohammed Al-Rashid, General Manager
P. O. Box 2309, Doha, State of Qatar
Phone: (974)326-611
Fax: (974)444-652

Arab Bank Ltd.
Mr. Ghassan Ahmed Bundakji, Senior Manager
P. O. Box 172, Doha, State of Qatar
Phone: (974)437-979
Fax: (974)410-774

Bank Saderat Iran
Mr. Mohammed Zamani, Manager
P. O. Box 2256, Doha, State of Qatar
Phone: (974)414-646
Fax: (974)430-121

Banque Paribas
Mr. Christian De La Touche, General Manager
P. O. Box 2636, Doha, State of Qatar
Phone: (974)433-844/7
Fax: (974)410-861

British Bank of the Middle East (now known as HSBC)
Mr. Chris Meares, Chief Executive Officer
P. O. Box 57, Doha, State of Qatar

Phone: (974)423-124/422-646
Fax: (974)416-353; 436-794 (CEO)

Commercial Bank of Qatar Ltd.
Mr. T. P. Nunan, General Manager
P. O. Box 3232, Doha, State of Qatar
Phone: (974)490-222
Fax: (974)443-807; 320-716 (Gm)

Doha Bank Ltd.
Mr. Mohammad Mustafa Jamjoum, General Manager
P. O. Box 3818, Doha, State of Qatar
Phone: (974)456-709; 456-710 (Gm)
Fax: (974)416-631; 310-416 (Gm)

Grindlays Bank Plc
Mr. John Fleming Murray, General Manager
P. O. Box 2001, Doha, State of Qatar
Phone: (974)473-700
Fax: (974)473-710

Mashreq Bank Psc
Mr. Assad Abdo Koshaish, General Manager
P. O. Box 173, Doha, State of Qatar
Phone: (974)413-213/7
Fax: (974)413-880

Qatar Industrial Development Bank
Mr. Maqbool Habib Khalfan, General Manager
P. O. Box 22789, Doha, State of Qatar
Phone: (974)421-600
Fax: (974)350-433

Qatar International Islamic Bank
Mr. Abdulbasit Al-Sheibi, Acting General Manager
P. O. Box 664, Doha, State of Qatar
Phone: (974)332-600
Fax: (974)444-101

Qatar Islamic Bank
Mr. Marwan Awad, General Manager
P. O. Box 559, Doha, State of Qatar
Phone: (974)438-000/439-498
Fax: (974)412-700

Qatar National Bank
Mr. John Finigan, General Manager

P. O. Box 1002, Doha, State of Qatar
Phone: (974)407-407
Fax: (974)413-753

Standard Chartered Bank Plc
Mr. Nick Ellison, General Manager
P. O. Box 29, Doha, State of Qatar
Phone: (974)414-251
Fax: (974)413-739

United Bank Ltd.
Mr. Mohammed Abdul Raouf, General Manager
P. O. Box 242, Doha, State of Qatar
Phone: (974)438-666
Fax: (974)424-600

STOCK EXCHANGE:

Doha Securities Market
Dr. Hussain Abdullah, Director
Dr. Ghanim Al-Hammadi, Manager of Brokers And Circulation Department
P.O. Box 22114
Doha, State of Qatar
Phone: (974) 325-737
Fax: (974) 326-470

ECONOMIC COMMERCIAL SECTION:

American Embassy, P.O. Box 2399, Doha, Qatar
Contact: Ambassador Elizabeth Mckune
Matthew Tueller, Deputy Chief of Mission
Darrin Hink, Economic Commercial Officer
Jiryis H. Khoury, Economic Commercial Advisor
Sima Carri, Commercial Clerk
Phone: (974) 884-101; Comm.: (974) 884-165
Fax: (974) 884-298; Comm: (974) 884-163
E-mail: bfif97@qatar.net.qa

TRADE EVENT SCHEDULE:

Qatar is not known as a regional or international center for trade events. However, a limited number of exhibitions are held each year at the State-owned Qatar International Exhibition Center. Scheduled events for each year are usually announced at the beginning of that year.

The latest available list of trade events for the year 1999 is provided on the following page.

For further information on trade events in Qatar, contact:
Mr. Abdullah Ibrahim Mohammed, Director, Fairs and Exhibitions Department, Ministry of Finance, Economy and Commerce, P.O. Box 1968, Doha, State of Qatar
Phone: (974) 834-450
Fax: (974) 834-480
E-mail: qiec@qatar.net.qa Internet: http://www.qiec.com

AGRICULTURAL TRADE EVENT SCHEDULE:

Event: MEFEX 2000 (Regional)
Sector: FOD
Date: February 26-29, 2000
Location: Manama, Bahrain
USG involvement in recruiting/promoting: No.

Event: The FMI 2000 Supermarket Industry Convention and Educational Exposition/NASDA U.S. Food Export Showcase
Sector: FOD
Date: May 7-10, 2000
Location: Chicago, IL
USG involvement in recruiting/promoting: Yes.

Event: The NRA 2000 Restaurant, Hotel, Motel Show
Sector: FOD
Date: May 20-24, 2000
Location: Chicago, IL
USG involvement in recruiting/promoting: No.

Event: Gulf Food 2001 Food & Equipment Exhibition (Regional)
Sector: FOD
Date: February 25-28, 2001
Location: Dubai, U.A.E.
USG involvement in recruiting/promoting: Yes.

TRADE EXHIBITIONS SCHEDULED TO BE HELD IN QATAR,

Name of Exhibition: School & Educational Accessories
Date: September 4-10, 1999
Organizers: Al-Marri & Public Relations, P.O. Box 3618, Doha, Qatar
Phone: (974) 447-740
Fax: (974) 441-146
E-mail: jaber@qatar.net.qa

Name of Exhibition: ISO 9000
Date: September 16-19, 1999
Organizers: World Trade Center Qatar, P.O. Box 6, Doha, State of Qatar
Phone: (974) 354-141
Fax: (974) 423-048
E-mail: wtcdoha@qatar.net.qa

Name of Exhibition: Tunisian Products Exhibition
Date: October 4-8, 1999
Organizers: Omnia Exhibition and Conference Organization Co.
Phone: (974) 438-240
Fax: (974) 433-695

Name of Exhibition: Money & Investment Exhibition (Q-Money)
Date: October 16-19, 1999
Organizers: Arabian Media Center,P.O. Box 22922, Doha, Qatar
Phone: (974) 369-955
Fax: (974) 449-920
E-mail: amc22922@qatar.net.qa

Name of Exhibition: Lebanese Economy Exhibition
Date: October 28-November 2, 1999
Organizers: Corniche Advertising
Phone: (974) 440-224
Fax: (974) 418-886

Name of Exhibition: Sports Products & Gifts Fair
Date: November 7-11, 1999
Organizers: Al-Noor Public Relations, P.O. Box 4408, Doha, Qatar
Phone: (974) 442-655
Fax: (974) 434-499
E-mail: mnoor@qatar.net.qa

Name of Exhibition: Real Estate Investment Exhibition
Date: November 25-28, 1999
Organizers: World Trade Center Qatar, P.O. Box 6, Doha, State of Qatar
Phone: (974) 354-141
Fax: (974) 423-048
E-mail: wtcdoha@qatar.net.qa

Name of Exhibition: Qatar International Toys Fair
Date: November 30-December 3, 1999
Organizers: World Trade Center Qatar, P.O. Box 6, Doha, State of Qatar
Phone: (974) 354-141
Fax: (974) 423-048
E-mail: wtcdoha@qatar.net.qa

Source: Fairs and Exhibitions Department, Ministry of Finance.

LIST OF MAJOR PUBLIC SECTOR PROJECTS

Note: This section is provided as a voluntary extension to the Country Commercial Guide, intended to serve as a quick reference on current major projects in the public sector in Qatar. For further details on these projects, interested parties may contact the following:

Embassy of the United States of America
Ambassador: Elizabeth McKune
Deputy Chief of Mission: Matthew Tueller
Economic Commercial Officer: Darrin Hink
Economic Commercial Advisor: Jiryis H. Khoury
Commercial Clerk: Sima Carri
P.O. Box 2399
Doha, State of Qatar
Phone: (Comm): (974) 884-165 or (Embassy): (974) 884-101
Fax: (Comm): (974) 884-163 or (Embassy): (974) 884-298
E-mail: bfif97@qatar.net.qa

I. Projects in engineering, procurement and construction (EPC) stage :
1. Ras Abu Fontas 'B' Power & Desalination Plant (Ministry of Electricity and Water)
2. Qatar Fertilizer Company (QAFCO) III & IV Ammonia & Urea Projects
3. Qatar National Cement Company (QNCC) Plant II
4. Qatar Steel Company (QASCO) Rolling Mill Expansion
5. Qatar Liquefied Natural Gas Co. (Qatargas)
6. Ras Laffan Liquefied Natural Gas Co. (Rasgas)
7. Qatar Steel Company (QASCO) New EAF No. 3
8. Qatar Fuel Additives Company (QAFAC) Methanol/MTBE Project
9. Doha International Airport

II. Projects in the early stages of pre-qualification, tender and bid evaluation:
1. Ras Abu Fontas 'C' Power & Desalination Plant (Ministry of Electricity and Water)
2. Qatar Clean Energy Company (QACENCO)
3. Qatar Industrial Manufacturing Company (QIMCO): Melamine Plant

4. Qatar Hot Briquetted Iron Company (QABICO): HBI Plant
5. National Oil Distribution Co. Expansion (NODCO)
6. Qatar Vinyl Co. (QVC)
7. Qatar Salt Company
8. Q-CHEM Ethylene/Polyethylene Complex (Phillips)
9. Qatar Primary Route Project
10. Doha Port: Container Cranes
11. NGL-4 Project

III. Projects in the proposal & study stage:
1. Qatar General Petroleum Corporation (QGPC)/Exxon Gas Conversion Plant
2. Qatar General Petroleum Corporation (QGPC)-Phillips-SASOL GTL Plant
3. Norsk Hydro-QGPC Aluminum Smelter
4. Qatar Steel Company (QASCO) Expansion Plans
4.1 Pelletizing Plant
4.2 Flat Rolled Products
5. Qatar-Iran Water Pipeline
6. Enron Liquefied Natural Gas (LNG) Project
7. Condensate Refinery - Mobil/Total/ Qatar General Petroleum Corporation (QGPC)
8. Enhanced Gas Utilization Project - NGL-5

**For additional analytical, business and investment opportunities information,
please contact Global Investment & Business Center, USA
at (202) 546-2103. Fax: (202) 546-3275. E-mail: rusric@erols.com
Global Business E-Books on Line: http://world.mirhouse.com**

SPEACHES OF THE EMIR

ON THE OCCASION OF THE RENDERING OF THE AWARD OF THE INTERNATIONAL COURT JUSTICE ON THE BORDER DISPUTE BETWEEN QATAR AND BAHRAIN

IN THE NAME OF GOD THE MOST COMPASSIONATE THE MOST MERCIFUL

Fellow Citizens,

I am addressing you today on the occasion of the rendering of the award of the international court of justice in the case of the border dispute between the two states of qatar and bahrain which we all have been waiting for since the conclusion of the oral pleadings at the court at the end of last june.

Undoubtedly, this long standing dispute of 62 years dominated relations between the two countries and their brotherly peoples throughout that period. During this dispute, these relations underwent several tensions and a few occasions of relaxation which would barely begin only to come to an end, with all the implications arising from the continuation and escalation of the dispute. Hence we became strongly convinced that we should pursue every possible course to put an end to this situation and settle for good the dispute between us and our brothers in bahrain, not only in the interest of relations between our two countries and peoples, but also in the interest of the security and stability of the gulf region as well as consolidating our gulf cooperation council.

In this context, qatar tried its best to find an objective settlement of this dispute by means of direct negotiation at one time, and the mediation of the sisterly kingdom of saudi arabia at another.

However, these endeavours were not successful due to the difference in positions and sensitivity of the disputed matters for either side. There remained no choice other than a judicial settlement, which was agreed upon by the two sides in1987 and 1990 under the patronage of my brother King Fahd Bin Abdulaziz Al Saud, the custodian of the two holy mosques, in the framework of his kind mediation which culminated in referring the matter to the international court of justice.

FELLOW CITIZENS,

As you know, the court has rendered its final award this evening. Although this award has many positive aspects that confirmed the rights of the state of qatar to its territorial lands, its maritime zones, its continental shelf, and its exclusive economic zone including the pearl banks, and in janan island, fasht dibal, and qitaat shajara and qitaat aarj and other maritime areas shown in the map attached to the award, yet it has awarded hawar islands to the state of bahrain.

Allow me to be frank with you as I have always been: the court award in this respect was not easy upon us. These islands have a great standing in the hearts of our people, a standing that is deeply rooted in the history of this country and the keenness of its sons to be bound to each grain of its soil.

However, despite the pain we feel, we think that the court award has, anyway, put an end to the dispute between the two states, and we can now put that dispute, which has become part of history, behind our backs.

While looking forward to the future, we realize that our sacrifice will not be in vain since it lays the foundation for closer and broader unblemished relations between qatar and bahrain and their brotherly peoples. Moreover, it will enhance the security and stability of our gulf states and contribute to strengthening the cooperation council for the gulf arab states (gcc) and consolidating the process of integration of its member states.

While congratulating the two peoples of qatar and bahrain on the ending of the dispute between the two countries, I extend to my brother, his highness sheikh hamad bin issa al-khalifa, amir of the sisterly state of bahrain, a hand that has always been full of fraternity and cordiality, so that we can together close that page and open a new chapter, where the two brotherly people take part in planning and deepening our future relations, where the two countries interact for their common interest and prosperity.

On this occasion, I would like to extend my thanks and appreciation to my brother, king fahd bin abdul aziz, the custodian of the two holy mosques, and my brother, his majesty Sultan Qaboos Bin Saeed, for their distinctive roles and efforts that have brought the two countries to the highest legal and judicial authority to have their dispute settled.

I also find this an opportunity to extend thanks and appreciation to all those who have sincerely contributed to the case of qatar, and to express all commendation and appreciation to the people of qatar for their strong backing and support of their national causes over the last six decades.

May the mercy of god be upon the martyrs of both countries: and eternal peace for our forefathers, our martyrs in damsah and wakra, and every martyr who fought for this country.

May the peace and mercy of god be upon you.

SPEECH ON THE ORDINARY SESSION OF THE ARAB SUMMIT

IN THE NAME OF GOD
THE MOST COMPASSIONATE THE MOST MERCIFUL

Your Majesty, Brother King Abdullah II Bin Al-Hussein Descendant of Hashem, The King of the sisterly Hashemite Kingdom of Jordan,

Your Majesties, Highnesses and Excellencies,

The U.N. Secretary-General,

The Arab League Secretary-General,

Members of the Delegations,

An optimistic analyst may not err much if he concludes that the Middle East region is going through one of the most critical juncture in its history and the most deteriorating in decades because of the very grave circumstances of the prime cause of the Arabs and Muslims: that is the cause of Palestine.

Would it take much effort from us to understand and then to analyse such Israeli violation of international legitimacy rules, the U.N. conventions and the principles of human rights? Has force, killing and siege become values and familiar, acceptable practices that do not contravene right and law?

This situation that seems to have emptied, or almost did so, the vocabulary of international law, the respect of sovereignty and human rights of every meaning and connotation, is the result of the flagrant contraventions of those international norms and conventions by the Israeli governments through their war machines.

Hence we are not surprised to have arrived at the conviction that the recurrent statements of condemnation and denunciation are not heeded by Israel, as you know, but its arrogance and intransigence prompted it to openly threaten the security of sisterly Arab countries and, thus, our national Arab security.

We, my brothers, as leaders and peoples, have a cause, and are champions of peace, not submission. Hence I address the co-sponsors of the peace conference, the other permanent members of the Security Council, The E.U. member states and all peace-loving powers, and say: Oppression portends the ruin of nations; it generates despair and relegates moderation. Maintaining stability in our region makes it necessary now to secure international protection for the unarmed Palestinian people and to curb Israeli intransigence – to apply similar measures taken in other less important cases in other parts of the world. Talking about international legality that is founded on equity and justice and realization of just and comprehensive peace requires the restoration of all Palestinian rights, withdrawal from all occupied Palestinian territories and the Syrian Golan Heights to the borders of June 4th and completion of withdrawal from the Lebanese territories to the internationally recognized borders.

We thank Almighty God to have guided us to endorse the convening of the Arab Summit Conference on a rotational basis, the idea of which has been inspired by the sons of the Palestinian Intifada. Such regular meetings will cement our cohesion, deepen avenues of joint cooperation among ourselves, armed with the necessary political will and our civilizational depth, to establish a new climate that adopts the culture of tolerance as an attitude, a course and a strong bond in our relations and practices.

Hence, all our peoples are waiting for positive positions and rational, practicable resolutions from us. They expect reinforcing of our political and economic support to our Palestinian brothers in their blessed Intifada, which is a legitimate exercise of self defence and for regaining the right to live in peace in an independent Palestinian State.

Moreover, our peoples expect us to close for ever the chapter of the second Gulf crisis, to restore confidence by confirming the rights of the sisterly State of Kuwait, and the return of brotherly Iraq to its natural place in the fold of the Arab family.

Our peoples are also looking to us to invigorate the role of the Arab League, the prime house of the Arabs, through reactivating its institutions, to renew its activity, its vigour and functions so as to respond to the requirements of the Arab nation at the beginning of the Third Millennium at the levels of political and economic integration and social development.

More than five decades have elapsed since the Arab League was formed. However, the Arab citizen has not found in it what he looks for and what he aspires to achieve. I have the feeling that this citizen has lost faith in the viability of such summits and the effectiveness of their resolutions. He has become indifferent to the decisions presented or adopted, considering them ineffective and not viable. This is a very serious matter which is contrary to our policy as leaders and officials. We believe that the way out of this situation necessitates the application of the principle of popular participation and the activation of the role of the constitutional institutions in Arab societies, because such participation symbolizes in the hearts of peoples a right and self-determination and the future of their generations.

Our pride in the Arab League spurs us to pursue serious, continuous action to develop it and reinvigorate its activity. We wish our new candidate for the Arab League Secretary-General post, Mr. Amr Mousa, all success to dedicate his personal skills and political experiences to the service of this Arab edifice.

We are, my brothers, faced with an unprecedented challenge that makes it incumbent upon us to shoulder our full responsibilities before God the Almighty and before our peoples. We have great confidence in this summit for which my brother, His Majesty King Abdullah II Bin Al-Hussein, and the Jordanian people have prepared all means of success, to put the basis for effective joint Arab action that develops gains and achieves aspirations.

May God lead us to success. And may the peace, mercy and blessings of God be upon you.

SPEECH AT THE EMERGENCY MEETING OF MINISTERS OF FOREIGN AFFAIRS OF THE ISLAMIC COUNTRIES

In the name of God The Compassionate, The Merciful

Your Excellency Brother Yasser Arafat, President of the State of Palestine,
Your Highnesses and Excellencies,
Dear Brothers,

You are welcome to this emergency meeting which is held in very critical circumstances. I do not wish to repeat that the region is going through grave escalation caused by the oppressive practices and continuous aggression carried out by Israel against the Palestinian people.

The initiative to call for this meeting was in response to a request by President Yasser Arafat and in line with the commitment of the Organization of Islamic Conference to its responsibilities towards the serious events in Palestine and the accelerating pace of deterioration resulting from them.

In fact the question that imposes itself on us in these difficult circumstances is: how can we support our Palestinian people? How can we protect these people from the aggression and harm they are exposed to? We can condemn and repeat that we are with them in their ordeal; but how can that convince the Palestinians who have a memory that we are really with them in their suffering? How can our thoughts and theirs, our positions and theirs, actually converge tangibly and not wishfully? It is undoubtedly not enough at all in this situation to repeat phrases of condemnation and denunciation, or issue resolutions that will have no response or effect on the actual reality.

God bless the people of Southern Lebanon who knew how to liberate their land, and by the means they chose and followed to reach their goal. If the people of Southern Lebanon were repeating what we repeat, could they have been able to achieve that victory?

Let us also ask ourselves: Could the action and practices undertaken by the Israeli government chaired by Sharon have been done if they had not already known that the Islamic reaction, and the Arab response in particular, will not go beyond condemnation and denunciation, and that while we demand peace from Israel we do not have the power that would help impose peace?

What is happening now in the Palestinian territories is first and foremost due to a feeling of injustice, frustration and loss of hope as a result of this Israeli policy and its oppressive practices. Since the first day of this Intifada, the Israeli response was excessively violent and brutal. There is no moral, political or security justification for responding to stones with air strikes, guns and rockets and all kinds of weapons of a sophisticated war machine against unarmed people who have nothing but their belief in the justice of their cause and their right to live in freedom and dignity.

Hence the Intifada is continuing and the Palestinian people wanted to completely depend on themselves. These struggling people are well aware that their brethren will not assist them with more that issuing statements of condemnation and denunciation, or some financial aids.

We are for peace; if the Intifada is the force that will dictate peace, we, as Muslims and Arabs, have to stand up bravely and provide material and moral support for this Intifada. It deserves every backing up from us. It has compelled us and its heroes have forced us to stand in all pride before their heroisms and pray for its martyrs. We have to move earnestly and effectively for the support of our brethren, and provide them with what they need in assistance and backing to alleviate their harsh suffering, and enable them to stand steadfast in the face of the aggression to which they are exposed under this grave imbalance of powers. In doing so, we do not only assist the Palestinians but also defend our sanctities and rights.

Brothers,

All of us have to expose to the international community this stark contradiction and double standards imposed by Israel at the level of international legality. Here is a United Nations member state which we see, as do all others, disavowing all its obligations and repudiating all its commitments.

We were hoping that with the growing concern of the international community with human rights and the fundamental developments in International Law in this field, and in other related domains such as the conventions regulating the rights and protection of civilians under occupation, that the international community will have a firm stance vis-à-vis the daily crimes committed by Israel against unarmed women and children in the occupied Palestinian territories. Yet what we see daily in Palestine, and the whole world sees, makes us doubt the credibility of those principles and values which we, as members of the international community, have blessed and endorsed.

That is why despite our appreciation for the international favourable response to the Mitchell Committee Report that has been welcomed by the Palestinian Authority and adopted by the United States as a course for its action, our experiences with Israel and its indifference to international resolutions, coupled with the inability of the international community to impose them upon it, make us fear that this report will be treated in the same way as several other international resolutions and agreements it has signed.

Hence, I hope that we emerge from this meeting with a unified Islamic strategy based on activation of the Doha Summit Conference resolutions in coping with the present circumstances, and material support to the Palestinian people in their legitimate struggle, while calling on the United Nations and the Security Council in particular to provide international protection for this people, and force Israel to halt all kinds of settlement activities in the Palestinian territories, and put an end to all forms of expansion and confiscation, and stop its constant violations of Islamic or Christian sacred placed. We have to seek in all earnest to activate the strategic role of the co-sponsors of the peace process, i.e. the United States of America and the Russian Federation, to carry out their fundamental responsibilities in this direction.

The United States of America, with the capabilities it has, has played a pivotal role in sponsoring the peace process since the 1991 Madrid Conference. This role helped strengthen confidence in its ability to bring this process to its desired goal, which made several Arab countries take part in it. It is, therefore, necessary that the United States continues to honour its commitments in the Arab-Israeli conflict, which will only end with the complete withdrawal of Israel from all the occupied Palestinian and Arab lands and recognition of the lawful national rights of their Arab people.

Hence I call upon the American administration and upon President George Bush in person, to the necessity of immediate intervention to put an end to this deteriorating condition which should no longer be kept silent about, and put pressure on the Israeli government to force it to halt its aggression and return without any prior conditions to abiding by the principles on which the peace process was based and the resumption of negotiations from the point where they have stopped. Israel cannot remain outside the framework of international legality, nor should it be beyond implementation of U.N. resolutions and conventions and the principles of human rights. If such resolutions and conventions and principles have to be executed, why are they not applied to Israel?

Arab and Islamic countries have been blockaded in the name of international legality. We have to wonder why this legality has been applied on some Arab and Islamic countries when it is not applied on Israel?

Where is this international legality that cannot provide security for an unarmed people, as is the case now in the West Bank and Gaza Strip?

We all know and always repeat double standards, while the double standards will always be applied on the weak peoples.

If these resolutions, conventions and principles are to be applied anywhere and to all crises and conflicts, they must necessarily be applied to the Arab-Israeli conflict and the Palestinian cause. The Palestinian people deserve to live like all other people of the world in freedom and dignity, and enjoy security and protection, and benefit from peace and prosperity in their homeland and on their land. Israel itself has to choose today between living in this region in security and peace or the continuation of this conflict for decades and generations, with all the resulting catastrophes and calamities that will fall on all states and peoples of the region.

Brothers,

In the face of these critical circumstances to which our brothers in Palestine are exposed, I propose that the Ministerial Committee formed at the 9th Islamic Summit should immediately resume its task by first calling for an emergency meeting of the Security Council to review the grave situation in the occupied Palestinian territories. The Committee should urgently proceed to the capitals of the five permanent member states of the Security Council, the European Union and the United Nations to discuss finding the necessary formulas and mechanisms for dealing with the deteriorating situation. I think it is necessary that the Committee should consider itself to be in continuous session to follow up the developments and propose the next steps.

May the Almighty God bestow His mercy on those who walked along the track of martyrdom and won it, and lead to triumph a people who believed and struggled and still is struggling to gain its right to live in freedom, with dignity and independence.

May the Peace and Blessing of God be upon you.

For additional analytical, business and investment opportunities information, please contact Global Investment & Business Center, USA at (202) 546-2103. Fax: (202) 546-3275. E-mail: rusric@erols.com Global Business E-Books on Line: http://world.mirhouse.com

THE MIDDLE EAST AND TERRORISM[4]

MIDDLE EAST OVERVIEW

Middle Eastern terrorist groups and their state sponsors continued to plan, train for, and carry out acts of terrorism throughout 2000. The last few months of the year brought a significant increase in the overall level of political violence and terrorism in the region, especially in Israel and the occupied territories. Much of the late-year increase in violence was driven by a breakdown in negotiations and counterterrorism cooperation between Israel and the Palestinian Authority. The breakdown sparked a cycle of violence between Israelis and Palestinians that continued to spiral at the end of the year.

Israeli-Palestinian violence also prompted widespread anger at Israel, as well as the United States, throughout the Middle East, demonstrated in part by numerous, occasionally violent protests against US interests in several Middle Eastern countries. Palestinian terrorist groups, with the assistance of Iran and the Lebanese Hizballah, took advantage of Palestinian and regional anger to escalate their terrorist attacks against Israeli
targets.

Other terrorists also keyed on Israeli-Palestinian difficulties to increase their rhetorical and operational activities against Israel and the United States. Usama Bin Ladin's al-Qaida organization, the Egyptian Islamic Jihad, and other terrorist groups that focus on US and Israeli targets escalated their efforts to conduct and promote terrorism in the Middle East. Several disrupted plans to attack US and Israeli targets in the Middle East purportedly were intended to demonstrate anger over Israel's sometimes disproportionate use of force to contain protests and perceptions that the United States "allowed" Israel to act.

Al-Qaida and its affiliates especially used their ability to provide money and training as leverage to establish ties to and build the terrorist capabilities of a variety of small Middle Eastern terrorist groups such as the Lebanese Asbat al-Ansar.

The most significant act of anti-US terrorism in the region in 2000--the bombing of the USS Cole in Yemen on 12 October--was not driven by events in the Levant. Although the joint US-Yemeni investigation into the savage bombing--which killed 17 US sailors and wounded 39 others--continued through the end of 2000, initial indications suggested the attack may have originated in Taliban-controlled Afghanistan, where al-Qaida, the Egyptian Islamic Jihad, and other terrorist groups are based and some of the alleged USS Cole attackers received training. The Yemeni Government, as much a victim of the attack as the United States, was working closely with the US Government to bring to justice those responsible for the act.

---

[4] Patterns of Global Terrorism -2000 Released by the Office of the Coordinator for Counterterrorism April 2001

Many other Middle Eastern governments also increased their efforts to counter the threat from regional and Afghanistan-based terrorists, including the provision of enhanced security for high-risk US Government targets. The Government of Kuwait, for instance, cooperated with regional counterparts in November to disrupt a suspected international terrorist cell. Kuwait arrested 13 individuals and recovered a large quantity of explosives and weapons. The cell reportedly was planning to attack both Kuwaiti officials and US targets in Kuwait and the region.

Algeria

President Bouteflika's Law on Civil Concord in 2000 initially contributed to a decrease in violence against civilians inside Algeria. Nonetheless, two main armed groups continued to reject the government's amnesty program for terrorists, and it is estimated that domestic terrorism kills between 100 to 300 persons each month. Antar Zouabri's Armed Islamic Group (GIA) actively targeted civilians, although such tactics caused his group to lose popular support. In contrast, Hassan Hattab's splinter faction--the Salalfi Group for Call and Combat (GSPC)--stated it would limit attacks on civilians, enabling it to co-opt Zouabri's supporters and eclipse the GIA as the most effective terrorist group operating inside Algeria.

Although at year's end the GSPC had not staged an anti-Western terrorist attack, various security services in January suspected Algerian extremists associated with the GSPC of planning to disrupt the Paris-Dakar Road Rally, leading organizers to reroute the race.

No foreign nationals were killed in Algeria during 2000, although in May GSPC troops crossed into Tunisia and attacked an outpost, killing three border guards. The GSPC frequently used false roadblocks to rob passengers of money. In one incident on 3 May, 19 persons were killed and 26 injured when militants sprayed a bus with bullets after the driver refused to stop.

Egypt

No terrorist attacks in Egypt or by Egyptian groups were reported in 2000. The Egyptian Government continued to regard terrorism as its most serious threat. Cairo tried and convicted numerous terrorists in 2000, including 14 al-Gama'a al-Islamiyya members, in connection with attempts to reactivate al-Gama'a in Egypt. Two Egyptian Islamic Jihad members, who were convicted in 1999 for planning an attack against the US Embassy in August 1998, were executed in February. Security forces attacked a terrorist hideout in Aswan in late October, killing two al-Gama'a members, including the group's military leader in charge of armed operations in Qina, Suhaj, and Luxor.

International counterterrorism cooperation remained a key foreign policy priority for the Egyptian Government throughout the year. In September, at the UN General Assembly Millennium Summit, Egypt signed the International Convention for the Suppression of Terrorist Financing.

The Egyptian Government worked closely with the United States on a broad range of counterterrorism issues in 2000. It cooperated with US authorities after the bombing in October of the USS Cole in Yemen, conducting a security survey of the Suez Canal and recommending measures to protect ships from possible terrorist attacks while transiting the canal. Egypt also played an important role in sharing its expertise at the Central Asian Counterterrorism Conference sponsored by the US Department of State and held in Washington in June.

In 2000, Egyptian security forces and government agencies continued to place a high priority on protecting US citizens and facilities in Egypt from terrorist attacks. The Egyptian Government increased security for the US Embassy and other official facilities in light of disturbances in Israel and the Palestinian territories and related threats against US interests.

Israel, the West Bank, and the Gaza Strip

Terrorism by Palestinian extremist groups opposed to the peace process increased in late 2000 against the backdrop of violent Palestinian-Israeli clashes. The Palestine Islamic Jihad (PIJ) and Islamic Resistance Movement (HAMAS) claimed responsibility for several attacks during the crisis, ending a period of more than two years without a large-scale successful terrorist operation. Both groups publicly threatened more anti-Israeli attacks to avenge Palestinian casualties.

In an operation almost certainly timed to mark the anniversary of the death of PIJ founder Fathi Shaqaqi in 1995, on 26 October a PIJ operative on a bicycle detonated an explosive device near a Jewish settlement in Gaza, killing himself and injuring an Israeli soldier. The PIJ also claimed responsibility for a car bomb that exploded near a Jerusalem market on 2 November, killing two Israeli civilians--including the daughter of Israeli National Religious Party leader Yitzhak Levy--and wounding nine. The bomb--which was concealed in a parked car--reportedly was remotely detonated; the perpetrators escaped. On 28 December, PIJ operatives detonated explosive charges near the Sufa crossing in Gaza, injuring four Israeli explosives-disposal experts, two of whom later died. The PIJ claimed the attack in honor of a PIJ member killed by Israeli forces earlier that month and promised further revenge attacks.

The PIJ stepped up its rhetoric condemning Israeli-Palestinian peace talks at Camp David and Israel for its role in clashes with the Palestinians and vowed to continue attacks against Israel. Before the crisis, PIJ leader Shallah had issued threats against US interests in response to speculation during the summer that Washington was considering moving the US Embassy from Tel Aviv to Jerusalem.

HAMAS also claimed responsibility for several attacks during the unrest, including the bombing of an Israeli bus on 22 November in downtown Hadera that killed two Israeli civilians and wounded more than 20. Resembling the car-bombing on 2 November, the bomb apparently also was hidden in a parked car and detonated as the bus passed; at year's end no suspects had been arrested for the attack. The group also took responsibility for launching an explosives-laden craft against an Israeli naval patrol boat

For additional analytical, business and investment opportunities information, please contact Global Investment & Business Center, USA at (202) 546-2103. Fax: (202) 546-3275. E-mail: rusric@erols.com Global Business E-Books on Line: http://world.mirhouse.com

off the Gaza coast on 7 November. The operative died in the explosion, according to a HAMAS statement, but the Israeli boat suffered no damage. A suicide bomber killed himself and injured three Israeli soldiers at a cafe in Moshav Mehola on 22 December; HAMAS's military wing claimed responsibility four days later.

Two Israeli civilians were killed when a powerful car bomb exploded next to this bus in the Northern Israeli town of Hadera on 22 November. The attack also injured more than 30 others.

Two Israeli civilians were killed when a powerful car bomb exploded next to this bus in the Northern Israeli town of Hadera on 22 November. The attack also injured more than 30 others.

In addition, other groups or individuals may have carried out terrorist attacks during the year. Three little-known groups--Palestinian Hizballah, Umar al-Mukhtar Forces, and the Martyrs of al-Aqsa--claimed responsibility for the bombing of an Israeli settler school bus in Gaza on 20 November that killed two Israelis. The al-Aqsa group also claimed responsibility for killing prominent Jewish extremist Binyamin Kahane, himself the leader of a terrorist organization, and his wife on 31 December. Kahane's death prompted heightened concern among Israeli security services that Jewish extremists would extend their violent attacks against Palestinian civilians to include "spectacular" operations, including against the Haram al-Sharif/Temple Mount. A group calling itself Salah al-Din Battalions claimed responsibility for bombing a bus in Tel Aviv on 28 December, injuring 13 persons. Israeli authorities accused Palestinian Authority (PA) security officials of facilitating the attack. The Salah al-Din Battalions reportedly also carried out a shooting attack in mid-November that killed at least one Israeli soldier.

In late summer, Israeli authorities arrested Nabil Awkil, a militant they suspect has links to HAMAS and Usama Bin Ladin. Israeli officials claim that Awkil underwent terrorist training in Bin Ladin-affiliated camps in Afghanistan before returning to the West Bank and Gaza to establish terrorist cells.

Earlier in the year, PA and Israeli security forces disrupted HAMAS networks that were planning several large-scale anti-Israeli attacks. On 10 February a botched bombing plot in Nabulus led to the discovery of a HAMAS explosives lab, several caches, and a multicell network in the West Bank. The network was preparing major terrorist operations designed to inflict mass casualties, including the bombing of a high-rise building in Jerusalem. The Israelis linked those arrested to a series of pipe-bomb attacks in Hadera in 1999. In March, an Israeli raid on a HAMAS hideout in the predominantly Israeli-Arab town of Et Taiyiba uncovered an extensive HAMAS network with ties to Gaza that was planning multiple terrorist attacks in Israel. The cell planned to carry out four-to-five simultaneous suicide bombings against Israeli targets, including bus stops and hitchhiking stations inside Israel frequented by Israeli soldiers. The PA discovered

For additional analytical, business and investment opportunities information, please contact Global Investment & Business Center, USA at (202) 546-2103. Fax: (202) 546-3275. E-mail: rusric@erols.com Global Business E-Books on Line: http://world.mirhouse.com

additional explosives in a Gaza kindergarten and arrested a bodyguard of HAMAS leader Shaykh Yasin on suspicion of having links to the Et Taiyiba cell. Israeli authorities arrested a Jewish settler and indicted an Israeli Arab for allegedly assisting the cell.

Israeli and PA security officials took additional measures, often coordinated, to further disrupt HAMAS terrorist planning. PA police in mid-March, following up on the Et Taiyiba raid, uncovered a HAMAS explosives lab in Tulkarm. Separate Israeli and PA operations disrupted HAMAS cells in Janin later that month. The PA also disrupted in mid-July another HAMAS explosives lab in Nabulus and made at least a dozen arrests. The PA inflicted additional damage on HAMAS's military wing with the arrest of two key leaders in 2000. In May, PA security forces arrested Gaza military wing leader Muhammad al-Dayf. In November, Dayf escaped from PA custody. West Bank military wing leader Mahmud al-Shuli (a.k.a. Abu Hanud) surrendered to PA security officials in August after a firefight with IDF soldiers in his hometown of `Asirah ash Shamaliyah near the West Bank town of Nabulus. Three IDF soldiers were killed by friendly fire in the incident. At year's end Abu Hanud remained in Palestinian custody, serving a 12-year sentence handed down by a PA security court.

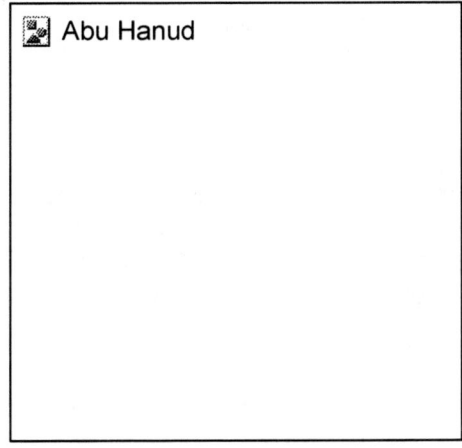
Abu Hanud

Abu Hanud

During the unrest HAMAS issued numerous statements calling for Palestinians to fight the Israelis with all means available and threatened to continue attacks to avenge Palestinian casualties. The group also vowed revenge for the killing of several HAMAS operatives during the unrest at year's end, including Ibrahim `Awda, who was killed on 23 November in Nabulus. HAMAS issued public statements accusing the Israelis of assassinating `Awda, who reportedly died when the headrest in the car he was driving exploded, although the Israelis claim he died transporting an explosive device. HAMAS vowed revenge for the killing of activist Abbas Othman Ewaywi, who was gunned down by Israeli security forces in front of a shop in Hebron on 13 December.

Despite demonstrated Palestinian efforts to uproot terrorist infrastructure earlier in the year, Israeli officials publicly expressed their dissatisfaction with PA counter-terrorism efforts during the crisis. The Israelis also accused PA security officials and Fatah members of facilitating and taking part in shooting and bombing attacks against Israeli targets, including the bus bombing in Tel Aviv on 28 December. The Israelis charged that the release of several prisoners during the crisis had facilitated terrorist planning by the groups and that Palestinian security officials had not been responsive to their calls for more decisive measures against the violence.

Israeli officials publicly expressed well-founded concern that Iran supported Palestinian rejectionist efforts to disrupt the Middle East peace process. The Israelis also stated Palestinian rejectionists increasingly were influenced by Lebanese Hizballah. Public statements by HAMAS, the PIJ, and other Palestinian rejectionist officials since the Israeli withdrawal from southern Lebanon in May lauded Hizballah's actions and called for emulating Hizballah's victory in the territories.

Jordan

Jordan remained vigilant against terrorism in 2000. On 18 September, the State Security Court convicted several Sunni extremists, some in absentia, for plotting terrorist attacks against US and Israeli targets during the millennium celebrations in late 1999. The accused allegedly acted on behalf of Usama Bin Ladin. The three-member military tribunal sentenced eight defendants to death but immediately commuted two of the sentences to life imprisonment at hard labor, citing family reasons. Six others, including a minor, were acquitted, while the remaining 14 received prison sentences ranging from seven-and-a-half to 15 years. Lawyers for 10 of the convicted men have appealed the verdicts.

On 9 December the State Security Court indicted Ra'id Hijazi, a US-Jordanian dual national who had been sentenced to death in absentia in January for having had a role in the millenial plot. He had been recently remanded by Syria. Khalil Deek, another US-Jordanian dual citizen, was brought to Jordan from Pakistan in December 1999 to face charges in the plot but at year's end had yet to be tried. Jordanian authorities were handling his case separately from the other suspects.

Two Israeli diplomats in Jordan were targets of shooting attacks in the latter part of the year. An unidentified gunman shot at Israeli Vice Consul Yoram Havivian outside his home in Amman on 19 November. On 5 December, an unidentified gunman wounded another Israeli diplomat, Shlomo Ratzabi, as he, his wife, and bodyguard left a grocery store in Amman. Both diplomats suffered minor injuries and returned to Israel soon after the attacks. By year's end, Jordanian authorities had detained several suspects and were continuing their investigation. Two previously unknown groups, the Movement for the Struggle of the Jordanian Islamic Resistance and the Holy Warriors of Ahmad Daqamseh, claimed responsibility for the attacks, which coincided with rising public sympathy in Jordan for Palestinians in ongoing violence with Israel. (Ahmad Daqamseh is a Jordanian soldier currently serving a life sentence for killing six Israeli schoolgirls in 1997.)

Jordan continued to ban all HAMAS activity, and the Supreme Court upheld the expulsion of four Political Bureau leaders. Jordan's Prime Minister reiterated the government's conditions for their return at a meeting with HAMAS leaders during the Organization of the Islamic Conference summit in Doha in November. The conditions reportedly included a renunciation of their HAMAS affiliation. In December, lawyers for

For additional analytical, business and investment opportunities information,
please contact Global Investment & Business Center, USA
at (202) 546-2103. Fax: (202) 546-3275. E-mail: rusric@erols.com
Global Business E-Books on Line: http://world.mirhouse.com

the group announced their intention to appeal once again to Jordan's Supreme Court to contest the deportation. Jordan refused to permit HAMAS military wing members to reside or operate in the country but allowed other lower-level HAMAS members to remain in Jordan provided they did not conduct activities on the group's behalf.

Several low-level incidents kept security forces focused on combating threats to Jordan. Police in the southern city of Ma'an in January detained 15 suspects in connection with two shooting attacks against a female dormitory at Al-Hussein University. Four women were injured slightly in one attack. Police sources reported that the suspects were affiliated with a group called the Islamic Renewal and Reform Organization. Before the attacks, leaflets denouncing coeducation and calling for women to wear veils were distributed on campus.

The Government of Jordan also regularly interdicted the smuggling across Jordan's borders of weapons and explosives, which, in many cases, may have been destined for Palestinian rejectionist groups in the West Bank and Gaza. The government prosecuted individuals suspected of such activity.

In March, the government expelled eight Libyans it suspected of having terrorist links, and in September it refused entry to the leader of Israel's Islamic Movement, Shaykh Ra'id Salah. The Israelis publicly claimed that followers of Shaykh Salah have links to HAMAS and were involved in plans to conduct terrorist operations against Israeli interests earlier in the year.

Jordanian security forces coordinated closely with the US Embassy on security matters and acted quickly to bolster security at US Government facilities in response to other threats, including one against the US Embassy in June 2000.

Kuwait

In November the Government of Kuwait disrupted a suspected international terrorist cell. Working with regional counterparts, Kuwaiti security services arrested 13 individuals and recovered a large quantity of explosives and weapons. The terrorist cell reportedly was planning to attack both Kuwaiti officials and US targets in Kuwait and the region.

Lebanon

Throughout the year, the Lebanese Government's continued lack of control in portions of the country--including parts of the Bekaa Valley, Beirut's southern suburbs, Palestinian refugee camps, and the southern border area--as well as easy access to arms and explosives, contributed to an environment with a high potential for acts of violence and terrorism.

A variety of terrorist groups--including Hizballah, Usama Bin Ladin's (UBL) al-Qaida network, HAMAS, the PIJ, the PFLP-GC, `Asbat al-Ansar, and several local Sunni extremist organizations--continued to operate with varying degrees of impunity, conducting training and other operational activities. Hizballah continued to pose the most potent threat to US interests in Lebanon. Although Hizballah has not attacked US targets in Lebanon since 1991, it continued to pose a significant terrorist threat to US interests globally from its base in Lebanon. Hizballah voiced its support for terrorist actions by Palestinian rejectionist groups in Israel and the occupied territories. While the Lebanese Government expressed support for "resistance" activities along its southern border, it has only limited influence over Hizballah and the Palestinian rejectionists.

UBL's al-Qaida network maintained a presence in Lebanon. Although the Lebanese Government actively monitored and arrested UBL-affiliated operatives, it did not control the Palestinian refugee camps where the operatives conducted terrorist training and anti-US indoctrination.

In the fall, Hizballah kidnapped an Israeli noncombatant whom it may have lured to Lebanon on a false pretense. Hizballah has been using hostages, including captured IDF soldiers, as bargaining chips to win the release of Lebanese prisoners in Israel.

In January, Lebanese security forces clashed in the north with a Sunni extremist movement that had ambushed and killed four Lebanese soldiers. The group had ties to UBL operatives. The same month, Asbat al-Ansar launched a grenade attack against the Russian Embassy. In October, the Sunni extremist group, Takfir wa Hijra, claimed responsibility for a grenade attack against a Christian Member of Parliament's residence, though there are indications others may have been behind this attack.

The Lebanese Government continued to support some international counterterrorist initiatives and moved against UBL-affiliated operatives in 2000. In February, Lebanese authorities arrested members of a UBL cell in Lebanon. In March, the government fulfilled a Japanese Government request and deported four Japanese Red Army (JRA) members after it had refused to do so for years. It allowed one JRA member to remain in Lebanon. It did not act, however, on repeated US requests to turn over Lebanese terrorists involved in the hijacking in 1985 of TWA flight 847 and in the abduction, torture, and--in some cases--murders of US hostages from 1984 to 1991.

Saudi Arabia

Several threats against US military and civilian personnel and facilities in Saudi Arabia were reported in 2000, but there were no confirmed terrorist incidents. At year's end Saudi authorities were investigating a shooting by a lone gunman who opened fire on British and US nationals near the town of Khamis Mushayt in early August 2000. The gunman fired more than 100 rounds on a Royal Saudi Air Force checkpoint, killing one Saudi and wounding two other Saudi guards. The gunman was wounded in the exchange of fire.

Terrorist Usama Bin Ladin, whose Saudi citizenship was revoked in 1994, continued to publicly threaten US interests in Saudi Arabia during the year. In a videotaped statement released in September, Bin Ladin once again publicly threatened US interests.

The Government of Saudi Arabia continued to investigate the bombing in June 1996 of the Khubar Towers housing facility near Dhahran that killed 19 US military personnel and wounded some 500 US and Saudi personnel. The Government of Saudi Arabia publicly stated that it still was looking for three Saudi suspects whom it wanted for questioning in connection with the bombing and whom authorities believed to be currently outside Saudi Arabia. The Saudis continued to hold in detention a number of Saudi citizens linked to the attack, including Hani al-Sayegh, whom the United States expelled to Saudi Arabia in 1999.

The Government of Saudi Arabia reaffirmed its commitment to combating terrorism. It required nongovernmental organizations and private voluntary agencies to obtain government authorization before soliciting contributions for domestic or international causes. It was not clear that these regulations were enforced consistently; however, allegations continued to surface that some international terrorist organization representatives solicited and collected funds from private citizens in Saudi Arabia.

Yemen

On 12 October a boat carrying explosives was detonated next to the USS Cole, killing 17 US Navy members and injuring another 39. The US destroyer, en route to the Persian Gulf, was making a prearranged fuel stop in the Yemeni port of Aden when the attack occurred. At least three groups reportedly claimed responsibility for the attack, including the Islamic Army of Aden, Muhammad's Army, and a previously unknown group called the Islamic Deterrence Force.

On 12 October an explosives-laden craft was detonated next to the destroyer USS Cole in Aden Harbor, killing 17 US service persons and injuring 39 others.

On 12 October an explosives-laden craft was detonated next to the destroyer USS Cole in Aden Harbor, killing 17 US service persons and injuring 39 others.

The Yemeni Government strongly condemned the attack on the USS Cole and actively engaged in investigative efforts to find the perpetrators. On 29 November, Yemen and the United States signed a memorandum of agreement delineating guidelines for joint investigation to further facilitate cooperation between the two governments. The Yemeni Government's ability to conduct international terrorism investigations was enhanced by joint investigative efforts undertaken pursuant to these guidelines.

Several terrorist organizations maintained a presence in Yemen. HAMAS and the Palestinian Islamic Jihad continued to be recognized as legal organizations and maintained offices in Yemen but did not engage in terrorist activities there. Other international terrorist groups that have an illegal presence in Yemen included the Egyptian Islamic Jihad, al-Gama'a al-Islamiyya, Libyan opposition groups, the Algerian Armed Islamic Group, and al-Qaida. Press reports indicated indigenous groups such as the Islamic Army of Aden remained active in Yemen.

The Government of Yemen did not provide direct or indirect support to terrorists, but its inability to control fully its borders, territory, or its own travel documents did little to discourage the terrorist presence in Yemen. Improved cooperation with Saudi Arabia as a result of the Yemeni-Saudi border treaty, concluded in June, promised to reduce illegal border crossings and trafficking in weapons and explosives, although border clashes continued after the agreement's ratification. The government attempted to resolve some of its passport problems in 2000 by requiring proof of nationality when submitting an application, although terrorists continued to have access to forged Yemeni identity documents.

OVERVIEW OF STATE-SPONSORED TERRORISM

The designation of state sponsors of terrorism by the United States--and the imposition of sanctions--is a mechanism for isolating nations that use terrorism as a means of political expression. US policy seeks to pressure and isolate state sponsors so they will renounce the use of terrorism, end support to terrorists, and bring terrorists to justice for past crimes. The United States is committed to holding terrorists and those who harbor them accountable for past attacks, regardless of when the acts occurred. The US Government has a long memory and will not simply expunge a terrorist's record because time has passed. The states that choose to harbor terrorists are like accomplices who provide shelter for criminals. They will be held accountable for their "guests'" actions. International terrorists should know, before they contemplate a crime, that they cannot hunker down in safehaven for a period of time and be absolved of their crimes.

The United States is firmly committed to removing countries from the list once they have taken necessary steps to end their link to terrorism. In fact, the Department of State is engaged in ongoing discussions with North Korea and Sudan with the object of getting those governments completely out of the terrorism business and off the terrorism list.

Iran, Iraq, Syria, Libya, Cuba, North Korea, and Sudan continue to be the seven governments that the US Secretary of State has designated as state sponsors of international terrorism. Iran remained the most active state sponsor of terrorism in 2000. It provided increasing support to numerous terrorist groups, including the Lebanese Hizballah, HAMAS, and the Palestine Islamic Jihad (PIJ), which seek to undermine the Middle East peace negotiations through the use of terrorism. Iraq continued to provide safehaven and support to a variety of Palestinian rejectionist groups, as well as bases, weapons, and protection to the Mujahedin-e-Khalq (MEK), an Iranian terrorist group that

For additional analytical, business and investment opportunities information, please contact Global Investment & Business Center, USA at (202) 546-2103. Fax: (202) 546-3275. E-mail: rusric@erols.com Global Business E-Books on Line: http://world.mirhouse.com

opposes the current Iranian regime. Syria continued to provide safehaven and support to several terrorist groups, some of which oppose the Middle East peace negotiations. Libya at the end of 2000 was attempting to mend its international image following its surrender in 1999 of two Libyan suspects for trial in the Pan Am 103 bombing. (In early 2001, one of the suspects was convicted of murder. The judges in the case found that he acted "in furtherance of the purposes of...Libyan Intelligence Services.") Cuba continued to provide safehaven to several terrorists and US fugitives and maintained ties to state sponsors and Latin American insurgents. North Korea harbored several hijackers of a Japanese Airlines flight to North Korea in the 1970s and maintained links to other terrorist groups. Finally, Sudan continued to serve as a safehaven for members of al-Qaida, the Lebanese Hizballah, al-Gama'a al-Islamiyya, Egyptian Islamic Jihad, the PIJ, and HAMAS, but it has been engaged in a counterterrorism dialogue with the United States since mid-2000.

State sponsorship has decreased over the past several decades. As it decreases, it becomes increasingly important for all countries to adopt a "zero tolerance" for terrorist activity within their borders. Terrorists will seek safehaven in those areas where they are able to avoid the rule of law and to travel, prepare, raise funds, and operate. The United States continued actively researching and gathering intelligence on other states that will be considered for designation as state sponsors. If the United States deems a country to "repeatedly provide support for acts of international terrorism," the US Government is required by law to add it to the list. In South Asia, the United States has been increasingly concerned about reports of Pakistani support to terrorist groups and elements active in Kashmir, as well as Pakistani support, especially military support, to the Taliban, which continues to harbor terrorist groups, including al-Qaida, the Egyptian Islamic Jihad, al-Gama'a al-Islamiyya, and the Islamic Movement of Uzbekistan. In the Middle East, the United States was concerned that a variety of terrorist groups operated and trained inside Lebanon, although Lebanon has acted against some of those groups. Lebanon also has been unresponsive to US requests to bring to justice terrorists who conducted attacks against US citizens and property in Lebanon in previous years.

Cuba
Cuba continued to provide safehaven to several terrorists and US fugitives in 2000. A number of Basque ETA terrorists who gained sanctuary in Cuba some years ago continued to live on the island, as did several US terrorist fugitives.

Havana also maintained ties to other state sponsors of terrorism and Latin American insurgents. Colombia's two largest terrorist organizations, the Revolutionary Armed Forces of Colombia and the National Liberation Army, both maintained a permanent presence on the island.

Iran
Despite the victory for moderates in Iran's Majles elections in February, aggressive countermeasures by hardline conservatives have blocked most reform efforts. Iran remained the most active state sponsor of terrorism in 2000. Its Revolutionary Guard Corps (IRGC) and Ministry of Intelligence and Security (MOIS) continued to be involved in the planning and the execution of terrorist acts and continued to support a variety of groups that use terrorism to pursue their goals.

For additional analytical, business and investment opportunities information,
please contact Global Investment & Business Center, USA
at (202) 546-2103. Fax: (202) 546-3275. E-mail: rusric@erols.com
Global Business E-Books on Line: http://world.mirhouse.com

Iran's involvement in terrorist-related activities remained focused on support for groups opposed to Israel and peace between Israel and its neighbors. Statements by Iran's leaders demonstrated Iran's unrelenting hostility to Israel. Supreme Leader Khamenei continued to refer to Israel as a "cancerous tumor" that must be removed; President Khatami, labeling Israel an "illegal entity," called for sanctions against Israel during the intifadah; and Expediency Council Secretary Rezai said, "Iran will continue its campaign against Zionism until Israel is completely eradicated." Iran has long provided Lebanese Hizballah and the Palestinian rejectionist groups--notably HAMAS, the Palestine Islamic Jihad, and Ahmad Jibril's PFLP-GC--with varying amounts of funding, safehaven, training, and weapons. This activity continued at its already high levels following the Israeli withdrawal from southern Lebanon in May and during the intifadah in the fall. Iran continued to encourage Hizballah and the Palestinian groups to coordinate their planning and to escalate their activities against Israel. Iran also provided a lower level of support--including funding, training, and logistics assistance--to extremist groups in the Gulf, Africa, Turkey, and Central Asia.

Although the Iranian Government has taken no direct action to date to implement Ayatollah Khomeini's fatwa against Salman Rushdie, the decree has not been revoked, and the $2.8 million bounty for his assassination has not been withdrawn. Moreover, hardline Iranians continued to stress that the decree is irrevocable. On the anniversary of the fatwa in February, the IRGC released a statement that the decree remains in force, and Ayatollah Yazdi, a member of the Council of Guardians, reiterated that "the decree is irrevocable and, God willing, will be carried out."

Iran also was a victim of Mujahedin-e-Khalq (MEK)-sponsored terrorism. The Islamic Republic presented a letter to the UN Secretary General in October citing seven acts of sabotage by the MEK against Iran between January and August 2000. The United States has designated the MEK as a Foreign Terrorist Organization.

Iraq

Iraq planned and sponsored international terrorism in 2000. Although Baghdad focused on antidissident activity overseas, the regime continued to support various terrorist groups. The regime has not attempted an anti-Western terrorist attack since its failed plot to assassinate former President Bush in 1993 in Kuwait.

Czech police continued to provide protection to the Prague office of the US Government-funded Radio Free Europe/Radio Liberty (RFE/RL), which produces Radio Free Iraq programs and employs expatriate journalists. The police presence was augmented in 1999, following reports that the Iraqi Intelligence Service (IIS) might retaliate against RFE/RL for broadcasts critical of the Iraqi regime.

To intimidate or silence Iraqi opponents of the regime living overseas, the IIS reportedly opened several new stations in foreign capitals during 2000. Various opposition groups joined in warning Iraqi dissidents abroad against newly established "expatriates' associations," which, they asserted, are IIS front organizations. Opposition leaders in London contended that the IIS had dispatched women agents to infiltrate their ranks and was targeting dissidents for assassination. In Germany, an Iraqi opposition figure denounced the IIS for murdering his son, who had recently left Iraq to join him abroad. Dr. Ayad `Allawi, Secretary General of the Iraqi National Accord, an opposition group, stated that relatives of dissidents living abroad are often arrested and jailed to intimidate activists overseas.

In northern Iraq, Iraqi agents reportedly killed a locally well-known religious personality who declined to echo the regime line. The regional security director in As Sulaymaniyah stated that Iraqi operatives were responsible for the car-bomb explosion that injured a score of passersby. Officials of the Iraqi Communist Party asserted that an attack on a provincial party headquarters had been thwarted when party security officers shot and wounded a terrorist employed by the IIS.

Baghdad continued to denounce and delegitimize UN personnel working in Iraq, particularly UN de-mining teams, in the wake of the killing in 1999 of an expatriate UN de-mining worker in northern Iraq under circumstances suggesting regime involvement. An Iraqi who opened fire at the UN Food and Agriculture Organization (FAO) office in Baghdad, killing two persons and wounding six, was permitted to hold a heavily publicized press conference at which he contended that his action had been motivated by the harshness of UN sanctions, which the regime regularly excoriates.

The Iraqi regime rebuffed a request from Riyadh for the extradition of two Saudis who had hijacked a Saudi Arabian Airlines flight to Baghdad, but did return promptly the passengers and the aircraft. Disregarding its obligations under international law, the regime granted political asylum to the hijackers and gave them ample opportunity to ventilate in the Iraqi Government-controlled and international media their criticisms of alleged abuses by the Saudi Arabian Government, echoing an Iraqi propaganda theme.

While the origins of the FAO attack and the hijacking were unclear, the Iraqi regime readily exploited these terrorist acts to further its policy objectives.

Several expatriate terrorist groups continued to maintain offices in Baghdad, including the Arab Liberation Front, the inactive 15 May Organization, the Palestine Liberation Front (PLF), and the Abu Nidal organization (ANO). PLF leader Abu `Abbas appeared on state-controlled television in the fall to praise Iraq's leadership in rallying Arab opposition to Israeli violence against Palestinians. The ANO threatened to attack Austrian interests unless several million dollars in a frozen ANO account in a Vienna bank were turned over to the group.

The Iraq-supported Iranian terrorist group, Mujahedin-e Khalq (MEK), regularly claimed responsibility for armed incursions into Iran that targeted police and military outposts, as well as for mortar and bomb attacks on security organization headquarters in various Iranian cities. MEK publicists reported that in March group members killed an Iranian colonel having intelligence responsibilities. An MEK claim to have wounded a general was denied by the Iranian Government. The Iraqi regime deployed MEK forces against its domestic opponents.

For additional analytical, business and investment opportunities information,
please contact Global Investment & Business Center, USA
at (202) 546-2103. Fax: (202) 546-3275. E-mail: rusric@erols.com
Global Business E-Books on Line: http://world.mirhouse.com

Libya

In 2000, Libya continued efforts to mend its international image in the wake of its surrender in 1999 of two Libyans accused of the bombing of Pan Am flight 103 over Lockerbie, Scotland, in 1988. Trial proceedings for the two defendants began in the Netherlands in May and were ongoing at year's end. (The court issued its verdict on 31 January 2001. It found Abdel Basset al-Megrahi guilty of murder, concluding that he caused an explosive device to detonate on board the airplane resulting in the murder of the flight's 259 passengers and crew as well as 11 residents of Lockerbie, Scotland. The judges found that he acted "in furtherance of the purposes of...Libyan Intelligence Services." Concerning the other defendant, Al-Amin Kalifa Fahima, the court concluded that the Crown failed to present sufficient evidence to satisfy the high standard of "proof beyond reasonable doubt" that is necessary in criminal cases.)

In 1999, Libya paid compensation for the death of a British policewoman[*], a move that preceded the reopening of the British Embassy. Libya also paid damages to the families of victims in the bombing of UTA flight 772. Six Libyans were convicted in absentia in that case, and the French judicial system is considering further indictments against other Libyan officials, including Libyan leader Muammar Qadhafi.

[*]In April 1984, a British policewoman was killed and 11 demonstrators were wounded when gunmen in the Libyan People's Bureau in London fired on a peaceful anti-Qadhafi demonstration outside their building.

Libya played a high-profile role in negotiating the release of a group of foreign hostages seized in the Philippines by the Abu Sayyaf Group, reportedly in exchange for a ransom payment. The hostages included citizens of France, Germany, Malaysia, South Africa, Finland, the Philippines, and Lebanon. The payment of ransom to kidnappers only encourages additional hostage taking, and the Abu Sayyaf Group, emboldened by its success, did seize additional hostages--including a US citizen--later in the year. Libya's behavior and that of other parties involved in the alleged ransom arrangement served only to encourage further terrorism and to make that region far more dangerous for residents and travelers.

At year's end, Libya had yet to comply fully with the remaining UN Security Council requirements related to Pan Am 103: accepting responsibility, paying appropriate compensation, disclosing all it knows, and renouncing terrorism. The United States remains dedicated to maintaining pressure on the Libyan Government until it does so. Qadhafi stated publicly that his government had adopted an antiterrorism stance, but it remains unclear whether his claims of distancing Libya from its terrorist past signify a true change in policy.

Libya also remained the primary suspect in several other past terrorist operations, including the Labelle discotheque bombing in Berlin in 1986 that killed two US servicemen and one Turkish civilian and wounded more than 200 persons. The trial in Germany of five suspects in the bombing, which began in November 1997, continued in 2000. Although Libya expelled the Abu Nidal organization and distanced itself from the Palestinian rejectionists in 1999, it continued to have contact with groups that use violence to oppose the Middle East Peace Process, including the Palestine Islamic Jihad and the Popular Front for the Liberation of Palestine-General Command.

North Korea

In 2000 the Democratic People's Republic of Korea (DPRK) engaged in three rounds of terrorism talks that culminated in a joint DPRK-US statement wherein the DPRK reiterated its opposition to terrorism and agreed to support international actions against such activity. The DPRK, however, continued to provide safehaven to the Japanese Communist League-Red Army Faction members who participated in the hijacking of a Japanese Airlines flight to North Korea in 1970. Some evidence also suggests the DPRK may have sold weapons directly or indirectly to terrorist groups during the year; Philippine officials publicly declared that the Moro Islamic Liberation Front had purchased weapons from North Korea with funds provided by Middle East sources.

Sudan

The United States and Sudan in mid-2000 entered into a dialogue to discuss US counterterrorism concerns. The talks, which were ongoing at the end of the year, were constructive and obtained some positive results. By the end of the year Sudan had signed all 12 international conventions for combating terrorism and had taken several other positive counterterrorism steps, including closing down the Popular Arab and Islamic Conference, which served as a forum for terrorists.

Sudan, however, continued to be used as a safehaven by members of various groups, including associates of Usama Bin Ladin's al-Qaida organization, Egyptian al-Gama'a al-Islamiyya, Egyptian Islamic Jihad, the Palestine Islamic Jihad, and HAMAS. Most groups used Sudan primarily as a secure base for assisting compatriots elsewhere.

Khartoum also still had not complied fully with UN Security Council Resolutions 1044, 1054, and 1070, passed in 1996--which demand that Sudan end all support to terrorists. They also require Khartoum to hand over three Egyptian Gama'a fugitives linked to the assassination attempt in 1995 against Egyptian President Hosni Mubarak in Ethiopia. Sudanese officials continued to deny that they had a role in the attack.

Syria

Syria continued to provide safehaven and support to several terrorist groups, some of which maintained training camps or other facilities on Syrian territory. Ahmad Jibril's Popular Front for the Liberation of Palestine-General Command (PFLP-GC), the Palestine Islamic Jihad (PIJ), Abu Musa's Fatah-the-Intifada, and George Habash's Popular Front for the Liberation of Palestine (PFLP) maintained their headquarters in Damascus. The Syrian Government allowed HAMAS to open a new main office in Damascus in March, although the arrangement may be temporary while HAMAS continues to seek permission to reestablish its headquarters in Jordan. In addition, Syria granted a variety of terrorist groups--including HAMAS, the PFLP-GC, and the PIJ--basing privileges or refuge in areas of Lebanon's Bekaa Valley under Syrian control. Damascus generally upheld its agreement with Ankara not to support the Kurdish PKK, however.

For additional analytical, business and investment opportunities information, please contact Global Investment & Business Center, USA at (202) 546-2103. Fax: (202) 546-3275. E-mail: rusric@erols.com Global Business E-Books on Line: http://world.mirhouse.com

Weapons-of-Mass-Destruction (WMD) Terrorism

At the dawn of a new millennium, the possibility of a terrorist attack involving weapons of mass destruction (WMD)--chemical, biological, radiological, nuclear (CBRN), or large explosive weapons--remained real. As of the end of 2000, however, the most notorious attack involving chemical weapons against a civilian target remained Aum Shinrikyo's sarin nerve agent attack against the Tokyo subway in March 1995.

Most terrorists continued to rely on conventional tactics, such as bombing, shooting, and kidnapping, but some terrorists--such as Usama Bin Ladin and his associates--continued to seek CBRN capabilities.

- *Popular literature and the public dialog focused on the vulnerability of civilian targets to CBRN attacks. Such attacks could cause lasting disruption and generate significant psychological impact on a population and its infrastructure.*

- *A few groups, notably those driven by distorted religious and cultural ideologies, showed signs they were willing to cause large numbers of casualties. Other potentially dangerous but less predictable groups had emerged, and those groups may not abide by traditional targeting constraints that would prohibit using indiscriminate violence or CBRN weapons.*

- *Some CBRN materials, technology, and especially information continued to be widely available, particularly from commercial sources and the Internet.*

Terrorist Use of Information Technology

Terrorists have seized upon the worldwide practice of using information technology (IT) in daily life. They embrace IT for several reasons: it improves communication and aids organization, allows members to coordinate quickly with large numbers of followers, and provides a platform for propaganda. The Internet also allows terrorists to reach a wide audience of potential donors and recruits who may be located over a large geographic area.

In addition, terrorists are taking note of the proliferation of hacking and the use of the computer as a weapon. Extremists routinely post messages to widely accessible Web sites that call for defacing Western Internet sites and disrupting online service, for example. The widespread availability of hacking software and its anonymous and increasingly automated design make it likely that terrorists will more frequently incorporate these tools into their online activity. The appeal of such tools may increase as news media continue to sensationalize hacking.

Although Syria claimed to be committed to the peace process, it did not act to stop Hizballah and Palestinian rejectionist groups from carrying out anti-Israeli attacks. Damascus also served as the primary transit point for terrorist operatives traveling to Lebanon and for the resupply of weapons to Hizballah. Damascus appeared to maintain its longstanding ban on attacks launched from Syrian territory or against Western targets.

SELECTED QATAR NEWS AND DEVELOPMENTS[5]

OFFICIAL

EMIR RECEIVES US SENATOR: HH the Emir, Sheikh Hamad bin Khalifa al-Thani, received at his Emiri Diwan office yesterday US Senator Richard Shelby and his accompanying delegation. The existing relations between the two countries were reviewed during the meeting, together with a host of regional and international issues.

The meeting was attended by the Emiri Diwan chief HE Sheikh Abdullah bin Mohamed bin Saud al-Thani, the acting director of the European and American Affairs Department at the Foreign Ministry Ali Saad al-Kharji and the US Ambassador to Qatar, Elizabeth McKune.

I Minister of State for Interior Affairs HE Sheikh Hamad bin Nasser bin Jassim al-Thani also conferred with senator Shelby and his accompanying delegation. They discussed bilateral relations.

NEW APPOINTMENT: HH the Emir, Sheikh Hamad bin Khalifa al-Thani, yesterday issued an Emiri decision appointing HE Sheikh Ahmed bin Mohamed bin Jabor al-Thani a secretary general of the Planning Council at the rank of ministry undersecretary. The decision enters into force and becomes operative as of the date of issue and is to be published in the official gazette.

MEETINGS: HE Sheikh Hamad bin Nasser bin Jassim al-Thani, the Minister of State for Interior Affairs, separately met yesterday Iraq's Ambassador to Qatar Fakhri Hamoud al-Dulaimi and Pakistan's Ambassador Arif Kamal. Qatar's relations with each of Iraq and Pakistan and means of promoting them were discussed during the meeting. - QNA

CABINET BRIEFED ON OIC TALKS

PRIME Minister HH Sheikh Abdullah bin Khalifa al-Thani yesterday presided over the weekly Cabinet meeting held at the Emiri Diwan.

---

[5] The Gulf Times

For additional analytical, business and investment opportunities information, please contact Global Investment & Business Center, USA at (202) 546-2103. Fax: (202) 546-3275. E-mail: rusric@erols.com Global Business E-Books on Line: http://world.mirhouse.com

After the meeting, Minister of State for Cabinet Affairs HE Ali bin Saad al-Kuwari gave the following statement:

At the outset of the meeting, the Prime Minister briefed the Cabinet on the talks between HH the Emir, Sheikh Hamad bin Khalifa al-Thani, who is also the current chairman of the Organisation of the Islamic Conference (OIC), and Palestinian President Yasser Arafat during their meeting on May 26, including a discussion of the latest developments on the Palestinian territories and a review of the most prominent items on the OIC ministerial meeting held in Doha last Saturday to address the grave situation in the occupied Palestinian territories resulting from Israel's on-going savage atrocities against the Palestinian people.

The Prime Minister then gave the floor to Foreign Minister HE Sheikh Hamad bin Jassim bin Jabor al-Thani to brief the Cabinet on the outcome of the extraordinary OIC ministerial meeting to address the grave situation in the occupied Palestinian territories.

The Cabinet ministers praised the final communique issued by the meeting. The Cabinet reiterated the support of Qatar and its people for the Palestinian brethren in their struggle to restore their legitimate rights urging the international community to provide international protection for Palestinian and to pressure Israel to honour the international legality's resolutions and the signed agreements as a prerequisite for a resumption of the Middle East peace process.

The Cabinet then considered items on the agenda and adopted the following decisions:

1 - To take necessary measures to issue a law regulating the practice of engineering after taking note of the Advisory Council's recommendations on the relevant draft law.

2 - To approve the draft law annulling the General Establishment of the Doha International Airport and to refer same to the Advisory Council.

3 - To endorse the draft law regulating real estate ownership by GCC nationals and to refer same to the Advisory Council.

4 - To take necessary measures to issue Cabinet decisions specifying the standard specifications for some goods and commodities.

5 - To approve the Interior Minister's draft decision amending some rules of the regulations incorporated in Law No 3 of 1995 concerning prisons, as issued by the interior minister's decision No 2 of 1999.

6 - To approve the Foreign Ministry's memorandum on the report prepared by the ad hoc committee set up by the Cabinet to consider ways to benefit from the regional, Arab and international organisations and groupings in which Qatar is a member, especially in the fields of training and qualifications and to obtain consultative services and technical assistance. - QNA

SHARIA COURTS CHIEF IN CAIRO

CAIRO: Sheikh Abdulrahman bin Abdullah al-Mahmoud, head of the Presidency of Sharia Courts in Qatar, and his accompanying delegation arrived here last night to attend the 13th conference of the Supreme Council for Islamic Affairs, opening here today and runs for four days. - QNA

Q-TEL TRANSFERS INQUIRY SERVICE

Staff Reporter

QATAR Telecom (Q-Tel) has transferred its billing inquiry service (146) to the Call Centre, which has put in place the interactive voice response (IVR) system.

Subscribers can seek details of their outstanding bills by dialling 146 and entering their telephone number, mobile number, pager number, internet account number or the QCV decoder number.

Customers who select a language provided by the system, will be guided to "individual bill options", a Q-Tel release last night said.

If a customer has more than one unpaid bill, the outstanding amount given indicates all the unpaid bills. However, the due date given by the system will be of the oldest bill.

Information about outstanding balance (in the case of those who have a limit for IDD calls) will be given if one inputs one's customer number.

To get a faster response, one must enter # key at the end of individual number or customer number.

While calls from any fixed line to 146 are free, calls from GSM numbers will be charged at standard rates.

In future, the IVR service will be available round-the-clock, Q-Tel said. Currently, it is not available between 9pm and midnight.

"We are confident that our subscribers will find the 146 service convenient. It will spare them of the trouble to visit our offices for billing details and clarifications. The facility will also enable them to avoid bill accumulation and eventual disconnection," Q-Tel said.

PATIENTS WARNED AGAINST HERBAL DRUGS

HAMAD Medical Corporation (HMC) has warned against use of herbs in treatment of diseases, especially diabetes.

An HMC official advised patients to consult doctors before using herbs, stressing that herbal medicine could only serve as an assisting factor.

In a statement to Qatar News Agency Dr Mahmoud al-Zari'e, consultant and head of endocrine glands and diabetes section, advised diabetic patients who take such herbal medicines to refrain from using herbs especially those made as powders and tablets. – QNA

OFFICIAL ALLOWS IDEAL SCHOOL TO RAISE FEES FOR NON-INDIAN PUPILS

Staff Reporter

"THE Ideal Indian School can raise the tuition fees of non-Indian students, who have their own community schools," Director of Private Education Hamad Ali al-Sulaiti told Gulf Times yesterday.

Al-Sulaiti had a meeting with school officials to seek clarification on the institution's proposal to raise tuition fees for non-Indian students from September 1.

In the wake of the Department of Private Education's sanction, students in the target group will have to pay a "nominal increase of not more than QR60 per month," said a statement issued by the school yesterday.

"We would like to reiterate that this decision has not been made to discriminate or show any disrespect to any community," school principal Ainsley L Edgar said.

Al-Sulaiti said that the Ideal Indian School was meant to serve the Indian community as it was a community school. "It is a non-profit organisation, set up to offer quality education to a particular community. So, if non-Indian students want to study in this school, despite having their own community school, they have to pay more for the service they are getting," he remarked.

However, the Director of Private Education was of the view that the case of non-Indian students whose communities did not have schools was different. "These students have a just cause. They don't have to pay the revised fees," the official added.

POETS INVITED FOR JUNE 14 SESSION

For additional analytical, business and investment opportunities information, please contact Global Investment & Business Center, USA at (202) 546-2103. Fax: (202) 546-3275. E-mail: rusric@erols.com Global Business E-Books on Line: http://world.mirhouse.com

HALQAE Adabe Islami, Qatar will hold a natiyah mushairah (poetic session) on June 14. All Urdu poets are welcome to take part, a spokesman for the organisation said in a press release. More information can be had from Amjad Ali Sarwar (Tel 4328000, 5867952).

WOMAN HURT IN ACCIDENT: An Arab woman was seriously injured when the Daewoo car she was driving jumped the central reservation after a tyre burst and hit a pick-up van coming from the opposite direction on the C Ring road, yesterday morning. Two occupants of the pick-up, both Asians, were also hurt in the accident. Both the vehicles were badly damaged.

QIIC TO HOLD HALF-DAY CAMP AND GATHERING

QATAR Indian Islahi Centre (QIIC) is to hold a half-day camp and a public gathering tomorrow in connection with the Second Qur'an Learning Courses Meet.

The camp, exclusively for the participants of the courses, will start after the Friday prayer and last until 6pm at the ICRC Auditorium. The gathering will take place at Shantiniketan Indian School in Mansoura at 6.30pm, according to a press release issued by the QIIC.

Distinguished personalities from the Ministry of Awqaf and Islamic Affairs, scholars Shamsudhin Palath of ISM and Abdul Sathar Koolimad, both from Kerala, are to speak at the gathering.

Certificates and prizes will be distributed to the top scorers in the examination held in conjunction with the meet. The meet was inaugurated by Aboobacker Karakkunnu, president of ISM (Ithihdhu Shubanil Mujahideen) of Kerala.a

NEW LANDFILLS FOR HAZARDOUS WASTES PLANNED

By Arvind Nair

THREE engineered landfills, including two designed for disposal of hazardous wastes, are being planned in Qatar. These will be at Ras Laffan Industrial City, Mesai'eed and Rukkia, in the south of the country.

The landfills at Ras Laffan and Messai'eed will be designed for disposing hazardous wastes while the one at the sand plant at Rukkia will be meant for domestic waste, Dr Khalid Ghanem al-Ali, secretary general of the Supreme Council for Environment and Natural Reserves, told Gulf Times.

Mesai'eed already has an engineered landfill for non-hazardous domestic, industrial and construction waste. The new dumpsite will be at 10km northwest of the industrial city. This is expected to be commissioned by the end of 2002 or early 3003, al-Ali said.

An engineered dump site is one where the various kinds of waste will be segregated according to their compatibility and other qualities. The facility also should have proper lining and ventilation to release the methane gas that might be produced by decomposing.

Such released gases could be either flared or used for producing electricity or other fuels.

The Rukkia landfill, near a sand plant located some 45km to the south of Doha, will replace the existing facility at Umm al-Affai, which literally means 'mother of snakes". The facility, a former limestone quarry, 20km from Doha, has had a few fires recently because of alleged "improper" dumping of waste.

All the domestic waste generated in the country will be eventually dumped at the new site, a study for which had just been commissioned.

A design for the engineered landfill at Ras Laffan, meant for storing hazardous wastes, is ready and the site is expected to be commissioned in about 11/2 years, said Dr Niranjan Bagchi, an environmental engineer, working for the Supreme Council for Environment.

Once the new landfill at Rukkia is ready, al-Ali said, the problems of Umm al-Affai will not be seen again elsewhere.

The fires and smoke at Umm al-Affai, he said, were normal. When organic materials degrade, under certain conditions, methane and other gases are produced. And when they remain trapped or stay under pressure, they can be easily ignited.

Though it is "normal", al-Ali said, "I don't want to see it happening anywhere else". There should be a system in place to monitor and to get the gases out.

CASTING A SPELL WITH GIFT OF THE GAB

By Nahla Nainar

LOVERS of the Tamil language and the art of 'Pattimandram' (Debating Forum) can expect to get a large-sized dose of humour as they gather to watch the Dindigul I Leoni team at the Doha Cinema today (Thursday).

Visiting Qatar for the first time under the auspices of the Qatar Tamizhar Sangam, Ali International Trading and Qatari Auto Parts, the team will debate on the topic of 'Which is the more popular sentiment in Tamil film songs:love or social awareness?' This will be interspersed with cultural presentations by local artistes.

Speaking to Gulf Times, Dindigul I Leoni, expressed great happiness to see the unity of Tamil-speakers in Doha. "Tamil lives in its purest form outside India. Some of the greatest literary traditions which we ourselves have lost in Tamil Nadu, are still practised abroad."

The 'Pattimandram,' a forum that allows speakers to thrash out the niceties of any topic under the sun, really came to public attention with the emergence of Leoni's team.

A science teacher from the historic city of Dindigul in Tamil Nadu state, his rise to fame has been pretty recent. "I used to be always interested in public speaking," he said. "But my real break came in 1992 when I released an audio cassette analysing old and new Tamil film songs."

Since then, his gift of the gab and his ability to combine zany humour with hard-hitting social messages has taken him on speaking engagements all over the world.

His most recent programme was held in Toronto, Canada. Before this, he has gone to countries such as Singapore, Malaysia, Saudi Arabia, UK and Germany. He is accompanied to Doha by four other speakers: Aranga Nedumaran, Kaviyan, Murugan and Paul Raj. They have been together for the past three years, and all testify to the sense of humour that keeps them working in tandem.

"We choose topics according to the appropriateness of the occasion," said Leoni. Aranga Nedumaran, the oldest member of the team, and also a teacher, says of the 'Pattimandram' tradition: "Everywhere we go, there is a tension we feel among our listeners. Our first goal is to undo that knot of tension, to make people laugh spontaneously. And then, while you are laughing, the messages are slipped in, subtly."

Leoni's speeches are known for their balanced nature, and an unrelenting stand against corruption and communalism.

Does it hurt him then, that a convicted politician is today the Tamil Nadu state's chief minister? "Election results are just public support drummed up within a week," he said. "But even those in power today are a little cautious now, because they know they have a lot going against them."

"My aim is to develop the sense of humour and social awareness in young minds," he added. "For that, a lot of ground needs to be covered."

Once the team decides its topic, and each member is assigned his share of work, the group separates to do what Leoni calls "homework." "It is important to be spontaneous," he said.

For additional analytical, business and investment opportunities information,
please contact Global Investment & Business Center, USA
at (202) 546-2103. Fax: (202) 546-3275. E-mail: rusric@erols.com
Global Business E-Books on Line: http://world.mirhouse.com

"We can't really practise anything, because it would spoil the flavour of the debate. But what we do is a lot of reading. We also observe the way people conduct themselves, the psychology behind public behaviour. This helps us when we are on stage. We also add mimicry and singing to our arguments, to make them more informal."

The rise of the satellite media has helped his group immensely. "Once we were just voices on audio tapes. Now, with televised programmes, our voices have got faces."

An accurate, if sometimes harsh, critic of Tamil films, Leoni's fan base is ironically spread out over the movie industry. "Our tapes are played in the editing rooms," he said. "Where people make the films, and then listen to us debating on their merits and demerits."

Leoni himself has acted in a Tamil film and three television serials.

What has helped the group's rise to fame is the absence of 'star' behaviour.

"I am from a small village," said Murugan, a lecturer. "This is my first time outside India. I used to see airplanes from my class as a child, and my heart would fly out of the window."

Kaviyan, the junior-most member of the group, and once a student of Leoni's, felt the group shares a unique relationship. "We all get along as a family, even when we are off stage. Many times, when I have stumbled, group members help me out. There is a feeling that everyone should get an equal share of the limelight."

"Like the string that gets scented with the flower it binds," said Paul Raj a bit poetically, "we all are part of one entity."

An avid reader of psychology texts, Leoni attributes a huge part of his success to his wife, Palaniammal, a lecturer by profession. "I was a chorus singer," he said, "My wife is the one who urged me to use that talent to better purpose." Has he ever been silent? "I've never had the time to think of it," he laughed.

MALAYALAM ARTISTES TO STAGE SHOW

Staff Reporter

A GROUP of Malayalam artistes, including film stars Vani Viswanath and Riza Bava, have arrived in Doha to take part in a show to be staged at the Amir Cinema at 9pm today.

The show, titled 'Atlas Comedy Star Wars', will also feature a bevy of singers and mimicry artistes.

For additional analytical, business and investment opportunities information,
please contact Global Investment & Business Center, USA
at (202) 546-2103. Fax: (202) 546-3275. E-mail: rusric@erols.com
Global Business E-Books on Line: http://world.mirhouse.com

The four-hour comedy and music show is organised by Dala.

"The show's chief attraction is Vani Viswanath, a nominee for the best actress award in India this year," Mohamed Ali Quilandi, the programme co-ordinator, said yesterday. Vani, he said, had won critical acclaim for her role in the Malayalam film Susanna. "The Doha show, which will include cinematic dances, comedy skits, Hasya Kathaprasangam and music, has received a very good response," Mohamed Ali said.

DOCTOR GIVES TIP FOR HEALTHY LIVING

Staff Reporter

DR Malini Chandrasekharen and Dr S Kumar gave tips for a healthy living at a seminar ohealth awareness, organised by the Doha chapter of the Institute of Chartered Accountants of India, at Ramada Hotel.

Dr Chandrasekharen, a private general medical practitioner in Doha for the last 15 years, talked about the life style adjustments required for a healthy living in the Gulf.

Adjustments are required at three levels: emotional, physical and dietary. She stressed the need for a family medical physician who can play the role of not only a doctor but also that of an elder who can advise on various personal matters.

She also spoke about three common health issues found in the Gulf: problems related to heart, peptic acid and kidney. She said the recommended life adjustments could significantly reduce occurrence of these diseases.

Dr Kumar, an ENT specialist attached to the Al-Mansour Polyclinic with more than seven years of Gulf experience, spoke about how to handle ENT problems. He gave tips on snoring problems, using mobile phones and listening to Walkman.

Earlier, Gopal Balasubramaniam, chairman of the Doha chapter, introduced the doctors. J P Narain Singh, vice chairman, proposed a vote of thanks.

GOAN MINISTER ATTENDS FAMILY CHARITY DINNER

Staff Reporter

MORE than 300 guests attended a Goan family charity dinner held in aid of Gujarat earthquake victims. It was organised by Goan Overseas Association.

Chief guest at the evening was Goa's Minister for Revenue and River Navigation, Jose Filipe De Souza. Other guests included charge d'affaires at the Indian embassy, Dr Ashok Amrohi, and John Van Deerlin.

Savio D'Silva, who flew in from Dubai, compered the show, keeping it lively until almost the next morning. The minister, who had come especially for the function, congratulated the Goan Overseas Association (GOA). In particular, he appreciated its efforts to organise such an event for the earthquake victims.

He asked the Goan community to prepare proposals aimed at their own welfare and forward them to Panaji. "The government is very keen to help and protect the NRIs' interests and provide business opportunities", he added. GOA president Simon D'Silva welcomed the guests and said the association has established links with similar bodies in other countries. John De Sa, chairman of GOA, thanked sponsors, co-sponsors, donors, well-wishers, and contestants for their support.

The musical band, Heat Wave, stirred up the mood of the guests with its performance. During the function, the minister also gave a memento to Queenie Fernandes, who won first prize in a 60m sprint for those aged eight to 12 years at the recent grand prix, conducted by Qatar Athletic Association.

KERALA HOSPITAL TO HOLD MEETING

Staff Reporter

A GENERAL meeting of the Central Travancore Specialists Hospitals Ltd (CTSHL) will be held today at 7pm at the Indian Cultural Centre.

Managing director of the hospital Dr Alexander Koshy, FRCP, will address the meeting.

CTSHL is a super speciality hospital located at Mulakuzha, near Chengannur in Kerala. The hospital has massive plans for installation of state of the art equipment and setting up of more departments to the existing facilities, a spokesman said.

The meeting is open to the public and all are cordially invited, he said.

More information can be had from Dr Abraham Kollamana (Bleep 2276705) or Sam Kuruvilla on telephone 4671148, 5811479.

MES, IDEAL SCORE 100% PASS IN CBSE X EXAM

IDEAL TOPPERS

For additional analytical, business and investment opportunities information, please contact Global Investment & Business Center, USA at (202) 546-2103. Fax: (202) 546-3275. E-mail: rusric@erols.com Global Business E-Books on Line: http://world.mirhouse.com

Staff Reporter

THE MES and Ideal Indian schools have yet again scored 100% results in the All India Secondary School (class X) examination of the Central Board of Secondary Education (CBSE), New Delhi. The results of the exam held in March this year were announced last night.

This was the 20th batch for the MES school and the 11th for the Ideal school. Of the 266 students who appeared for the exam at the MES school, 114 secured distinction (75% marks and above) and 103 first class (between 60% and 74%). At the Ideal school 123 wrote the exam. Of them 31 bagged distinction and 80 got first class.

The MES acting principal Dr B K Abdul Azeez complimented the students and teachers on the impressive achievement. "This is the fourth in a series of excellent results the school has bagged this academic year in various public examinations," he pointed out. The Ideal school principal Ainsley L Edgar also congratulated the students of his school, who gave a good performance.

Toppers at MES: Sheethal Anto (457/500, 91.4%), Mimi George (446, 89.2%) and Qaisar Sibtain Choudhary (445, 89%).

Subject toppers at MES: English - Bastian Nonginiyil Chacko (94%), Hindi - Sai Megha Menon (92), French - T Regina Claire Oreta Padero (90), mathematics - Qaisar Sibtain Choudhary (99), Pearl Mary Varughese (99), Jenson John Thomas (99) and Renash Chandran (99), science - Harshvardhan Vathsangam (99), social science - Harshvardhan Vathsangam (97) MES students who won A1 in all subjects Sheethal Anto, Trupti Balakrishnan Madgeri, Neha Dattatraya Kharsikar, Prasanth Karat, Nitya Zachariya Mathew, Sheba Elizabeth Kurien and Cinderella Williams.

MES students who won distinction: Sheethal Anto, Mimi George, Qaisar Sibtain Choudhary, Omkar Uday Kawalekar, Trupti Balakrishnan Madgeri, Harshvardhan Vathsangam, Parijat Mukherjee, Neha Dattatraya Kharsika, Prasanth Karat, Nitya Zacharia Mathew, Pearl Mary Varughese, Teenu Ann Thomas, Shameem Usman, Sai Megha Menon, Anand Abraham, Bensy Kareelamannil John, Sheba Elizabeth Kurien, Cinderella Williams, Maria Joseph Kurian, Jinu Susan Varughese, Tanya Chopra, Sushant Malhotra, Rohit Babu Suresh Nair, Kruthi Murali, Nahda Abdul Azeez, Penny Susan Johns, Bilky Baeb Eapen, Thasneem, Gureet Singh Chandhok, Anjali Gopalakrishnan, Mary Jose Purackal, Bastian Nonginiyil Chacko, Pooja George, Sumaiya Shahoo, Siby P Daniel, Soumya Dash, Fazil Mohamood, Jees Joseph, Syed Khalid Kabli, Hadia Hussain, Samiha Sooppi, Fazil Moidu, Febin Vadakkeyil, Bhavana Sudhakaran, K R Remya, Amith George Jacob, Asma Ghulam Mohammed Raj, Jimla Mariam John, Neethu Unnikrishnan, Surya Cicily Sebastian, Mohammed Afham, Sijo Varghese, Aysha Ismail, Mini Mathew, Aswathy Asok Nair, Ramya P M, Sabna Abdul Salam, Arun Sugadhan, Philip Abraham, Kim Fernandes, Joceylin P Jose, R Nithya, Reeja Thankam Jolly, Jenson John Thomas, Rejo Joby Peter, Chaitanya Kiran Konher, Imran K Patanwala, K M Rency, Shagun Jain, Arun David D'Souza, Rashmi Arun Kadam, Shiney Rachel Rajan, Taresh Ramesan, Binal Lalitkumar Joshi, Amruta A Patel,

Mariamma Thomas, Samson Philip, Shawn Bartholomew Fernan, Thomas P Paul, Anie Jacob Mundenchira, Gauri Ganesan, R Meenakshi Menon, Aditi Chakrabarti, Kirthiga Muthusamy, Kiran Koshy Jerry, Rajesh Nair, Shashank Bhandari, Neenu Jose K, Silby Jacob, Sini, Yasir Shoaib, Surumi Mammu, Parkar Abdulaffo Hanif, Gikku Rachel George, Rahana Ashraf, Najla Mohammed Easa, Helen Christina Kutty, Shamna Ahammed Sageer, Arun Chacko Varghese, Swati Francis, Lemiya Rasheed, Sandhya Mahadevan, Arun John Thomas, Gigoo Thomas George, Shabna Mohideen, Linta Mathew, Shamimbanu Gulamhusen Duwaida, Jini Deena Varughese, Neethu T M, R P Rashma, Sharon Kurien, Veena Aleyamma Wilson, Shamseer M K and Raji Pappachan Philipose.

Toppers at Ideal: Nishita Dayanand Shenoy (439/500), Anupama Jayathilakan (426) and Anish Mathew Thomas (425).

Subject toppers at Ideal: Hindi - Sameena Abdul Kareem (90/100), Malayalam - Safwa Abdul Latheef (82), French - Sawsan Abdus Samad (89), English - Nishita Dayanand Shenoy and Anupama Jayathilakan (89), mathematics - Rahul Rajan (99), science - Nishita Dayanand Shenoy (97), social science - Anupama Jayathilakan (91).

Ideal students who won distinction: Nishita Dayanand Shenoy, Anupama Jayathilakan, Anish Mathew Thomas, Preeti Charanya, Hari A Ravindran, Ashfaq Fathema Mehmood Jafer, Maimuna Sadulla Khatib, Nikhil Manjunath Shanbhag, Cynthia Susan Elizabeth, Safwa Abdul Latheef, Rahul Rajan, Mithun George Mathew, Sameena Abdul Kareem, Roji Thomas, Sawsan Abdus Samad, Maria Suelee Joylma Correia, Ayesha Tarannum, Sangeeta Lilly Samson, Sharon Valankani Mathias, Dolan Bhowmik, Ameya Subash Jambavalikar, Pinku George, Ashwin Renju, Neha Sharma, Nazia Shafi, Harpreet Singh Doad, Leny Thomas Mathew, Umera Bashir Ahmed, Lakshmi Vijay, Thanuja Salam and Tony Mathew.

MIDEAST HAS 'HIGH PREVALENCE' OF ALZHEIMER'S

By Pratap John

THE fight against Alzheimer's disease may get a fillip if scientists at the National Institute of Health in the United States are able to isolate genes responsible for the illness.

A research project on Alzheimer's, funded by the United States government, has given promising indications, said Dr Robert P Friedland, a renowned American neurologist.

Alzheimer's disease, the most common cause for dementia in adults in many parts of the world, is considered an "approaching epidemic". Some 5% of people above 60 world-wide have this illness. And it is the fourth leading cause of death after heart failure, cancer and stroke, he said in an interview with Gulf Times yesterday.

Alzheimer's patients have memory disturbances, as well as defects in mental abilities such as judgement, abstract thinking or use of words. However, a recent study by Dr Friedland, who works at the Alzheimer Center of the University Hospitals of Cleveland, revealed that some 20% of people above 60 in Palestine suffer from Alzheimer's disease.

The incidence rate in Palestine is very high, Dr Friedland points out and cites consanguinity as a major reason. The study is the only one carried out so far among 225mn Arabs world-wide, he points out.

The renowned American neurologist, who was in Doha at the invitation of the Hamad Medical Corporation, said Alzheimer's disease can affect any adult, though a number of factors determine its onset. The most prominent early symptom of the disease is the gradual onset of progressive memory loss.

It is also characterised by a steady progression of "intellectual deterioration". In the later stage, all intellectual capabilities are lost and difficulty in movement becomes apparent with urinary incontinence.

"Forgetting is normal. But if one forgets certain crucial things, it is abnormal," Dr Friedland said.

He said: "If I rush to the airport to catch a scheduled night flight without my baggage or travel documents, I am abnormal. Again it is an abnormal behaviour, if I continue enjoying a dinner completely forgetting about a scheduled night flight".

Those who have had similar experiences must contact a neurologist, he suggests. Besides genetic reasons, smoking, alcoholism, hypertension, cardiac problems, diabetes, and a sedentary lifestyle are the factors for Alzheimer's disease. Dr Friedland said he had seen some 30 patients with problems of dementia at the HMC.

"But I don't remember having seen anyone with Alzheimer's disease here".

He, however, admits that his assessment based on the five-day stay in Qatar may not be correct. "There may be Alzheimer's cases here. For, the Middle East region is considered having a high prevalence rate".

Asian countries and Africa have only a very low incidence rate. A study in India shows the incidence of Alzheimer's in the country is well below the world average of 5%. Many causes of dementia are completely reversible, the neurologist points out. And Alzheimer's disease itself is treatable to a large extent.

"Though Alzheimer's patients may not be able to lead a normal life, their overall condition can be improved by a special drug," Dr Friedland said.

For additional analytical, business and investment opportunities information, please contact Global Investment & Business Center, USA at (202) 546-2103. Fax: (202) 546-3275. E-mail: rusric@erols.com Global Business E-Books on Line: http://world.mirhouse.com

Asked whether only elderly people are prone to Alzheimer's, he said he was yet to see any patient below 40. "Our research indicates young people are not vulnerable to Alzheimer's disease," the doctor said.

He suggests the setting up of a research project on Alzheimer's at the HMC. HMC facilities are world class. The system for filing records is also exemplary. Qatar being a rich country can easily fund such a project.

"I am more than happy to associate with such a project," Dr Friedland said.

KERALA ORATOR TO ADDRESS DOHA MEETING

Staff Reporter

NOTED orator and scholar Prof P P Shahul Hameed will deliver the keynote address at the annual general body meeting and family get-together of South Kerala Islamic Association, Qatar, to be held tomorrow at the ICRC hall.

Nissar Kocheri, a legal expert will inaugurate the family meet while Shareef, managing director of Inter Food Group of Companies will give the felicitation speech. Association president Mohamed Qutub will preside.

For registration, members can contact Qutub on 4352599 or 5806700.

INDIAN DANCER'S JEWELLERY STOLEN ON WAY TO DOHA

By Arvind Nair

RENOWNED Odissi dancer, Monalisa Ghosh will be performing today in Doha with borrowed jewellery, hurriedly put together by the organisers of the concert.

When no dancer worth her salt ever goes out for a recital without her own costume and jewellery, how come a veteran dancer like Ghosh does not have her own adornments?

Ghosh indeed had her own set of earrings, necklaces, waistband and other pieces, made of silver, when she started the journey from Kolkatta. But, when she arrived in Doha yesterday morning, via Dhaka, her jewel box was empty!

"I saw my new suitcase coming through the conveyer belt. Its security tape had already been cut. When I picked up the case I saw that it was half open," she related the incident to Gulf Times last night. On inspection, she found that her jewellery box had been opened and all the contents were missing. Fortunately for her, her costume had been spared.

In terms of money, the loss of jewels was no big deal for a successful dancer like Ghosh, though it had taken about seven years for her to collect them. But, aesthetically, it was a big blow for her.

"It will take years for me to put together once again something like that. It will be difficult to collect", said the petite dancer, with a tinge of sadness.

Ghosh, who had been dancing for three decades, is accompanied by Subhankar Chatterjee, the vocal artiste who will also be singing Ghazals, and Uttam Mandal, on the tabla.

The concert today, at the Ministry of Education Auditorium, will start at 7pm.

PEACE MOVES MUST BE BASED ON UN RESOLUTIONS: SHARA

DAMASCUS: Syrian Foreign Minister Farooq al-Shara said yesterday that any peace moves in the Middle East must be based on UN resolutions, which call for Israel to withdraw from land it captured in 1967.

Shara made his comments as he received Jordanian Foreign Minister Abdel Ilah el-Khatib, whose country and Egypt are co-sponsors of a plan to end eight months of deadly Israeli-Palestinian clashes and bring the sides back to the negotiating table.

Asked by reporters about his opinion on the Jordanian-Egyptian initiative, Shara said: "We won't oppose any initiative that would take into consideration UN resoluor the principles of Madrid."

He was referring to the 1991 peace conference in the Spanish capital that launched now-moribund US-sponsored peace talks between Israel and its Arab neighbours, along with the Palestinians.

The plan by Egypt and Jordan, the only two Arab countries to have signed peace treaties with Israel, calls for a halt to the violence that has killed 575 people since September, a freeze to Jewish settlements in the Palestinian territories and talks to lead to a final settlement.

The Palestinians have publicly backed the plan, but Israel has criticised the points on settlements.

The Jordanian-Egyptian plan was proposed shortly before the publication of the Mitchell report on the violence, which recommends a complete halt to the violence followed by a freeze on settlements and a Palestinian crackdown on terrorism.

For additional analytical, business and investment opportunities information, please contact Global Investment & Business Center, USA at (202) 546-2103. Fax: (202) 546-3275. E-mail: rusric@erols.com Global Business E-Books on Line: http://world.mirhouse.com

Jordan and Egypt have long backed UN Security Council Resolutions 242 and 338, which call for Israel to withdraw from land it captured from the two countries and Syria in the 1967 Six-Day War.

Separately, Khatib said he had "very good" talks with Syrian President Bashar al-Assad, who he said gave "an evaluation of the situation in the region," and presented him with a message from Jordanian King Abdullah II.

An official in Amman said earlier that the message deals with "the entire situation in the region and bilateral ties between the two countries." - AFP

GLOSSARY

Al

> Uppercased, it connotes family of, or belonging to, as in Al Sabah, Al Khalifa, Al Thani, Al Nuhayyan, Al Maktum, Al Qasimi, and Al Said. Lowercased, it represents the definite article *the*, as in Ras al Khaymah.

amir

> Literally, commander. In many of the Arab states of the gulf, amir often means ruler or prince.

amirate

> Political entity under the rule of an amir. Analogous to a shaykhdom and, if an independent state, to a kingdom.

Bahraini dinar (BD)

> Consists of 1,000 fils. Bahrain has maintained a fixed exchange rate according to which in 1993 US$1 equaled BD0.376.

barrels per day (bpd)

> Production of crude oil and petroleum products is frequently measured in barrels per day. A barrel is a volume measure of forty- two United States gallons. Conversion of barrels to tons depends on the density of the specific product. About 7.3 barrels of average crude oil weigh one ton. Heavy crude is about seven barrels per ton. Light products, such as gasoline and kerosene, average close to eight barrels per ton.

downstream

> The oil industry views the production, processing, transportation, and sale of petroleum products as a flow process starting at the wellhead. Downstream includes any stage between the point of reference and the sale of products to the consumer. Upstream (*q.v.*) is the converse.

gross domestic product (GDP)

> A value measure of the flow of domestic goods and services produced by an economy over a period of time, such as one year. Only output values of goods for final consumption and investment are included because the values of primary and intermediate production are assumed to be included in final prices. GDP is sometimes aggregated and shown at market prices, meaning that indirect taxes and subsidies are included; when these have been eliminated, the result is GDP at factor cost. The word *gross* indicates that deductions for depreciation of physical assets have not been made. *See also* gross national product (GNP).

gross national product (GNP)

For additional analytical, business and investment opportunities information, please contact Global Investment & Business Center, USA at (202) 546-2103. Fax: (202) 546-3275. E-mail: rusric@erols.com Global Business E-Books on Line: http://world.mirhouse.com

The gross domestic product (*g.v.*) plus the net income or loss stemming from transactions with foreign countries. GNP is the broadest measurement of the output of goods and services by an economy. It can be calculated at market prices, which include indirect taxes and subsidies. Because indirect taxes and subsidies are only transfer payments, GNP is often calculated at factor cost by removing indirect taxes and subsidies.

hadith

Tradition based on the precedent of Muhammad's words and deeds that serves as one of the sources of Islamic law (sharia).

hijra

Literally, to migrate, to sever relations, to leave one's tribe. Throughout the Muslim world, hijra refers to the migration of the Prophet Muhammad and his followers to Medina. In this sense, the word has come into European languages as hegira. The year of Muhammad's hijra constitutes the beginning of the Islamic calendar.

ibn

Literally, son of; *bint* means daughter of; and *bani* is literally sons of, hence clan or tribe.

imam

Word used in several senses. In general use, it means the leader of congregational prayers; as such it implies no ordination or special spiritual powers beyond sufficient education to carry out this function. It is also used figuratively by many Sunni (*q.v.*) Muslims to mean the leader of the Islamic community. Among Shia (*q.v.*) the word takes on many complex meanings; in general, however, and particularly when uppercased, it indicates that particular descendant of the House of Ali who is believed to be God's designated repository of the spiritual authority inherent in that line. The identity of this individual and the means of ascertaining his identity have been major issues causing divisions among Shia. Among the Ibadis of Oman, the imam was elected to office and was regarded by all as the spiritual leader of the community and by some as the temporal ruler as well. Claims of various Omani imams to secular power led to open rebellions as late as the 1950s.

import-substitution industrialization

An economic development strategy that emphasizes the growth of domestic industries, often by import protection using tariff and nontariff measures. Proponents favor the export of industrial goods over primary products.

International Monetary Fund (IMF)

Established along with the World Bank (*q.v.*) in 1945, the IMF is a specialized agency affiliated with the United Nations and is responsible for stabilizing international exchange rates and payments. The main business of the IMF is the provision of loans to its members (including industrialized and developing countries) when they experience balance of payments difficulties. These loans frequently carry conditions that require substantial internal economic adjustments by the recipients, most of which are developing countries.

jihad

The struggle to establish the law of God on earth, often interpreted to mean holy war.

Kuwaiti dinar (KD)

The national currency, consisting of 1,000 fils. The exchange rate of the Kuwaiti dinar to the United States dollar has fluctuated somewhat; in March 1992 the exchange rate was US$1 = KD0.295.

majlis

Tribal council; in some countries the legislative assembly. Also refers to an audience with an amir (q.v.) or shaykh (q.v.) open to all citizens.

Omani rial (RO)

Monetary unit of Oman, divided into 1,000 baizas. Oman has maintained a fixed exchange rate according to which in 1993 US$1 equaled RO0.3845.

Qatari riyal (QR)

The national currency consisting of 100 dirhams. Qatar has maintained a fixed exchanged rate according to which in 1993 US$1 equaled QR3.64.

shaykh

Leader or chief. Applied either to a political leader of a tribe or town or a learned religious leader. Also used as an honorific.

Shia (from Shiat Ali, or Party of Ali)

A member of the smaller of the two great divisions of Islam. The Shia supported the claims of Ali and his line to presumptive right to the caliphate and leadership of the world Muslim community, and on this issue they divided from the Sunnis (q.v.) in the major schism within Islam. Later schisms have produced further divisions among the Shia over the identity and number of imans (q.v.). Most Shia revere twelve Imams, the last of whom is believed to be in hiding. *See also* Twelve Imam Shia.

special drawing rights (SDR)

An International Monetary Fund (IMF--q.v.) unit of account made up of a basket of major international currencies consisting of the United States dollar, the German deutschmark, the Japanese yen, the British pound sterling, and the French franc.

Sunni

The larger of the two great divisions of Islam. The Sunnis, who rejected the claims of Ali's line, believe that they are the true followers of the *sunna*, the guide to proper behavior composed of the Quran and the hadith (q.v.).

Twelve Imam Shia

The majority group among Shia (q.v.), who believe that the Imamate began with Ali, the fourth caliph, or successor ruler, in Islam. The line continued through his sons until the Twelfth Imam, who is believed to have ascended to a supernatural state to return to earth on Judgment Day.

UAE dirham (Dh)

National currency of the United Arab Emirates (UAE), consisting of 100 fils. The UAE has maintained a fixed exchange rate according to which in 1993 US$1 equaled Dh3.671.

ulama

Collective term for Muslim religious scholars.

upstream

The converse of downstream (q.v.), it includes the exploration and drilling of wells in the petroleum production process.

Wahhabi

Name used outside Saudi Arabia to designate adherents to Wahhabism (q.v.).

Wahhabism
> Name used outside Saudi Arabia to designate official interpretation of Islam in Saudi Arabia. The faith is a puritanical concept of unitarianism (the oneness of God) that was preached by Muhammad ibn Abd al Wahhab, whence his Muslim opponents derived the name. The royal family of Qatar and most indigenous Qataris are Wahhabis (*q.v.*)

World Bank
> Informal name used to designate a group of four affiliated international institutions that provide advice and assistance on long-term finance and policy issues to developing countries: the International Bank for Reconstruction and Development (IBRD), the International Development Association (IDA), the International Finance Corporation (IFC), and the Multilateral Investment Guarantee Agency (MIGA). The IBRD, established in 1945, has as its primary purpose the provision of loans at market-related rates of interest to developing countries at more advanced stages of development. The IDA, a legally separate loan fund but administered by the staff of the IBRD, was set up in 1960 to furnish credits to the poorest developing countries on much easier terms than those of conventional IBRD loans. The IFC, founded in 1956, supplements the activities of the IBRD through loans and assistance specifically designed to encourage the growth of productive private enterprises in the less developed countries. The president and certain officers of the IBRD hold the same positions in the IFC. The MIGA, which began operating in 1988, insures private foreign investment in developing countries against various noncommercial risks. The four institutions are owned by the governments of the countries that subscribe their capital. To participate in the World Bank group, member states must first belong to the International Monetary Fund (IMF--*q.v.*).

Abstract: Qatar Minister of Foreign Affairs Sheik Hamed Bin Jassim Bin Jabr Al-Thani discusses Persian Gulf economic and military developments. He states Qatar's readiness to market its energy products to China and urged countries involved in the Middle East peace process to negotiate a comprehensive Arab-Israeli peace settlement.

For more information see: http://www.rice.edu/rtv/speeches/19990223qatar.html

قطر وعملية السلام في الشرق الأوسط

ملاحظات وتطلعات

١) نحن في قطر نتطلع إلى تحقيق السلام في الشرق الأوسط بإعتباره هدفا إستراتيجيا يصبّ في صميم مصالحنا ويستجيب لطموحاتنـــا وآمالنا . فالسلام بالنسبة لنا هو المدخل الذي لا بــد منـــه نحـو الوصول إلى وضع جديد في منطقتنا يخرجها من أتون النزاعـات والحروب ودوّامات العنف والتصعيد التي لا طائل منها . كمـــا أنّ السلام في نظرنا هو الشرط الأول والأساسي الذي يجب أن يتوافر حتى يصبح في مقدورنا أن نتصور وضعا إقليميا تقوم العلاقـــات بين دول المنطقة فيه على أسس ثابتة من التعاون والصداقة والأمن والإستقرار . فمن دون سلام عادل ودائم وشامل وثابت ، لا يمكن أن نتحدث عن شرق أوسط جديد تتركز فيه الموارد والطاقات على تحقيق أولويات التنمية والإزدهار والرخاء والإستقرار السياسـي والإقتصادي ، والتفاعل الحضاري والإجتماعي ، والثقة المتبادلـة بين جميع شعوب المنطقة ودولها من دون إستثناء ، عوضا عـــن إهدار هذه الموارد وتبديد هذه الطاقات على أغـــراض الصـراع والتقاتل التي لا تخدم أحدا . فالسلام بالنسبة لنا هو الحد الفـــاصل الذي يجب أن يفرقنا عن الماضي الكئيب الذي عانت منه منطقتنـا

— ١ —

طويلا ، وبين المستقبل المشرق الذي يحق لنا ولشعوبنا أن نحلم به وأن نتطلع إليه .

٢) من هذا المنظور الواسع والبعيد الأمد ، إلتزمنا في قطر بتأييد الجهود الهادفة إلى تحقيق السلام ، ودعم مسيرة المفاوضات الرامية إلى التوصل إلى تسوية الصراع العربي – الإسرائيلي الذي اعتبرناه على الدوام مصدرا رئيسيا من مصادر العنف والتوتر وعدم الإستقرار في منطقتنا . كما أننا نظرنا دائما إلى التسوية المنشودة على أساس أنها يجب أن تكون أوسع وأشمل بكثير من مجرد إتفاقات ورقية تتعلق ببعض الأراضي هنا ، أو بعض المواقع هناك . فهذه التسوية الإقليمية ، على أهميتها ، لن تكون كافية وحدها ، بل لا بدّ لها حتى تكون ذات معنى أن تؤدي إلى مصالحة تاريخية بين الجانبين تضع حدّا نهائيا للصراع وتفتح آفاق التعاون والثقة المتبادلة والمصالح المشتركة التي نعتقد أنها كثيرة ومتعددة بينهما .

وحتى تكون هذه التسوية المصالحة التاريخية التي ننشدها ، إعتبرنا منذ البداية أن السلام الذي سينتج عنها لا بدّ أن يكون شاملا وعادلا حتى يكون دائما ونهائيا . وأسس هذا السلام الشامل والعادل والدائم يجب أن تقوم ، ببساطة كلية ، على مبادئ الشرعية الدولية ومبادلة الأرض بالسلام وتوفير الأمن والإستقرار لجميع شعوب المنطقة ودولها . وهذا يعني ، في نظرنا ، إنسحاب إسرائيل من الأراضي العربية التي إحتلتها عام ١٩٦٧ م ، ومن جنوب لبنان ، وعودتها إلى الحدود الدولية المعترف بها ، وحصول الشعب الفلسطيني على حقوقه الوطنية والسياسية المشروعة ، مثله مثل غيره من شعوب العالم ، حتى تحصل إسرائيل بدورها على ضمانات الأمن والسلام والإستقرار التي يستحقها شعبها ، ولكي تصبح بالتالي جزءا طبيعيا وكاملا من المنطقة ، لننعم جميعنا عندئذ بفوائد السلام وعوائده على أسس ثابتة من علاقات حسن الجوار والصداقة والتعاون الإقتصادي والتفاعل الإجتماعي والثقافي والحضاري .

ولأن نظرتنا إلى التسوية المطلوبة والسلام المنشود كانت دائمـا ، وهي لا تزال على رغم كل الصعوبات والنكسات التي واجهتـهـا عملية السلام خلال السنوات الماضية ، قائمة على هـذه الأسـس الثابتة ، فقد كنا دائما في قطر على إستعداد لقطع تلـك "المسافة الإضافية" ، بل وحتى "المجازفة" في سبيل السلام ، لأن هذا كـان دائما ولا يزال ما نؤمن به إيمانا عميقا .

ولذلك ، دعمنا بقوّة المسارات التفاوضيـة الثنائيـة بيـن إسـرائيل وجيرانها العرب من فلسطينيين وسوريين ولبنـانيين ، وأعربنـا باستمرار عن أملنا في أن تحقق هذه المسارات الثنائية أهدافـهـا . ورحّبنا بالإتفاقات التي تم التوصل إليـهـا تباعـا علـى المسـار الفلسطيني الذي نعتبره بالغ الحيوية بالنسبة إلى مجمـل العمليـة السلمية ، وكان آخرها طبعا إتفاق "واي" الذي تم التوصـل إليـه بفضل الجهود المكثفة والمشكورة التي بذلها مسؤولو الإدارة ، وفي مقدمتهم الرئيس كلينتون ووزيرة الخارجية السـيـدة أولـبـرايت ، ودعونا الجانبين إلى ضرورة التقيد ببنـوده ووضعهـا موضـع التطبيـق في أسرع وقت ممكن من أجل المحافظة علـى زخـم التقدم والبناء عليه . وشدّدنا أيضـا علـى ضـرورة إستئناف المفاوضات على المسارين السوري واللبناني بغيـة وضـع حـد للجمود الحاصل عليهما مع ما يحمله ذلك من إحتمالات سلبية على العملية السلمية وعلى الإستقرار في المنطقة .

وإنطلاقا من نظرتنا الإقليمية الشاملة إلى السلام وفوائده المرجوّة ، دخلنا طرفا في المفاوضات المتعدّدة الأطراف التي كنا نأمل في أن تؤدي إلى وضع الأطر الواسعة المطلوبـة للتعاون الإقليمـي ، خصوصـا فـي مجـالات التنميـة والتطويـر الإقتصـادي والإجتماعي ، واستضفنا في الدوحة ، في هذا الإطار ، إجتمـاع لجنة الحدّ من التسلح . وذهبنا بعيدا فـي مواجهـة الكثيـر مـن الإنتقادات والتحفظات ، فإستضفنا في الدوحـة أيضـا المؤتمـر الإقتصادي لدول الشرق الأوسط وشمال إفريقيا ، على رغم إنعقاده في ظروف سياسية صعبة وغير مؤاتية . . وحافظنا على علاقة

عمليـــة السـلام بالشكل والوتيرة التي كنا نتمناها بإتجـــاه تحقيـق أهدافهـــا . لكن ذلك لم يحدث ، للأسـف الشـديد ، نظـرا لمــا إعتبرناها مواقف سلبية وسياسـات متصلبة إتبعتهـا الحكومـة الإسرائيليـــة برئاسة السيد بنيامين نتانياهو منـــذ وصولـها إلـى السلطة ، فلم تخدم أهداف السلام ولم تكن في مصلحـة الجهود الرامية إلى تحقيقه في المنطقة .

ونحن على أمل كبير في أن تسفر الإنتخابات الإسرائيلية المقبلـــة قريبا عن نتائج إيجابية تكون في مصلحة العملية السلمية ، حتــى يصبــح من الممكن إعادة إحيـاء المفاوضـات علـى جميـع مساراتها ، وتحريكها من جديد نحـــو إحـراز التقـدم الحقيقي والملموس الذي طال إنتظاره في هذه العملية . والأهم من ذلـك ، نرجو أن تؤدي هذه الإنتخابات إلى تحويل السلام ، على الساحة السياسية الإسرائيلية بمختلف إتجاهاتها وتياراتـــها ، إلـى خيار إستراتيجي نهائي وسياسة حكومية ثابتة لا تظل خاضعة للتقلبـات والتــرددات والتحولات المبنية على إعتبـارات حزبيـة وفئويـة ضيّقة . فالعرب ، بالذات أطرافهم وقواهم الرئيسـية والمؤثّـرة ، إعتمدوا السلام خيارا إستراتيجيا ثابتا ، وهم يحتاجون إلى شـريك إسرائيلي اعتمد السلام بدوره خيارا إستراتيجيا ثابتا . وفي إعتقادنا أن شراكة كهذه ستكون كفيلة تماما بتمكين عمليـة السـلام مـن الوصول إلى نتائجها المنشودة .

٤) على رغم الصعوبات والنكسات ، والمواقف السلبية من أي جهـــة أتت ، فإننا لا نزال مؤمنين بعملية السلام ، ومقتنعيــن بجدواهـا وضرورتها ، وبنجاحها في نهاية المطاف . فالسلام بالنسبة لنا هو ضرورة لا بدّ منها . كما أنه بالنسبة لنا ، كما هو الحال بالنسبة إلى الأكثرية الساحقة من العرب ، خيار إستراتيجي ثابت لا تراجع عنه .

وسأسمح لنفسي هنا أن أتطرق إلى نقطة مهمة تتعلق تحديدا بهـذه المسألـــة . لأقول أنه خلافا للإنطباع المؤسف ، والخاطئ تمامـا

المتحدة بالذات ، ومفاده أن العرب منقسمون حول السلام ، أو أنّ الحكومــات العربية تريــد السلام في حيــن أن الشــعوب لا تريده ، وإلى ما ذلك من مقولات مشابهة ، دعوني أؤكد لكــم أن الأمر ليس كذلك ، بل اننا على إقتناع كامل بــأن الأكثرية مــن قطاعات المجتمعات العربية وشعوبها تؤيد السلام وتنشده .

ولا شك لديّ على الإطلاق بأن أكثريــة الشــعب الإسرائيلي ، ومؤسساته السياسية ، تنشد بدورها السلام وترغب في تحقيقه .

لكن للسلام ، كما سبق وذكرت ، أسس ومتطلّبات جوهرية لا بـد من تلبيتها ومراعاتها حتى يكون سلاما ذا معنى وجدوى تجعلـه قابلا للعيش وقادرا على الإستمرار . وأهم هذه الأسس والمتطلبات في رأينا ، هو إحترام حق الشعوب في العيش بحرية وكرامة وأمن وإطمئنان إلى المستقبل . وهذا الحق يجب أن ينطبق علــى كـل الشعوب وعلى الأطراف كافة ، لا على طرف من دون الآخــر ، وهو بالتالي يجب أن ينطبق على الفلسطينيين كما إنطباقــه علــى الإسرائيليين ، والعكس صحيح .

فنحن نجد من الصعب كثيرا ، كأصدقاء للولايــات المتحـدة فـي المنطقة، أن نقبل عدم تمييز السياسة الأمريكية في منطقتنـا بيــن الارهاب الذي يستهدف الأبرياء ، والذي ندينه جميعا ونستنكره ، وبين طموحات الشعوب الى تحرير أرضها وإستعادة حقوقها. ولهذا ، ندعو دائماالى التفريق ما بين الارهاب وحركات التحرر ومقاومة الاحتلال. كما أننا نرفض بشدة الربــط السـاذج الـذي نشهده أحيانا للأسف في وسائل الاعلام وغيرها من المؤسسات من الغرب بين الارهاب وديننا الحنيف الاسلام. فالاسلام بريء مـن الارهاب والتطرف والتعصب ، بل أنه دين يقوم علــى التسـامح والمحبة واحترام الأديــان السماوية الأخــرى ، أي المسـيحية واليهودية. أما ما نشهده أحيانا من نزعات متعصبــة أو متشـددة لدى بعض المجموعات الاسلامية ، فانها لاتختلف عــن تيـارات متطرفة مشابهة موجودة في المسيحية واليهودية على حد سواء كما

وهنا سأكون صريحا فنحن على إقتناع بأن الوسيلة المثلى لمكافحة ظواهر التطرف والانغلاق هي من خلال المزيد من الانفتاح والمشاركة الشعبية والديمقراطية ومصارحة الرأي العام. وربما وجدتم في بعض ما سأقوله موضع إستغراب ، عندما أؤكد لكم بأن الرأي العام في بلادنا ومنطقتنا أصبح له ثقل وشأن وتأثير على سياسات الحكومات التي لم يعد في مقدورها تجاهله أو القفز من فوقه. ونحن نرى أن من مصلحة الولايات المتحدة نفسها ومن مصلحة علاقاتها بدول المنطقة أن تحرص على مخاطبة الرأي العام العربي والاسلامي ومراعاته بالدرجة نفسها التي تحرص فيها على مخاطبة الرأي العام الاسرائيلي ومراعاته.

ونرى أن اعتماد هذا المنهج في علاقاتنا وفي السياسة الأمريكية حيال منطقتنا يجب أن يكون الوسيلة المطلوبة لكسب الرأي العام العربي والإسلامي وجذب تأييده.

كما أنه لا بدّ من اعتماد التوازن والعدل في توجيه اللوم وتحميل المسؤولية على الطرف ، أو الأطراف ، التي تعرقل العملية السلمية ، أو تتراجع عن إلتزاماتها حيالها ، أو تخلّ بالإتفاقات المعقودة في إطارها . فلا يظلّ هذا اللوم مقتصرا على جانب واحد ، كما هي الحال في معظم الأحيان بالنسبة إلى الفلسطينيين ، بل نعتقد أنه من الضروري أن يوضع الإسرائيليون أيضا أمام مسؤولياتهم . وكم نتمنى لو تعمد الولايات المتحدة ، باعتبارها راعية عملية السلام في المنطقة ، إلى توجيه اللوم علانية إلى أي طرف يعيق هذه العملية أو يلحق الضرر بها ، ومن دون ممالأة أو مراعاة . وفي إعتقادي أنه عندما يصبح هذا المفهوم متوازيا ومتوازنا ومتبادلا ، نكون قد أصبحنا فعلا على الطريق الصحيح نحو إحلال السلام الحقيقي في المنطقة .

(٥) من أجل هذه الأسباب ، يتعين علينا أن نتحلى بالصراحة وأن نعترف بأن هذه الأكثرية ، التي أودّ أن أطلق عليها إسم "الأكثرية من أجل السلام" على الجانبين ، تشعر حاليا ، وهي

الإحتقـــان والغضب ، ومنهما أيضا تتبـع أوضاع وممارسـات مؤلمة ومؤسفة تفسح المجال واسعا أمام أعداء السلام ، وهم فـي نظري أقلية على الجانبين ، للتهجّم على السلام وعرقلة فـرص التوصّل إليه بهدف إرجاع المنطقة ، لا قدّر الله ، إلى دوامة العنف والخراب والكراهية . وهذا بالذات ما يجب أن لا نسمح بحصولـه على الإطلاق ومهما كان الأمر أو كلف الثمن .

دعـــونا نتذكر أنه كانت هناك ، عند بدايـة المسيرة السـلمية ، مرحلة إرتفعت فيها آمالنا وطموحاتنا عاليا جدا بإمكانيــة تحقيـق السلام وسرعة التوصل إليه . وربّما كانت تلك المشاعر مغالية في تفاؤلها أنذاك ، لكنها نتجت عـن توجّـهات وسياسـات حكيمـة وخيارات صعبة وقرارات شجاعة إتخذها القادة على الجانبين فـي ذلك الوقت ، ومنهم من دفع حياته ثمنا لها في ما بعد .

كما لا بدّ لي أن أشير هنا إلى الخسارة الفادحة التي شـعرنا بـها برحيل العاهل الأردني الملك حسين رحمــه الله . فـإلى جـانب العـــلاقات الودّيّة المميّزة التي تربــط بلدينـا بصورة تقليديـة وتاريخية ، كان الملك حسين ركنا أساسيا من أركان السـلام فـي المنطقة ، ومكافحا مخلصا من أجل إحلاله وتكريسـه ، ومؤمنـا إيمانا عميقا بأن السلام هو الطريق الوحيد أمام منطقتنا لتحقيق مـا تأمـل به وتتطلّع إليه من تقدّم ورخاء وطمأنينة لدولها وشعوبها كافة . ولا يجب أن ننسى الشجاعة التي اتسم بها موقـف الملـك حسين في السعي الى تحقيق حلمه التاريخي بالتوصل الى تسـوية سلمية عادلة ومشرفة للصراع العربي الاسرائيلي ، ومدى استعداده للمجازفة من أجل ذلك الهدف النبيل . فلنعمل معا من أجل تحويـل هذا الحلم الى حقيقة تخلد ذكرى جلالته وتكرس إنجازاته في تاريخ منطقتنا وشعوبها. وبودي في هذا المجال ، أن أدعو بقوّة أصدقاءنا في الولايات المتحدة ، وكل الحلفاء والأصدقاء في العــالم ، إلـى توفير الدعم والمساندة التي يحتاجـها فـي مواجهـة الصعوبـات والتحدّيات إلى خليفة الملك حسين ، نجله الملك عبد الله ، متمنيا له كلّ النجاح والتوفيق في مهمته ، ومتمنيا للأردن وشـعبه الشّـقيق

وإذا كان السياسيون ، أو بعضهم ، غير قادرين أو راغبين حاليـا بإنتهاج مثل تلك السياسات الحكيمة وإتخـاذ القرارات الصعبة والشجاعة المطلوبة لإحداث الخرق الحقيقي الذي ننتظره جميعا من أجـل إعادة إحياء العملية التفاوضية في إتجـاه السـلام ، فإنـهم يكونوا بذلك يرتكبون أفدح الأخطاء بحق شـعوبهم وأوطانـهم ، ويساهمون عن قصد أو غير قصد في تعزيز روح التطرّف وزيادة التصلـب ، وتشجيع أعداء السلام على التحـرك والعمـل ضـد السلام . وهذا ما يفرض علينـا جميعـا ، عربا وإسرائيليين وأميركيين وكل الراغبين في رؤية الأمن والإستقرار والتطوّر كمعالم ثابتة ودائمة لمستقبل المنطقة ، أن نضاعف جهودنا ونكرّس تمسكنا بالأهداف السامية التي حددناها لنفسـنا ولمنطقتنـا ، بـل وللعالم أجمع .

٦) من هنا ، ومن على هذا المنبر ، أدعو الأصدقاء فـي الولايـات المتحدة ، التي طالما قدرنا دورها ومساعيها فـي دفـع العمليـة السلمية إلى الأمام وإدارة مسـاراتها التفاوضيـة ، إلـى تكثيـف جهودها وعزمها على الإستمرار على ذلك . وأدعو كـل أنصـار السلام ، على جانبي النزاع ، عربا وإسرائيليين ، إلى تجميع قواهم وطاقاتهم ، وأدعو معهم أصدقاءنا الأميركيين ، حكومة وإعلامـا ومعاهـد بحث ودراسات وفي كل قطاعات الرأي العـام ، إلـى رص الصفوف وتوحيد الجهود في إطار ما سـأطلق عليـه إسـم "تحالف شامل من أجل السلام" من أجل رفع صوت معسكر السلام عاليا ، وتغليبه على ضجيج أعداء السلام وممارساتهم وأفعالـهم ، وقبل كل شيء ، من أجل حمل السياسيين أنفسهم علـى الإرتقاء بسياساتهم وقراراتهم وخياراتهم إلـى المسـتوى الـذي يـوازي طموحات شعوبهم وآمالها وأحلامها .

فلعلنا نكون عندئذ قد وفينا بواجباتنا تجاه شعوبنا وبلادنا ، وخطونا الخطوات الحاسمة المطلوبة نحو السلام الذي نتّمناه لمنطقتنا فـي القرن المقبل الذي نقف الآن على أعتابه .

A Brookings Leadership Forum

The Saban Center for Middle East Policy
presents

H.E. SHEIKH HAMAD BIN JASSIM BIN JABR AL-THANI
Foreign Minister of Qatar

"An Arab Leader's View of Post 9-11 Challenges"

The Brookings Institution
Thursday, September 12, 2002

AMBASSADOR MARTIN INDYK: Sheikh Hamad, members of the diplomatic corps, ladies and gentlemen, good morning. I'm Martin Indyk, the Director of the Saban Center for Middle East Policy at The Brookings Institution. On behalf of the Saban Center I'm delighted to have an opportunity to welcome you all here this morning for a very special session of the Brookings Leadership Forum with His Excellency Sheikh Hamad Bin Jassim Bin Jabr Al-Thani, the Foreign Minister of the state of Qatar.

Sheikh Hamad was named Minister of Foreign Affairs by the Emir of Qatar in 1992. Since then, over ten years, he has been the architect of Qatar's new foreign policy, expanding its relations outside the Arab world with the leading nations of Asia, Africa and Europe, guiding Qatar to a leadership role in the Islamic world, in the organization of Islamic countries, and playing a critical supportive role in promoting Arab-Israeli peace.

At the same time Qatar has also dramatically strengthened its political, economic and security ties to the United States. As the Washington Post reported today on its front page in a story that highlighted the transfer of 600 U.S. personnel to the multi-billion dollar airbase that's being built at Al-Udeid in Qatar, and the transfer of these personnel from Central Command in Tampa, Florida. The Washington Post referred to Qatar as emerging as a "key strategic ally" of the United States in the Gulf.

It is a special pleasure for me personally to welcome Sheikh Hamad to Brookings and to the Saban Center. I had the distinct honor of working with him over many years in the U.S. government and saw close-hand how skillfully he steered his country's foreign policy. He is a true friend of the United States and he has a real and strong commitment to strengthening the relations between the United States and the Arab world, and promoting peace in his troubled region.

I'm also especially grateful for the support that his government is providing to The Brookings Institution's project on U.S. relations with the Islamic world, including the hosting of a very important conference that the Islamic Project of Brookings will be organizing with the government of Qatar in Doha in October of this year.

Ladies and gentlemen, yesterday was a very sad day for the United States and for all people who love freedom, and today we look ahead to the President's speech at the United Nations to phase two of the war on terror and the question about what to do with Saddam Hussein's flaunting of the U.N. Security Council Resolutions. It is therefore very timely for Sheikh Hamad to address us on the issues that confront U.S. relations with the Arab world and the Islamic world in the wake of September 11th.

Ladies and gentlemen, please join me in welcoming to the Saban Center at Brookings and its leadership forum Sheikh Hamad Bin Jassim Bin Jabr Al-Thani.

[Applause]

SHEIKH HAMAD BIN JASSIM AL-THANI: Good morning ladies and gentlemen. First of all I would like to convey the condolences of His Highness the Emir of Qatar and the people of Qatar about the tragedy which happened on the 11th of September.

This country is a great country and I think they can get over this more stronger and they can concentrate on how to help the world, and not themselves, to look ahead for new future especially in the countries which they need help in education, as the countries in Africa and Asia which suffer from sickness and other due to lack of financing and lack of education.

First of all I would like to say that what happened on 11th of September is a tragedy not only for the American people, but for the American people and for ourselves. The people which did or planned 11th of September, they wanted not to harm you only, they wanted to harm you and to harm us by making this big void between the two nations, between the Arab world and the United States, between the Arab world and the Western countries.

For that reason we have to ask hard, both sides, how we can build the bridge and where is the weakness and from where is the weakness? If it's from our side we have to correct it, if it's from our side, if it is from the American side, they have to correct it.

No doubt that we have mistakes. No doubt that the relationship in the beginning which we enjoyed some time doesn't go to the depth to build a base so it could continue when we have crisis like this.

I think it is very important that we reform ourselves in a new kind of relationship and we cannot reform ourselves without building a bridge and see what is the difference.

I think the most important thing which we have to look at is first of all how we can build the confidence now and how we show each other that we are partners to fight the terrorism and to fight the people which are against these relations between the two nations. We cannot do this without confidence. We cannot do this without kind of, democratic countries which they can talk in different language between the both sides. So we have to upgrade ourselves also in the Arab world and to understand what's going on.

I don't put all the blame on ourselves, but also we have to let the people in United States know us more and know what is the problem.

First I would like to talk about the Middle East problem which is between the Palestinians and the Israelis. I think this problem we have to give more effort, especially from the United

States, to stop the bloodshed and the violence between both sides. Both sides are human beings and I think the Palestinians have the right to live in their country in peace as the Israelis have to live in peace. We cannot say this by words. We have to do something on the ground. I think the United Nations, with support of the United States, has to take a role and to play a role in this.

I am not going to do a long speech because I would like to lay the ground and then to answer some questions.

Second thing about Iraq, or the third thing about Iraq. The Gulf area has been in crisis more than 20 years. During the Iran-Iraq War, after that the invasion of Kuwait, and now. We are waking up to a new crisis it seems to me in the Gulf. We in Qatar are trying to avoid any military action in the Gulf. This sometimes has a lot of interpretation which is some of it's right, some of it's wrong.

I have been to Baghdad a few weeks ago, less than a month ago, and I saw Saddam Hussein, and I talked to him very closely and told him that he has to let the inspectors in without any conditions, to avoid another crisis in the area. We are continuing this dialogue with the Iraqis.

As small country we are doing our best in this, but I can see there is a big momentum going on and we need to see how we can slow down this process.

No doubt that we are supporting peace in the region and our relationships with the United States is not a secret relation in Qatar. From the beginning everything between us and the United States has been known to the world and to the people. His Highness' policy is not to hide this relation. As we always say, I don't think we like to have a secret wife or a secret lover. If we have a relation, everybody will know it. If action will be taken from Qatar everybody will know about it. So there is nothing to be learned from other sources on this aspect.

I will stop here and I am ready to take questions.

QUESTION: Are you willing to allow U.S. troops [inaudible]?

SHEIKH HAMAD: That is a very direct question. First of all, as I told you we are working hard not to let a war happen, and at the same time the United States and ourselves and the Iraqis know that we have a very special relation with the United States and it is not secret that they are already in Al-Udeid.

The United States has not asked us up until now for any support or any permission for an attack from Qatar to Iraq. If they ask us we will look at this seriously, but at the moment there is no decision because nobody has asked us about it.

QUESTION: Sir, would Qatar place any conditions on the use of Al-Udeid base if it comes to that? That's one.

The second part, you said you met with Saddam Hussein in Iraq. Did you get any feeling about his willingness to allow the inspectors in and under what conditions? And I'll leave it at that.

SHEIKH HAMAD: I think there is hope that Saddam could accept the inspectors. He is just worried that if he allows the inspectors in, the military action will still be carried out. So he said why should I do it if the military action will be done with or without the inspectors? That' what he said to me when I met him. We have to look at this point seriously, if he will allow them according to the United Nations Resolution, I think that's a big step for Saddam and we are wishing and still hoping that he takes this action.

QUESTION: Christian Boers with United Press International.

One of the stated policies of, at least information that's come out of the U.S. government, has been the need for, towards the Middle East region, the Arab nations in particular, the need for a growth of democratic states and democracy within the individual countries but there's a lot of disagreement whether this is really a potential for true democracy in the Western sense within countries in the region. I was wondering if you could address that issue.

SHEIKH HAMAD: Well as you know His Highness the Emir when he came to power in '95, had this on the agenda. Part of the agenda, was how to move the country to a democratic state. I think last year, three years ago we have been working on this hard. This year we finish our constitution in Qatar. I think by year 2003 we will have a parliamentary election. With that we will complete our democratic body in Qatar. I think by the year 2005 we will have a full system in Qatar, run through a democratic, of course monarchy, but democratic country. This is the will of His Highness.

And I think the trend is this. The trend is this because the people are well educated now. We have to educate ourselves as a responsible people how to deal with people in a democratic country. And I think we need to make a big effort to try to educate ourselves and our people for democracy. That doesn't mean that they don't know democracy, they know it well. But how to practice the democracy. And our decision in Qatar has very clearly been made that we will have a democratic country, we will have a parliament, free election, and we have already a [ministerial] election, and free elections. We have a free press. I think the time is due to continue in this line.

We cannot talk with you as a democratic country in the future if we are not a democratic state. There will be big differences in our view.

Before, I think people looked maybe more for business, the people who are business minded either here or on other side. There is mutual interest between both sides but I don't think this could continue without a democratic base on both sides, which they will have dealing either commercial dealing or political dealing or any other dealing between two states.

AMBASSADOR INDYK: Can I just follow up on that for a moment, Sheikh Hamad? Some people say that the danger of democratic government in the Arab world is that the people that will benefit most from that in the early stages are the extremists and it will help the extremists come to power and they have no interest in democracy. How do you respond to that kind of concern that in fact democratic governing will create instabilities rather than a stable process?

SHEIKH HAMAD: Well I wish we can run the country like before, and if you think that in every country the extremists will come, this is because of the way matters were handled in other countries. I think there are extremists everywhere. Even in United States there are extremists, in Europe there are extremists. But how will we handle them and how you will work with them? Democratic system I think is important and you will have an up and down in it until it settles. It will not settle for first 20 or 30 years. People need to be educated how to deal in a democratic society.

I mean we need to educate ourselves how to deal with this when it comes up next year. We don't know how to deal with a parliament, or present our case as a government. So it's not an easy task. Yes, maybe the example that you have, what happened in Algeria. But I think you might find that some extremists come to power, but they have to play according to the rules, according to the international rules. If they don't play according to the international rules there is the United Nations and there is all the world that will be against them. We saw examples of this in the world.

So this could happen, but I think extremists are part of our society and we have to deal with them. We have to convince them and they convince us when they are right, that we need to be convinced by them and when we are right we have to convince them.

QUESTION: Barbara Slavin of USA Today.

You say that the United States has not asked for permission to use facilities in Qatar yet against Iraq. Will it be sufficient if you get this request from the United States or do you need a U.N. Resolution, approval from the Arab League? What will be required for Qatar to be part of a coalition against Saddam? Thank you.

SHEIKH HAMAD: You want to drag me to this. [Laughter] And I promised myself before I came here that I will not be dragged to it so I will keep my promise to myself.

Let me tell you this. What I answer, to be more frank and I hope you will know it, I answer as a diplomatic answer, that nobody has asked us. We did not give permission, because nobody has asked us. But you have to realize that we have a very special relation with the United States. This relation will always be in our consideration in any decision that will be taken by the state of Qatar. That is my answer.

QUESTION: My name is Andrei Shivoval with the Russian News Agency Tass.

Let me try to ask that in a different way though. No, no, no, sir.

You are going to the General Assembly right? Do you feel the U.N. can still do something to maintain peace in the region which is your goal? Who do you regard as your natural allies in those efforts at the U.N.? What efforts do you want to put into that?

And on a different subject, the head of the Russian Parliament when he recently visited Qatar said that the Qatari side suggested creating a gas OPEC. Can you tell us what he meant, whether that was true or not? Thank you.

SHEIKH HAMAD: We didn't suggest a gas OPEC. The Russians suggested that. We are cautious about this up until now. We did not make up our mind.

Let me tell you one thing, the United Nations have to play a role in the conflict between Iraq and let us say the international arena or with the United Nations [sic]. I think we have to work, all of us, to make an effort with the United Nations to say what they want exactly from the Iraqis. I think we should tell the Iraqis look, this is what we want. If you do this you will avoid any military action. But we have to know that United States has also their own opinion. You have to ask the United States if they will cooperate through the United Nations or they want to do it alone. We don't know about that.

QUESTION: [inaudible] Capitol Hill. I know you've got several meetings. Specifically what do you plan to discuss with them?

SHEIKH HAMAD: Well, first of all as you know I usually come to United States twice a year, so that is not a special occasion at the moment. Usually when I come here we discuss our relation with the United States which is growing not only in the military sphere and economic aspects and education. As you know there are university exchanges often in Qatar from the United States. And also we will discuss the latest crises, the Middle East crisis and the Iraqi crisis. We would like to share our view with their view, how they are looking at these problems and how they are looking to solve this problem. We know that in your country, this is thanks to the democracy, you have many different opinions here. And sometimes you need to know all these opinions to make a judgment because from far away we cannot judge what you are going to do.

QUESTION: [inaudible]

SHEIKH HAMAD: The message which I would like to say is that our area is an important region for, not for us only, for the world because of the energy there. The message that we know that United States after 11th of September have some comments or some questions about our area and I think they are right to have these questions and we have the right also to answer these questions and we have to cooperate how to get out of this matter. I know it is not concerning Qatar immediately, but we are part of the region. So it is concerning us.

The message also which I would like to take, is that any military action will destabilize the area and we have to know, as a small country we have to know where we are and that's important for us.

QUESTION: -- Insight Magazine.

Mr. Foreign Minister, two questions. One, is the Palestinian use of suicide bombers justified? And two, Al Jazeera TV has been accused of promoting radical Islam, so what do you think of Al Jazeera?

SHEIKH HAMAD: I am here not as a pokesman of Al Jazeera, but I will try to give you our opinions and the government's.

First of all the suicide bombing, we are not supporting the suicide bombing in Qatar as a government. I think human beings have respect, he is a Palestinian or he is an Israeli. Both sides have to respect each other and not to kill each other. This problem cannot be solved through this tragedy. It has to be solved on the table. We all know through history even if there is a war and there is a victory, the end is at the table to discuss what they are going to do. This we know from World War I and II, that always they sit at the table to discuss what they are going to do after the victory.

My opinion, my advice for the Israelis, that they have the upper hand. They are the strongest. They are more stronger than the Palestinians. If they are thinking, strategic thinking for the long term -- I am not talking about 10 or 20 years -- they have to sit and to give what they promised to give. The world also has to deliver what they promised in the Madrid Conference and through United Nations resolution 242. Why don't we implement that, why the Israelis don't accept to implement it. They say yes we will implemen,but we need to discuss it. Okay, what do you want to discuss and how many years do you want to discuss this problem?

I think the most important thing which if we need to avoid many more crisis in our area and many more areas is to give rights to the Palestinians, to give them their land according to the

'67 border, and according to resolution 242.

We are supporting United Nations Resolutions so we should support this resolution and let the Israelis implement it. That's one thing.

If I am talking about Al Jazeera, Al Jazeera is a private and not private because it's financed by the government at the moment. It doesn't cover its expenses as far as I know. So the government when they would like to have a free press, they thought that they have to have a TV, a free TV in Qatar. And believe me, we are suffering as a government from this channel because we have a lot of friends, a lot of brothers which don't like what s on Al-Jazeera.

But we are not supporting or directing Al-Jazeera to attack somebody else or to attack a country like some of the other states. This is not our policy, not His Highness' government policy. Our policy is to have free TV. But I cannot say that it is fair, what is presented in Al-Jazeera. It is only six years old, Al Jazeera. It needs time to settle. There are many mistakes there. I can see there is many mistakes. But these mistakes are not meant to be done as mistakes as far as I know. Maybe some of them were meant to be done but not by us, maybe by one of the employees, who would like to accuse this guy or accuse that country. But this is not the policy of the government of Qatar, it doesn't present our policy of Qatar.

The other part of your question if it supported any, about Al-Jazeera if it supported any?

QUESTION: [inaudible]

SHEIKH HAMAD: No, no. We did an assessment of this that some of our friends says that we are supporting. Tell me how are we supporting radicals and have an office for the Israeli government or for the Israeli state in Doha. Tell me how we can support this, while so loudly they know our relationship with the United States which has used Qatar for actions in Afghanistan, and for other purposes everywhere. It doesn't work together.

But in our region, in our area people always think, we have been educated to say and to repeat what the government says. To change that, the government, not the people, will be against you. What you hear here I know is part of government lobbying, many governments lobby and I don't blame them. If I am on their side I would lobby against Al Jazeera. But we have to give it time to settle. That's one thing.

Radical? No. We are a monarchy country. Yes, we are a Muslim country and we are proud about our religion, but we are a moderate Islamic country. You can go in Qatar, you can see the women driving, the women working, the women wear whatever they wear here, they wear it in the street in Qatar. So we are not a radical country. But yes, we are proud that we are an Islamic country.

For that reason it doesn't fit. And we looked at a percentage of the programs which we show on Al Jazeera. And it shows that this is a very small percentage, what you call radical programs. But people usually focus on them and then they say oh, most of the programs is radical because you hear one or two programs a day so you think that Al Jazeera is talking in behalf of radicals. That we will not allow it, we are not part of it. Our line is completely different than this.

QUESTION: -- Engel of the Guardian, London.

Sir, from your meeting with Saddam can you tell us something about your assessment of his mood? Do you feel that he has weapons that he could use in a last resort and do you believe that he would use them?

SHEIKH HAMAD: I wish he told me. [Laughter] I asked him and he said no, he doesn't have, but he doesn't tell me -- [Laughter]

QUESTION: Did you sort of make an assessment of what you felt his situation was?

SHEIKH HAMAD: I am not a military guy so I cannot make an assessment if he has or not. But I can make an assessment that I will not be surprised if he will accept the inspectors to be in Baghdad. I would not be surprised from my conversation with him.

QUESTION: Can I just follow up on that? When you say you're not surprised, are you saying basically he's looking now at conditions for inspectors to come in? Some kind of guarantee that he's not going to be attacked?

SHEIKH HAMAD: I told him conditions will not be allowed, but I think he is looking for a guarantee that if he allows them in, that he will not be hit militarily until the inspectors see what they have to see.

AMBASSADOR INDYK: Can I just ask one other question about this?

The United States, not just President Bush but President Clinton also, expressed a great deal of concern about Saddam Hussein's efforts to acquire weapons of mass destruction. We see that as a threat to our vital interests, and now after September 11th we see it as a potential threat to Americans at home here in the United States.

You live in his neighborhood. Does Qatar and the other neighbors of Saddam Hussein see the threat in the same way? After all he invaded Kuwait, he invaded Iran, he used chemical weapons. You live next to him. How do you evaluate the threat that he poses in your neighborhood?

SHEIKH HAMAD: As I told you, more than 20 years now we are at war in the area, or we are alert for a war so we get used to it. It may be a very serious threat but we don't feel it sometimes. I think we are worried but not from Saddam only, to be very frank. We are worried about the region completely. And we are not only worried from military action but we are worried from changing or reforming the area. We are looking in Qatar to reform the area. Before we are pushed to reform with a crash program, so I think the best thing is for the area to start reforming themselves and the countries reforming themselves in the region.

I think that's the most important thing which could avoid a lot of things in the region.

Threats, as a small country we will always feel that we have threats. This is why we have part of our relations with the United States. Sometimes people blame us for this. We say we are the last end in this relationship, but maybe it's become more strong and this is because we work in a very clear basis with the United States. You never do any action from Qatar without hearing it in the news, and we don't deny it. If it is right we don't deny it. But I hope that will be the case everywhere because that could let the people understand what their government's doing. And I think if they understand, they have nothing to add more. That's the big problem which we have in the area.

QUESTION: [inaudible]

SHEIKH HAMAD: I am not defending Saddam, and I am not with him or against him. I was against him when he was invading Kuwait. At the moment I'm not with him or not against him. I am with the Iraqi people and our government is with the Iraqi people, helping to avoid the Iraqi people from any crisis.

Do you think Saddam is the only obstacle for the democracy in our region? I think you know the answer.

QUESTION: Al Millikan, Washington Independent Writers.

How do you see other Muslims who are serious about Islam wrestling with the future of their religion? And how do you explain reports claiming terrorists were recruiting at mosques, targeting the most devoted, disciplined, serious young men who want to submit to Allah?

SHEIKH HAMAD: This is part of the problem in our region. Why are people being driven to this way? They have frustrations. To be very frank, we have to see what is the problem in our region? Sometimes we push them to the mosques, sometimes we don't want them to go to the mosques. We have to make up our minds. Religion is free for everybody to choose as a religion and which grade or level he wants to have his religion. That's fair. But you shouldn't push the others or try to dominate the others by your religion by force. That I think which shouldn't be accepted and we will not accept it. We cannot force somebody to be a Muslim or to show him how he lives. We respect the other religions and we hope that the others respect our religion.

In the end people which go to the mosques, imagine if they don't have work and they finish their university? Sometimes they have, either they sleep in the house or go to the mosque. We have to create jobs for the people in our region. We have to educate them, educate them well. The universities which we have, it's not on the level, it doesn't help us to educate our people. We have to change our education policy. I mean if you let him learn these nasty things which does not belong to the Islam and later you want to fight him, why do you let him learn these things from the beginning? I think is very important that we educate our young generation to avoid these things happen.

AMBASSADOR INDYK: I just want to follow up on that because one of the trustees of Brookings when she heard that you were going to speak today she sent me a whole range of e-mails of sermons that have been delivered from mosques in your country. And also broadcast on state television. There's something in common with all of these sermons. I'll give them to you afterwards, in which the "Imampraise to God" is in the conclusion of all the sermons and I'll quote from one of them. "O God, destroy the usurperes and avowed Christians. O God, destroy the Jews, pour your anger on them, destroy them, support our Palestinian brothers, give them courage and have mercy on them and their martyred children and women."

So given what you've just said about the importance of education and tolerance and so on, how do you deal with this coming from a religious leader?

SHEIKH HAMAD: Let me tell you one thing. It's been said to me by one of my friends yesterday when I came at night about these kind of speeches in the mosques. In Qatar, and in some countries in the region, all the speech in the mosque is written by somebody else who is anti-faith. This has caused the people go underground.. What will be said in Qatar will be said and will be announced, so nothing will be built underground, which is more dangerous in my opinion than what's being said in speech in the mosque or in the newspaper or in the TV.

Of course I totally disagree with this type of speech,and we have a big dialogue in Qatar discussing this matter with the religious leaders. It's become much less and less. I don't know when the speech happened, but I know it is almost now finished. But this happened when the wave of the killing happened in Palestine between the Israelis and the Palestinians. And we know, as I said in the beginning, that the upper hand is for the Israelis so they have to consider that they are strong and they can kill the Palestinians but what is the use of it because they will behave not in Palestine country but in the international arena or at least in the Middle East or in the Muslim world.

We should kill this head, we should not build a [tail] between the Jews, between the Christians, between the Muslims. That's not an easy task. This task needs all of us to work.

I cannot say that this is right. It is wrong. But it is better than to have somebody plant something under table.

QUESTION: Ken Pollock from the Saban Center.

Sheikh Hamad, Qatar is also very close to Saudi Arabia and Saudi Arabia would also be a key country in any U.S. war against Iraq. Right now we're hearing a great deal of disagreement from the Saudi government over American plans. Help us to understand better what you think Saudi Arabia's concerns are about a war with Iraq and what it might take for the United States to assuage those Saudi concerns and bring them on board to a war.

SHEIKH HAMAD: I cannot talk on behalf of our brothers in Saudi Arabia, but I could say Saudi Arabia is a major and important country in our region, a big country. I'm sure if they have a concern it's a legitimate concern and it has to be discussed between them and the United States. We might agree with them in some of it, we might not agree in some of it. But let me put it this way. All of us are against the war. I am not with the war and I say this from the beginning, but we have to work hard to convince the Iraqis, the United States, the United Nations how to wotogether and to bring it under the international arena.

QUESTION: Richard Andereig, La je Fis, Swiss Financial Newspaper.

Is the Palestinian uprising in your view or the view of the Qatari government something that is being maneuvered by Islamic extremists? Or is it, although nobody say so officially, essentially an anti-colonial political war of national liberation in the tradition of say French Algeria, Indochina, or the Netherlands-East Indies?

SHEIKH HAMAD: Let me tell you one thing. First of all we or the Israelis in the international arena, if there there extremists in Palestine we supported them because when we were talking to the moderate people among the Palestinians from Madrid until now and they give us what we need and they give up their claims and throwing Israel in the sea and accepting the land of '67, and all the world knows, then the Israelis come to bargain in the land of '67. Then we let the extremists take the lead. I think we helped the extremists for this lead because we didn't give the Palestinians their rights to the moderate people and the right people which they are talking in the peace and they sign the peace treaties. So I think we are pushing people to be extremists because we don't give them their right to talk. That's bad.

AMBASSADOR INDYK: The last question is from your competition, Radio Sawa --

QUESTION: Sheikh Hamad, I hope you did not make a promise to yourself not to talk about it. What is the status of the Saudi-Qatari relationship today? [Laughter]

SHEIKH HAMAD: Okay. First of all if there is any misunderstanding it is between family. Between us and the Saudis and we are very close family. We can work out this difference, if there is a difference, we can work it out between us. We respect the Saudis. We assume that they respect us. And the difference, it's not a difference which is not, it cannot be corrected. Maybe there is difference of view between us and them where we respect their view and I wish that they respect our view and with the wisdom of both sides we can work it out between us as usual. I don't think there is a big problem that could concern you or concern the others. It will be solved between us and our brothers the Saudis.

Is very important to know that sometimes people exaggerate these kinds of difference of opinion. This difference of opinion doesn't mean that we don't like them or we hate them. It's a difference of opinion, that's all. But in the end we are brothers and we respect them and I am sure they respect us and we will work it out.

Thank you very much.

AMBASSADOR INDYK: Sheikh Hamad, I want to on behalf of all of us here today thank you very much for a very interesting and candid response to some tough questions. I think everybody here greatly appreciates the spirit that you have brought to this dialogue and the importance that you attach to it and we are very grateful for everything that you have told us today.

Thank you very much.

SHEIKH HAMAD: Thank you very much.

[Applause]

# # # # #

2002 DOHA CONFERENCE
on
U.S. RELATIONS
WITH THE ISLAMIC WORLD
October 19-21, 2002

THE BROOKINGS INSTITUTION

THE SABAN CENTER *for* MIDDLE EAST POLICY

STATE OF QATAR

DOHA 2002 CONFERENCE PARTICIPANTS

ALGERIA
Rachid Tlemcani — *Professor of Political Science, University of Algiers*
Saad Jbarra — *Associate Fellow, Chatham House*

BAHRAIN
Munira Fakhro — *Professor of Sociology, University of Bahrain*

EGYPT
Gehad Auda — *Professor of Political Science, Helwan University, Cairo*
Mona Makram Ebeid — *Professor of Political Science, American University, Cairo; Former Member of Parliament*
Mohamed Kamal — *Professor of Political Science, Cairo University*

GERMANY
Wolfgang Von Erffa — *German Foreign Office, Head of Interregional Issues Central/South Asia*

INDIA
Hamid Ansari — *Former Ambassador to Afghanistan, United Arab Emirates, United Nations; Former Vice-Chancellor, Aligarh Muslim University*

INDONESIA
Bachtiar Effendy — *Professor, State Islamic University*
Mohammad Farjul Falaakh — *Vice-Dean for Academic Affairs University of Gadjah Mada Law School; Deputy Chairman of Nahdlatul Ulama*

IRAN
Sadegh Zibakalam — *Associate Professor, Political Science Department, Tehran University*

JORDAN
Rami Khouri — *Senior Regional Analyst, International Crisis Group*

KUWAIT
Saad Bin Taflah Al-Ajmi — *Former Minister of Information, Government of Kuwait*

LEBANON
Paul Salem — *Director, Fares Foundation*
Jamil Mroue — *Editor-in-Chief and Publisher, The Daily Star*

MALAYSIA
Karim Raslan — *Senior Partner, Raslan Loong*

MOROCCO
El Hassan Bouqentar   *Professor, University of Mohammed V, Rabat, Morocco*
Abdelhadi Boutaleb   *Former Adviser to King Hassan II; Former Ambassador to the U.S.*

OMAN
H.H. Yusif bin Alawi   *Foreign Minister of Oman*

PAKISTAN
Khaled Ahmed   *Writer, The Friday Times*
Ejaz Haider   *News Editor, The Friday Times*
Khalid Mahmood   *Scholar, Institute of Regional Studies*

PALESTINIAN AUTHORITY
Mahdi Abdel Hadi   *Director, Palestinian Academic Society for the Study of International Affairs*

PHILIPPINES
Amina Rasul-Bernardo   Fellow, *Asian Institute of Management, United States Institute of Peace*

QATAR
Abdul Qader Al-Aamri   *Former Ambassador to the U.S. and Algeria*
Maher Abdullah   *Al Jazeera Satellite Network*
Abdel Hameed Al-Ansari   *Dean of Sharia College, University of Qatar*
Hassan Al-Ansari   *Director of Gulf Studies, University of Qatar*
Mohammad Al-Haiki   *Consul General, Houston*
Ghassam Jaffar   *Diplomatic and Strategic Affairs Analyst*
Hamad Abdulaziz Al-Kawari   *Columnist and Political Analyst, Former Minister of Information*
Mohammad Giham Al-Kawari   *Ambassador-at-Large, Ministry of Foreign Affairs*
Khaled Fahd Al-Khater   *Director of Strategic Studies Center, Doha*
Abdulla bin Saleh Al-Khulaifi   *President, University of Qatar*
Nasser bin Hamad Al Khalifa   *Qatari Ambassador to the United Kingdom*
Yousef Al Qaradawi   *University of Qatar*
Ali Al-Thani   *First Secretary, Embassy of Qatar, Washington D.C.*
Ali Hilal   *Al Jazeera Satellite Network*

SUDAN
Ghazi Salahuddin Atabani   *Cabinet Member and Advisor to the President of Sudan on Peace Affairs*
Dafallah El Hag Yousif   *Fellow, University of Khartoum*

SYRIA
Imad Moustapha   *Director of Information Technology, Damascus University*

THAILAND
Surin Pitsuwan   *Member of Parliament, former Foreign Minister of Thailand*

TUNISIA
Hicham Djaït   *Professor Emeritus, University of Tunis*
Ahmed al-Ghudaidi   *University of Qatar*

TURKEY
Ayse Saktanber   *Professor, Middle East Technical University*

UNITED ARAB EMIRATES

Ahmed Hassan Makkawi
Research Fellow, Zayed Center for Coordination and Follow-up Political Cooperation-Arab League

Jamal S. Al-Suwaidi
Director, Emirates Center for Strategic Studies and Research

Azeeza Al-Zaabi
Research Assistant, Zayed Center for Coordination and Follow-up Political Cooperation-Arab League

UNITED STATES

Khaled Abou el Fadl
Alfi Fellow, University of California Los Angeles Law School

Hady Amr
Senior Advisor, Search for Common Ground

Daniel Brumberg
Professor, Georgetown University and Carnegie Visiting Fellow

Shaul Bakhash
Professor, George Mason University

Stephen Cohen
Senior Fellow, The Brookings Institution

Steven Cook
University of Pennsylvania and former Brookings Research Fellow

Thomas Friedman
Foreign Affairs Correspondent, The New York Times

Philip Gordon
Senior Fellow, Director U.S.-France Center, The Brookings Institution

Mouafac Harb
Program Director, Radio Sawa

Martin Indyk
Director, Saban Center for Middle East Policy at The Brookings Institution

Ibrahim Karawan
Professor, University of Utah and Director of Middle East Center

Bert Kleinman
Radio Sawa

Martin Kramer
Editor of Middle East Quarterly

Haim Malka
Saban Center for Middle East Policy at The Brookings Institution

John Paden
Professor, George Mason University

Jillian Schwedler
Professor, University of Maryland

Peter W. Singer
Coordinator, Brookings Project on U.S. Policy Towards the Islamic World; Olin Fellow, The Brookings Institution

Shibley Telhami
Professor, University of Maryland, Senior Fellow, The Brookings Institution;

Peter Theroux
Policy Planning Analyst, U.S. State Department

Fareed Zakaria
Editor-in-Chief, Newsweek International

UZBEKISTAN

Babajanov Bahtiyar
Professor, Al-Biruni Institute of Oriental Studies

YEMEN

Nasr Taha Mustafa
Board Chief and Editor-in-Chief, Saba, national news agency of Yemen

GLOBAL BUSINESS & INVESTMENT LIBRARY

PRICE $129.95

Ultimate directories for export-import, investment, government and

GLOBAL LAW FIRMS DIRECTORY
ISBN 0739767089

GLOBAL BUSINESS CONTACTS DIRECTORY
ISBN 073976702X

GLOBAL CHAMBERS OF WORLD
ISBN 0739767054

GLOBAL CHAMBERS OF COMMERCE USA
ISBN 0739767046

GLOBAL SLAVIC LIBRARIES DIRECTORY
ISBN 0739767100

GLOBAL BUSINESS AND INDUSTRIAL DIRECTORIES PUBLISHERS DIRECTORY
ISBN 0739767003

AFRICA UNIVERSITY LIBRARIES
ISBN 0739700936

UNITED KINGDOM UNIVERSITY DIRECTORY
ISBN 0739700928

GLOBAL OFFSHORE INVESTMENT & BUSINESS
ISBN 0739767097

GLOBAL BUSINESS ASSOCIATIONS DIRECTORY
ISBN 0739767011

GLOBAL TAX GUIDE EUROPE
ISBN 0739767119

GLOBAL INVESTMENT FUNDS DIRECTORY
ISBN 0739767070

GLOBAL US ECONOMIC
ISBN 0739767143

GLOBAL WORLD TRADE
ISBN 073976716X

WORLD TRADE ORGANIZATION
ISBN 0739707426

KOREA UNIFICATION HANDBOOK
ISBN 0739700936

GLOBAL OFFSHORE INVESTMENT & BUSINESS
ISBN 0739767097

GLOBAL OFFSHORE BUSINESS CONTACTS
ISBN 0739739336

GLOBAL TAX GUIDE ASIA
ISBN 0739767127

GLOBAL OFFSHORE BUSINESS LAW HANDBOOK
ISBN 0739739344

GLOBAL OFFSHORE TAX HANDBOOK
ISBN 0739739352

GLOBAL TRANSPORTATION BUSINESS CONTACTS
ISBN 073970091X

UNITED STATES TV BROADCASTIN
ISBN 0739707442

PORTUGAL TELECOM INDUSTRY INVESTMENT & BUSINESS GUIDE
ISBN 0739707434

US REGIONAL INVESTMENT & BUSINESS LIBRARY-2000

Investment and Business are available for the following states and cities

ALASKA INVESTMENT & BUSINESS GUIDE

Price: $99.95 each

1. Alabama
2. Alaska
3. Arizona
4. Arkansas
5. Atlanta
6. Boston
7. California
8. Chicago
9. Colorado
10. Connecticut
11. Dallas
12. District of Columbia
13. Florida

15. Hawaii
16. Idaho
17. Illinois
18. Indiana
19. Iowa
20. Kansas
21. Kentucky
22. Los Angeles
23. Louisiana
24. Maine
25. Marylamd
26. Massachusetts
27. Miami
28. Michigan
29. Minnesota
30. Mississippi
31. Missouri
32. Montana
33. Nebraska
34. Nevada
35. New Hampshire
36. New Jersey

38. New York City
39. New York
40. North Carolina
41. North Dakota
42. Ohio
43. Oklahoma
44. Oregon
45. Pennsylvania
46. Philadelphia
47. Rhode Island
48. San Francisco
49. South Carolina
50. South Dakota
51. Tennessee
52. Texas
53. Utah
54. Vermont
55. Virginia
56. Washington
56. West Virginia
57. Wisconsin
58. Wyoming

GLOBAL ECONOMIC, FINANCIAL DEVELOPMENT ORGANIZATIONS
ISBN 0739767062
Intl economic development agencies and investment funds in over 100 countries

GLOBAL CENTRAL BANK
ISBN 0739767038
Central banks in about 100 countries

GLOBAL INTERNATIONAL HUMANITARIAN ORGANIZATIONS DIRECTORY
ISBN 0739767186
International organizations worldwide

WORLD EXPORT-IMPORT & BUSINESS LIBRARY

Ultimate directories for conducting export-import operations in the country. Largest exporters and

Directories are available for the following countries

RUSSIAN Export-Import BUSINESS DIRECTORY

Armenia	Israel	Switzerland
Austria	Italy	Tajikistan
Azerbaijan	Kazakhstan	Turkmenistan
Belarus	Kyrgyzstan	Ukraine
Belgium	Latvia	UK
Czech Rep	Liechtenstein	USA
Denmark	Lithuania	Uzbekistan
Estonia	Luxemburg	
France	Moldova	
Georgia	Netherlands	
Germany	Pakistan	
Greece	Portugal	
Ireland	Russia	
	Spain	

Price: $99.95 each

Please contact International Business Publications, USA for ISBN numbers
Please send your order to International Business Publications, USA.
P. O. Box 15343, Washington, DC 20003
Phone: (202) 546-2103. Fax: (202) 546-3255. E-mail: rusric@erols.com
Selected guides are available in electronic format on CD-ROM
Global Markets on Line: http://world.mirhouse.com

US FEDERAL GOVERNMENT LIBRARY-2003

ULTIMATE INFORMATION ON US FEDERAL GOVERNMENT AGENCUES

The ultimate handbook with detailed information on US Federal Government Agencies and more

Price: $99.95 each

Title *	ISBN
1. Overseas Private Investment Corporation (OPIC) Handbook	0739731835
2. The White House Handbook	0739731815
3. U.S. House Committee on Agriculture	0739727370
4. U.S. House Committee on Appropriations	0739727389
5. U.S. House Committee on Armed Services	0739727397
6. U.S. House Committee on Education and the Workforce	0739727710
7. U.S. House Committee on Energy and Commerce	0739727435
8. U.S. House Committee on Financial Services	0739727745
9. U.S. House Committee on Government Reform	0739727443
10. U.S. House Committee on House Administration	0739727788
11. U.S. House Committee on International Relations	0739727451
12. U.S. House Committee on Resources	0739727486
13. U.S. House Committee on Rules	073972780X
14. U.S. House Committee on Science	0739727494
15. U.S. House Committee on Small Business	0739727729
16. U.S. House Committee on Standards of Official Conduct	0739727737
17. U.S. House Committee on the Budget	0739727419
18. U.S. House Committee on the Judiciary	073972746X
19. U.S. House Committee on Transportation and Infrastructure	0739727453
20. U.S. House Committee on Veterans Affairs	0739727761
21. U.S. House Committee on Ways and Means	073972777X
22. U.S. House Joint Committee on Printing	0739727699
23. U.S. House Joint Committee on Taxation	0739727362
24. U.S. House Joint Economic Committee	0739727354
25. U.S. House Permanent Select Committee on Intelligence	0739727796
26. U.S. Senate Agriculture, Nutrition, And Forestry Committee	0739727818
27. U.S. Senate Appropriations Committee	0739727826
28. U.S. Senate Armed Services Committee	0739727834
29. U.S. Senate Banking, Housing, And Urban Affairs	0739727842
30. U.S. Senate Budget Committee	0739727850
31. U.S. Senate Commerce, Science, And Transportation	0739727869
32. U.S. Senate Committee On Indian Affairs	0739727990
33. U.S. Senate Energy And Natural Resources Committee	0739727877
34. U.S. Senate Environment And Public Works Committee	0739727885
35. U.S. Senate Finance Committee	0739727893

To order and for additional analytical and marketing information, please contacrt
International Business Publications, USA at:
P.O. Box 15343, Washington, DC 20003, USA. Phone: (202) 546-2103. Fax: (202) 546-3275.
E-mail: rusric@erols.com

Title *	ISBN
36. U.S. Senate Foreign Relations Committee	0739727907
37. U.S. Senate Governmental Affairs Committee	0739727915
38. U.S. Senate Health, Education, Labor And Pensions Committee	0739727931
39. U.S. Senate Joint Committee On Taxation	0739728644
40. U.S. Senate Joint Economic Committee	0739728636
41. U.S. Senate Judiciary Committee	0739727923
42. U.S. Senate Rules And Administration Committee	073972794X
43. U.S. Senate Select Committee On Ethics	0739727982
44. U.S. Senate Select Committee On Intelligence	0739727974
45. U.S. Senate Small Business Committee	0739727958
46. U.S. Senate Special Committee On Aging	0739728628
47. U.S. Senate Veterans' Affairs Committee	0739727966
48. US African Development Fund Handbook	073973184X
49. US AGENCY FOR INTERNATIONAL DEVELOPMENT BUSINESS OPPORTUNITIES HANDBOOK	0739731866
50. US Agency for International Development Handbook	0739731874
51. US Arms Control and Disarmament Agency Handbook	0739739832
52. US CENTRAL INTELLIGENCE AGENCY (CIA) HANDBOOK	0739732757
53. US Civil Rights Policy Handbook	073976201X
54. US Commodity Futures Trading Commission Handbook	0739762028
55. US Congressional Budget Office Handbook	0739762036
56. US Defense Intelligence Agency Handbook	0739711709
57. US Department of Agriculture Business Opportunities Handbook	0739762044
58. US Department of Agriculture Handbook	0739762052
59. US Department of Commerce Handbook	0739762079
60. US Department of Defense Handbook	0739762087
61. US Department of Energy Business Opportunities Handbook	0739762095
62. US Department of Energy Handbook	0739762109
63. US Department of Health and Human Services Handbook	0739762117
64. US Department of Housing and Urban Services Handbook	0739762125
65. US Department of Interior Handbook	0739762133
66. US Department of Justice Handbook	0739762141
67. US Department of Labor Handbook	073976215X
68. US Department of State Handbook	0739762168
69. US Department of the Air Force Handbook	0739762060
70. US Department of the Army Handbook	0739762176
71. US Department of the Navy Handbook	0739762184
72. US Department of the Treasury Handbook	0739762192
73. US Department of Transport Handbook	0739762206
74. US Department of Veteran Affairs Handbook	0739762214
75. US Environmental Protection Agency Handbook	0739762222
76. US Export-Import Bank Handbook	0739762230

To order and for additional analytical and marketing information, please contacrt
International Business Publications, USA at:
P.O. Box 15343, Washington, DC 20003, USA. Phone: (202) 546-2103. Fax: (202) 546-3275.
E-mail: rusric@erols.com

Title *	ISBN
77. US FBI ACADEMY HANDBOOK	0739731858
78. US Federal Bureau of Investigation (FBI) Business Opportunities Handbook	0739762370
79. US Federal Bureau of Investigation (FBI) Handbook	073976246X
80. US Federal Communication Commission Handbook	0739733494
81. US Federal Election Commission Handbook	0739762400
82. US Federal Energy Sector Regulations Handbook	0739762419
83. US Federal Executive Government Handbook	0739731823
84. US Federal Maritime Commission Handbook	0739762427
85. US Federal Mine Safety and Health Commission Handbook	0739762435
86. US Federal Reserve System Handbook	0739762532
87. US Federal Trade Commission Handbook	0739762451
88. US Food and Drug Administration Handbook	0739762397
89. US Food Assistance to Russia Handbook	0739762478
90. US Information Agency Handbook	0739762486
91. US Intelligence Policy Handbook	0739762494
92. US Internal Revenue Service Handbook	0739762508
93. US Libraries and Information Science National Commission Handbook	0739762516
94. US National Academy of Science and Research Policy Handbook	0739762524
95. US National Aeronautics and Space Administration Handbook	0739762249
96. US National Drug Control Policy Handbook	0739762389
97. US National Institute of Health Handbook	0739762443
98. US National Science Foundation Handbook	0739762362
99. US National Security Policy Handbook	0739762354
100. US Navy Seals Handbook	0739762540
101. US Office of Management and Budget Handbook	0739762346
102. US Office of Personnel Management Handbook	0739762338
103. US Peace Corp Handbook	073976232X
104. US Postal Service Handbook	0739762311
105. US Science and Technology Policy Handbook	0739762303
106. US Securities and Exchange Commission Handbook	073976229X
107. US Small Business Administration Handbook	0739762281
108. US Special Combat Fources Handbook	0739762001
109. US Submarine Force Hnadbook	0739764136
110. US Trade and Development Agency Handbook	0739762273
111. US Trade Representative Office Handbook	0739762265
112. WORLD BANK BUSINESS OPPORTUNITES HANDBOOK	0739762257

To order and for additional analytical and marketing information, please contacrt
International Business Publications, USA at:
P.O. Box 15343, Washington, DC 20003, USA. Phone: (202) 546-2103. Fax: (202) 546-3275.
E-mail: rusric@erols.com
.

VLADIMIR PUTIN

PRESIDENT OF NEW RUSSIA
LEADERSHIP, POLICY, REFORMS

NEW WORLD POLITICAL LEADERS LIBRARY-2003
ULTIMATE INFORMATION ON LOLITICAL AND BUSINESS LEADERS OF FOREING COUNTRIES

The ultimate handbook with detailed information on foreign leaders, including biographic data, position on domestic and international issues, economic policy and more

Price: $99.95 each

TITLE
1.   Albania President Rexhep Meidani Handbook
2.   Angola President José Eduardo dos Santos Handbook
3.   Armenia President Robert Kocharian Handbook
4.   Austria President Dr. Thomas Klestil Handbook
5.   Azerbaijan President Heydar Aliyev Handbook
6.   Bangladesh Prime Minister Khaleda Zia Handbook
7.   Belarus President Alexander LUKASHENKO Handbook
8.   Brunei Sultan Haji Hassanal Bolkiah Mu'izzaddin Waddaulah Handbook
9.   Canada Prime Minister Joseph Jacques Jean Chrétien Handbook
10.   China President Jiang Zemin Handbook
11.   Cuba President Fidel Castro Handbook
12.   Egypt President Hosny Mubarak Handbook
13.   France President Jacques Chirac Handbook
14.   Germany President Johannes Rau Handbook
15.   Guyana President BHARRAT JAGDEO Handbook
16.   Iran President Hojjatoleslam Seyed Mohammad Khatami Handbook
17.   Iraq President Saddam Hussein Handbook
18.   Israel Prime Minister Ariel Sharon Handbook
19.   Japan Prime Minister Junichiro Koizumi Handbook
20.   Korea North General Secretary Kim Jong Il Handbook
21.   Korea South President Kim Dae-jung Handbook
22.   Libya President Muammar Muhammad Abd as-Salam al-Gaddafi Handbook
23.   Norway Queen Sonja Handbook
24.   Pakistan President Pervez Musharraf Handbook
25.   Palestine President Yasser Arafat Handbook
26.   Philippines President Gloria Macapagal Arroyo Handbook
27.   Poland President Aleksander Kwasniewski Handbook
28.   Russia President Vladimir Putin Handbook
29.   Saudi Arabia King Fahd bin Abdul Aziz Handbook
30.   Syria President Bashar Hafez Al-Assad Handbook
31.   Taiwan President Chen Shui-bian Handbook
32.   Thailand King Bhumibol Adulyadej Handbook
33.   United Arab Emirates Ruler Sheikh Zayed bin Sultan Al Nahyan Handbook
34.   United States President George W. Bush Handbook
35.   Uzbekistan President Islam Karimov Handbook
36.   Yugoslavia President Vojislav Koštunica Handbook

**To order and for additional analytical and marketing information, please contacrt
International Business Publications, USA at:
P.O. Box 15343, Washington, DC 20003, USA.
Phone: (202) 546-2103. Fax: (202) 546-3275. E-mail: IBPUSA@comcast.net**

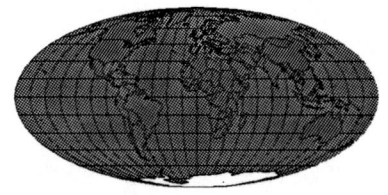

WORLD DIMPOLMATIC AND CUSTOMS GUIDE LIBRARY
2004

Price: $99.95 Each

TITLE	ISBN 1
1. Afghanistan Customs, Trade Regulations and Procedures Handbook	0739757075
2. Afghanistan Diplomatic Handbook	0739757032
3. Africa Countries Mineral Industry Handbook	0739757083
4. Africa Telecom & Internet Business Opportunities Handbook	0739757091
5. Albania Customs, Trade Regulations and Procedures Handbook	0739757109
6. Albania Diplomatic Handbook	0739757040
7. Albania Fishing Industry Business and Investment Opportunities Handbook	0739757113
8. Albania National Defense and Armed Forces Handbook	0739757121
9. Algeria Customs, Trade Regulations and Procedures Handbook	073975713X
10. Algeria Diplomatic Handbook	0739757059
11. Angola Customs, Trade Regulations and Procedures Handbook	0739757148
12. Angola Diplomatic Handbook	0739757067
13. Anti-Globalizm Movement Handbook	0739757156
14. Antigua and Barbuda Customs, Trade Regulations and Procedures Handbook	0739757164
15. Antilles (Netherlands) Customs, Trade Regulations and Procedures Handbook	0739757172
16. Antilles (Netherlands) Diplomatic Handbook	0739757180
17. Argentina Customs, Trade Regulations and Procedures Handbook	0739757199
18. Argentina Diplomatic Handbook	0739757202
19. Armenia Customs, Trade Regulations and Procedures Handbook	0739757210
20. Armenia Diplomatic Handbook	0739755781
21. Aruba Customs, Trade Regulations and Procedures Handbook	0739757229
22. Australia Army, National Security and Defense Policy Handbook	0739757237
23. Australia Customs, Trade Regulations and Procedures Handbook	0739757245
24. Australia Diplomatic Handbook	073975579X
25. Austria Customs, Trade Regulations and Procedures Handbook	0739757253
26. Austria Diplomatic Handbook	0739757261
27. Azerbaijan Customs, Trade Regulations and Procedures Handbook	073975727X

For additional analytical, business and investment opportunities information,
please contact Global Investment & Business Center, USA
at (202) 546-2103. Fax: (202) 546-3275. E-mail: rusric@erols.com

TITLE	ISBN 1
28. Azerbaijan Diplomatic Handbook	0739757288
29. Bahamas Customs, Trade Regulations and Procedures Handbook	0739757296
30. Bahamas Diplomatic Handbook	073975730X
31. Bahrain Customs, Trade Regulations and Procedures Handbook	0739757318
32. Bahrain Diplomatic Handbook	0739757326
33. Baltics Countries (Estonia, Latvia, Lithuania) Mineral Industry Handbook	0739757334
34. Bangladesh Army, National Security and Defense Policy Handbook	0739757342
35. Bangladesh Customs, Trade Regulations and Procedures Handbook	0739757350
36. Bangladesh Diplomatic Handbook	0739757369
37. Barbados Customs, Trade Regulations and Procedures Handbook	0739757377
38. Belarus Customs, Trade Regulations and Procedures Handbook	0739757385
39. Belarus Diplomatic Handbook	0739757393
40. Belgium Customs, Trade Regulations and Procedures Handbook	0739757407
41. Belgium Diplomatic Handbook	0739757415
42. Belize Customs, Trade Regulations and Procedures Handbook	0739757423
43. Belize Diplomatic Handbook	0739757431
44. Benin Customs, Trade Regulations and Procedures Handbook	073975744X
45. Benin Diplomatic Handbook	0739757458
46. Bermuda Customs, Trade Regulations and Procedures Handbook	0739757466
47. Bermuda E-Commerce Guide	0739757474
48. Bermuda Investment and Business Contacts Directory	0739757482
49. Bhutan Customs, Trade Regulations and Procedures Handbook	0739757490
50. Bhutan Diplomatic Handbook	0739757504
51. Bolivia Customs, Trade Regulations and Procedures Handbook	0739757512
52. Bolivia Diplomatic Handbook	0739757520
53. Bosnia and Herzegovina Customs, Trade Regulations and Procedures Handbook	0739757539
54. Bosnia and Herzegovina Diplomatic Handbook	0739757547
55. Botswana Customs, Trade Regulations and Procedures Handbook	0739757555
56. Botswana Diplomatic Handbook	0739757563
57. Botswana Telecom Industry Investment and Business Opportunities Handbook	0739757571
58. Botswana Telecom Industry Laws and Regulations Handbook	073975758X
59. Brazil Customs, Trade Regulations and Procedures Handbook	0739757598
60. Brazil Diplomatic Handbook	0739757601
61. Brunei Customs, Trade Regulations and Procedures Handbook	073975761X
62. Brunei Diplomatic Handbook	0739757628
63. Bulgaria Customs, Trade Regulations and Procedures Handbook	0739757636
64. Bulgaria Diplomatic Handbook	0739757644

**For additional analytical, business and investment opportunities information,
please contact Global Investment & Business Center, USA
at (202) 546-2103. Fax: (202) 546-3275. E-mail: rusric@erols.com**

TITLE	ISBN 1
65. Burkina Faso Customs, Trade Regulations and Procedures Handbook	0739757652
66. Burkina Faso Diplomatic Handbook	0739757660
67. Burundi Diplomatic Handbook	0739757687
68. Burundi Peace Agreements Handbook	0739757695
69. Cambodia Customs, Trade Regulations and Procedures Handbook	0739757679
70. Cambodia Diplomatic Handbook	0739757709
71. Cambodia Tax Guide	0739757717
72. Cameroon Customs, Trade Regulations and Procedures Handbook	0739757725
73. Cameroon Diplomatic Handbook	0739757733
74. Canada Customs, Trade Regulations and Procedures Handbook	0739757741
75. Canada Diplomatic Handbook	073975775X
76. Cape Verde Diplomatic Handbook	0739757768
77. Caribbean Countries Mineral Industry Handbook	0739757776
78. Caribbean Development Bank Handbook	0739757784
79. Cayman Islands Diplomatic Handbook	0739757792
80. Central African Republic Diplomatic Handbook	0739757806
81. Central America Mineral Industry Handbook	07397577814
82. Central European Countries Mineral Industry Handbook	0739757822
83. Chad Diplomatic Handbook	0739757830
84. Chile Customs, Trade Regulations and Procedures Handbook	0739757849
85. Chile Diplomatic Handbook	0739757857
86. China Army, National Security and Defense Policy Handbook	0739756818
87. China Customs, Trade Regulations and Procedures Handbook	0739757865
88. China Diplomatic Handbook	0739757873
89. Colombia Customs, Trade Regulations and Procedures Handbook	0739757881
90. Colombia Diplomatic Handbook	073975789X
91. Commonwealth of Independent States (CIS) Handbook	0739757903
92. Comoros Customs, Trade Regulations and Procedures Handbook	0739757911
93. Comoros Diplomatic Handbook	073975792X
94. Congo Diplomatic Handbook	0739757938
95. Congo, Democratic Republic Diplomatic Handbook	0739757946
96. Cook Islands Diplomatic Handbook	0739757954
97. Costa Rica Customs, Trade Regulations and Procedures Handbook	0739757942
98. Costa Rica Diplomatic Handbook	0739757970
99. Costa Rica Ecological and Nature Protection Handbook	0739757989
100. Costa Rica Trade Policy Handbook	0739757997
101. Cote d'Ivoire Diplomatic Handbook	0739756001
102. Croatia Customs, Trade Regulations and Procedures Handbook	073975601X

**For additional analytical, business and investment opportunities information,
please contact Global Investment & Business Center, USA
at (202) 546-2103. Fax: (202) 546-3275. E-mail: rusric@erols.com**

	TITLE	ISBN 1
103.	Croatia Diplomatic Handbook	0739756028
104.	Croatia Financial & Banking Law and Regulations Handbook	0739756036
105.	Cuba Army, National Security and Defense Policy Handbook	0739756826
106.	Cuba Customs, Trade Regulations and Procedures Handbook	0739756044
107.	Cuba Diplomatic Handbook	0739756052
108.	Cuba Export-Import and Business Directory	0739756060
109.	Cyprus Customs, Trade Regulations and Procedures Handbook	0739756079
110.	Cyprus Diplomatic Handbook	0739756087
111.	Cyprus Financial Market Investment and Business Opportunities Yearbook	0739756095
112.	Cyprus Parliament Guide	0739756109
113.	Czech Republic Customs, Trade Regulations and Procedures Handbook	0739756117
114.	Czech Republic Diplomatic Handbook	0739756125
115.	Czech Republic Army, National Security and Defense Policy Handbook	0739756133
116.	Denmark Customs, Trade Regulations and Procedures Handbook	0739756141
117.	Denmark Diplomatic Handbook	073975615X
118.	Djibouti Diplomatic Handbook	0739756166
119.	Dominica Diplomatic Handbook	0739756176
120.	Dominican Republic Diplomatic Handbook	0739756184
121.	Dubai Customs, Trade Regulations and Procedures Handbook	0739756192
122.	Dubai Export-Import and Business Directory	0739756206
123.	Dubai Jebel Ali Free Zone Business Opportunities and Regulations Handbook	0739756214
124.	Ecuador Customs, Trade Regulations and Procedures Handbook	0739756222
125.	Ecuador Diplomatic Handbook	0739756230
126.	Egypt Customs, Trade Regulations and Procedures Handbook	0739756249
127.	Egypt Diplomatic Handbook	0739756257
128.	El Salvador Customs, Trade Regulations and Procedures Handbook	0739756265
129.	El Salvador Diplomatic Handbook	0739756273
130.	Equatorial Guinea Diplomatic Handbook	0739756281
131.	Eritrea Diplomatic Handbook	073975629X
132.	Eastern European Countries Mineral Industry Handbook	0739756303
133.	Estonia Army, National Security and Defense Policy Handbook	0739756311
134.	Estonia Customs, Trade Regulations and Procedures Handbook	073975632X
135.	Estonia Diplomatic Handbook	0739756338
136.	Ethiopia Diplomatic Handbook	0739756346
137.	Falkland Islands Diplomatic Handbook	0739756354

**For additional analytical, business and investment opportunities information,
please contact Global Investment & Business Center, USA
at (202) 546-2103. Fax: (202) 546-3275. E-mail: rusric@erols.com**

	TITLE	ISBN 1
138.	Faroes Diplomatic Handbook	0739756362
139.	Fiji Customs, Trade Regulations and Procedures Handbook	0739756370
140.	Fiji Diplomatic Handbook	0739756389
141.	Finland Army, National Security and Defense Policy Handbook	0739756397
142.	Finland Customs, Trade Regulations and Procedures Handbook	0739756400
143.	Finland Diplomatic Handbook	0739756419
144.	France Army, National Security and Defense Policy Handbook	0739756427
145.	France Customs, Trade Regulations and Procedures Handbook	0739756435
146.	France Diplomatic Handbook	0739756443
147.	France Senate Handbook	0739756451
148.	Gabon Diplomatic Handbook	073975646X
149.	Gambia Diplomatic Handbook	0739756478
150.	Georgia (Republic) Customs, Trade Regulations and Procedures Handbook	0739756486
151.	Georgia Diplomatic Handbook	0739756494
152.	Germany Army, National Security and Defense Policy Handbook	0739756508
153.	Germany Customs, Trade Regulations and Procedures Handbook	0739756516
154.	Germany Diplomatic Handbook	0739756524
155.	Ghana Banking and Financial Sector Business and Investment Opportunities Handbook	0739756532
156.	Ghana Customs, Trade Regulations and Procedures Handbook	0739756540
157.	Ghana Diplomatic Handbook	0739756559
158.	Ghana Financial Market Business Opportunities and Regulations Handbook	0739756567
159.	Gibraltar Diplomatic Handbook	0739756583
160.	Gibraltar Offshore & Customs, Trade Regulations and Procedures Handbook	0739756575
161.	Global Aviation Industry Handbook	0739756605
162.	Global E-Commerce Laws and Regulations Handbook	0739756753
163.	Global Embassy Contacts Directory	0739756613
164.	Global Leather Exporters & Importers Directory	0739756621
165.	Global Mining, Oil and Gas Industry Directory	073975663X
166.	Global Mobile & Cellular Communications Industry Directory	0739756648
167.	Global National Libraries Directory: EUROPE	0739756656
168.	Global Non Profit Organizations Directory	0739756664
169.	Global Offshore Financial Services Providers Directory	0739756672
170.	Global Oil & Gas Industry Directory	0739756680
171.	Global Pharmaceutical Industry Directory	0739756699
172.	Global Privatization Handbook	0739756702

	TITLE	ISBN 1
173.	Global Sea Food Industry Directory	0739756718
174.	Global Senate Handbook	0739756729
175.	Global Shipbuilding Industry Directory	0739756737
176.	Global Telecom Industry Handbook: Regulations and Contacts	0739756745
177.	Global Transpiration Contacts Directory	0739756761
178.	Greece Customs, Trade Regulations and Procedures Handbook	073975677X
179.	Greece Diplomatic Handbook	0739756788
180.	Greenland Diplomatic Handbook	0739756796
181.	Grenada Diplomatic Handbook	073975680X
182.	Guatemala Diplomatic Handbook	0739756834
183.	Guernsey Diplomatic Handbook	07397566842
184.	Guinea Diplomatic Handbook	0739756850
185.	Guinea-Bissau Diplomatic Handbook	0739756869
186.	Guyana Diplomatic Handbook	0739756877
187.	Guyana President BHARRAT JAGDEO Handbook	0739756885
188.	Haiti Customs, Trade Regulations and Procedures Handbook	0739756893
189.	Haiti Diplomatic Handbook	0739756907
190.	Honduras Customs, Trade Regulations and Procedures Handbook	0739756915
191.	Honduras Diplomatic Handbook	0739756923
192.	Hungary Army, National Security and Defense Policy Handbook	0739756931
193.	Hungary Customs, Trade Regulations and Procedures Handbook	073975694X
194.	Hungary Diplomatic Handbook	0739756958
195.	Iceland Customs, Trade Regulations and Procedures Handbook	0739756966
196.	Iceland Diplomatic Handbook	0739756974
197.	India Army, National Security and Defense Policy Handbook	0739756982
198.	India Customs, Trade Regulations and Procedures Handbook	0739756990
199.	India Diplomatic Handbook	0739755005
200.	Indonesia Customs, Trade Regulations and Procedures Handbook	0739755013
201.	Indonesia Diplomatic Handbook	0739755021
202.	International Telecommunication Union Handbook	073975503X
203.	Iran Customs, Trade Regulations and Procedures Handbook	0739755048
204.	Iran Diplomatic Handbook	0739755056
205.	Iraq Diplomatic Handbook	0739755064
206.	Iraq Economic Sanctions, Customs, Trade Regulations and Procedures Handbook	0739755072
207.	Ireland Army, National Security and Defense Policy Handbook	0739754440
208.	Ireland Customs, Trade Regulations and Procedures Handbook	0739755080
209.	Ireland Diplomatic Handbook	0739755099

**For additional analytical, business and investment opportunities information,
please contact Global Investment & Business Center, USA
at (202) 546-2103. Fax: (202) 546-3275. E-mail: rusric@erols.com**

	TITLE	ISBN 1
210.	Israel Army, National Security and Defense Policy Handbook	0739755110
211.	Israel Customs, Trade Regulations and Procedures Handbook	0739755102
212.	Israel Diplomatic Handbook	0739755129
213.	Italy Customs, Trade Regulations and Procedures Handbook	0739755137
214.	Italy Diplomatic Handbook	0739755145
215.	Jamaica Diplomatic Handbook	0739755161
216.	Jamaica Offshore Customs, Trade Regulations and Procedures Handbook	0739755153
217.	Japan Army, National Security and Defense Policy Handbook	073975517X
218.	Japan Customs, Trade Regulations and Procedures Handbook	0739755188
219.	Japan Diplomatic Handbook	0739755196
220.	Jordan Customs, Trade Regulations and Procedures Handbook	073975520X
221.	Jordan Diplomatic Handbook	0739755218
222.	Kazakhstan Customs, Trade Regulations and Procedures Handbook	0739755226
223.	Kazakhstan Diplomatic Handbook	0739755234
224.	Kenya Customs, Trade Regulations and Procedures Handbook	0739755242
225.	Kenya Diplomatic Handbook	0739755250
226.	Korea North Army, National Security and Defense Policy Handbook	0739755307
227.	Korea South Army, National Security and Defense Policy Handbook	0739755315
228.	Korea, North Customs, Trade Regulations and Procedures Handbook	0739755269
229.	Korea, North Diplomatic Handbook	0739755277
230.	Korea, South Customs, Trade Regulations and Procedures Handbook	0739755285
231.	Korea, South Diplomatic Handbook	0739755323
232.	Kuwait Customs, Trade Regulations and Procedures Handbook	0739755331
233.	Kuwait Diplomatic Handbook	073975534X
234.	Kyrgyzstan Customs, Trade Regulations and Procedures Handbook	0739755358
235.	Kyrgyzstan Diplomatic Handbook	0739755366
236.	Laos Customs, Trade Regulations and Procedures Handbook	0739755374
237.	Laos Diplomatic Handbook	0739755382
238.	Latvia Army, National Security and Defense Policy Handbook	0739755390
239.	Latvia Customs, Trade Regulations and Procedures Handbook	07397554404
240.	Latvia Diplomatic Handbook	0739755412
241.	Lebanon Army, National Security and Defense Policy Handbook	0739755420
242.	Lebanon Customs, Trade Regulations and Procedures Handbook	0739755439
243.	Lebanon Diplomatic Handbook	0739755447
244.	Lesotho Diplomatic Handbook	0739755455
245.	Liberia Diplomatic Handbook	0739755463
246.	Libya Customs, Trade Regulations and Procedures Handbook	0739755471

	TITLE	ISBN 1
247.	Libya Diplomatic Handbook	073975548X
248.	Liechtenstein Diplomatic Handbook	0739755498
249.	Lithuania Army, National Security and Defense Policy Handbook	0739755501
250.	Lithuania Customs, Trade Regulations and Procedures Handbook	073975551X
251.	Lithuania Diplomatic Handbook	0739755528
252.	Luxembourg Diplomatic Handbook	0739755536
253.	Macao Customs, Trade Regulations and Procedures Handbook	0739755544
254.	Macau Diplomatic Handbook	0739755552
255.	Macedonia Customs, Trade Regulations and Procedures Handbook	0739755587
256.	Macedonia Diplomatic Handbook	0739755595
257.	Macedonia National Security, Army and Defense Policy Handbook	0739755560
258.	Macedonia Parliament and Legislative Activities Handbook	0739755579
259.	Madagascar Customs, Trade Regulations and Procedures Handbook	0739755609
260.	Madagascar Diplomatic Handbook	0739755617
261.	Malawi Diplomatic Handbook	0739752625
262.	Malaysia Army, National Security and Defense Policy Handbook	073975565X
263.	Malaysia Customs, Trade Regulations and Procedures Handbook	0739755633
264.	Malaysia Diplomatic Handbook	0739755641
265.	Maldives Diplomatic Handbook	0739755668
266.	Mali Diplomatic Handbook	0739755676
267.	Malta Customs, Trade Regulations and Procedures Handbook	0739755684
268.	Malta Diplomatic Handbook	0739755692
269.	Man Diplomatic Handbook	0739755706
270.	Marshall Islands Diplomatic Handbook	0739755714
271.	Mauritania Diplomatic Handbook	0739755722
272.	Mauritius Customs, Trade Regulations and Procedures Handbook	0739755730
273.	Mauritius Diplomatic Handbook	0739756749
274.	Mexico Customs, Trade Regulations and Procedures Handbook	0739755757
275.	Mexico Diplomatic Handbook	07397557675
276.	Micronesia Diplomatic Handbook	0739755773
277.	Middle East and Arabic Countries Copyright Law Handbook	0739755811
278.	Middle East Countries Mineral Industry Handbook	0739755803
279.	Middle East and Arabic Countries Design Law Handbook	073975582X
280.	Middle East and Arabic Countries Patent Law Handbook	0739755838
281.	Middle East and Arabic Countries Trademark Law Handbook	0739755846
282.	Moldova Customs, Trade Regulations and Procedures Handbook	0739755854
283.	Moldova Diplomatic Handbook	0739755862
284.	Monaco Diplomatic Handbook	0739755870

	TITLE	ISBN 1
285.	Mongolia Customs, Trade Regulations and Procedures Handbook	0739755889
286.	Mongolia Diplomatic Handbook	0739755897
287.	Morocco Customs, Trade Regulations and Procedures Handbook	0739755900
288.	Morocco Diplomatic Handbook	0739755919
289.	Mozambique Diplomatic Handbook	0739755927
290.	Myanmar (Burma) Energy Sector Business Opportunities Handbook	0739755935
291.	Myanmar Army, National Security and Defense Policy Handbook	0739754041
292.	Myanmar Customs, Trade Regulations and Procedures Handbook	0739755943
293.	Myanmar Diplomatic Handbook	0739755951
294.	Namibia Diplomatic Handbook	073975596X
295.	NATO Enlargement Handbook	0739755978
296.	Nepal Customs, Trade Regulations and Procedures Handbook	0739755986
297.	Nepal Diplomatic Handbook	0739755994
298.	Netherlands Customs, Trade Regulations and Procedures Handbook	0739754009
299.	Netherlands Diplomatic Handbook	0739754017
300.	New Zealand Army, National Security and Defense Policy Handbook	073975405X
301.	New Zealand Customs, Trade Regulations and Procedures Handbook	0739754025
302.	New Zealand Diplomatic Handbook	0739754033
303.	Nicaragua Customs, Trade Regulations and Procedures Handbook	0739754068
304.	Nicaragua Diplomatic Handbook	0739754076
305.	Niger Diplomatic Handbook	0739754084
306.	Nigeria Customs, Trade Regulations and Procedures Handbook	0739754091
307.	Nigeria Diplomatic Handbook	0739754106
308.	North America Mineral Industry Handbook	0739754114
309.	Norway Army, National Security and Defense Policy Handbook	0739754122
310.	Norway Customs, Trade Regulations and Procedures Handbook	0739754130
311.	Norway Diplomatic Handbook	0739754149
312.	Norway Tax Treaties with Foreign Countries Handbook	0739754157
313.	Oman Customs, Trade Regulations and Procedures Handbook	0739754165
314.	Oman Diplomatic Handbook	0739754173
315.	Oman Royal Police Handbook	0739754181
316.	Pacific Countries Mineral Industry Handbook	073975419X
317.	Pakistan Army, National Security and Defense Policy Handbook	0739754203
318.	Pakistan Customs, Trade Regulations and Procedures Handbook	0739754211
319.	Pakistan Diplomatic Handbook	073975422X
320.	Palestine Diplomatic Handbook	0739754238
321.	Panama Customs, Trade Regulations and Procedures Handbook	0739754246

For additional analytical, business and investment opportunities information,
please contact Global Investment & Business Center, USA
at (202) 546-2103. Fax: (202) 546-3275. E-mail: rusric@erols.com

	TITLE	ISBN 1
322.	Panama Diplomatic Handbook	0739754254
323.	Papua New Guinea Diplomatic Handbook	0739754AZZZ ZZZZZZZZZZZ ZZZZZZZZZZZ ZZZZZZZZZZZ Z262
324.	Paraguay Diplomatic Handbook	0739754270
325.	Peru Customs, Trade Regulations and Procedures Handbook	0739754289
326.	Peru Diplomatic Handbook	0739754297
327.	Philippines Agricultural Sector Business Opportunities Handbook	0739754300
328.	Philippines Army, National Security and Defense Policy Handbook	0739754319
329.	Philippines Customs, Trade Regulations and Procedures Handbook	0739754327
330.	Philippines Diplomatic Handbook	0739754335
331.	Philippines Financial Market Business Opportunities Handbook	0739754343
332.	Philippines National Police Force Handbook	0739754386
333.	Philippines Science and Technology Policy Handbook	0739754351
334.	Philippines Trade Policy Handbook	073975436X
335.	Philippines Transportation and Communication Policy Handbook	0739754378
336.	Poland Army, National Security and Defense Policy Handbook	0739754394
337.	Poland Customs, Trade Regulations and Procedures Handbook	0739754408
338.	Poland Diplomatic Handbook	0739754416
339.	Portugal Customs, Trade Regulations and Procedures Handbook	0739754424
340.	Portugal Diplomatic Handbook	0739754432
341.	Qatar Customs, Trade Regulations and Procedures Handbook	0739754467
342.	Qatar Diplomatic Handbook	0739754475
343.	Romania Army, National Security and Defense Policy Handbook	0739754483
344.	Romania Customs, Trade Regulations and Procedures Handbook	0739754491
345.	Romania Diplomatic Handbook	0739754609
346.	Russia and NIS Central Eurasia) Mineral Industry Handbook	0739754513
347.	Russia Army, National Security and Defense Policy Handbook	0739754521
348.	Russia Customs, Trade Regulations and Procedures Handbook	073975453X
349.	Russia Diplomatic Handbook	0739754548
350.	Russian KGB Handbook: Past and Present	0739754556
351.	Russian Navy Handbook: History and Modern Situation	0739754564
352.	Russia-NATO Cooperation Handbook	0739754572
353.	Rwanda Diplomatic Handbook	0739754580
354.	Samoa (Western) Diplomatic Handbook	0739754599
355.	Saudi Arabia Customs, Trade Regulations and Procedures Handbook	0739754602
356.	Saudi Arabia Diplomatic Handbook	0739754610

**For additional analytical, business and investment opportunities information,
please contact Global Investment & Business Center, USA
at (202) 546-2103. Fax: (202) 546-3275. E-mail: rusric@erols.com**

	TITLE	ISBN 1
357.	Scotland Central Police Handbook	0739754645
358.	Scotland Customs, Trade Regulations and Procedures Handbook	0739754629
359.	Scotland Diplomatic Handbook	0739754637
360.	Senegal Diplomatic Handbook	0739754661
361.	Seychelles Diplomatic Handbook	0739754653
362.	Sierra Leone Diplomatic Handbook	073975467X
363.	Singapore Government Encyclopedic Directory	0739754688
364.	Singapore Army, National Security and Defense Policy Handbook	0739754459
365.	Singapore Customs, Trade Regulations and Procedures Handbook	0739754696
366.	Singapore Diplomatic Handbook	0739754718
367.	Slovak Republic Army, National Security and Defense Policy Handbook	0739754742
368.	Slovak Republic Customs, Trade Regulations and Procedures Handbook	0739754750
369.	Slovak Republic Customs, Trade Regulations and Procedures Handbook	0739754726
370.	Slovak Republic Diplomatic Handbook	0739754769
371.	Slovak Republic Diplomatic Handbook	0739754734
372.	Solomon Islands Diplomatic Handbook	0739754777
373.	Somalia Diplomatic Handbook	0739754785
374.	South Africa Army, National Security and Defense Policy Handbook	0739754797
375.	South Africa Customs, Trade Regulations and Procedures Handbook	0739754807
376.	South Africa Diplomatic Handbook	0739754815
377.	South Africa Environmental Business Opportunities Handbook	0739754831
378.	South America Mineral Industry Handbook	073975484X
379.	South America Police Handbook	0739754823
380.	Spain Customs, Trade Regulations and Procedures Handbook	0739754858
381.	Spain Diplomatic Handbook	0739754866
382.	Sri Lanka Army, National Security and Defense Policy Handbook	0739754890
383.	Sri Lanka Customs, Trade Regulations and Procedures Handbook	0739754874
384.	Sri Lanka Diplomatic Handbook	0739754882
385.	Sri Lanka National Police Handbook	0739754904
386.	Sudan Customs, Trade Regulations and Procedures Handbook	0739754912
387.	Sudan Diplomatic Handbook	0739754920
388.	Suriname Customs, Trade Regulations and Procedures Handbook	0739754939
389.	Suriname Diplomatic Handbook	0739754947
390.	Swaziland Diplomatic Handbook	0739754955
391.	Sweden Customs, Trade Regulations and Procedures Handbook	0739754963
392.	Sweden Diplomatic Handbook	0739754971

**For additional analytical, business and investment opportunities information,
please contact Global Investment & Business Center, USA
at (202) 546-2103. Fax: (202) 546-3275. E-mail: rusric@erols.com**

	TITLE	ISBN 1
393.	Switzerland Army, National Security and Defense Policy Handbook	073975498X
394.	Switzerland Customs, Trade Regulations and Procedures Handbook	0739754998
395.	Switzerland Diplomatic Handbook	0739759000
396.	Syria Customs, Trade Regulations and Procedures Handbook	0739759019
397.	Syria Diplomatic Handbook	0739759027
398.	Taiwan Army, National Security and Defense Policy Handbook	0739759035
399.	Taiwan Customs, Trade Regulations and Procedures Handbook	0739759043
400.	Taiwan Diplomatic Handbook	0739759051
401.	Taiwan National Police Handbook	073975906X
402.	Taiwan President Chen Shui-bian Handbook	0739758978
403.	Tajikistan Customs, Trade Regulations and Procedures Handbook	0739759086
404.	Tajikistan Diplomatic Handbook	0739759094
405.	Tanzania Diplomatic Handbook	0739759108
406.	Thailand Customs, Trade Regulations and Procedures Handbook	0739759116
407.	Thailand Diplomatic Handbook	0739759124
408.	Thailand Royal Army, National Security and Defense Policy Handbook	0739759132
409.	Thailand Royal Police Handbook	0739759140
410.	Togo Diplomatic Handbook	0739759159
411.	Tunisia Customs, Trade Regulations and Procedures Handbook	0739759167
412.	Tunisia Diplomatic Handbook	0739759175
413.	Turkey Army, National Security and Defense Policy Handbook	0739759205
414.	Turkey Customs, Trade Regulations and Procedures Handbook	0739759183
415.	Turkey Diplomatic Handbook	0739759191
416.	Turkey National Intelligence Organization and Policy Handbook	0739759213
417.	Turkmenistan Customs, Trade Regulations and Procedures Handbook	0739759221
418.	Turkmenistan Diplomatic Handbook	073975923X
419.	Uganda Diplomatic Handbook	0739759248
420.	UK Bank of England Handbook	0739759337
421.	UK British Monarchy Handbook	0739759345
422.	UK Department for International Development (DfID) Handbook	0739759353
423.	UK Department for Transport, Local Government and the Regions (DTLR) Handbook	0739759361
424.	UK Department of Trade and Industry (DTI) Handbook	073975937X
425.	UK Foreign and Commonwealth Office (FCO) Handbook	0739759388
426.	UK Her Majesty's Treasury (HMT) Handbook	0739759396
427.	UK Immigration and Nationality Policy Handbook	073975940X
428.	UK Intelligence & Counterintelligence Handbook	073975470X

**For additional analytical, business and investment opportunities information,
please contact Global Investment & Business Center, USA
at (202) 546-2103. Fax: (202) 546-3275. E-mail: rusric@erols.com**

	TITLE	ISBN 1
429.	UK Intelligence and Security Policy Handbook	0739755418
430.	UK National Intelligence Service Handbook	0739759426
431.	UK National Police Handbook	0739759442
432.	UK Northern Ireland Office (NIO) Handbook	0739759434
433.	UK Royal Air force Handbook	0739759450
434.	UK Royal Army Handbook	0739759469
435.	UK Royal Navy Handbook	0739759477
436.	Ukraine Army, National Security and Defense Policy Handbook	0739759256
437.	Ukraine Customs, Trade Regulations and Procedures Handbook	0739759264
438.	Ukraine Diplomatic Handbook	0739759272
439.	United Arab Emirates Customs, Trade Regulations and Procedures Handbook	0739755280
440.	United Arab Emirates Diplomatic Handbook	0739759299
441.	United Kingdom Army, National Security and Defense Policy Handbook	0739759302
442.	United Kingdom Customs, Trade Regulations and Procedures Handbook	0739759310
443.	United Kingdom Diplomatic Handbook	0739759329
444.	United States Customs, Trade Regulations and Procedures Handbook	0739759485
445.	United States Diplomatic Handbook	0739759493
446.	Uruguay Diplomatic Handbook	0739759507
447.	US Arms Sales to Foreign Countries Handbook	0739759515
448.	US Defense Policy Handbook	0739759523
449.	US Economic and Political Assistance to Macedonia Handbook	0739759531
450.	US Federal Depository Libraries Directory	073975954X
451.	US Federal Government Directory	0739759558
452.	US Federal Grant Management Handbook	0739759666
453.	US Immigration Policy and Programs Handbook	0739759574
454.	US Ocean Transportation Companies Directory	0739759582
455.	US War Against Iraq Handbook: Political Strategy and Operations	0739750655
456.	US-Russia Cooperation Against Terrorism Handbook	0739759590
457.	US-Russia Economic & Financial Cooperation Handbook	0739759604
458.	US-Russia Military Cooperation Handbook	0739759612
459.	US-Russia Political Cooperation Handbook	0739759620
460.	US-Russia Scientific & Technological Cooperation Handbook	0739759639
461.	US-Russia Space Cooperation Handbook	0739759647
462.	Uzbekistan Customs, Trade Regulations and Procedures Handbook	0739759663
463.	Uzbekistan Diplomatic Handbook	0739759671

**For additional analytical, business and investment opportunities information,
please contact Global Investment & Business Center, USA
at (202) 546-2103. Fax: (202) 546-3275. E-mail: rusric@erols.com**

	TITLE	ISBN 1
464.	Venezuela Diplomatic Handbook	073975968X
465.	Vietnam Diplomatic Handbook	0739759698
466.	Vietnam Financial and Trade Policy Handbook	0739759779
467.	Western European Countries Mineral Industry Handbook	073975971X
468.	World Trade Organization Handbook	0739759701
469.	Yemen Diplomatic Handbook	0739759728
470.	Yugoslavia Customs, Trade Regulations and Procedures Handbook	0739759736
471.	Yugoslavia Diplomatic Handbook	0739759744
472.	Zambia Diplomatic Handbook	0739759752
473.	Zimbabwe Diplomatic Handbook	0739759760

**For additional analytical, business and investment opportunities information,
please contact Global Investment & Business Center, USA
at (202) 546-2103. Fax: (202) 546-3275. E-mail: rusric@erols.com**

CPSIA information can be obtained at www.ICGtesting.com
Printed in the USA
BVOW01s1453061213

338393BV00003B/218/A